With Best Compliments

Think Tank Initiative

ukaid
from the British people

BILL&MELINDA
GATES *foundation*

THE WILLIAM AND FLORA
HEWLETT
FOUNDATION

Norad

✳ IDRC | CRDI
International Development Research Centre
Centre de recherches pour le développement international

Canada

STRENGTHENING
POLICY
RESEARCH

Thank you for choosing a SAGE product!
If you have any comment, observation or feedback,
I would like to personally hear from you.

Please write to me at **contactceo@sagepub.in**

Vivek Mehra, Managing Director and CEO, SAGE India.

STRENGTHENING POLICY RESEARCH

Role of Think Tank Initiative in South Asia

Edited by
Sukhadeo Thorat
Ajaya Dixit
Samar Verma

Los Angeles | London | New Delhi
Singapore | Washington DC | Melbourne

The research presented in this publication was carried out with the aid of a grant from the International Development Research Centre, Ottawa, Canada. The views expressed herein do not necessarily represent those of IDRC or its Board of Governors.

First published in 2019 by

SAGE Publications India Pvt Ltd
B1/I-1 Mohan Cooperative Industrial Area
Mathura Road, New Delhi 110 044, India
www.sagepub.in

SAGE Publications Inc
2455 Teller Road
Thousand Oaks, California 91320, USA

SAGE Publications Ltd
1 Oliver's Yard, 55 City Road
London EC1Y 1SP, United Kingdom

SAGE Publications Asia–Pacific Pte Ltd
18 Cross Street #10–10/11/12
China Square Central
Singapore 048423

Published by Vivek Mehra for SAGE Publications India Pvt Ltd, typeset in 10.5/13 pt Bembo by AG Infographics, Delhi and printed at Chaman Enterprises, New Delhi.

Library of Congress Cataloging-in-Publication Data Available

ISBN: 978-93-532-8216-5 (HB)

SAGE Team: Abhijit Baroi, Sandhya Gola, Syeda Aina Rahat Ali and Anupama Krishnan

Contents

List of Tables   ix
List of Figures   xi
List of Abbreviations   xiii
Foreword by Anindya Chatterjee   xxi
Foreword by Peter Taylor   xxv
Preface   xxvii
Acknowledgements   xxxi

Part I: Introduction

Chapter 1   Think Tank Initiative: A Bold Experiment in
               Strengthening Think Tanks   3
               Andrew Hurst, Seema Bhatia-Panthaki and
               Samar Verma

Part II: The Journey of Think Tanks: Bangladesh, Nepal, Pakistan and Sri Lanka

Chapter 2   BRAC Institute of Governance and
               Development   29
               Sultan Hafeez Rahman and *Kaneta Zillur*
Chapter 3   Centre for Policy Dialogue   42
               Fahmida Khatun
Chapter 4   Centre for Poverty Analysis   57
               Udan Fernando
Chapter 5   Institute of Policy Studies   67
               Dushni Weerakoon
Chapter 6   Institute for Social and Environmental
               Transition-Nepal   79
               Ajaya Dixit
Chapter 7   Sustainable Development Policy Institute   94
               Abid Q. Suleri

Chapter 8   Social Policy and Development Centre   109
                 Khalida Ghaus

Part III: The Journey of Think Tanks: India

Chapter 9   Centre for Budget and Governance
                 Accountability   129
                 Subrat Das and *Happy Pant*
Chapter 10   Centre for Policy Research   140
                 Yamini Aiyar
Chapter 11   Centre for the Study of Developing Societies 153
                 Sanjay Kumar
Chapter 12   Center for Study of Science, Technology
                 and Policy   163
                 Anshu Bharadwaj
Chapter 13   Indian Institute of Dalit Studies   180
                 G. C. Pal and *Sanghmitra S. Acharya*
Chapter 14   National Council of Applied Economic
                 Research   195
                 Shekhar Shah
Chapter 15   Public Affairs Centre   209
                 Meena Nair and *Gurucharan Gollerkeri*

Part IV: Social Science Research and TTI: Country-Level Synthesis

Chapter 16   Social Science Research and TTI: Bangladesh 225
                 Fahmida Khatun
Chapter 17   Social Science Research and TTI: India   236
                 Sanghmitra S. Acharya, Chandrani Dutta
                 and *G. C. Pal*
Chapter 18   Social Science Research and TTI: Nepal   253
                 Ajaya Dixit and *Ashutosh Shukla*
Chapter 19   Social Science Research and TTI: Pakistan   279
                 Abid Q. Suleri
Chapter 20   Social Science Research and TTI: Sri Lanka   286
                 S. Sirimevan Colombage and
                 P. R. M. P. Dilrukshi Ranathunge

Part V: The Role of Think Tanks in South Asia: A Synthesis

Chapter 21   The Role of the Think Tank Initiative in
              South Asia   303
              Sukhadeo Thorat, Ajaya Dixit and
              Samar Verma

Part VI: Life After TTI: Challenges and the Way Forward

Chapter 22   Life After TTI: Challenges and
              the Way Forward   365
              Ajaya Dixit, Samar Verma and
              Sukhadeo Thorat

Bibliography   372
About the Editors and Contributors   379
Index   388

List of Tables

13.1   Percentage Change in Theme- and Group-Wise
Completed Research Projects Before (2003–2010)
and After (2011–2017) TTI   185

15.1   SATs Pioneered/Developed by PAC   211
15.2   PAC's Approaches and Their Applications   214

17.1   Indian Think Tanks and Areas of Research   244
17.2   Ranking of SDGs as per Thematic Areas of Policy
Influence by Think Tanks in India   249

20.1   Gross Expenditure on R&D   293
20.2   National GERD by Sources of Funding, 2010   294
20.3   Sector-Wise Allocation of Government Expenditure
on Research and Collection of Statistics   295
20.4   Sri Lanka: GERD by Discipline   297

21.1   Main Sources of Funding for 34 Think Tanks in South
Asia, 2009   310
21.2   State-Wise Distribution of Autonomous Research
Institutes with Social Science in India   312
21.3   Cluster of Activities That Grantees Undertook with
the Funding   318
21.4   Methods to Improve Research Quality   322
21.5   Internal Research Quality Control Process of
Think Tanks, 2017   323
21.6   Activities Undertaken to Improve Research Quality   324
21.7   Cluster of Strategies Used by Think Tanks to
Improve Policy Influence and Impact   329

21.8   Strategies Adopted by Think Tanks for Sustainability   348

A21.1   Think Tanks in South Asia: An Overview   351

A21.2   TTI Contribution Across Five Dimensions of
        Sustainability   355

List of Figures

7.1   Policy Briefs/Papers (1992–2017), SDPI   100

7.2   Working Papers (1992–2017), SDPI   100

8.1   Representation of RAI Model, SPDC   125

12.1   CSTEP Successfully Used the Core Grants to Raise Project Grants for Growth   167

12.2   Share of Government, Domestic and Foreign Funding in CSTEP's Cumulative Funding   178

13.1   Percentage Change in Publications and Capacity-Building Programmes Before (2003–2010) and After (2011–2017) TTI   185

13.2   Percentage Change in Policy Engagement Outputs Before (2003–2010) and After (2011–2017) TTI   187

16.1   Proportion of Published Research Documents in South Asia (1996–2017)   232

16.2   Number of Published Research Documents and Citations per Document in South Asia (1996–2017)   233

16.3   Relationship Between Number of Documents Published and Citations per Document in Bangladesh (1996–2017)   234

21.1   Thematic Diversity of South Asian Think Tanks Selected for TTI   313

List of Abbreviations

ACCCRN   Asian Cities Climate Change Resilience Network
ADB   Asian Development Bank
AG   Accountants General
AI   Accountability Initiative
AI   artificial intelligence
AIN   Association of INGOs
AMQ   annual monitoring questionnaire
ARTNeT   Asia-Pacific Research and Training Network on Trade
ASCI   Administrative Staff College of India
ASF   Asian Scholarship Foundation
ASHA   Anti Sexual Harassment
ASSA   Asian Social Science Association
BBRMs   brown bag research meetings
BBS   Bangladesh Bureau of Statistics
BCIM   Bangladesh, China, India, Myanmar
BEE   Bureau of Energy Efficiency
BIGD   BRAC Institute of Governance and Development
BIMSTEC Bay of Bengal Initiative for Multi-Sectorial Technical
         and Economic Cooperation
BMGF   Bill & Melinda Gates Foundation
BMZ   German Federal Ministry for Economic Cooperation
         and Development
BSG   BIGD Study Group
BSSRC   Bangladesh Social Science Research Council
BYS   Bangladesh Youth Survey
CAG   Comptroller and Auditor General
CAP   communications and policy
CAREC   Central Asia Regional Economic Cooperation Program
CARIAA   Collaborative Adaptation Research Initiative in Africa
         and Asia

CARP	Council for Agriculture Research Policy
CASS	Chinese Academy of Social Sciences
CBGA	Centre for Budget and Governance Analysis
CBR	Central Board of Revenue
CCSC	Climate Change Score Card
CEPA	Centre for Poverty Analysis
CFAR	Centre for Advocacy and Research
CGE	computable general equilibrium
CIDA	Canadian International Development Agency
CLEIA	Community-Led Environment Impact Assessment
CMI	Chr. Michelsen Institute
CoP	Conference of the Parties
CoR	Community of Researchers
CORAM	Community-based Rainfall Measurement
CPD	Centre for Policy Dialogue
CPR	Centre for Policy Research
CRC	Chair, Research Committee
CRC	Citizen Report Card
CREEs	community rural electricity entities
CSC	Citizens' Score Card
CSDS	Centre for the Study of Developing Societies
CSG	Core Support Group
CSOs	civil society organizations
CSR	corporate social responsibility
CSS	Centre for Social Studies
CSSs	centrally sponsored schemes
CSTEP	Centre for Study of Science, Technology and Policy
CTTN	CAREC Think Tanks Network
DANIDA	Danish International Development Agency
DARPAN	Decision Analysis for Research and Planning
DBTs	Direct Benefit Transfers
DFID	Department for International Development
DGIS	Dutch Ministry of Foreign Affairs
DIE	German Development Institute
EC	Executive Committee
ECHO	European Commission-Humanitarian Aid and Civil Protection
ED	executive director

EDACE	Enhanced Democratic Accountability and Civic Engagement
ESID	Effective States and Inclusive Development
EU	European Union
FAA	finance and administration
FBR	Federal Board of Revenue
FES	Friedrich-Ebert-Stiftung
FPCCI	Federation of Pakistan Chambers of Commerce & Industry
GDN	Global Development Network
GDP	gross domestic product
GIS	geographic information system
GM	genetically modified
GNI	gross national income
GoN	Government of Nepal
GoP	Government of Pakistan
GoSL	Government of Sri Lanka
GRB	gender-responsive budgeting
GST	general sales tax
GTZ	German Technical Cooperation Agency
HCM	human capital management
HEC	Higher Education Commission
HKC	Himalayan Knowledge Conclave
HR	human resource
IAG	International Advisory Group
IAS	Indian Administrative Service
ICC	Internal Complaints Committee
ICCG	International Centre for Climate Governance
ICDS	Integrated Child Development Services
ICIMOD	International Centre for Integrated Mountain Development
ICM	India Centre for Migration
ICPSR	Inter-university Consortium for Political and Social Research
ICRIER	Indian Council for Research on International Economic Relations
ICSSR	Indian Council of Social Science Research
ICT	information and communication technology

IDRC	International Development Research Centre
IDS	Institute of Development Studies
IGC	International Growth Centre
IGNTU	Indira Gandhi National Tribal University
IGS	Institute of Governance Studies
IHDS	India Human Development Survey
IIAS	Indian Institute of Advanced Studies
IIDS	Indian Institute of Dalit Studies
IIGMF	intersectionality informed gender mainstreaming framework
IIM	Indian Institute of Management
ILO	International Labour Organization
ILP	Indian Languages Programme
IMF	International Monetary Fund
INGO	international non-governmental organization
IPCC	Intergovernmental Panel on Climate Change
IPE	Institute of Public Enterprises
IPF	*India Policy Forum*
IPoA	Istanbul Programme of Action
IPS	Institute of Policy Studies
IRBD	International Review of Bangladesh's Development
ISDE	International Society of Doctors for the Environment
ISET-I	Institute for Social and Environmental Transition-International
ISET-N	Institute for Social and Environmental Transition-Nepal
ISPM	International Social Policy and Macroeconomic Model
KIAS	Kathmandu Institute of Applied Sciences
KIET	Korea Institute for Industrial Economics and Trade
KP	Khyber Pakhtunkhwa
KPIs	key performance indicators
LAPA	Local Adaptation Plan of Action
LBSNAA	Lal Bahadur Shastri National Academy of Administration
LDC	less developed country
LEAD	Leadership for Environment and Development
LOGIN	Local Governance Initiative and Network
LSE	London School of Economics
LUMS	Lahore University of Management Sciences
M&E	monitoring and evaluation

MDGs	Millennium Development Goals
MEL	monitoring, evaluation and learning
MGG	Managing Global Governance
MIS	management information system
MIT	Massachusetts Institute of Technology
MJF	Manusher Jonno Foundation
MNRE	Ministry of New and Renewable Energy
MoA	Memorandum of Agreement
MoEFCC	Ministry of Environment, Forest and Climate Change
MoFALD	Ministry of Federal Affairs and Local Development
MoPME	Ministry of Primary and Mass Education
MoUs	memorandums of understanding
MPs	members of parliament
MSEs	Micro and Small Enterprises
NA	National Assembly
NACEUN	National Association of Community Electricity Users-Nepal
NARESA	National Resources, Energy and Science Authority
NASC	Nepal Administrative Staff College
NCAER	National Council of Applied Economic Research
NCERT	National Council of Educational Research and Training
NCS	National Conservation Strategy
NFC	National Finance Commission
NGO	non-governmental organization
NHRC	National Health Research Council
NHRC	National Human Rights Commission
NIPFP	National Institute of Public Finance and Policy
NITI Aayog	National Institution for Transforming India
NOAA	National Oceanic and Atmospheric Administration
NORAD	Norwegian Agency for Development Cooperation
NRA	National Reconstruction Authority
NRC	National Research Council
NRRDA	National Rural Roads Development Agency
NSC	National Science Council
NSF	National Science Foundation
NSHIE	National Survey of Household Income and Expenditure
N-SIPI	NCAER State Investment Potential Index
NSRLC	National Strategy for Resilient Local Communities

NSU	North South University
NTBs	non-tariff barriers
NTMs	non-tariff measures
NWCF	Nepal Water Conservation Foundation
OBCs	Other Backward Classes
OCB	Organisational Capacity Building
ODI	Overseas Development Institute
OECD	Organisation for Economic Co-operation and Development
OP	organizational performance
P&DD	Planning and Development Department
PA	PAISA associates
PAC	Public Affairs Centre
PAI	Public Affairs Index
PAISA	Planning, Allocations and Expenditures, Institutions Studies in Accountability
PAT	Perform Achieve and Trade
PCP	Pakistan Centre for Philanthropy
PCS	policy community survey
PEC	policy engagement and communications
PEF	Punjab Economic Forum
PERC	post-event review capability
PETS	public expenditure tracking systems
PFs	permanents funds
PGIS	Postgraduate Institute of Science
PGRG	Participatory Governance Research Group
PIDE	Pakistan Institute of Development Economics
PIL	public interest litigation
PIMU	Poverty Impact Monitoring Unit
PL	policy linkage
PMGSY	Pradhan Mantri Gram Sadak Yojana
PMO	Prime Minister's Office
PO	Program Officers
R&D	research and development
RAI	research–advocacy–implementation
RBI	Reserve Bank of India
REDS	Rural Economic Demographic Survey
RfPs	requests for proposals

RHF	Resources Himalaya Foundation
RM	regional meeting
RMG	ready-made garment
RPC	Research and Publications Committee
RQ	research quality
SAG	Strategic Advisory Group
SAM	social accounting matrix
SAP	structural adjustment programme
SAPs	Social Action Plans
SATs	social accountability tools
SBM	Swachh Bharat Mission
SC	Scheduled Caste
SchEMS	School of Environmental Science and Management
SCSP	Scheduled Caste Sub Plan
SDC	Sustainable Development Conference
SDGs	Sustainable Development Goals
SDPI	Sustainable Development Policy Institute
SECP	Securities and Exchange Commission of Pakistan
SEI	Stockholm Environment Institute
SERC	Social and Environment Research Centre
SIAS	South Asia Institute of Advanced Studies
SLRC	Sustainable Livelihoods Research Consortium
SNA	System of National Accounts
SoC	*State of Cities*
SoG	*State of Governance*
SPDC	Social Policy and Development Centre
SSA	Sarva Shiksha Abhiyan
SSR	social science research
STs	Scheduled Tribes
TE	Talking Economics
TSP	Tribal Sub Plan
TTI	Think Tank Initiative
TU-CDES	Central Department of Environmental Science at Tribhuvan University
TV	television
UCL	University College London
UGC	University Grants Commission
UK	United Kingdom

UMass Amherst	University of Massachusetts Amherst
UMCP	University of Maryland, College Park
UNDEF	United Nations Democracy Fund
UNDP	United Nations Development Programme
UNESCAP	United Nations Economic and Social Commission for Asia and the Pacific
UNFCCC	United Nations Framework Convention on Climate Change
UNHCR	United Nations High Commissioner for Refugees
UPPI	University of the Philippines Population Institute
USA	United States of America
USAID	United States AID
VAWG	violence against women and girls
WB	World Bank
WCAR	World Conference Against Racism
WDD	Women Development Department
WTO	World Trade Organization

Foreword

By Anindya Chatterjee

While the Think Tank Initiative (TTI) was being implemented over the last decade, a number of developments were occurring in South Asia. Taking the risk of overgeneralizing, let me try to capture some of these developments. This may help us in understanding the dynamic and somewhat frenzied policy environment where this experiment on institutional strengthening through core support to a cohort of institutions over 10 years was taking place. Over the last decade, South Asia made significant strides in poverty reduction, access to safe drinking water, primary school enrolment, control of HIV and tuberculosis, and under-five and infant mortality, among others. While the regional economy showed resilience at the face of global financial crisis, inequality increased. Infrastructure deficit in the region started getting more attention through establishment of the New Development Bank and the Asian Infrastructure Investment Bank.

Sharp polarization of policy positions between political actors and political processes that drive these took place during this time. This was characterized in some contexts with the rise of newer varieties of authoritarianism. This showed no clear regional pattern, however, with increasing and decreasing trends from one administration to the other over time in different countries. Attempts to control discourses and debates often spilled over outside the political arena and negatively impacted civil society. South Asia also bore its share of spread of misinformation through social media platforms. Investments were made in institution building. Institutions were also under attack driven by short-sighted and immediate political imperatives of the day. Think tanks were co-opted, sometimes willingly and at other times by governments, to advance their agendas of economics and foreign policy objectives. Such convening of political nature by the think tanks led to palpable discomfort in national and regional partners where interests and positions differed. It is not that these did not happen before in the region. What differed is the scale and spread.

In the meanwhile, regional fragmentation (barriers to travel, trade, low-intensity conflict, terrorism and collapse of regional coordination mechanism) increased significantly over last 10 years or so in South Asia. Practically, this meant that travel, visa, holding meetings, moving money from one country to the other and sharing thoughts and approaches, all became more difficult. Often regional meetings, including those in TTI, had to be held outside South Asia due to difficulties of travel and convening. New regional groupings became prominent, such as the Bay of Bengal Initiative for Multi-Sectoral Technical and Economic Cooperation (BIMSTEC), the Chinese One Belt, One Road initiative and ASEAN Plus, to name a few. This meant more fluid and evolving regional configuration and newer platforms of dialogue and cooperation.

Think tanks received more attention in Asia during this period and were in a dynamic phase of development. Other networks were established, for example, ADB-Asian Think Tank Network (with some common institutions with TTI). China has committed to build a new generation of think tanks 'with Chinese characteristics'. Foreign funding (and hence perceived influence) from time to time was politically sensitive. At other times, Asian think tanks in the TTI cohort avoided accepting funding from the national government for exactly the same reason—to maintain independence from government influence. This was also a time for diversifying funding sources for think tanks, particularly from private, corporate or philanthropy sources. There are a few positive examples here. And the story is a mixed one.

The TTI institutions witnessed and made sense of what it meant to build more resilient institutions in this fluid and dynamic landscape. Insights are captured in the book.

There had also been rumblings for some time that whether investment in institution and capacity building was akin to sponsoring substandard research in the global south, including South Asia. Arguments were made that research enterprise is after all a meritocratic one where only the best ideas should prevail. This was the time to address such half-cooked notions. International Development Research Centre's (IDRC) own Research Quality Plus approach has demonstrated that research produced in the global south was robust and well-positioned for use and challenged assumptions of a default north–south gradient in capacity building. There was also significant correlation between capacity building and scientific rigour.[1] Understanding and improving research quality had remained a major preoccupation in TTI.

Independence or embeddedness (in policy processes of the day) of think tanks was the other question. This is not necessarily an either-or issue, however. Research needs to be locally grounded and contribute to national priorities. There is no question about that. It may also be necessary to be part of a policy process to optimize research uptake and impact. Reading and understanding local contexts and political appetite are all important. But national systems and the messy nature of policy-making often generate blind spots, where insights are generated only much later. This is why a look from outside is often necessary. Here, the initiative has again played some significant role.

This book not only captures the changes outside but also, and more importantly, within the institutions. These changes are sometimes transformational and at other times incremental. Stories of change, successes, trials and tribulations, leadership transition, strengthening governance and communication, and addressing emerging policy issues through core support, all make it an interesting volume. Institutional change, after all, is less written about. The book captures experiences of this decade-long experiment.

Support to institutions to conduct high-quality research to inform policy continues to and should remain a highly relevant issue for both national and international funders. The think tanks, in the meanwhile,

---

[1] Lebel and MacLean, 'A Better Measure of Research', 23–26.

must continue to do three things: (a) speak truth to power, (b) speak truth to those who seek power (i.e., those who want to be at the table of policy-making, representing their constituencies) and (c) speak truth to other truth seekers. The last one will generate lot more debate than what we ever thought it would.

Anindya Chatterjee
Regional Director
IDRC, Asia Regional Office
New Delhi, India

Foreword
By Peter Taylor

We live in a rapidly changing world. The universal and transformative 2030 Agenda of the Sustainable Development Goals (SDGs) emphasizes the importance of giving our collective attention to the future of people, planet and prosperity. As we see major global, regional and national shifts constantly taking place, South Asia continues to make extraordinary strides towards improving the lives of its citizens, tackling huge environmental challenges and creating conditions for vigorous economic growth. Yet even with this major progress taking place, many people in the region still remain left behind, as deep economic and social inequities continue to persist.

For almost 50 years, IDRC has sought to help address development challenges such as these by working to support the generation of knowledge, innovation and solutions. As part of its efforts, it has engaged with development actors worldwide to help strengthen locally generated evidence, policy engagement and debate. One of its largest programmes, TTI, has aimed to encourage evidence-informed and locally grounded policy-making processes by helping policy research organizations move along a path towards sustainability in all aspects of their work. Through a multi-donor partnership since 2009, TTI's efforts have been targeted to not only help support individual policy research organizations but also help build strong communities and networks whose role will continue to be central to successful achievement of the SDGs and to 2030 Agenda overall.

Think tanks will continue as key development actors in the South Asia region, even though the spaces in which they operate are sometimes constrained. This book, representing the stories and accounts of think tank leaders from across South Asia who have participated in TTI, is a wonderful reminder of why their work matters so much. It demonstrates, from both organizational and national perspectives, just why IDRC and its partners have supported think tanks for 10 years. As the chapters in this book reveal, think tanks do make a difference. They influence and shape national policy priorities and implementation; provide interdisciplinary approaches and draw on a variety of perspectives; convene stakeholders around public debates; support sustainable implementation measures; provide independent analyses and evaluations; and engage in policy dialogues from sub-national to regional and even global levels.

As TTI draws to an end, we look back and feel proud that this immensely important group of organizations continues to thrive and strive for better conditions for all people in their countries. This book reminds us clearly that think tanks are living proof of the power of evidence-informed policy to influence positive change and transformation.

Peter Taylor
Former Associate Director
Think Tank Initiative (TTI) Program, IDRC
Ottawa, Canada

Preface

Among the key lessons learnt from international development experience is that public policies work best when they are designed and implemented by local actors. Unless they are informed by locally generated data and analysis, well-intentioned programmes often do not respond to realities on the ground. Although national and international donors recognize the critical importance of local ownership to the success of development interventions, they often fail to invest in those national organizations that undertake the research and analysis needed by policy-makers and the wider community to effect societal change.

To address this gap, TTI was designed as a long-term, well-structured programme to support southern think tanks so that they could strengthen their autonomy, credibility and effectiveness and thereby enhance their impact on policy. TTI's core aims were to strengthen the organizational capacities of a group of local, independent think tanks based in East and West Africa, South Asia and Latin America so that they could produce and communicate high-quality, contextualized, objective and timely evidence that could be used to inform and influence policy and practice. TTI was designed with a 10-year horizon divided into two 5-year phases—Phase 1 from 2009 to 2014 and Phase 2 from 2014 to 2019—to strengthen three areas of think tanks: research quality, policy engagement and organizational performance. Through open competition, TTI selected and began to support 43 think tanks in 20 countries: 11 think tanks in Latin America, 14 in South Asia (this is in Phase 2; it was 16 in Phase 1) and 18 in sub-Saharan Africa. The selected think tanks are diverse in terms of establishment, history, size, areas of research, capacity, outreach and strategies of engagement.

The 22 chapters of this book tell the stories of the 14 South Asian think tanks and their journey of strengthening in their specific contexts.

The first chapter introduces the TTI programme, while Chapters 2–15 present the reflections of think tank leaders as the TTI programme evolved. Next five chapters describe the status of social science research in the countries of Bangladesh, India, Pakistan, Nepal and Sri Lanka and outline the broad canvas of social science research in each country. They also highlight issues dealing with research infrastructure that have links to public policy-making. Chapter 21 presents a summary of the experiences of all 14 think tanks in relation to the three areas of TTI support: organizational performance, quality research and policy outreach. The last chapter considers broad lessons and ways forward for the policy research community, particularly funding agencies.

The idea of publishing this book was mooted as the journeys of the TTI cohort began to unfold and the cohort realized the need to document them. It emerged in response to the widely felt need by the TTI-supported think tanks to capture the experiences of and lessons from this innovative programme combining core and complementary capacity-building support. This need was first expressed by the think tanks at the 2012 TTI regional meeting in Mysore and reiterated at subsequent annual regional gatherings. The most recent expression of that need found voice at the sixth regional meeting of the 14 South Asian think tanks in Bangkok in December 2016. There, the TTI participants highlighted the strong need for capturing and documenting the transformative role that TTI support had played in their organizations over the previous eight years (2010–2018). They collectively expressed a strong desire to capture the stories of transformative change in think tanks in a volume which would then be disseminated to help demonstrate the value of core support in strengthening think tanks in ways unseen through project funding. In particular, TTI core funding was unique in creating conditions for long-term sustainability, strengthening organizational systems, enhancing the effectiveness of think tanks and for long-term sustainability. The aim was not only to document a legacy—for little literature exists on the role of think tanks in developing countries in public domain—but also to shift funders' thinking about the modalities that best strengthen think tanks as well as to guide the design of similar programmes in future. IDRC, as one of TTI's several funding agencies and the manager of TTI, readily agreed to support the call to document and share experiences and lessons learned under the leadership of the Institute for Social and Environmental Transition-Nepal (ISET-N).

A small group of executive directors from the cohort expressed an interest in constituting the working group (later called the Core Support Group [CSG]) which would coordinate and deliver this project. Ajaya Dixit from ISET-N and Professor Sukhadeo Thorat from the Indian Institute of Dalit Studies (IIDS) volunteered to jointly lead the CSG. To take this decision forward and to discuss this idea in detail and then develop a road map, a round table of CSG members was organized in Kathmandu on 28 July 2017. TTI staff joined the deliberations to support the project's shape and direction and to facilitate linkages with ongoing global TTI programmatic communication efforts. An initial draft proposal and detailed work plan were agreed upon at the round table, and through subsequent iterations with all leaders of the TTI cohort, a final proposal was prepared. This volume is the result of that proposal.

The chapters in this book provide a picture of the developmental challenges each South Asian country faces and the efforts independent knowledge production institutes have made to tackle those challenges. The book demonstrates that critical knowledge production is fundamental to making an effective policy in and fostering the well-being of South Asian societies. It underscores the fact that South Asian knowledge-providing organizations produce high-calibre research and tackle the social, economic and political problems facing each country using rigorous research. However, they find it very difficult to access funds to support such research. The book also presents the diverse ways in which each organization has engaged in policy outreach. Its 22 chapters present a rich range of approaches to policy influence that will be useful in discerning lessons about the policy-making spheres of South Asian countries. The themes researched by each organization include economic development, poverty alleviation, food security, energy, public dialogue, trade, climate change, governance, disaster risk reduction, urbanization, critical social studies and historiography, though the specific details vary across the five South Asian countries. The book emphatically highlights the need to maintain the momentum created by TTI in new forms and architectures in order to respond to the complexities that South Asian countries and societies face.

Through the persuasive narratives articulated by the South Asian think tank leaders supported by TTI and through the extremely rich diversity of approaches and strategies that think tanks have employed to achieve change through organizational strengthening, the editors hope to remind the donors of the need for and role of core funding for think tanks if they are to help find local solutions to local challenges. As global challenges become increasingly complex and multidisciplinary, governments need rigorous analysis and research so that they can draft effective public policies which can achieve their SDGs. Think tanks, as key providers of evidence-based policy recommendations, continue to play an increasingly key role as credible purveyors of the new knowledge required for policy-making. To become more effective and sustainable, think tanks need long-term, untied core support. The TTI programme effectively demonstrates this possibility through the rich collection of organizational journeys presented in this volume. Governments and donors need to pay heed.

Acknowledgements

A volume of this breadth and depth can scarcely be produced without contributions from not only a large number but also a huge variety of scholars, organizations and individuals drawn from diverse disciplines and backgrounds. This is specially so in this volume which is a result of deep collaboration among 14 think tanks leaders and staff drawn from five South Asian countries, over past eight years. Directors and staff of all 14 think tanks have worked tirelessly and to an extremely ambitious deadline to eventually produce this volume in less than a year. They are as much the authors of their respective chapters in this volume as co-travellers who have made the eight years of the TTI journey since 2010 in South Asia worthwhile. We offer our thanks to all 14 think tank directors—Dushni Weerakoon, Institute of Policy Studies; Udan Fernando, Centre for Poverty Analysis; Khalida Ghaus, Social Policy and Development Centre; Abid Qaiyum Suleri, Sustainable Development Policy Institute; Sultan Hafeez Rahman, BRAC Institute of Governance and Development; Fahmida Khatun, Centre for Policy Dialogue; Gurcharan Gollerkeri, Public Affairs Centre; Anshu Bharadwaj, Centre for Study of Science, Technology and Policy (CSTEP); Sanghmitra S. Acharya, IIDS; Shekhar Shah, National Council of Applied Economic Research; Yamini Aiyar and Pratap Bhanu Mehta, Centre for Policy Research; Subrat Das, Centre for Budget and Governance Accountability; and Sanjay Kumar, Centre for the Study of Developing Societies—for so eloquently sharing their experiences of the TTI journey. Many eminent scholars and staff from research and non-research side from each think tank, and others associated with TTI in countless ways, have contributed to make this journey enjoyable in many different ways. We owe a deep debt of gratitude to them all.

We owe special thanks to CSG of select directors from the TTI cohort who volunteered to steer this project and spent a full day at Kathmandu in July 2017, brainstorming the proposal and work plan for this volume, coordinated and hosted by ISET-N.

This volume is an outcome of eight years of the TTI programme since 2009 in South Asia. Conceived as a global programme by the William and Flora Hewlett Foundation, TTI was initiated with IDRC of Canada—which both funds and manages its implementation globally—and supported by UK government's Department for International Development (DFID), the Bill & Melinda Gates Foundation, the Dutch Ministry of Foreign Affairs (DGIS) and Norwegian government's Norwegian Agency for Development Cooperation (NORAD). But for their progressive vision and path-breaking initiative, a programme of long-term, untied core support of TTI would not have been possible. To each of them, we owe huge gratitude.

As a funder and manager of the TTI programme, we owe special gratitude to many IDRC staff whose unflinching support to strengthening think tanks have enabled building up of a huge social capital in the region. We would particularly like to thank Anindya Chatterjee, Regional Director of Asia Regional Office, for being a constant guide and mentor, and Peter Taylor, Acting Director, Inclusive Economies Program, and Andrew Hurst, Program Leader, TTI, for their continuous support and encouragement to steadfastly uphold the programme values and principles. Seema Bhatia-Panthaki, Senior Program Officer, TTI, deserves a particular mention as an invaluable colleague in Delhi who made the TTI journey enjoyable through her enthusiastic support and critical feedback at all stages of the work. We also thank Sheeba Varghese specially for help in preparing tables.

Multiple rounds of chapter reviews, editorial support, and persuading and coordinating with the publisher were a gigantic task. G.C. Pal and Chandrani Dutta of IIDS played a remarkable role in getting all these done seamlessly, and in record time. We remain deeply grateful for their untiring support, often working until very late evenings and early mornings.

Many staff members at ISET-N have played a key role in coordination of a complex project across seven different cities in five countries.

They have worked relentlessly to complete this work in a very short time. Particular mention must be made of Kanchan Mani Dixit, Rabi Wenju, Anustha Shrestha, Ratna Deep Lohani, Sushila Ghimire, Bishnu Lakhe, Yogendra Subedi, Sheela Bogati, Anurag Pokhrel, Vibustuti Thapa, Ankan Subedi, Prarthana Dixit, Saisha Dixit and Shrabya Singh Karkee for their inputs at different stages. And we owe sincere gratitude to Perry Thapa for her input at different stages. We also thank Jayendra Rimal for his support. Our sincere gratitude also goes to Merlin Francis at CSTEP for her editorial support, working to an ambitious timeline.

Needless to write, this volume would not have seen the light of the day had it not been for the prompt and enthusiastic support from SAGE. They reposed complete trust in us, providing all support as required in ensuring the quality of the product. They rose remarkably to the challenge of standing by our side and completing the entire publication cycle in a record period of three months to meet our requirements. We remain indebted to SAGE in taking up the manuscript on an urgent basis to publish it within an ambitious time frame.

Recognizing the contribution of individuals and organizations limited to making possible the publication of this volume would be myopic. Countless intellectuals, thinkers, scholars, practitioners and visionaries, from past and present, have, in many different ways not always attributable or even explicitly known, have contributed to making the TTI journey possible and enjoyable. What we have learnt, and what we are yet to learn, is the product of thoughts, practices and actions of many. We take this opportunity to thank all who helped us see far and beyond.

The thoughts and experiences included in this volume are testimony to the vision of the funders of TTI and other similar core support programmes, including in the past. Equally, we hope that the evidence and stories in this volume will emphatically shift the mainstream thinking in the funding community—from public and private philanthropic sectors—and reignite their long-term commitment to strengthen think tanks as crucial public policy interlocutors.

PART I

Introduction

Chapter 1

Think Tank Initiative: A Bold Experiment in Strengthening Think Tanks

Andrew Hurst, Seema Bhatia-Panthaki and Samar Verma

CONTEXT

The role of local actors and institutions, such as think tanks, in generating locally relevant evidence and knowledge, providing inputs into the design of policies and programmes best suited to contextual realities, and engaging with a range of locally invested stakeholders is increasingly well-documented in development literature. Donors, both international and domestic, have increasingly recognized that local ownership is critical to successful development interventions and their future sustainability. Despite this recognition, however, investments in local organizational capacities and their institutional landscapes to set, shape and implement locally relevant development agendas have not always been a high priority for donors. This increases the risk of ineffectiveness and failure of development interventions, no matter how well-meaning the interventions may be.

The Think Tank Initiative (TTI) was set up in response to bridge the gap in the market for locally informed, context-specific public policies. The initiative's core aims were to strengthen the organizational capacities of a group of local, independent policy research organizations, or think tanks, based in East and West Africa, South Asia and Latin America to produce and communicate high-quality, contextualized, objective and timely evidence that informs and influences policy and practice. The donors of this programme understood the long-term commitment required to do this and subsequently designed the initiative with a 10-year time horizon, divided over two 5-year phases—Phase 1 from 2009 to 2014 and Phase 2 from 2014 to 2019—which allowed the funders to take stock of grantee performance, revisit the core principles of the initiative and make any design tweaks required at the end of Phase 1.

FUNDERS

Conceived by the William and Flora Hewlett Foundation, TTI was initiated in 2008 by the International Development Research Centre (IDRC), which both funds and manages its implementation in the three regions. Subsequently, three other funders came on board to join the initiative. These were the UK government's Department for International Development (DFID), the Bill & Melinda Gates Foundation (BMGF) and the Dutch Ministry of Foreign Affairs (DGIS) for Phase 1 (2009–2014). Following a review at the end of Phase 1, all donors except DGIS[1] remained on board to support this work over the next five-year period. The Norwegian government's Norwegian Agency for Development Cooperation (NORAD) joined the initiative as a funding partner for the final year of Phase 1 and committed to support it along with the Hewlett Foundation, IDRC, BMGF and DFID until the end of its cycle in September 2019.

PROGRAMME MISSION, DESIGN AND APPROACH

TTI's mission is to strengthen the capacity of local think tanks to produce objective, high-quality research and evidence that can be utilized by policy-makers to support interventions that contribute to more equitable and prosperous societies. Following through on this

[1] A change in their organizational priorities led to DGIS' decision to not join Phase 2.

ambition required investments in building local capacities over a longer time horizon as compared to usual development programme cycles. In order to contribute to context-specific development priorities, think tanks had to be able to establish their own research agendas to fill specific evidence gaps, stay invested within research portfolios over a period of time in a planned and strategic way, and be ready to respond to emerging opportunities within the local development context.

Strengthening organizational research quality mechanisms, improving organizational performance, and sharpening policy outreach and communication of think tanks' outputs were identified as the three core areas or pillars for support in the initiative's design. To enable this, the support provided to think tanks included a combination of core, or flexible, non-earmarked funding and complementary, targeted and supplementary capacity-building support explained as follows:

1. **Core funding support:** This component formed 60 per cent of the funding provided to think tanks over the life cycle of the initiative. It comprised flexible, non-earmarked, long-term funding support, allocated across the three pillars against a set of objectives determined by the think tanks themselves in consultation with TTI programme officers. This ensured that the think tanks owned and remained committed to building capacities across the organization in line with their mission and priorities.

2. **Technical support:** In addition to core support grants, TTI provided technical support to the grantee think tank. While the technical support provided in both the phases was linked directly to the TTI Results Framework, the modalities of its delivery were starkly different. In the first phase, targeted technical support was provided in the area of policy engagement and communications. It was designed and delivered through TTI selected agencies. A review of this support at the end of Phase 1 revealed that this format was not well-suited to such a diverse grantee group with different needs, priorities and expertise in the area. Therefore, in Phase 2, a more concerted effort was made to design and deliver the capacity-building support, taking into account these differences and better aligning with grantee needs and priorities across all three pillars of TTI.

In addition to such targeted capacity offerings in both phases, additional support was made available, including on developing new research portfolios and encouraging research collaborations, through two other specific modalities—the Matching Fund calls in Phase 1 and the Opportunity Fund calls in Phase 2.

Key learning events have also facilitated capacity building through peer learning for the TTI grantees across the three pillars of the initiative. These include the TTI Exchanges that took place in Cape Town (2012) and Istanbul (2015) and the seven regional meetings (RMs) in South Asia that have enabled open spaces for think tanks to learn lessons emerging on the opportunities and challenges faced within the peer network and the sector in other contexts.

THE SELECTION PROCESS

At its global launch in 2008,[2] the programme selected a cohort of think tanks. It had the following specific aims:

1. Assist them to assess critical areas of strength and weakness, and identify opportunities for improved organizational performance.
2. Provide a combination of general support funding or core support and access to training and technical support to achieve improvements in research quality, policy linkages and other aspects of organizational performance.
3. Capture and share programme learning about strategies for supporting and managing policy research organizations in order to influence the future activities of the funding partners, think tanks and other development actors.

Four geographic clusters of countries in the three continents were identified globally for the work of the initiative on the basis of five broad criteria: need (based on income per capita), population size (since very small countries may not have a sufficient range of research organizations to warrant support), political openness (since willingness

---

[2] The programme was first launched in Africa in 2008 and then in Latin America and South Asia in 2009. Grants were initiated with selected organizations in 2009.

of governments to make use of independent research results is critical), political stability, and extent of local funding of research and development (as an indicator of the ability of local governments to contribute over the longer term to the work of independent think tanks). These regions/countries included the following:

- East Africa: Ethiopia, Kenya, Rwanda, Tanzania and Uganda
- West Africa: Benin, Burkina Faso, Ghana, Mali, Nigeria and Senegal
- South Asia: Bangladesh, India, Nepal, Sri Lanka and Pakistan
- Latin America: Honduras, Bolivia, Ecuador, El Salvador, Guatemala, Peru and Paraguay

A rigorous selection process across the globe produced a mixed portfolio consisting of independent think tanks that varied in size (large, mid-sized and small), age (young and established), areas of policy focus (themes as well as local, national and international) and division of work between research and advocacy projects. Of the total 52 selected think tanks, 16 were based in South Asia.[3] To understand the diversity of the selected South Asian cohort at the start of the initiative, consider the following:

1. The age of the selected think tanks ranged from 5 to 54 years, with total number of staff ranging from 15 to 131. Full-time researchers also ranged from 8 to 51 across the cohort in 2010.
2. Their annual budget ranged from less than CAD 500,000 to over CAD 2.5 million.
3. Of the 16 think tanks, 4 had no previous relationship of working with IDRC, whereas 2 had over seven projects each from IDRC worth CAD 4 million.
4. The huge dependence of think tanks on international sources of funding was also observed during institutional visits to 34 think tanks as part of the selection process in the five South Asian countries. Of the total annual funding for all the 34 think tanks

---

[3] The selected think tanks are based in five South Asian countries: Bangladesh, India, Nepal, Pakistan and Sri Lanka.

combined, 54 per cent came from international sources. While this was 44 per cent for Indian think tanks, it was significantly higher at 84 per cent for the other four South Asian countries combined. Only 20 per cent of all funding for Indian think tanks came from the government, and it was much less (an average of 3%) for the other four countries in the region. While the share of domestic philanthropy in the annual budgets of the grantee think tanks in India was 12 per cent, it stood at a meagre average of 3 per cent in the neighbouring four countries.

5. A huge diversity was also noticed across the thematic areas that the 14 selected think tanks were working in, which was a result of the programme design being theme-agnostic.[4] All selected think tanks worked in multiple areas of policy research, ranging from agriculture, food security and climate change to energy, technology, budgets, inclusion, and discrimination, governance and gender.

GOVERNANCE STRUCTURE

The governance structure for this multi-year, multi-country and multi-donor initiative reflected the composition of funders active in TTI. The Executive Committee (EC), comprising representatives from each of TTI's five funders, was the main body for discussion and joint decision-making by all donors. It focused on strategic decision-making and learning, leaving most of the operational decision-making to IDRC. An International Advisory Group (IAG) consisting of eminent scholars from different parts of the world was also constituted to guide the design and implementation of the programme at its start. Over the course of the implementation period, the IAG's role was found to overlap with that of the EC, thus it was dissolved. Subsequently, the EC took the lead on all strategy decision-making and learning for most of Phase 2.

---

[4] This was a criterion of the selection process; that is, the call was designed to encourage applications from think tanks working in several policy areas, with a general focus on those active in socio-economic research. As a result, think tanks dedicated to working on several issues within a single thematic area, such as gender or climate or trade, did not qualify.

MID-PROGRAMME: PHASE 2 REVIEW (2014)

A reassessment of the organizations selected for grants on the completion of the first five-year phase in 2014 was built in at the design stage of the grant call. This meant that the think tanks for support in Phase 1 had to demonstrate continued commitment and considerable improvements in their operational capacities, research quality and policy engagement, and communication capabilities at the end of the phase to be considered for continued funding.

After looking at the results of the programme and strategic deliberations, the EC decided to restrict the eligibility of think tanks to receive TTI support in Phase 2 to those that had already won the competition in Phase 1. It was felt that funding grantees from within the existing cohort was appropriate, given that the original country selection criteria still held, and in light of TTI's rationale as a long-term institutional capacity development programme.

A number of lessons learnt from the experience of Phase 1 were identified which, combined with the findings of the external evaluation and valuable inputs from the EC, grantees and other stakeholders, have been instrumental in steering the design and strategy of Phase 2 approach. Thus, at the programme level, prominent lessons that informed the Phase 2 approach included the following: the need to preserve the regional diversity of the cohort, the importance of further encouraging and catalysing peer-learning and regional collaboration, the acknowledged value and benefits of core support (strongly buttressed by the results of the external evaluation), and an imperative to further improve the suite of monitoring tools based on the varied and enriched understanding of what 'success' meant to different grantees and donors.

It was also decided that the support to grantees that were unable to fully benefit from participation in the programme and experienced difficulties in their leadership and governance—despite the efforts of programme staff—be discontinued. In a few cases, Phase 2 support was made contingent on achievement of certain specific milestones by midway through the phase. As a result, 14 of the 16 South Asian TTI grantees were chosen to receive support for a further five years.

PROGRAMME MONITORING

The provision of core support had an element of trust in organizations and organization building, no matter how rigorous the process
of selection of the think tanks was. It was critical to maintain a balance
between detailed monitoring for accountability purposes on the one
hand and allowing enough flexibility and space for think tanks to know
and exercise real ownership in the use of the core support on the other.
Considerable efforts have, therefore, gone into thinking strategically
and then designing and refining the multiple tools to monitor progress
both of the think tanks' use of core grant and of the programme results.

The TTI's vision of promoting the production and use of high-
quality evidence to inform and influence policy-making is also reflected
in its programming. The initiative's monitoring and learning tools are
premised on collecting evidence on performance to be utilized both
by the grantees and TTI to address accountability needs of both as well
as to learn from the data to tweak objectives and programme design in
real time. It has also been used to inform other funders already engaged
in, or interested in undertaking, organizational strengthening efforts.

GRANTEE-LEVEL TOOLS

At the start of each phase, a set of long-term, organizational change
objectives across the three pillars of TTI's support were negotiated and
agreed to with each think tank for the duration of that phase, that is,
five years. These were tailored to the specific needs and ambitions of
each grantee. The objectives were then broken down into annual work
plans with clear milestones. These helped the think tanks periodically
assess their own progress towards the set objectives. The approach was
designed to be flexible enough to allow think tanks to re-evaluate priorities and respond to changing demands within their national policy
contexts over the course of the programme. The tailored objectives
thus formed the basis for the assessment of progress and improvement
at the individual think tank level.

The monitoring tools to collect data against these objectives were
designed to help not just generate evidence on performance but also

help make self-assessments and reflect on the progress made year on year. These included the following:[5]

1. **The annual technical and financial reports:** These enabled data gathering for the purposes of monitoring progress made towards achieving the tailored objectives, managing risks from implementation and designing of the work plans and budgets for the following year.

2. **The annual monitoring questionnaire (AMQ):** This collected grantee-level data around the common indicators outlined in the TTI Results Framework, identified after extensive consultations with grantees, TTI staff, IDRC's in-house evaluation experts and donors. In Phase 2, this monitoring instrument was revised to include a smaller number of indicators that were more closely aligned with what grantees themselves and the programme found useful in informing their budget–allocation choices over time.

3. **Institutional monitoring visits:** These underpinned the 'trust factor' of the core funding relationship built with the think tanks over the years. The annual monitoring visits enabled TTI programme officers to formally visit grantee organizations and take stock of progress towards the objectives with the think tanks themselves. These visits provided in-depth, critical feedback on performance and allowed for the sharing of lessons from other similar think tanks on how they responded to challenges and opportunities emerging within their national policy contexts. These conversations, underpinned by the data collected in the technical and financial reports and the AMQ, formed the basis for honest, if sometimes difficult, conversations.

PROGRAMME-LEVEL TOOLS

1. **Programme snapshot:** Limited to the implementation of Phase 1 of the programme, the snapshot provided an overview of

---

[5] In addition to the tools listed, there were other reporting tools designed for internal learning purposes highlighting the performance of think tanks, capturing their stories of success and their challenges, and capturing reflections of programme staff from the extensive interactions they had with the think tanks.

programme performance across four main areas, including grantee progress, grantee spending, a newsfeed of grantee activities and TTI spending, showing the annual progress on spending against the budget by line item. As all data for the snapshot were available from regular TTI monitoring tools, this required no additional data collection. In Phase 2, the information they contained was compiled on an 'as needed' basis for particular organizations, rather than annually for the whole programme.

2. **TTI technical and financial reports to donors:** The technical and financial reports for TTI as a programme were sent annually to funders using the same common technical reporting framework that was agreed upon by all funders in Phase 1. The technical report provided an overview of TTI's programme activities over the year, progress towards the implementation of the programme in relation to the Results Framework and to the annual work plan reviewed by the EC, lessons learned over the year and challenges ahead.

LEARNING TOOLS

1. **Grantee scorecard:** The grantee scorecard included self-assessments by grantees as well as assessments by the programme officers in the form of numeric scores on progress made towards yearly milestones within each tailored objective. Scores were allocated to each milestone and to each tailored objective as a whole. This scoring mechanism allowed the programme to scale up the analysis of grantee progress at country, regional and cohort levels. These scores were shared back with the think tanks in order to help them track progress, and as a basis for identifying capacity development needs.

2. **Peer review:** The peer review generated a score for up to four research papers produced by each grantee. This review, conducted by external reviewers, was undertaken for all grantees at the beginning of Phase 1, then towards the end of Phase 1 and finally towards the end of Phase 2. A sample of grantees were reviewed in the second, third and fourth years with the intent of having two data points for each grantee in Phase 2, and four data points overall. The peer review exercise was designed to track grantee progress in the

area of research quality. The outcomes of peer reviews undertaken in Phase 1 informed each think tank's Phase 2-tailored objectives related to research quality. As is customary, peer review scores and feedback were shared back with the grantee think tanks to help them strengthen their research quality processes.

3. **Policy community survey (PCS):** PCS is a perception survey that was administered to a wide variety of policy stakeholders in each country where TTI was active. Targeted respondents included senior-level policy-makers (both elected politicians and unelected bureaucrats), media, civil society and union leaders, and other researchers and academics. PCS was designed with three objectives in mind. First, it was intended to shed light on the nature of the demand for research by the wider policy community within which the selected think tanks operate and to capture perceptions of each think tank's contribution to national policy processes. Second, it provided a basis for reflection by each think tank on its own performance as seen through the eyes of its key constituents. This, it was hoped, would help them identify critical organizational capacity needs that required attention. For instance, if respondents indicated a poor awareness of a think tank's work, this was a sign that the think tank in question should invest more in connecting with and engaging the stakeholders who were supposed to be the consumers of its research. Finally, it was felt that PCS would capture shifts or broad changes in the policy community in a particular country over time, and by extension serve as a basis to judge the extent to which each think tank is perceived to have adapted to those changes. PCS was administered at the beginning of and towards the end of Phase 1, and again in the final year of Phase 2, allowing for longitudinal comparisons of change in the policy contexts within and across countries.

PROGRAMME EVALUATION

Over the two phases of TTI, independent, external evaluations were commissioned twice—a mid-term summative evaluation at the end of Phase 1 and an accompaniment evaluation, which began at the start of Phase 2 as a way to inform ongoing implementation of the initiative.

Key lessons from this independent, external evaluation of Phase 1,[6] applicable to the programme globally and not just in South Asia, indicated that the TTI model of support has provided compelling results across its key areas of support to think tanks, that is, research quality, policy engagement and communication, and organizational performance. For instance, it found that most think tanks invested in improved research capacity through staff training, investments in analytical software and improved internal peer review systems as a result of this long-term funding. It also found strong evidence of increased research breadth and depth among funded think tanks, and more regular publications.

Several lessons from this Phase 1 evaluation informed the design of Phase 2 of TTI and helped to set its implementation priorities. The following were some of these lessons:

1. **Collaboration:** The Phase 1 evaluation highlighted that while think tanks often work on similar themes, pooling and scaling this work through collaboration was not always feasible due to resource and capacity constraints. TTI recognized this issue towards the end of Phase 1 and made subsequent funding available that required think tanks to collaborate on multi-country or regional projects, build targeted research capacities, seed new areas of thematic research and strengthen wider networks with non-TTI partners.
2. **Data collection:** The evaluation in Phase 1 highlighted the need to focus on the collection of better data on policy engagement and outreach of think tanks. Monitoring tools were accordingly modified at the beginning of Phase 2.
3. **Design of the capacity-building component:** The evaluation also raised questions about the extent to which targeted, supplemental capacity development support in Phase 1 was adequately needs-based. As a result, Phase 2 followed more of a demand-led approach, with the intention of increasing ownership by the think tanks of the modality and better linking of these activities to the think tanks' strategic objectives. This also resulted in increased

---

[6] Drawn from TTI's internal document, 'The Think Tank Program: Strengthening Policy Research for Development Phase 2', May 2013.

engagement of local service providers and allowed for think tanks themselves, where they had the demonstrated capacity, to get involved in delivering this supplemental technical assistance.

4. **Cohort selection and flexibility in implementation:** The evaluators confirmed the validity of selecting the original think tank cohort and the diversity in terms of their size, age, thematic expertise and the regional spread that resulted. They also confirmed the value of the open and flexible approach in defining what the three pillars of the initiative (research quality, policy engagement and communications, and organizational performance) looked like for each organization, as this accommodated the different national contexts. In turn, this made the organizational strengthening objectives more relevant for each organization and aided the learning process on how best to use core and technical support. The same approach was, therefore, adopted in Phase 2.

REFLECTIONS ON THE PROGRAMME'S IMPLEMENTATION IN SOUTH ASIA

This section captures reflections from the IDRC's TTI team on what has worked and what has been challenging in the initiative's implementation, specifically in South Asia. These reflections are based on the experience of implementing the initiative on the ground, some of which are corroborated by the evidence cited in the Phase 2 independent evaluation reports.[7]

ON CORE FUNDING: USE, SIZE, OWNERSHIP AND LONG-TERM SUSTAINABILITY USE

As also highlighted by the evaluators at the end of Phase 1, core funding has played a critical role in the strengthening of think tanks. The long-term, non-earmarked and predictable nature of 'core' funding, combined with principles of flexibility, ownership and a focus on both accountability and learning for the TTI and the grantees, has enabled a cohort of South Asian think tanks to make a step change in the way

[7] Report available at http://www.thinktankinitiative.org/blog/new-findings-tti-evaluators (accessed on 17 August 2018).

organizations work. For instance, assuring research quality, implementing prudent financial and human resources practices, resourcing policy engagement and communications teams, and undertaking strategic planning exercises at set intervals are now a core part of the business of grantee think tank management.

The Phase 2 evaluation reports highlight the links among core grants, think tanks' independence and strategic planning, leadership and governance, and how they are positioned for influencing policy and practices within given contexts.

Think tanks' credibility to work in contested political spaces stems from their ability to remain independent. While how think tanks defined what independence meant varied—from the ability to set their own research agenda independent of donor and/or government priorities to the ability to maintain an impartial, evidence-based stance in political debates—core funding played a crucial role in helping the organizations define this sense of independence and confidence for themselves. Closely connected to this was the positioning of think tanks, or their ability to influence policies within the given context. We observed that both independence and positioning were significantly driven by the investments made in strategic planning processes, strengthening thematic leadership practices, and having in place organizational structures and systems that were fit for the purpose.

Size

There has been some discussion on what constitutes the right amount of core funding in proportion to the think tanks' organizational budgets. In the absence of any preceding evidence and guidelines, we decided to provide typically one-third of the total organizational budget as core grants. This was based on the principle that the core grant support should be large enough to enable the think tanks to make a transformative difference in their organizational effectiveness and yet small enough to not make them dependent on this core grant in the long run. There were arguable important exceptions to this thumb rule, where a small think tank needed a larger dose to overcome critical challenges as identified in institutional assessment reports, or where the organization's budget was too large for TTI to meet the thumb rule without compromising on the quality of support to many other smaller and younger think tanks. Overall, despite the thumb rule, the decision was based on institutional assessment reports—areas of identified and expressed (by think tanks) strengthening—as well as the TTI team's assessment of critical factors needing support for a transformative change. On balance, this approach based on the principle of optimum support seems to have worked well.

Ownership

Another important nuance in this approach that also worked well is worth noting. The think tanks were allowed to distribute the total grant spread over two multi-year instalments (of five years each) in the manner that they thought best but after having to make a persuasive case to TTI. Some think tanks chose to front-load their grant distribution, while some others back-loaded this. Many were comfortable with an equal distribution over the grant period. This flexibility and assurance of being able to draw down their total grant in a way most useful to them was a source of tremendous confidence to the think tanks. But it was not an unfettered freedom they enjoyed—they had to make a persuasive case to be able to carry forward, or defer, expenses. Annual monitoring visits by TTI programme officers combined with regular conversations during the year played an important role in this mechanism working seamlessly.

An interesting observation from the initial year of TTI grant making relates to the challenges many think tanks faced in drawing up an independent set of objectives for the entire grant period as was required of them. Several think tanks realized that the process was challenging because for many of the executive directors, handling a TTI core grant was a 'first-in-their-lifetime' experience, while for several others, there was little existing organizational mechanism to develop a set of grant objectives that was owned by the entire organization—from governing board members and directors to research staff as well as administration, human resources, communications, library and IT staff. The process of setting up such mechanisms and getting them to function was reported as an important organizational strengthening by many think tanks. Most think tanks could do it in months, but few took longer.

From our experience, and from think tanks' reports, we know how they have transformed themselves not only as a result of the use of core funding but also due to the processes that have been set in place to handle the grant's objective—setting and organizational ownership of such objectives for core grants.

Long-Term Sustainability

Would this flush of core grants over a decade make them sustainable forever? While the core grants have made them stronger, more effective, more confident, more credible and independent, organizations require sustainable sources of such funding to be able to maintain similar levels of credibility and effectiveness. Decade-long TTI core grants have transformed the business of think tanks in the cohort—it has propelled them into a higher orbit of effectiveness, organizational efficiency, influence, credibility and strategic positioning. However, we have argued at multiple forums on the need for strengthening research ecosystems and enhanced public funding for policy research which is a public good.[8] This public funding could come from public sources, or public–private partnerships, especially in India where there is a rich tradition of corporate funding of many top institutions of higher learning and research, and where a recent central government law, mandating a fixed proportion of earnings in private and public sector to be spent on corporate social responsibility (CSR), has created a significant opportunity. This highlights the fact that to ensure longer sustainability of think tanks, it is not enough to strengthen the think tanks' capacities alone; this requires investments in the ecosystem within which think

---

[8] One example of such efforts is programme engagement with Indian Council of Social Science Research (ICSSR) that resulted in a pioneering work—Thorat and Verma, *Social Science Research in India*. Others include Srinivasan and Verma, 'Public Policy Research in South Asia', 58–61; Verma, 'Social Science Research', 88–102; Verma, Vaidyanathan, and Bharadwaj, 'Corporate Social Responsibility in India'; and a blog to advocate for the TTI model as guide to fund Indian think tanks.

tanks work. Indeed, our efforts[9] to create awareness on the need for a vibrant national research ecosystem for think tank sustainability were drawn from our early learning in the TTI programme.

ON PROGRAMME TOOLS, INCLUDING EVALUATION

TTI's data collection tools were designed to encourage the grantees' use of evidence and data generated in planning for their own organizational journeys. As a matter of fact, the processes of institutional assessments were reported by many think tanks as very useful in helping them put in place organizational systems and processes as knowledge management system as well as management information system (MIS) tools at the organizational levels.

In the case of the use of the peer review process, a standard tool to assess research quality of academic products, however, the tool did not successfully translate as a means to map research quality of think tanks' products. Grantees typically submitted research outputs that were already published or completed, which meant feedback could not be incorporated into the outputs themselves. Further, peer review proved to be an imperfect tool for measuring non-academic products like policy briefs or reports, as reviewers found it difficult to judge these outputs on grounds other than academic rigour. Moreover, think tanks themselves frequently operated with different priorities and different quality principles, which meant they often put greater weight on factors such as accessibility and timeliness of research products rather than purely on academic rigour. These differences reflect broader

---

[9] Two notable efforts are TTI catalysing the creation and launch in September 2014, of Asian Social Science Association (ASSA), a pan Asian knowledge platform for peer-learning and enhanced international and interdisciplinary collaboration, to promote social science research in Asia, consisting of representatives of social science research councils, government bodies, fraternal members and associate members from many Asian countries and TTI catalysing the tri-national (Bangladesh, India and Nepal) effort to introduce regional pedagogy and discourse on public policy, first concrete outcome of which is a regional public policy and governance conference organized by Nepal Administrative Staff College (NASC), a premier government agency that trains senior public officials in Nepal. The second annual conference was organized in June 2018.

debates, both about the different ways of measuring research quality in individual policy research outputs and the challenges of measuring improvements in organizational research quality.

The global programme evaluation was a major learning tool for TTI to understand and learn systematically about the impact of core funding on think tanks' organizational performance and subsequently their contribution towards better informed policy-making processes as a result of such strengthening. With four in-depth case studies from the South Asia region included in the report, the evaluation provided both a helpful feedback on the programme's ongoing implementation in the region and a valuable basis for learning for those case study organizations. The evaluation methodology was also able to reaffirm more rigorously what programme officers judged intuitively through their work.

ON THE RM PLATFORM

The RM of the South Asian cohort of TTI-supported think tanks has been a major, and unique, knowledge-sharing platform ('network effect', as one think tank has mentioned) for think tankers. Prior to the TTI RMs, think tanks engaged with each other on thematic issues through policy forums but lacked a platform for discussion on the 'business of managing think tanks'. The annual RM in South Asia—a unique platform—was set up in response to the demand from think tank leadership to learn from their peers on issues of organizational and management practices and responding to changes in the regulatory and policy contexts. It provided an opportunity to understand common and different challenges faced in undertaking policy research and informing and influencing narratives based on evidence and data. We have consistently been told by think tanks how valuable this platform has been, and how TTI RMs were the only platform for discussion of institutional matters.

A total of seven RMs were held in Asia over the duration of TTI's two phases. Over the years, the scope and scale of the platform also changed to respond to requests for greater participation from different groups or communities of practice within think tanks such as researchers, communications teams and policy engagement teams. From our experience of combining the RMs with bespoke capacity building on issues such as resource mobilisation, we learnt the need to be more inclusive and demand driven in our approach, and also customize the delivery of capacity building to reflect the diversity in needs and abilities across the 14 think tanks in South Asia. The last two meetings provided the scope to undertake targeted, demand-led capacity-building activities around data visualization and gender in think tank research and organizations that link back to strategic priorities within the cohort and help widen the communities of practice in this sector. These have been well received and reported to have been useful by think tank participants.

We also learnt along the journey and widened the scope of the membership at the meetings to include younger staff in addition to coupling the meetings with capacity building-activities in Phase 2.

There are at least two reflections that are worth considering in the design of such platforms. First, the fifth RM opened up a space for discussion on thematic discussions, but this received a tepid response from participants as most felt that the value of the platform was in the discussion on institutional matters, rather than thematic issues for which other more specialized forums were available. Second, while the capacity-development activities were demand driven and delivered using South Asian experts and through peer learning processes, these could have been more explicitly and better linked to overall capacity-building framework for the region for enabling the learning from the activities to be more sustainable.

ON BALANCING LEARNING AND ACCOUNTABILITY WITHIN THINK TANKS

While TTI has been successful in helping translate core funding to improve internal and external accountability systems, particularly with regard to human resources and financial systems management, strategic planning exercises and research quality management processes, it is less clear how this has helped transform think tanks into hubs with significant expertise on knowledge management to promote learning on themes.

The think tanks worked on multiple themes within their own organizations and linking data and evidence across themes and over time would have enhanced the quality of research to support policy and practice.

However, think tanks focused on the use of core and complementary support to set up and strengthen accountability systems and process for much of the TTI period and less so on transforming into learning organizations with strong knowledge management systems in place. This is reflected in the second interim report of the evaluators, which, for instance, has recommended that in future, think tanks should focus on developing more analytical narratives describing their organization's conceptual and strategic positioning rather than the instrumental use of their stories of impact narratives. An organizational structure focused on learning as a key goal would have been able to use the data being produced to do just that.

This again brings an important issue to the fore. Given the contextual constraints within which think tanks grow, and do so in stages, balancing the accountability and learning functions would require resourcing over a longer-term time frame than the TTI's 10 years.

ON THE PROGRAMME OFFICER ACCOMPANIMENT MODEL

Grant-making is both an art and a science. The approach to grant-making that IDRC adopts in its programming is known as the 'grants-plus' model, which includes technical expertise provided by programme officers in addition to the financial grants provided for projects. In the case of TTI, programme officers provided active support to each institution in shaping their objectives, often acting as sounding boards to provide critical, objective and constructive inputs through their development journey. Such inputs were grounded not just in the technical expertise and training of the programme officers but also knowledge of the changing dynamics of the ecosystems within which think tanks worked. This approach is in sharp contrast to many other funders who restrict their engagement strictly to administering and monitoring the grant or those that tend to be very directive in the way the projects are conceptualized, designed and delivered. In the case of TTI, each grant was administered separately, customized to the specific requirements of the think tank as articulated by the think tanks, combined with objective inputs provided by the programme officers.

Capacity-building grants deal with sensitive issues such as organizational leadership, governance and people management and are premised on relationships based on principles of trust and ownership. For the TTI programme officers, this required balancing the responsibilities around grant management in the three support areas and respecting each think tank's decision-making sovereignty around these sensitive issues early on in the implementation of the initiative.

There is no single recipe to create the deep sense of trust and ownership required in this case, but it became clear very early in the programme that both these would be crucial to the successful implementation of the initiative. Monitoring visits by programme officers, therefore, focused on working with the research, non-research, management, leadership and governance staff at think tanks to get their buy-in for the programme, and establishing mutual respect and space for honest conversations and ideas. This was not a time-limited process—trust building for honest feedback remained a process all through the programme's implementation phases for both the think tanks and the programme officers.

This relationship served the achievement of programme objectives as well as the purpose of strengthening the grantee think tanks themselves. It took time, but eventually we learnt what is now strongly confirmed in literature:[10] deep and trusted interpersonal relationship based on mutual learning and appreciation is key to policy influence.

As informed interlocutors and trusted critics, we were frequently asked to share our insights and reflections with think tanks to help them perform better, set up bespoke institutional research quality assurance mechanisms, identify and address their areas of vulnerabilities and challenges as they grew rapidly,[11] help them mobilize resources

---

[10] See http://www.ids.ac.uk/news/social-relationships-are-at-the-heart-of-knowledge-for-development (accessed on 17 August 2018).

[11] http://www.thinktankinitiative.org/blog/adolescence-adulthood-managing-growth-think-tanks (accessed on 17 August 2018).

for financial sustainability, or engage their governing boards on ways to improve governance and organizational leadership, and redesign organizational structures and systems for stronger organizations. These relationships developed across think tanks created a huge source of social capital for the IDRC and TTI's funders as well as the think tanks themselves—these will prove to be an amazing asset that will long outlive the programme's life. While the extent and depth of engagement with the think tanks varied by institution, the 'soft' power of persuasion, developed through deep and regular engagement, enabled us to achieve the outcomes of TTI grant better and more effectively. The same power also helped us in the programme to tweak our programming approach and modify our modalities and tools better and quicker to suit the needs and interests of the think tanks as we learnt from them while walking the journey together with them.

However, by the very nature of such human transactions, much of this relationship remained undocumented[12] but constituted an important pillar of programme achievement and think tank effectiveness. It required playing multiple roles at different times—that of task masters to ensure deadlines and standards of grant reporting were met, as well as that of informed knowledge interlocutors, objective counsels, respected peers and trusted confidants as needed. The TTI's first interim evaluation report of June 2017 also highlighted the important 'coaching' role of programme officers and reported their valuable 'nudging' role in the region. The second interim report went on to say that

> The accompaniment role [of the POs) in ... [strategic planning] ... was particularly appreciated and there are initial signs that this may help the grantees in reflecting, over time, about the ways that a business model should bridge concerns about resource mobilization with overall strategic planning.[13]

---

[12] Referred to as 'secret ingredient' by a TTI programme staff in her blog. Available at: http://www.thinktankinitiative.org/blog/programme-officers-tti%E2%80%99s-secret-ingredient (accessed on 17 August 2018).

[13] 'External Evaluation of TTI Phase 2', Second Interim Report, 5 December 2017 (TTI internal document).

CONTINUING THE JOURNEY

Over nearly a decade, TTI has demonstrated that think tanks can, and do, influence policies and practice in their countries, regions and internationally. We know that research and evidence foster vibrant policy landscapes and accelerate development progress, and IDRC has for long been working to get knowledge into the hands of those who can use it. The TTI programme was a bold step in that direction; bold because at the time when TTI was conceptualized, there was precious little donor funding available as core support for think tanks' strengthening. The role of think tanks in development processes, such as in the achievement of the Sustainable Development Goals (SDGs), was clearly recognized and supported by TTI.[14] TTI has remarkably demonstrated that long-term development research is done and leveraged best when think tanks have the bandwidth to define their long-term research agenda independently and have the confidence to resource this decision in a sustainable manner. TTI has not only strengthened think tanks but has also equally contributed to strengthening the research ecosystem through its support to and engagement with national research granting councils, thus building the knowledge landscape as well as creating conditions for sustainable production of good-quality, collaborative social science research, as in Asia. As contributors in the SDGs process, many think tanks in low- and middle-income countries have combined rigorous research with locally rooted citizen and policy engagement. They have bridged the local with the global, connected citizens with decision-makers and generated creative yet grounded solutions.

A lot has changed since TTI started in 2009. A dramatic set of political and economic events globally has brought rapid changes to the national, regional and international policy landscape. In many countries, donor and government ideologies and priorities have changed significantly, risks of increased fragility from climatic shocks have increased and global governance that seemed relatively assured

---

[14] One example of this initiative is the 'Southern Voice' network of 48 think tanks from around the globe that was catalysed by the TTI programme to bring evidence-based voice from the global south into agenda setting for SDGs. See http://southernvoice.org (accessed on 17 August 2018).

now seems less certain with major political upheavals in a wide range of contexts, both traditional donor and recipient countries alike. At the same time, in many quarters, the value of evidence as a key input towards informed policy- and decision-making is increasingly recognized. 'No public policy can be developed, no market interaction can occur, and no statement in the public sphere can be made, that does not refer explicitly or implicitly to the findings and concepts of social and human sciences.'[15] The experience of TTI has shown that support for evidence-based policy-making by strengthening think tanks can help achieve inclusive, transparent and rigorous action around development challenges as defined by the SDGs in a more sustainable manner and through organizations that are resilient to tough times and challenging institutional contexts.

---

[15] See Wittrock (2010: 207) in Bastow, Dunleavy, and Tinkler, *The Impact of the Social Sciences.*

PART II

The Journey of Think Tanks: Bangladesh, Nepal, Pakistan and Sri Lanka

Chapter 2

BRAC Institute of Governance and Development

Sultan Hafeez Rahman and Kaneta Zillur

INTRODUCTION

Bangladesh, despite many adversities and challenges, has emerged as a lower middle-income country. With a GDP growth exceeding 6 per cent per year and sound macroeconomic management for nearly three decades, it has consistently beaten downside risks, signalling increasing economic resilience. The performance of the agriculture sector has been perhaps the most impressive on the supply side. From being the largest food grain importer in the world at independence in 1971, Bangladesh achieved self-sufficiency by the late 1990s. Farm incomes and productivity increased while the sector diversified. A large amount of scarce foreign exchange resources was released for priority investment elsewhere in the economy. Poverty declined from 41 per cent in 1991 to 15 per cent in 2016. The share of agriculture in total GDP declined steadily to below 20 per cent by 2010, contributing to resilience of the economy. The robust GDP growth was accompanied by impressive social indicators, allowing the country to achieve all the core Millennium Development Goals (MDGs) targets. Primary and secondary school enrolment rates are over 85 per cent for male and female students and, significantly, the large gender gap at these levels has been eliminated, female participation in the labour force has increased along with improvement in maternal health, and there has been a sharp decline in infant mortality rate and rise in average life expectancy (68 years currently). Upward social mobility has driven a burgeoning middle class. The foreboding challenges Bangladesh faced at independence led many to doubt the economic viability of the nascent country. Viewed against the backdrop of such grave concerns about its future, Bangladesh's economic and social transformation has been nothing less than spectacular.

As impressive as Bangladesh's development has been, however, its future development trajectory will be constrained by unaddressed past challenges and new challenges: weak governance, weak political will in reforming institutions, including civil service reform and corruption, degradation of the natural environment (water, air, solid waste, noise, wet lands and forest cover), weakening rule of law and law enforcement, political polarization, unplanned urbanization and migration, and overall 'reform paralysis'. In recent years, inequality, especially in urban areas, has increased. Besides dealing with these challenges, Bangladesh, for its continued growth, also needs to invest in energy, including renewable sources, infrastructure, ICT, especially to increase the reach of public service delivery; accelerate policy reforms to increase domestic private sector investment and FDI, prioritizing incentives to develop efficient land markets and competitive financial markets, both banking and capital; and invest in human and knowledge capital and not just in skills development apart from energy and infrastructure.

Over the last decade, especially in the last five years, the BRAC Institute of Governance and Development (BIGD), with support from the Think Tank Initiative (TTI), has grown into a full-fledged and reputed policy research institute in Bangladesh. The institute's journey started in 2006 as the Centre for Governance Studies within BRAC University. It was strengthened and renamed the Institute of Governance Studies (IGS) in 2008 when it was included as a member of the TTI programme. However, it faced many challenges as a new institution. It conducted research on a small scale due to funding constraints; dependence on project funding severely restricted recruitment of high-performing researchers and skilled operations staff. A substantial part of its work was done by short-term consultants, with support from the institute's staff, and it depended on sporadic availability of donor-funded projects. There was very limited focus on establishing long-term institutional agendas and research priorities. The small scale of its operations, however, also enabled a sharp focus on governance research, an area in which it quickly established a unique niche, although the link with policy mostly remained remote. IGS, as an 'organic' part of the university, was directly supervised in its operations—finance, human resources and administration—by the university. A major downside of such a 'business model' was that the incentives of the institute's operational units were not aligned to provide the support it needed to achieve its objectives and aspirations.

In 2013, following an evaluation by an international and independent panel of three eminent persons commissioned by the Board of Trustees of BRAC University, the university resolved to merge two of its institutes, that is, IGS and the BRAC Development Institute, into one institution—BIGD—essentially due to their overlapping mandates. The objective was to create a high-quality, effective and efficient policy research institute. The TTI assistance played a crucial role in sustaining the newly established IGS and supporting its growth as a reputed think tank in the initial years. Among the most important aspects of the TTI funding was the 'space' it provided for IGS and later BIGD to shift the emphases of their work to longer-term strategic planning, from working on a project-focused short-term 'survival' mode of operation. Second, it provided substantial flexibility in strengthening operational efficiency and planning. The motivation behind TTI was a desire to build and support institutions that could affect change in their societies. The TTI assistance played a much more significant role in the evolution of BIGD in the last five years, that is, since its inception, with its work being forcefully driven by that motivation.

ORGANIZATIONAL PERFORMANCE

One of the key areas of influence of the TTI funding has been on the organizational capacity of the institute. BIGD seized the opportunity to revamp its organizational structure underpinned by a new organogram and strategic thinking. The position of the head of the institute was elevated from 'director' to 'executive director' (ED) with much greater responsibilities and executive authority. This was complemented by providing autonomy to BIGD to run its own affairs not only in planning and executing its research but also on the operational management side, that is, in the areas of finance, administration and human resources. The ED had much more authority not only in interactions within the university but also with the external institutions, including donor agencies. The only key link with the university that remained was its function of awarding degrees for the postgraduate academic courses of BIGD, as required by the law. The new organogram had the ED at its apex, four main departments, namely research, academics and training, communications, and operations. To strengthen operational efficiency, a position of head of finance was created to coordinate and lead the three operational units—finance, administration and human resources.

The most important contribution of the TTI funding to BIGD's development into a lasting institutional set-up was the joint determination by BIGD's senior management and TTI's administration of setting challenging key performance indicators (KPIs) to be monitored closely and evaluated at a midterm review, that is, two years after the initiation of the second phase of funding. A fully committed BIGD leadership successfully achieved all the KPIs to attain new-found confidence in their collective capacity as an institution. The KPIs resulted in rapid formulation of an institutional strategy with a clearly articulated vision, mission and objectives—detailed financial and human resources plan and guidelines, medium-term financial sustainability plan applicable also in a post-TTI era, guidelines for administrative decisions, guidelines for travel, a communications strategy and other protocols—giving BIGD a firm institutional foundation for the present and the future. The strategies, guidelines and protocols helped the creation of a more rules-based work culture, transparency and accountability at BIGD and significantly improved its operational efficiency and effectiveness. As a result, BIGD could also plan and implement a more ambitious research and academic agenda.

BIGD emphasized investment in training and developing skills in its human resources in research and operations which 'paid rich dividends' and research staff access control system with attendance monitoring to promote a stronger accountability process. Monitoring and controlling staff attendance was a challenge for the institute before the introduction of this system.

In 2014, the conceptual basis for assessing staff performance was fundamentally altered from an 'evaluative' mechanism to one which mainly emphasized recognizing and highlighting the essentials for high performance, recognizing high performers and providing 'feedback' to improve performance to achieve goals set by staff themselves. The new performance management system was linked to annual work plans prepared by each staff, both of which are reviewed annually with staff assessing their own performance followed by the supervisor's assessment and feedback. A more sophisticated performance management system has improved work incentives and aligned them to institutional goals and objectives, as well as promoting a meritocratic environment.

STRENGTHENING OF RESEARCH QUALITY

BIGD has progressed significantly since its inception. As noted above, in the pre-TTI period, BIGD relied solely on individual projects funded mainly by international donors. While it served short-term sustenance of the institute at that time, it could not lead to the creation of a financially sustainable, lasting institution, capable of quality research and effective policy influence and advocacy. This restricted the type and extent of research that BIGD could undertake, focusing primarily on project-based studies and less on independent research work. However, the programmatic funding provided by TTI allowed deep-seated institutional reform and restructuring. On the research management side, BIGD organized its research around four clusters, that is, politics and governance; economic growth; gender; and urban, environment and climate change, each led by a cluster head. Located within the gender cluster, the Centre for Gender and Social Transformation conducts research in the areas of violence against women, women's participation in local government, women's labour market participation, adolescent and livelihood issues, women empowerment, etc.

In undertaking research, the flexibility enabled BIGD to set its research agenda independently in line with its strategic vision and objectives, strengthen its research capacity and extend it to the use of more advanced methodologies by investing in human capital, and change the skills mix to support its research agenda. The built-in flexibility of TTI's funding also enabled BIGD to stay relevant—it could adapt to changing dynamics of the country's political, social and economic context. This cluster-based structure has aided in expanding the scope of research of the institute as well as helped to more efficiently assign researchers across the institution in line with their area of expertise or interest. With effective stewardship by the senior management team and the commitment of researchers supported by the operations and communications team, BIGD has successfully increased the number of research outputs to over 200 publications with steadily rising quality.

BIGD greatly values research collaboration with local and international partners and has used it effectively as a means to strengthen its own capacity. Several important research outputs have been the result of collaboration with national and international academic institutions such as BRAC University; the University of Manchester's Effective States and Inclusive Development (ESID) programme; the London School of Economics (LSE), the School of Oriental and African Studies and King's College of University of London; the University of Sussex; International Labour Organization; University College of London; United Nations Development Programme (UNDP); the University of Illinois at Chicago; the University College of London; and International Growth Centre (IGC), and local institutes such as Bangladesh Institute of Development Studies; Power and Participation Research Centre; South Asian Network on Economic Modeling; and Anti-corruption Commission, among others.

The two annual publications of BIGD, that is, the *State of Governance* (SoG) and the *State of Cities* (SoC) reports, supported by TTI, have emerged as the most authentic reports in the two broad fields of governance and urbanization in the country, raising BIGD's profile, and enhanced its reputation as a centre of excellence. The reports' launches are eagerly awaited each year by stakeholders, and they spark lively public discussion and debate on public policies in print, TV, e-media and social media. Senior civil servants, ministers, members of parliament (MPs), academics, think tanks and NGOs attend the launches and participate in the discussions that follow. Both reports often evoke op-eds and editorials in the highest circulation newspapers of the country and are the subject of 'talk shows' in the country. They, therefore, directly influence public opinion and indirectly contribute to policy-making as evidenced by the presence of ministers, MPs and senior civil servants and their high demand for the reports. The two reports have helped 'branding' of BIGD as a top-notch policy research institute and are thus BIGD's flagship reports.

The SoG reports are devoted to the analysis of critically important contemporary issues of public policy in governance. Recent reports have assessed concerns around democratic institutions, including the political party system, its financing and confrontational politics that has characterized democracy in Bangladesh for three decades. The reports' salient finding that the country's majoritarian parliamentary system was consistent with 'partyarchy' (à la Fukuyama) had generated public debate on a scale not experienced by BIGD before. The SoG reports have been devoted to an important thematic issue with the chapters assessing a set of key dimensions of the overall theme. Since 2015, a systematic effort was made in the SoG reports towards analysing trends in a set of important indicators reflecting critically important thematic areas of governance. The intent was to develop governance indicators to compute indexes of meaningful sub-categories and, eventually, a composite index of democratic governance of the country as a whole. The systematic effort in the last three years to this end has been a major contribution to the analysis of governance in the country and a subject of significant public discussion.

Given the massive surge in population in urban areas and the new challenges that emanate from the migration, the SoC report provided a unique opening to address the newly emerging policy challenges around the rapid and 'chaotic' growth of cities. The SoC report views urban concerns through the 'lens' of institutions and governance, and by doing so has carved out a 'niche' area of specialization in the broader urban agenda. By addressing some of the most pressing policy issues around solid waste management, transportation of large numbers of people across the cities, traffic congestion, solid waste management and the 'crisis' of housing in Dhaka, one of Asia's largest mega cities, along with the challenges in the growth of secondary cities of Bangladesh, the SoC report has attained a stellar reputation as both a repository of knowledge and a critical policy analysis. Each year, it also sparks animated public discussion and debate across the entire media spectrum. By analysing relevant policy concerns, it has drawn the attention of stakeholders, including policy-makers, and established itself as an eminently influential report on urban issues in the public domain. The institute plans to construct a comprehensive urban livability index in the coming years that incorporates all these different issues. Both the SoG and SoC reports have been crucial in BIGD's policy engagement and influencing agenda.

A major contribution of TTI funding has been the significant growth in BIGD's policy research capacity. Apart from the SoG and SoC chapters, researchers publish individual or joint working papers based on the priorities of each of BIGD's four clusters. These include papers on a wide range of issues—effectiveness of parliament, integrity in government, dispensation of justice, law enforcement, urban governance, public procurement, electoral process, municipal finances, decentralizing public finance, local resource mobilization, political violence, violence against women, women's agency in political, and social and economic institutions—which are published electronically and made available on the BIGD website. From just 1 working paper in 2012, BIGD researchers had added 50 working papers until 2017. Committing and delivering about 10 working papers each year under the TTI work plan has instilled a culture of in-house research and growth of capacity hitherto unknown. Some of these working papers with further value addition have been published as articles in national and international journals. Other publications include research reports, books, book chapters, policy briefs and notes, as well as journal articles. The ED actively participates in and monitors the annual research programme of BIGD.[1] The BIGD blog, Magna Carta, started in 2017, has also provided a platform for BIGD researchers as well as external parties to share their thoughts and have constructive debates on relevant and emerging topics. Participation in national and international conferences, again mainly a direct contribution of TTI, has been a major vehicle for capacity building of BIGD researchers.

[1] For further information on BIGD publications, please visit http://bigd.bracu.ac.bd/ (accessed on 20 August 2018).

Quality assurance is one of the key priorities, and over the years, BIGD has developed new mechanisms to assure the quality of its research outputs. The Research and Publications Committee (RPC) was established to develop and monitor the institutional annual research programme as well as conduct quality checks. BIGD proactively provides ethical and technical guidance to researchers and conducts plagiarism checks on research outputs. The entire research process, from the concept of note preparation to publication of the output, is closely monitored by the RPC. Further, BIGD enforces internal and external peer reviewing and language editing of research outputs as a method to ensure better quality. BIGD has instituted a bi-weekly brown bag seminar series that not only permits rigorous peer review of individual research but also encourages active debate and dialogue. The institute has developed a strong culture of continuous self-learning and applications of advanced research methods to improve rigour and quality of its research.

As a step towards realizing its vision of creating a just and prosperous society, BIGD has made strenuous efforts to foster a generation of younger researchers capable of undertaking independent, quality research which can be published, as well as to encourage vibrant debate on a wide range of national and international policies of contemporary national, regional and international significance. BIGD's involvement in TTI has been a key factor in driving this effort. It has made collaboration at all geographical levels possible, allowing capacity building of young researchers through training programmes in qualitative and quantitative methods at frequent intervals. In 2017, the BIGD Study Group (BSG) was initiated, where researchers convene to discuss theory; learn new and advanced research methods, software applications and data analytics; debate on contemporary issues; and watch relevant documentaries. BSG is popular among the staff due to the learning and nurturing environment it provides in an informal setting.

POLICY ENGAGEMENT AND INFLUENCE

Given its goal of establishing itself as a policy research institute, BIGD has been devotedly connecting its research to policy. One key constraint of BIGD during its early years was its limited institutional capacity to engage and influence. However, with the TTI funding, and a well-thought-out strategy, BIGD increased the 'space' for policy dialogue and engagement substantially. Increasing the number of seminars and conferences which were attended by key policy-makers and influencers, that is, cabinet ministers, MPs, senior civil servants, academics and opinion makers; effecting a step increase in the reach of its publications; publishing op-eds and articles; expanding its social media presence; and redesigning its website, the institute greatly increased its profile, reputation and influence. Simultaneously, the institute expanded its research capacity, in terms of both the size of in-house researchers and the quality of its research. As part of its strategy, senior researchers also worked on government-funded projects, as well as other funded research, directly involving one or more government agencies. This paid rich dividends in achieving direct policy impact. Examples of these are BIGD's work in training government officials in e-procurement and the follow-on project on designing and piloting a third-party monitoring model (involving local citizens) for small infrastructure projects tendered through the e-procurement system in four *upazilas* of Bangladesh. The concerned BIGD team was highly successful in piloting the model and won a regional award for its work from the World Bank (WB). Following the success of the pilot model, the government took a policy decision to scale up the 'social account-ability' or citizen's engagement model to all upazilas of the country in phases over 5–10 years. BIGD has been selected to undertake this project by the government with WB funding. Another example of direct policy impact is BIGD's work in partnership with the Copenhagen Consensus Center, a think tank, in which it analysed three government digitization interventions of public service delivery, led by the Prime Minister's Office (PMO). Its studies on the digitization of land records, e-procurement and village courts were ranked among the top 10 priority interventions the government should invest in, in its 7th Five-Year Plan. These were exemplary policy impacts achieved by BIGD in which TTI's support augmented the research and helped train the researchers in the required research methods. Earlier, in 2012, BIGD (then IGS) assisted the government in preparing the National Integrity Strategy.

One key area of influence has been through BIGD's partnerships with national and international research institutes and thinks tanks to conduct research as well as to organize national and international seminars and conferences as a key dissemination strategy. The institution has equally prioritized the partnerships and engagement with many government agencies and departments. Furthermore, BIGD has built and maintained strong relationships with relevant civil society members, whose interest and work align with that of the institute. These linkages have assisted in establishing BIGD's authority and credibility as a policy-oriented research institute.

In 2011, BIGD, in collaboration with the University of Colombo, conducted the Bangladesh Youth Survey (BYS), which was partially funded by TTI. Findings from BYS were disseminated nationally as well as internationally at a regional conference in Sri Lanka. This allowed the institute to showcase its research in front of a global audience. In 2014, BIGD organized a three-day international conference on political economy, accountability and governance in collaboration with TTI, International Development Research Centre (IDRC), IGC, LSE and ESID, which successfully attracted national and international participation of key figures in the area of development from the USA, UK, Japan, India, Nepal and Bangladesh. In 2015, BIGD collaborated with the Copenhagen Consensus Center to identify smart solutions for Bangladesh, identifying village courts, land digitization and e-procurement as some of the key priorities. The latter was later referred to in the 7th Five-Year Plan and the national budget for FY 2016–2017 set by the government. During the same year, BIGD partnered with the Central Procurement Technical Unit of the Ministry of Planning to develop a piloting strategy for citizen engagement in the implementation of public procurement, which was later approved for a nationwide roll-out by the government. In 2016, BIGD was assigned as one of the core members of the National Governance Assessment Framework, run by the Governance Innovation Unit of the PMO. This allowed the institute to be engaged in various divisional workshops and conferences held in Dhaka city. BIGD also collaborated with the National Institute of Local Government to strengthen the guidelines set by ward *shobhas* (ward council) under the Helvetas-supported Sharique project. These diversified collaborations and partnerships are a direct result of the institutional growth and capacity building that was made possible under TTI. These partnerships and effective dissemination through seminars and the media have facilitated the policy engagement agenda of the institute and strengthened BIGD's voice in the development sector.

The communications unit, along with the research team, has played an important role in building the brand of BIGD and in increasing its visibility in the country. Frequent opinion pieces for national Bangla and English newspapers based on current and ongoing research, as well as appearances of BIGD researchers in television talk shows, have helped to make a greater community, more familiar with the institute and its work. Over the years, BIGD has also modified its dissemination strategy to swiftly reach a greater audience, especially through the use of social media, like Facebook. Coverage of seminars, workshops, launching events and conferences are all featured on the BIGD website as well as on the BIGD Facebook page. One challenge in this process has been in presenting the research—which is oftentimes highly technical—in a way that is comprehensible to the general public.

SUSTAINABILITY: GAPS, CHALLENGES AND THINKING AHEAD

The core motivation for TTI was to nurture and support organizations that can have a positive impact in their communities through research and policy engagement. More importantly, TTI aimed to help these organizations become more effective and help them become sustainable. BIGD's journey so far, from infancy to an established policy research institute, exemplifies TTI's goal and demonstrates its achievement. The institute has remained focused on its goal to produce research that can affect change in the governance and development fronts of the country. From very modest beginnings, BIGD has grown in terms of its operational capacity, research and policy engagement and flourished into the country's premier governance research institute. Over the years, it has modified and strengthened its core strategies to improve efficiency and quality of research. TTI allowed BIGD to completely reshape and frame its research agenda, thus giving authority to those who were in the best position to understand the objectives of their research undertakings and who had the knowledge about the relevant ground realities. Furthermore, the financial support from TTI made it possible for BIGD to attract medium-term funding and to engage with a greater number of donor agencies, as well as academic and research institutions, and to negotiate from a position of strength when doing so. From contributing over 70 per cent of its total expenditure in 2013, its contribution had dropped to 18 per cent in 2017 and is likely to drop further in 2018. In the current year, that is, 2018, BIGD has signed USD 8 million worth of contracts for a four-year period. Only one of the three projects is yet to start; the other two have started. This is a 'story of revival' that TTI must be proud of as is its partner, BIGD.

In 2016, BRAC University awarded BIGD in endowment of BDT100 million. This endowment will be crucial in BIGD's sustainability as an institute beyond the TTI grant period. While this is a start, greater endowment will be needed to ensure the institute's sustainability, especially in the retention of skilled employees. In terms of operational capacity, BIGD has demonstrated greater efficiency in the operation of its units. In the foreseeable future, BIGD will have to encounter the challenges of operating in a shrinking resource environment, a challenge of both national and international emergencies (Rohingya crisis), while maintaining independent quality research. Thinking ahead, the institute needs to build a stronger research base and increase the quality of research to meet international standards. This will mean investing more resources in growing a pool of qualified mid-level researchers. In addition, BIGD will have to further improve the standard of its publications and aim to bring about a more direct impact on government policies and influence public opinion through a much larger footprint on social media. One major challenge that BIGD continues to face is having to compete for talent with not only other national think tanks but also, to a greater extent, the rest of the world due to migration. Therefore, while the challenge of maintaining financial stability is presently not a challenge, the search for resources and increasing the endowment will remain a major challenge in the future.

Above all, maintaining a high-quality research environment through continuous learning processes and attracting first-rate younger and mid-level researchers arguably will be BIGD's biggest challenges. Without this, the institution's hard-won capabilities in all areas will be at risk of decline.

Chapter 3

Centre for Policy Dialogue

Fahmida Khatun

INTRODUCTION

In 1993, Professor Rehman Sobhan, an eminent economist and civil society leader in Bangladesh, took the initiative to establish the Centre for Policy Dialogue (CPD). His initiative was in response to the growing need of a civil society platform after Bangladesh returned to democracy in the early 1990s. It was perceived that CPD would contribute to strengthening the country's process of democratization. The centre would do so by promoting demand-driven developmental agendas and enabling stakeholders to have a say in developmental policies. To achieve this goal, CPD would focus on (a) making citizens aware about policy issues that affect their lives and livelihoods and the future of their country, (b) facilitating public discussions on those policy issues with a view to building a broad-based support for policies and (c) influencing the process and outcome of policy-making in Bangladesh through proactive advocacy.

CPD has four operational areas: (a) 'knowledge generation' through research and analysis, (b) 'policy awareness' through dialogues, net-working, dissemination and mobilizing support of the civil society, (c) 'policy influencing' at national, regional and international levels by involving policy-makers in dialogue and (d) 'strengthening' in-house capacities and organizing policy appreciation events for policy-makers and key stakeholders.

CPD focuses on issues critical to Bangladesh in shaping and influencing the country's development prospects in the mid-term horizon. CPD's journey over the years is reflected by enhanced organizational strength, higher research quality, effective outreach and better-equipped infrastructure. These investments have helped CPD gain national prominence as an effective think tank and enabled it to lead two global networks.

WHERE IS CPD NOW?

Organizational Performance

CPD has made significant strides in ensuring higher quality of activities, capacity development of researchers, institutional sustainability and leadership transition. It has made effort in institutionalization of the centre through development of service rules, retirement benefits, participatory management system, modern financial management, performance-based rewards and equal opportunity practices. Think Tank Initiative (TTI) support was used in strengthening organizational capacity to meet the challenges emanating from the centre's expanded work and its global initiatives. The centre's finance management, internal audit and administrative procedures needed updating.

The TTI support has contributed to build capacity of CPD researchers in conducting both qualitative and quantitative research through in-house and external training and workshops on social accounting matrix (SAM) and computable general equilibrium (CGE) modelling. CPD researchers can now use CGE modelling techniques to forecast various indicators of the economy. The efficiency of CPD's finance division has improved through training and recruitment of an internal auditor. CPD has benefited from additional support for mutual learning through the exchange of staffs (CPD and Sustainable Development Policy Institute [SDPI] under TTI Matching Grant). Through participation in training programmes, the capacity of communication unit has been further strengthened.

The centre's overarching objective is to contribute good governance in Bangladesh by promoting accountability and transparency and ensuring development with equity and justice. In this journey to attain its vision, CPD will deploy instruments such as research, dialogue and networking. CPD identifies research priorities in a demand-driven and consultative manner and mobilizing funds for prioritized research activities, rather than bidding for supply-driven projects. The centre avoids funds that may create potential conflict of interest and has largely avoided funds from the government and international financial institutions. At the same time, it has tried to reduce dependence on a single source of funding.

The TTI grant has allowed CPD to raise the quality of delivery on all three areas. Thus, more emphasis has been given to quality of research. The number of papers submitted for publication in reputed peer-reviewed journals indicates this trend. Thanks to the TTI support, organizational strength of CPD has been consolidated through strengthening of human resource management, putting in place internal audit mechanisms, linking incentives with delivery quality, introduction of a more structured decision-making system, making better use of ICT through revamping of the website, strengthening of management information system (MIS) and more modern logistics. With regard to policy linkages, by using the TTI support and the networking opportunities offered through the TTI events, CPD has been able to achieve global presence.

RESEARCH
Strategy and Focus

During its formative years, CPD focused on organizing dialogues and discussions around issues of macroeconomic management, governance and donor–recipient relationships in Bangladesh. However, the need for input of research to the dialogue process and its outcome were gradually felt. Thus, research themes that reflected felt needs were identified. CPD's flagship research programme, the Independent Review of Bangladesh's Development (IRBD), was envisaged early on and provided home-grown development alternatives. Thus, CPD began preparing research proposals in areas perceived important from the national perspective and where its functionaries had relevant competencies. CPD thus built its niche on three pillars: research, dialogue and outreach.

While identifying its research agenda, the centre tended to focus more on issues that were policy-tailored and policy-relevant. Both strategic themes and issues of immediate relevance were taken up. CPD's research programmes cover governance, economic reforms, environmental sustainability and financial sector analysis. CPD is also engaged in a study of issues around the World Trade Organization (WTO) processes with special emphasis on study of challenges faced by least developed countries (LDCs) in general and Bangladesh in particular. CPD also pursues issues of regional importance, such as trade, investment, connectivity and trade facilitation in South Asia, in its research themes.

The support by TTI has helped CPD expand the remit of its goals in terms of both depth and breadth in order to increase effectiveness of its activities. CPD's major goals include the following: (a) to serve needs of the country through quality research analysis and disseminate findings among larger sections of the society, (b) to consolidate its position as a leading think tank in Bangladesh and (c) to become a think tank comparable to its peers in terms of capacity, competence and credibility. The centre undertakes rigorous research based on primary data on issues that have direct effect on the lives and livelihoods of the marginalized people. The findings have direct policy implications.

COLLABORATION

From the very beginning, CPD has partnered with other organizations in implementing its research and dialogue programmes. The partnerships have allowed CPD to make use of expertise not available in-house, and also use the opportunity as a way of building capacity of its staff through joint research. The centre has taken on board Bangladeshi scholars with specific expertise working in research and academic institutions in Bangladesh as partners and also inducted Bangladeshi experts working in various international institutions and organizations to take part in its research. It has partnered with international organizations and global think tanks in implementing joint surveys and research programmes.

The centre has strived to maintain global presence since many of the issues Bangladesh faces are of relevance to both regional and global developments. Assisted by predictability of TTI's capacity-building support, and taking advantage of the additional TTI windows, CPD has expanded its activities to embrace regional and global issues as part of attaining its aim of being a think tank with local roots and global outreach. The centre, thus, has strengthened its activities to promote economic cooperation and integration in the South Asian region and to strengthen global integration of low-income countries through its research, dialogue and outreach. CPD's two global initiatives, 'Monitoring the Implementation of the Istanbul Programme of Action (IPoA) for the LDCs' (in short, LDC IV Monitor initiative) and 'Southern Voice on Post-MDG International Development Goals' (in short, Southern Voice on post-MDGs initiative), have helped it pursue its objective of achieving global recognition.

CPD's focus on consolidation of its networking has strengthened bilateral and multilateral cooperation in South Asia. This strategy has also helped articulate Bangladesh's interest in the various global forums including WTO and the UN system. Through Indo-Bangladesh dialogues, and organizing of regional, international and LDC dialogues, CPD has established itself as a leading civil society organization in Bangladesh. Its senior staff members were invited to be members of a number of national committees and negotiating delegations.

RESEARCH QUALITY

Although the research products were of high quality, there was little time to convert research outputs into publishable journal articles. With the TTI support, CPD researchers were able to put additional efforts towards converting their research outputs into journal articles in peer-reviewed journals. Publications by CPD researchers have increased in both quantity and quality. In 2017, CPD had 166 publications of various types, including journal articles, books, book chapters, occasional papers, working papers, issue papers and op-eds. More emphasis was put on enhancing research quality because it initiated global networks and its own research strength had to be at par with some of the best global organizations.

POLICY ENGAGEMENT
Dialogue Activities

CPD's dialogue programme is designed to avoid exchange of rhetoric and opinions and instead promote and stimulate constructive engagement and informed sharing of views. The dialogues are designed to come up with specific recommendations that would redefine policies as well as ensure their effective implementation. These recommendations are then placed before the country's current and prospective policy-makers for action.

In practice, on a regular basis, the centre brings together high-level government officials, senior executives, members of parliament (MPs), the business community, professionals, academics, non-governmental organizations (NGOs), activists and donor representatives to discuss policy issues. CPD also initiates policy dialogues with public interest groups such as trade unions, peasant organizations, women's organizations, professional associations and local community groups. Eventually, in cooperation with other organizations, the idea was shared with grass-roots groups by locally holding the dialogue process. Policy-makers and academics were invited to such platforms and encouraged to interact with people who actually face consequences of a particular policy. In such meetings, new ideas as well as concerns about the validity of the policy were discussed.

The centre remains non-partisan in its outlook and retains independence in the designing and conducting of its dialogues. Such a stance has enabled the centre to bring together Cabinet ministers and opposition leaders around the same table when these contending parties are not communicating with each other in the parliament. CPD dialogues proceed in an environment where controversial issues are discussed in a non-confrontational manner and solutions are jointly explored. These initiatives that bring political protagonists together have extended over three successive political regimes.

CPD can take credit for playing an important role in creating the tradition of multi-stakeholder consultations in Bangladesh. Its dialogue provides a platform for all relevant stakeholders for constructive engagement around various issues. CPD's target groups are diverse and include both policy-makers and those for whom policies are designed in the first place.

The broad groups of stakeholders are engaged in exchanging views in three phases of CPD's activism: (a) identification of socially relevant issues, (b) generating inputs for the purpose of policy analysis and (c) validation of policy recommendations. Even at times when opposition parties were boycotting the parliament, CPD dialogues provided opportunities for major political forces to come together and be engaged in informed debates. CPD research outputs have served as the evidence to inform the discussions.

Whilst dialogues tended to be organized around CPD's researches, increasingly the need was felt to organize events to discuss issues that required urgent attention. Thus, CPD dialogues started to include frank and open discussions on such issues as labour unrest, input needs of farmers and price hike of essentials.

In 2001, CPD took initiatives to prepare a set of policy proposals for the then upcoming government. Two years later, in 2003, CPD reviewed the progress made in the context of these proposals and, in 2006, began pre-election campaign for honest and capable candidates. Ten years later, in 2016, CPD launched a new initiative, namely 'Citizen's Platform for SDGs'. Thus, over the years, CPD has systematically been engaging and contributing to the broader issues of policy-making and governance in Bangladesh. The centre's ability to bring on board a broad spectrum of stakeholders in these initiatives added to effectiveness of its outreach activities. The centre coordinated such efforts implemented through participation of broad-based civil society organizations.

Policy Linkages

Meeting the objective of policy linkages, communication and networking requires a strong dialogue and communications division within the organization. Such a division also must be endowed with adequate staff with capacity and modern equipment. The TTI support helped CPD build these capacities.

In recent times, the demand for evidence-based research, as a tool for policy-making, has increased significantly. Given Bangladesh's social and economic transition, there is a continuous need for maintaining policy discourse on issues critical to the country. In addition to holding dialogues, preparing policy briefs, popular write-ups in the print media and discussions in the electronic media also play a role in policy outreach. Similarly, outreach activities targeted to policy stakeholders and policy advocacy groups need to use various communication tools. In view of CPD's expanded activities in recent years, at national, regional and global levels, the demand on communication and outreach activities has increased and the centre maintains such capacities.

CHALLENGES AND LESSONS LEARNT

As a research institution and a think tank engaged in policy activism, CPD faces several challenges. The centre is prone to contending point of views particularly from the government officials whenever CPD undertakes an assessment including projections on gross domestic product (GDP) growth. Policy-makers seem unhappy when policies and outcomes are put under larger public scrutiny. Similarly, the private sector has also been critical of CPD when it published its research results. The results of CPD's studies on living wage of the workers of the ready-made garment (RMG) and banking sector crises were two such examples. Because of its evidence-based research, sound analysis and effective use of media, CPD was able to withstand the pressure. The centre's experience thus underscores that the key to effective policy influence is evidence-based research backed by analytical rigour. Otherwise, findings may not pass scrutiny and think tanks may not be able to defend their position. This would compromise their legitimacy.

Internally, CPD's major challenge was to strengthen human resource capacity. Limited pool of quality researchers within the country posed a major challenge. CPD has tried to overcome this challenge through professional development of its researchers by organizing in- and out-of-country training, involving outside faculties for dedicated research, through motivation supported by appropriate incentives. The TTI grant has been a major support towards implementation of this plan.

Retention of senior researchers and training programme on SAM and CGE modelling conducted with the TTI grant have given confidence to CPD researchers. They now undertake quantitative and modelling exercise contributing to the analytical rigour of CPD outputs.

CPD learned that the professional competency draws strength from networks and is capable of maintaining independence and will be able to address the risks in its journey. Thus, for effective policy influence, CPD has partnered with major advocacy players on these issues. In this endeavour, CPD undertakes research, its uses and the combined strength of the partnership for policy influence.

The civil society initiative on monitoring of post-Rana Plaza disaster is one example. On 24 April 2013, the plaza in Dhaka collapsed, killing 1,132 garment workers who were trapped in the rubble. This tragedy drew the attention of concerned citizens regarding persistence and non-compliance of workplace safety rules in the garment sector. CPD, in partnership with a number of civil society organizations and eminent personalities in Bangladesh, began systematic monitoring of the actions that major stakeholders in RMG took on safety. After the release of two monitoring reports on the catastrophe, policy-makers at the highest level took initiative to scrutinize implementation of promises that stakeholders of the industry made about workplace safety. The 'Citizen's Platform for SDGs' initiative was launched in 2016 with the objective to contribute to the delivery of the Sustainable Development Goals (SDGs) and enhance transparency and account-ability at the country level.

MEDIA AS A STRATEGIC PARTNER

CPD has developed a strategic partnership with the print and electronic media of the country. Media is an important conduit in extending out-reach and disseminating its research and outputs in building awareness on policy challenges. CPD holds regular press briefings on topical issues, launches global reports and prepares press releases on events organized by the centre. CPD professionals take help from the print and elec-tronic media to provide comments through interviews, writing short write-ups and even editorials. International media also interviewed senior CPD staff members. Since 2006, CPD's analysis of the national budget is broadcasted live via local television stations.

PUBLICATION AND DISSEMINATION

CPD pursues an extensive programme for disseminating its research and dialogue outputs through regular publications and website postings. This is a useful way of extending outreach—a key tool for policy influence— and an effective way of contributing to informed policy discussions.

POLICY CONTRIBUTIONS

CPD has two and a half decades of experience in policy research, analysis and advocacy. It has worked with successive governments and served as a unique platform for constructive engagements involving conflicting interest groups. The centre has been able to connect national research to global discourse and interpret consequences of global developments for the country. The centre has successfully engaged diverse policy actors on specific debates. During the successive political regimes, it has been able to maintain its credibility as a non-partisan, open and constructive platform.

The role of CPD as a policy actor has been strengthened by its good working relationship with high-level policy-makers including ministers, MPs and senior government officials. Senior CPD researchers are members of various high-level consultative committees and task forces set up by various ministries including ministries of finance, commerce, planning and agriculture. The centre derives its legitimacy from its close relationship with the community of non-state actors and is looked upon by citizens of Bangladesh as a credible source of analytical resources.

SUCCESS STORIES

Monitoring of Rana Plaza Collapse

On 18 May 2013, CPD convened a meeting with a number of leaders of the civil society organizations to discuss what they could do to

improve compliance. The meeting explored that whether in partnership with a number of organizations and individuals CPD could come
together to systematically monitor the actions undertaken by the major
stakeholders. The idea was to undertake an audit of what is being done,
to identify the gaps and to put pressure on key stakeholders so that
appropriate and adequate actions are taken.

The report titled *100 Days of Rana Plaza Tragedy: A Report on
Commitments and Delivery* was presented at a dialogue in Dhaka. MPs,
civil society organizations, representatives from business chambers and
trade unions, human rights organizations and legal forums, NGOs and
media, all took part in the discussion. Several victims of the tragedy
also shared their plight at the dialogue. The report provided a detailed
stocktaking of the commitments in response to Rana Plaza collapse and
their deliveries. A number of recommendations from various parts of
the society surfaced towards improving compliance.

IMPROVING REGIONAL CONNECTIVITY

CPD took the initiative to involve policy-makers in its effort towards
improving regional connectivity. The 11th BCIM (Bangladesh, China,
India, Myanmar) Forum organized by CPD in Dhaka on 23–24 February
2013 is a testimony to this. The theme of this forum was 'New
Opportunities and New Challenges for BCIM Cooperation'. Over
the past several years, governments of the participating countries have
started to show interest in the forum. The 11th BCIM Forum organized
a car rally which started in Kolkata and ended in Kunming (popularly
coined as K2K Car Rally). The Dhaka forum brainstormed ways of
giving institutional shape to accelerated collaboration and cooperation
among the BCIM countries.

ESTIMATING WOMEN'S CONTRIBUTION TO THE ECONOMY

In Bangladesh, women undertake a large part of the economic activities including household chores, family care and agriculture. The work
remains unaccounted for in conventional measures such as GDP and

transmits wrong signals to policy-makers whose decisions on allocations and distribution are influenced by the prevailing model. Family members' attitude towards women without an income is often discriminatory and occasionally leads to violence.

In view of the above, CPD felt the need to capture, in value terms, the contribution that women make to the economy. In doing so, CPD partnered with a civil society organization, Manusher Jonno Foundation (MJF), to survey 8,320 women and 5,320 men aged 15 years and above, across Bangladesh. The study provided new findings that have implications for the System of National Accounts (SNA). First, it showed that the time spent on non-SNA activities by a female member of a household is about three times higher than that by a male household member. Second, the study estimated that in FY 2013–2014, the value of women's unpaid non-SNA activities was equivalent to 76.8 per cent of Bangladesh's GDP, based on the replacement cost method, and 87.2 per cent of the GDP, based on the willingness-to-accept method.

CPD organized a dialogue on 25 October 2014 to disseminate the findings of the study. Mr A. H. M. Mustafa Kamal, Minister for Planning, Government of Bangladesh, attended the dialogue as the chief guest. Officials from Bangladesh Bureau of Statistics (BBS) also attended, among others. The minister assured the audience that the government would take measures to estimate women's unpaid contribution. The issue was discussed in the national parliament where the minister also mentioned about women's contribution to the economy. BBS also took note of the findings and informed that they would start measuring women's unaccounted work. The study monograph has been published and copies have been distributed to policy-makers, activists, researchers and media.

GLOBAL LEADERSHIP

CPD currently leads two important global initiatives, namely LDC IV Monitor initiative and Southern Voice initiative. The centre provides conceptualization and content to both the initiatives. It has built partnerships with institutions to chalk out activities and programmes to take the initiatives forward. These activities indicate CPD's transition into a think tank with local roots and global outreach. This transition, to a large extent, has been made possible by the support provided by TTI.

CITIZEN'S PLATFORM ON SDGs

A group of individuals in Bangladesh established the Citizen's Platform for SDGs, Bangladesh. CPD functions the secretariat of the platform to implement 2030 Agenda at the national level with enhanced in-country transparency and accountability. Formally launched in June 2016, the platform has 74 NGOs working on SDGs. The platform organizes dialogues on these themes across the country and has produced many publications. It has also produced a video on SDGs with a theme 'Leave No One Behind'.

SUSTAINABILITY: GAPS, CHALLENGES AND THINKING AHEAD

CPD has emerged as a leading think tank of Bangladesh that actively engages in issues of concern to citizens. It pursues these efforts through its own initiative and draws synergies by building networks and part-nerships. It has remained as one of the few platforms where stake-holders of different perceptions agree to come together and interact constructively.

The centre is fully aware of the challenges that it needs to overcome to realize its aspiration of becoming a leading regional think tank with a global outreach. It must be more proactive to reach this goal and address many challenges in that journey. Its strategies of institution-building efforts need to consolidate CPD's achievements so far and build them further. Some of the gaps that remain to be fulfilled are as follows:

- **Publish more in Bangla:** Increasing publication in Bangla is a less fulfilled area for CPD. Language is a major barrier in policy aware-ness building and policy advocacy. Most of the research outputs of CPD are in English and efforts will be made to produce products in both English and Bangla.

- **Proactive engagement in gender-sensitive issues:** In the past, CPD has endeavoured to focus on gender issues, in both research and dialogue. Costing domestic violence against women, women's representation in parliament and gender issues in apparels sector are some examples of our past work. CPD will put more focus on gender issues.
- **Participation of more youth in the dialogues:** CPD recognizes that active participation of young people in its dialogue programme is important. It was observed that due to the limited number of participants that can be accommodated in the dialogues, only a few young professionals could be invited to CPD events. Often, they did not express their views. On the other hand, in dialogues and consultations organized exclusively for young professionals, they were proactive. In future, CPD will attract more young people in dedicated dialogues, covering issues of particular interest to youths.

Sustainability has always been a challenge for CPD. The centre has underwritten its expenses with support for implementing research programmes, both on its own and in collaboration with partners. Most donors do not want to provide overhead or administrative costs. CPD has attempted to secure an endowment fund from donors but has not been successful. Hence, the centre's financial sustainability faces challenges in maintaining the current momentum of organizational growth.

To overcome the challenge, CPD plans to take a proactive approach to seek opportunities for generating financial resources. The approach will include (a) undertaking high-value long-term research programmes, (b) leveraging its track record of quality research and encouraging its research staff to explore if funding priorities of CPD's donors' and the organization's priority themes match, (c) building strategic regional and global partnerships with research organizations and universities for joint projects and programme implementation opportunities, (d) participating in international bidding for research grants on a stand-alone or partnership basis, specifically in themes that match CPD's priorities, (e) securing an endowment fund through partnership with the national and international private sector and philanthropic foundations and (f) exploring if the organization can take advantage of government resources in a manner that does not compromise its independence.

CPD is involved in civic activism for which funds are not readily available. A significant part of the expenditure incurred in civic activism is underwritten with CPD's core funds. CPD plans to continue these activities using its own funding sources even though it will imply drain on its financial reserves. CPD is confident that the transformative changes it has achieved in the last two and a half decades will help take the journey forward in the post-TTI period.

Chapter 4

Centre for Poverty Analysis

Udan Fernando

INTRODUCTION

It is almost eight years since the Centre for Poverty Analysis (CEPA) in Sri Lanka embarked on an institutional partnership with the Think Tank Initiative (TTI) administered and managed by International Development Research Centre (IDRC), Canada. In this chapter, CEPA takes stock of its overall experience of interacting with both the TTI and the cohort of fellow TTI-supported think tanks from South Asia in particular and Latin America and Africa in general. On the eve of the end of a relatively long-term institutional partnership and collaboration, CEPA reflects on its own evolution and assesses the exact nature of the relational outcomes and impacts generated during the past eight years. This chapter also examines the particular contributions of the TTI partnership, which leave CEPA with a legacy of capacity to continue in its journey.

FORMATIVE YEARS AND THE ORIENTATION

The centre was established in 2001 as a sequel to a project of the Poverty Impact Monitoring Unit (PIMU) of German Technical Cooperation Agency (GTZ, now GIZ) in Sri Lanka. A pilot project jointly implemented by the Sri Lankan and German governments,

PIMU had been provided high flexibility of operation and a small number of staff implemented PIMU. PIMU was mandated to develop methodologies for both poverty impact monitoring and a market-oriented service package for clients.[1] Its conceptualization was based on the understanding that development interventions often lacked a sound understanding of their impacts. At its inception, CEPA was profiled as an 'independent service provider, to offer services in the areas of Applied Research, Advisory Services, Training and Dialogue & Exchange within four programme areas: Poverty Impact Monitoring, Poverty & Conflict, Poverty & Youth and Poverty Assessment & Knowledge Management'.[2] In a generic sense, CEPA was also profiled as a 'professional' organization with a title for its staff designated as senior professional, professional and junior professional. CEPA's programme themes and the overarching identity were thus arguably influenced by the orientation and legacy of the PIMU project. In fact, some of the staffs of PIMU were recruited to senior/leadership positions at CEPA and, as such, a common thread could be observed running through PIMU and CEPA.

Over time, however, CEPA evolved—the result of being governed by a Sri Lankan board of directors, the expanding number of staff who brought in diversity and new ideas. Close engagement with a variety of stakeholders including a diverse group of clients and bureaucrats also contributed to CEPA's evolution. The emphasis on the programme areas also underwent some changes as PIMU morphed into CEPA. However, CEPA still retained its overall identity as a professional organization providing services on applied research, training and exchanges.

During 2007–2008, CEPA faced a financial crisis and its very existence was threatened. CEPA undertook various short-term assignments that fell within its mandate as a way to mitigate the financial crunch. Although such an approach to funding for projects was provided for relatively short spans of time, typically, one to two years, this strategy, together with stringent financial measures, enabled CEPA to gradually overcome the crisis and establish a minimum level of

---

[1] Gunetilleke and Jafferjee, *Triangulation Squared*, 34.
[2] Ibid., 273.

stability. In these initial years, CEPA would hardly qualify as a think tank. It should also be noted that at this stage, very little attention was accorded to the challenges of communicating and disseminating research findings.

ENTER THE (THINK) TANKS

It is at this juncture that the TTI funding opportunity opened up in 2009, prompting CEPA to apply for a grant. CEPA's selection as a recipient of the grant further eased its financial crisis and helped the organization move forward. CEPA aimed to maintain a balance among responding to the demand of the market, policy needs and the accumulation of knowledge. In this transition, CEPA had to systematically address the gaps in its organizational capacity and enhance research quality (RQ).[3] TTI's support was utilized in CEPA's three areas of work: (a) RQ, (b) organizational performance (OP) and (c) policy linkages (PL), communications and outreach. The following sections explain CEPA's institutional journey from this point, followed by a discussion of the overall impactful experience resulting from the eight years of interface with TTI as well as from the interactions with the cohort of fellow think tanks.

SECTORAL SUPPORT

The objectives of TTI support were aligned with CEPA's own organizational strategy when implementation of CEPA's strategy began. Over the course of the grant, some objectives were achieved, while changes in the grant request were made to achieve other objectives, for example, the work under PL. The changes were incorporated.

One of CEPA's main objectives under RQ was to develop a coherent research agenda with clear thematic focus. The selected themes thus reflected the important areas of development in Sri Lanka, and where CEPA had a clear niche in terms of knowledge and experience. To enable this to happen effectively, CEPA had to reorganize the

---

[3] De Silva and Fernando, 'Change from Within', 132.

management of its structure. Once the transformation had taken place (through structural changes and the development of thematic strategies), CEPA needed to refocus on the RQ objectives to support the thematic area and put in place a mechanism that would ensure that the research and evidence generated would be of high quality.

The same was true for the objectives under OP. The new research agenda required an effective organizational strategy to back it up. Initially, meeting this objective required the restructuring of the organization and recruiting qualified senior staff. In order to achieve a high level of OP, it was important that CEPA put in place financial, administrative and human resource development systems that enabled effective research management. Subsequently, OP objectives were set that focused on this objective: supporting the research agenda through developing the capacity of staff in research and organization management; strengthening financial management support through improved accounting systems and audit processes and a resource mobilization strategy; and enabling the effective monitoring of performance at both organizational and individual levels through the establishment of a management information system (MIS).

The objectives of the PL processes were also changed. Initially, the objectives were narrowly conceptualized in terms of support to CEPA's research agenda, particularly the thematic research. However, by the end of the first year of the grant period, and following the setting up of a communications and policy (CAP) team (the result of the organizational restructuring objective), the objectives of the PL section were considerably broadened. It included the development of a CAP influence strategy. The strategy envisaged more effective communication channels to different audiences, established systems for tracking and directing information both within CEPA and externally, and developed an agenda for policy outreach. It also included a three-language (English, Sinhala and Tamil) policy of communication. Overall, the TTI grant objectives came together to enable CEPA to work towards strengthening itself as an organization with the ability to generate independent and rigorous poverty analysis and inform and influence policy and decision-making within Sri Lanka and the South Asian region.

SIGNIFICANT CHANGES

The following areas of work supported by TTI core funding stimulated the most significant changes at CEPA.

After the new management structure was put in place in the first year of the grant, the emphasis was shifted from poverty impact monitoring and poverty assessments to the development of research that focused on key thematic areas. These were post-conflict context, infrastructure, migration, vulnerability, environment and climate change. A dedicated team of researchers began to work on communicating findings with the objective of influencing policy. The CEPA team also began to focus on long-term research agendas and key issues. Under its post-conflict theme, the centre established collaboration with international agencies (Overseas Development Institute [ODI] and Department for International Development [DFID]) as part of the Secure Livelihoods Research Consortium (SLRC). The CAP team was able to go beyond informing, to influencing and inspiring stakeholders and decision-makers. CEPA thus worked with the network with diverse actors. This dynamism helped build organizational confidence to the recruitment and retention of senior staff. The creation of a programme development position provided support for researchers to obtain funding for their work and kept CEPA abreast of new opportunities. The restructuring of the organization thus ensured a long-term, coherent research agenda, strong communication and policy outreach, and a diversified resource base.

- **The development (in collaboration with the Organisational Capacity Building [OCB] project of TTI) of an RQ framework:** Parallel to the development of thematic research, CEPA was also engaged in a process of serious reflection and capacity building on RQ. Led by the poverty impact monitoring team, the process was stimulated by CEPA's participation in the OCB project with other TTI grantees. CEPA now has an RQ framework that covers the whole research cycle from conceptualization to dissemination of research findings, backed by guidelines, practice notes, as well as guidelines for all communication products and processes. The interest in having quality markers to assess outputs and services has now spilt over to the finance and administration (FAA) team. At the same time, a set of quality indicators for administrative support has also been drawn up. SLRC, of which CEPA is a member, is adapting this framework to maintain quality in its research and products.

- **The generation of robust financial and operational management information through the creation of the MIS and other related activities:** CEPA always had good and transparent financial management and governance. This was strengthened significantly through the establishment of an MIS. The MIS is a self-management system and is part of a broader effort by the FAA team to have strong financial, administration and human resource systems that will support the performance of the organization. The MIS enabled CEPA to be more realistic in managing time, which is its main resource. With TTI funding, CEPA has also been able to establish the safeguards proposed by the organization's Audit Committee and to improve policies on human resources.

REIMAGINING DEVELOPMENT

The cutting edge of a think tank is the generation of ideas that are critical as well as creative. The former involves an evaluative task with a critical lens supported by a robust body of empirical evidence. Creative ideas are triggered by critical assessments. Yet such ideas need to go a step ahead, questioning or challenging the problem in a way that is different from the conventional wisdom. This would generate the context for reimagining the problem and seeking out-of-the-box solutions. In a narrow sense, the outcomes would be specific solutions and recommendations, but in a broader sense, the outcome can be creation of new concepts or even new paradigms that challenge the status quo.

One of the creative results of the CEPA–TTI collaboration was the opportunity to be involved in the inspiring space of incubation of new ideas. At its inter-regional meeting held in South Africa in 2012, TTI facilitated a platform to collectively ideate and incubate novel thinking. At this platform, CEPA pitched the idea of 'reimagining development', a critique of the current development paradigm which is clearly obsolete and does not serve the interests of the sections of society that CEPA is mandated to work for. The critique was followed by a plea to establish a process of creative and progressive imagination for a transformative change that better serves the planet as well as societies irrespective of the degree of power they hold.

TTI supported CEPA in launching this new idea, initially by holding an international symposium in Colombo in December 2012, which brought a large delegation of fellow TTI-supported think tanks. In addition, a large and representative participation was ensured from different constituencies within Sri Lanka. The symposium triggered interest in the premise of reimagining development. CEPA has prepared a concrete plan of action to take the conversation forward and continue the enquiry. CEPA carried this work with a group of organizations and networks which shared the vision of a need for a change of thinking in development.

Reimagining development became an overarching impetus for CEPA's thematic work and has created 'positive discomfort'. Such an orientation continuously shakes CEPA's entrenched thinking on a particular theme and prevents the organization from becoming intellectually complacent. Looking back, this initiative has been one of the most significant contributions of the partnership between CEPA and TTI. It has kept CEPA at an advantageous position in the landscape of think tanks, giving its particular niche and recognition as capitals for its continuation and future.

BEING PART OF A FRATERNITY OF THINK TANKS

As mentioned in a previous section, a partnership with TTI/IDRC is not merely a bilateral relationship. Instead, the initial partnership led to a membership and an active network with a diverse set of think tanks from Asia, Africa and Latin America/Caribbean. The TTI-initiated regional meetings, inter-regional meetings, and specific thematic/technical sessions bring think tanks together from time to time. TTI made a deliberate effort to allow ample exchange of ideas among think tanks. Some of these exchanges led to collaborative endeavours encouraged and sometimes supported by TTI. In addition, think tanks, on their own, either individually or collectively, initiate activities—research, training, conferences and publications—for which other TTI-supported think tanks were invited.

These opportunities enabled CEPA to actively exchange and engage with quite a few think tanks whose work was of interest to CEPA and vice versa. The exchanges ranged from knowledge sharing and cross-fertilization of ideas to concrete forms of collaboration. Two prominent examples are highlighted below. CEPA collaborated with the Public Affairs Centre (PAC) in Bangalore. CEPA adopted PAC's substantive expertise on Citizens' Score Cards (CSCs). Prior to adoption, PAC staff provided series of trainings to CEPA staff. These trainings and field experiments were carried out in Bangalore and Colombo. As a result, CEPA was able to secure two prominent and consecutive contracts from the European Union (EU), implemented by a lead agency, an international non-governmental organization (INGO) functioning in Sri Lanka.

CEPA's services as the research and technical partner sought in two assignments. These assignments, spanning about six years, not only brought in substantive revenue for CEPA but also widened its outreach of influence to carry out work in the severely poor districts of Sri Lanka's north, east and some parts of the south. The second collaboration was established with the Southern Voice initiative. This collaboration initially focused on the Millennium Development Goals (MDGs) and subsequently on the Sustainable Development Goals (SDGs) that were set in 2015. A senior researcher of CEPA functions as the Sri Lankan liaison with the Southern Voice initiative. This responsibility entails a great deal of SDG-related work at global and regional levels. This involvement, for example, has led to the United Nations Development Programme (UNDP) office in Colombo signing a contract with CEPA to obtain technical advice for its work on the SDGs. Being part of the Southern Voice network has enabled CEPA to expand its exposure and influence beyond Sri Lanka.

CONCLUDING REMARKS

The TTI support has helped CEPA to achieve organizational change in a way that is more sustainable. The organizational transformation has led to emergence of a relevant research agenda, stronger RQ orientation, better research management and a greater capacity to generate resources for research activities. Over the years, CEPA's Development Fund has grown by 30 per cent—a positive movement towards CEPA's having sufficient funds for independent research. CEPA's FAA team now has a set of indicators that enable self-monitoring of the quality of their performance.

The strengthening of the research agenda has also enabled CEPA to stimulate its own staff to improve their academic credentials. The idea of 'growing CEPA's own PhDs' has now taken root among staff who, in the past, were not so keen on pursuing higher educational qualifications. It is also attracting researchers from a range of universities, following their own PhD degrees, to work at CEPA.

CEPA's recognition as a credible research organization has spurred new collaborative work, notably with ODI, London; the Universities of Oxford and Sussex; and the Commonwealth Foundation. While these relationships cannot be directly attributed to TTI support, the involvement with other TTI grantees through global initiatives such as the OCB project, the Southern Voice initiative, the reimagining development work and focused exchanges of ideas and partnerships (e.g., PAC's support to CEPA's work) have stimulated the centre's thinking, broadened the skill base and contributed to greater RQ. They have also increased CEPA's international visibility.

CEPA's credibility and visibility for policy engagement and communications were enhanced through TTI support. The centre's communication team has benefited significantly from TTI support and increased the organization's outreach. For CEPA's staff, the TTI grant has provided opportunities to be more strategic about identifying a relevant research agenda—something CEPA had little control over while it chased consultancy opportunities for survival. The grant has also made research management more effective and, in multiple ways, improved the individual and collective capacities of both research and non-research staff.

Overall, CEPA's journey with TTI has enabled it to build a particular niche in Sri Lanka but beyond TTI, as well as a think tank that undertakes evidence-based, policy-oriented research with high-quality, context-sensitive research. This capacity is backed up by an effective and creative communication strategy that targets various constituencies and stakeholders. CEPA's 'positive discomfort' with the mainstream and conventional wisdom pushes the organization to seek and generate novel ideas. A flexible, relevant and creative partnership with TTI helped CEPA build these attributes, creating a solid foundation for its continued journey.

Chapter 5

Institute of Policy Studies

Dushni Weerakoon

INTRODUCTION, CONTEXT AND BRIEF HISTORY

The Institute of Policy Studies (IPS) of Sri Lanka was already a fairly well-established think tank regionally, with over two decades of experience in public policy engagement, when it succeeded in qualifying for the Think Tank Initiative (TTI) grant in 2010. In the South Asian cohort of grantees, IPS had the distinction of being the sole semi-autonomous organization, with formal financial and administrative links to the Government of Sri Lanka (GoSL). Despite these links and its legal status under an Act of parliament, IPS had worked on the premise of financial autonomy as an important element of maintaining its integrity and independence in research. With approximately 10 per cent–15 per cent of its annual budgetary requirements met by the GoSL as earmarked spending for non-research-related expenses, IPS relied on commissioned research and interest income from its accumulated reserves to meet its expenditure needs.

There were three key challenges facing IPS at the time when TTI was launched in 2009. After a decade of pursuing the GoSL for a piece of land to be allocated to construct its building and seeking donor assistance for building construction costs, the institute was successful in starting construction work in 2007. Unforeseen delays, however, meant that cost overruns had begun to stretch available funding and IPS had to tap its own resources to ensure that work was completed by 2010.

IPS was also facing another internal challenge in terms of depletion of its senior research staff. Around five of its most experienced researchers began to leave for extended periods of 3–4 years to pursue PhD studies overseas from 2007 onwards. Whilst the institute recognized the potential long-term value of granting leave of absence to allow its staff to pursue further postgraduate studies, there were no certainties that the researchers would return to take up their former positions at IPS. Thus, the overall in-house research capacity was quite limited by 2009–2010.

A third factor was external to IPS in the context of changes in Sri Lanka's policy landscape. With the successful military win by the GoSL to conclude a simmering 30-year internal separatist conflict, post-war elections saw the emergence of a strong mono-centric government. As a result, Sri Lanka's development priorities and policies began to undergo a transformational change, while at the same time there was a slow but steady erosion of policy engagement by the government more broadly. While IPS still had a degree of access to policy-making, it lacked a focused policy engagement and outreach strategy to navigate these new developments for maximum impact.

Thus, in many respects, the TTI funding came at a critical juncture for IPS. Instead of attempting to manage these challenges within available resources, and facing a worst-case scenario of downsizing some activities, the availability of the TTI funding from 2010 brought about a rethinking on how best to use these resources in a fresh setting for IPS, that is, new facilities from a custom-built office and a new policy environment in the country at large. Over the years, the benefits of the TTI funding have been manifold across all three pillars of support. It has enabled the institute to emerge stronger and significantly more resilient eight years later. Some of the more specific areas of innovation and successes as well as continuing gaps are detailed under each of the three main pillars of support.

ORGANIZATIONAL PERFORMANCE

The most significant change in IPS' organizational improvements from TTI has come about in the approach to monitoring and evaluation (M&E) processes that we identified and adopted. Indeed, much of this process originated from specific questions posed at the outset when IPS applied for the TTI grant. These questions related to performance indicators surrounding not only research and policy outcomes but also more crucially questions of overall institutional governance and accountability.

As a result, IPS made significant investments in streamlining its financial management modules, research costing and human resource (HR) management systems, throughout the grant period, in incremental steps. To a large extent, these were areas of investment that received least priority when IPS was running on a tight budget, where research costs and investments in critical areas such as information technology took precedence. Indeed, to an extent, the pillars around which TTI itself was built forced IPS to study its organizational structures as never before.

For the first time in its existence of more than two decades, IPS undertook a systematic five-year strategic planning exercise with the TTI funding, led by a core steering group from within the institute and facilitated by an external party of consultants. Key areas of focus were identified from internal one-to-one interviews across the organization and group discussions. The identified focus areas included research performance, visibility, HR management, financial management and administration oversight.

The objectives and key performance indicators (KPIs) identified for action in each of these areas fed into strengthening organizational performance activities identified in the TTI work plan of IPS in successive years. Two of the most critical improvements that came about as a result relate to project costing and overall M&E of outcomes, at both individual and institutional levels, through new HR management systems.

Both internal and external financial auditors had in the past highlighted gaps in IPS' internal processes to capture accurate costing of research activities with implications for the overall financial strengthening of the organization. Thus, a compelling case was made for investments towards strengthening financial management and staff performance through an integrated system. As a first step, investments were made in new online financial accounting systems. As a second step, an integrated online HR system to manage attendance and leave, as well as time allocation for research and support function activities, was introduced. A follow-up important step was the creation of a new administrative post for HR personnel for the first time, funded with the TTI grant.

The gains to IPS were twofold. The new systems allowed a better costing of overheads, and the institute is now able to cost research activities accurately when preparing research proposals. It is also able to better account for and cross-subsidize research activities not deemed profitable in monetary terms but important in other contexts of policy engagement or networking. The HR system has allowed IPS to better understand the actual time allocation of staff in both research and non-research activities. For researchers, information such as the allocation of time between funded and non-funded activities, time spent on research and policy engagement activities, among others, is easily accessible at individual, team or organizational levels. IPS firmly believes that these innovative systems have allowed for improved medium- to long-term planning in all the most important areas such as research, policy outreach, finance and human resources. The value addition and importance of these process changes will outlive the TTI grant period and are most important from the perspective of organizational change.

Aside from the financial aspects of TTI that made investments in process changes possible, the rethinking on organizational issues facilitated by TTI—most especially the regional forums—and sharing of experiences have been perhaps even more invaluable to design and implement changes. Managing the introduction of changes to the day-to-day running of an organization can be challenging. Oftentimes, the challenges can appear insurmountable and generate its own sense of lethargy. In this regard too, the TTI experiment was groundbreaking. It offered the organization not only the chance to draw on peer learning from others but also an added inducement of a think tank cohort striving for positive changes collectively. As such, individual efforts were also driven by group dynamics.

Today, IPS is a much better managed and efficiently run organization. This is reflected in all the institute's internal and external financial audits when compared to the start of TTI. While causation is difficult to establish as a definite factor, IPS is of the opinion that individual and collective learning through TTI has much to do with the positive changes seen in the institute over the last eight years.

RESEARCH QUALITY

Like most other TTI grantees, from the outset itself, IPS prioritized the recruitment of senior research staff. Unfortunately, it was less than successful in its endeavours in the initial years. Young, dynamic and postgraduate qualified researchers of the calibre that IPS was seeking were not plentiful in the immediate post-war environment in Sri Lanka. Thus, efforts were put into recruiting promising junior-level researchers and providing them with more targeted in-house training.

One of the most important changes that the institute has experienced through the TTI grant period is the approach and methods of training research staff. Prior to the TTI grant, the institute depended on funded training offered by various organizations, on the basis of supply rather than demand. With funds at its disposal, IPS was able for the first time to conduct periodic in-house surveys of methodological and other soft skills training demanded by researchers, prioritize these and deliver an annual training schedule. Indeed, it was surprising to note that IPS' own senior researchers could deliver many of the training needs identified. What had held them back previously in offering training was the inability to allocate sufficient time to design and deliver training. With TTI funds set aside to cover such research costs, the institute was able to relieve senior researchers from proposal writing and searching for commissioned research; instead, better overall management of research activities could be planned and implemented.

For instance, research methodological training was packaged with actual proposal writing and proposals deemed to have merit were converted to research studies and IPS working paper publications through TTI funds. This allowed junior researchers to gain a gamut of skills, with clear outcomes identified for M&E.

Efforts to raise in-house research capacity were complemented by a rethinking of IPS' medium-term research agenda. This factor was also a key outcome of the strategic planning exercise. A new medium-term research programme was developed with a focus on Sri Lanka's post-war development challenges. The IPS' flagship annual report *Sri Lanka: State of the Economy*, which previously drew on ongoing research, was revamped and rebranded with original research around a thematic area each year. Its already wide readership has since expanded, and the report is now recognized as perhaps the most credible and independent analysis of the Sri Lankan economy and its medium-term development challenges.

The new research programme also identified emerging areas that IPS must begin to explore. One of the most critical among them were issues of urbanization as Sri Lanka embarked on an ambitious public infrastructure development programme that included urban regeneration as a key component. While these emerging policy areas for research were identified, IPS was also continually searching for appropriate senior researchers for recruitment. Here again, the funding space that opened with the TTI grant was critical to enable the institute to bring various strands of activities together with a common overall objective within the three pillars of funding.

IPS was able to record a large degree of success in getting its researchers on postgraduate studies overseas to return full time to the institute. Additional incentives could be offered to returning senior researchers by way of core funding to restart their research agenda and carry out studies, publish their research work, reconnect with networks and other partners, and recruit research assistants and interns. Funding activities were interconnected to facilitate these in a holistic fashion. For example, a pool of TTI funding was set aside each year to support core research—encompassing new areas, issues considered to be of high policy priority, research that is adopting new methods and tools, etc.—with proposals evaluated on a competitive basis. Funding for publications was provided, including covering staff time for journal submissions. Researchers could also tap into funding for stakeholder meetings and conference presentations to network and obtain feedback on their research. New forms of quality assessments and refereeing were adopted by allocating funds for external peer review.

The expansion of such core funded research activities also allowed IPS to build national research capacity by absorbing more interns from the local universities. The quality of student learning at national universities is often felt to be inadequate, with little or no exposure to research or policy. As a first step, IPS organized a university forum, engaging both lecturers and students from Sri Lanka's 16 public universities spread across the country over a two-day forum that included organized interactions with key economy policy-makers. Three memorandums of understanding (MOUs) were signed initially with more established universities to absorb a given number of interns each year, but the institute now receives such requests from universities across the country, including from the former conflict-affected areas in the north and east of Sri Lanka. In any given year, IPS trains about 10–15 interns for periods ranging from two to six months each.

Overall, the quality of IPS' research over the TTI grant period has seen a substantive change, be it in the research areas covered, the volume of publications, the types of publications or presentation of research papers, at both local and international forums. This was made possible because the supporting environment to conduct high-quality and policy-relevant research was strengthened, thanks to TTI support. Arguably, these are areas that the institute would have invested in as a priority even without the additional support of TTI funds. The difference that TTI brought was to give the space for senior management to take a step back from day-to-day operations and work through a programme of interconnected activities that would build on one another for maximum gain to the organization. The fact that a pool of funds were available to invest in the identified activities simultaneously, rather than apportioning on a phased basis owing to tight financial constraints, meant that the results also became more visible and quantifiable. Again, instead of an isolated organizational endeavour, the fact that a cohort of think tanks were engaged in discussions, designs and implementation meant that the process received an added impetus at an individual organization-level to galvanize the activities.

POLICY ENGAGEMENT

For IPS, the most fundamental change from its engagement with TTI has come under the policy engagement pillar of support. As a semi-government organization that has always considered national-level policy actors in the government as its main stakeholder group, IPS was primarily focused on producing quality, policy-relevant research, rather than on dissemination and advocacy. At the outset of TTI, IPS relied mostly on traditional tools for policy engagement. Dissemination of research was done largely through printed materials in the form of books, working papers or journal publications, and presentation of research papers at conferences. It had branched to developing an in-house blog—Talking Economics (TE)—in 2009. This is a work-in-progress and at a nascent stage in terms of the numbers of researchers who are engaged in writing blogs.

Policy engagement—or the visibility aspect as per IPS' strategic planning exercise—was considered one of the weaker areas of activity within the organization. While good-quality research was being done, the forms in which it was tailored to different stakeholders was inadequate, as was IPS' efforts to reach out to other important stakeholders such as the general public.

Over the last seven years, a communication strategy was developed incrementally. A new post in the organizational set-up for communications was created and funded via TTI monies. A more strategic communications plan was crafted thereafter with the help of external facilitators, whereby IPS' main stakeholders and the targeted communication strategies and tools to reach out to them effectively were mapped out. Complementing these efforts, the public website and blog site were also revamped. Customized training programmes for researchers were developed and rolled out with the assistance of external consultants. Some of the critical areas of training aimed to strengthen blog writing skills, engaging in new social media platforms such as Twitter and more general training on effective communication of research to different audiences.

Throughout this process, the institute benefited to some extent from tailor-made policy engagement and communications training and capacity-building efforts rolled out by TTI at a programme level. What was perhaps more beneficial was the peer learning from the other TTI grantees, many of whom were far more advanced in communications and policy advocacy than IPS. Thus, the mix of institutes within the cohort was a distinct advantage in this context.

Today, IPS' communications and strategic outreach is an integrated element of the entire research process. At the start of the year, a detailed communications plan is mapped out per researcher on the basis of ongoing and expected research activities over the year. Where possible, a communications strategy is outlined for some research studies from the outset. All publications also have complementary communications targets, including blogs, media interviews and one-to-one meetings with relevant government ministers or other policy-makers.

A key activity identified by IPS to strengthen policy linkages that failed to gain much traction was in encouraging more collaborative advocacy work with other organizations, including the private sector. In retrospect, it could be argued that the limited number of think tanks working on issues of economic policy in Sri Lanka and IPS' own status as a semi-government entity hampered progress in this area.

Policy Contribution

At the time that IPS qualified for the TTI grant, it already had an established reputation for quality, independent research that was sought after by policy-makers. Clearly, the organizational status also gave the institute an edge in terms of access to government officials unlike the case of non-governmental organizations (NGOs), for example. What the TTI grant brought to these initial conditions was a qualitative improvement in the manner in which IPS thought of policy influence and the manner in which it set about influencing policy.

A clear example of the impact of the TTI exercise can be offered in the area of urban policy research at IPS. As infrastructure development and urban regeneration efforts took off rapidly in post-war Sri Lanka, it was identified as a critical research gap in the medium-term research agenda. When IPS was able to attract a promising senior researcher—recruited full time under the TTI programme—seed money was provided to develop a research agenda through a consultative process with stakeholders. Given the newness of urban sector policy research to IPS, it was considered more prudent to adopt this strategy.

Once a research agenda was developed and prioritized, core funding from TTI was made available to conduct a study on how urban populations are to be quantified, looking at best practices globally to correct obvious limitations in Sri Lanka's existing practice of adopting an administrative definition. Through the course of the research, Sri Lanka's national data-gathering agency and other interested parties were consulted. In addition, training and guidance were also provided where required.

The communications and policy linkages built into the research study proposal were a continuous process, unlike previously, where such efforts began only with the formal publication of a research paper. Here, the initial findings were written up in blogs and were further disseminated through IPS' social media channels as well as with wide publicity on the research findings reported by the local media. A one-to-one targeted meeting was held with the government minister in charge of the subject portfolio with two objectives in mind: to brief about the research study and recommendations, but even more importantly to brief about the inclusion of this new area of research at IPS. Indeed, the eventual outcome is that the study helped galvanize Sri Lanka's data agencies and other relevant bodies to begin work on formally working out a new definition to capture the country's grow-ing urban population to inform the macro-level planners on urban development issues.

The above is only one example of the many ways in which the different activities supported through the three pillars of TTI came together to help achieve the primary objective of helping to shape and fashion economic policy. The approach of the initiative as much as the funding is a key driver of change. Rather than be reactive, IPS was proactive in identifying research gaps and actively working to bring it to the attention of a multiple stakeholders. This is qualitatively very different to the initial conditions and thinking that prevailed prior to the TTI grant.

There are many other examples of impact stories, most prominent is IPS' research in areas of migration and trade policy formulation. However, IPS' story is perhaps also a little different to its other part-ner grantees. Aside from its research output, by virtue of its semi-government status, IPS' involvement in policy formulation is likely more intense than that of NGOs. Indeed, it can often be disruptive to an ongoing work plan as requests for policy inputs often have a short-time horizon. To ease the burden on researchers as well as to make the contributions more effective, IPS has experimented by providing core funding for some select activities. These include, among others, the provision of funds to sit on policy-making committees that the researchers choose to engage in, if they are considered very useful, and the preparation of research inputs requested on short notice by the GoSL. As a result, there is better tracking and awareness of the many policy engagements, the costs involved and the eventual outcomes to inform IPS about future engagements on a particular committee or agency. Thus, scarce resources can be more effectively deployed in follow-up engagements.

SUSTAINABILITY: GAPS, CHALLENGES AND THINKING AHEAD

The sustainability of organizations dependent on a range of funding options is an ongoing concern. Sustainability relates to retaining human resources and building a buffer of financial resources that will support independent agenda setting and its implementation.

After an exploratory assessment of funding options during IPS' strategic planning exercise, the most practical option followed was to consolidate and build its financial savings base through professional fund managers. This strategy was aimed to ensure that there will be internal resources that can be channelled to absorb the costs of activities initiated under TTI which the institute wishes to pursue over the medium to long term. In addition, efforts to seek programme funding for thematic areas of research will act as a complementary measure.

For IPS, continuity in the provision of core funding to pursue new areas of research or conduct policy relevant research, a separate training budget that meets internally identified training needs, and supporting communications and policy engagement activities are the three key areas where continuity of activities initiated with the TTI funding must continue as a priority.

Very tangible benefits have accrued to the organization in these areas and they will continue to be the backbone for continued growth of the organization.

Sustainability will be an ongoing and continuous challenge. IPS, however, is firmly of the view that the organization has emerged from the TTI exercise stronger in research capacity, more efficient in internal management and more resilient in financial autonomy to manage these challenges more effectively. An often overlooked factor in the TTI journey is the learning and value addition that has come about through a peer group exchange, dedicated regional programme officers and support from a global partner like International Development Research Centre that has extensive experience and expertise in understanding country-specific as well as region-specific challenges of think tanks operating in developing countries. Those insights clearly helped shape a programme that not only gave enough autonomy at individual level for grantees to set their objectives and activities but also introduced important accountability measures in their M&E methods. From the outset of the initial application process, the engagement with TTI provided fertile grounds for learning about systematically aiming to improve the way organizations function, produce good-quality research, and maximize policy impact and influence to better development outcomes in a country.

Chapter 6

Institute for Social and Environmental Transition-Nepal

Ajaya Dixit

THE START

On 29 and 30 August 2009, on behalf of the Institute for Social and Environmental Transition-Nepal (ISET-N), I coordinated a regional conference called 'Adapting to Climate Change in Asia' in Kathmandu.[1] At this conference, ISET-N's researchers made a presentation of learning from a study on climate change adaptation in Nepal conducted by the ISET network. Researchers from Nepal, the United States of America (USA), Bangladesh and Pakistan were involved in this study. After this conference, on 31 August and 1 September, with support from the Asian Development Bank (ADB), Danish International Development Agency (DANIDA), Department for International Development (DFID) and World Bank (WB), the Government of

---

[1] Supported by the International Development Research Centre ((IDRC) and the National Oceanic and Atmospheric Administration (NOAA), ISET-N organized the conference in partnership with ISET, the International Centre for Integrated Mountain Development (ICIMOD) and the Stockholm Environment Institute (SEI). About 100 scholars from Nepal, India, the USA, Canada, Pakistan, the United Kingdom (UK), Kenya, Bangladesh and China took part in the conference.

Nepal (GoN) organized a conference on climate change as a prelude to Nepal's participation in the Conference of the Parties (CoP) in Copenhagen. In the evening of 1 September, we found out about a forthcoming 'call for proposals' for the Think Tank Initiative (TTI) grant. A few days later, the IDRC), Canada, made the call public. We then applied for the grant and became one of the recipients.

The study on climate change adaptation presented in the regional conference was published in 2009 as a book, *Vulnerability Through the Eyes of the Vulnerable*. The study used the perspectives of both natural and social sciences to highlight how critically vulnerable Nepal is to climate change and how imperative it is for the country to pursue various adaptive strategies. Between its establishment in 2001 and 2010, ISET-N, in partnership with its US-based sister organization, the Institute for Social and Environmental Transition-International (ISET-I), Nepal Water Conservation Foundation (NWCF) and other research groups in South Asia,[2] worked on local water and other community-based natural resource management, food security, resilience and as the front-line defence against climate change vulnerabilities and disaster risk reduction in the region. The partners' 10 years of lessons are documented in many publications by ISET-N, ISET-I and other members of the network, notably *The Fluid Mosaic: Water Governance in the Context of Variability, Uncertainty and Change* (2003), *Adaptive Capacity and Livelihood Resilience* (2004), *Winds of Change* (2007), *From Risk to Resilience* (2008), *From Research to Capacity* (2008) and *Re-imagining the Rural–Urban Continuum* (2008).

These books and other research products gave us a sense of accomplishment. We had, it seemed, contributed our bit towards expanding the frontiers of the world's understanding of our evolving adaptation to anthropogenic climate change. At that stage, ISET network's products had contributed to two outcomes: one at the national and one at global levels. In 2010, with the support of DFID and the European

---

[2] Madras Institute of Development Studies, Institute of Development Studies, Vikram Sarabhai Centre for Development Interaction, International Institute for Environment and Development, London, and Gorakhpur Environmental Action Group were some of the other organizations.

Union, ISET-N partnered with ISET-I and the International Institute for Environment and Development, London, and other local organizations in designing Nepal's Local Adaptation Plan for Action (LAPA). This design was based on the premise that local communities with improved access to services from both the natural ecosystem and human-built systems would be better able to respond to shocks due to climate change. The GoN approved the LAPA framework in 2011.[3] In addition, ISET-I used lessons from above-mentioned studies to initiate another adaptation study, one on urban adaptation research that was conducted in selected cities in India and Southeast Asia through the Asian Cities Climate Change Resilience Network (ACCCRN) programme. Funded by the Rockefeller Foundation, ACCCRN helped to expand the ISET network's learning and develop the exposure–system–agent–institution framework as a heuristic to unpack vulnerability to various shocks and build resilience; this framework is now widely used. Since 2013, Zurich Insurance's Flood Resilience Alliance has adopted this framework in its post-event review capability (PERC) method as a part of the organization's corporate responsibility programme. PERC is used for disaster forensics—post-disaster analysis focusing on how a specific hazard event became a disaster—to collect and share lessons to improve resilience.[4]

At this point, ISET-N had neither focused on developing its capacity to manage a research organization nor systematically packaged research results for effective policy outreach. We were primarily researchers; thus, when ISET-N was awarded the TTI grant in 2010, its governance and organization management was ad hoc, a reality that dawned on us immediately after we began implementing the activities with TTI support.

In 2010, Nepal was going through two major political transitions: the Maoist-led armed rebellion had ended and the institution of

---

[3] See GoN, *National Framework on Local Adaptation Plans for Action.*

[4] Zurich Insurance launched the Flood Resilience Alliance in 2013 with the goal of linking academia with the humanitarian sector, private sector and communities to improve dialogue around and generate mechanisms for enhancing flood resilience. To date, PERCs have been conducted for floods in Central and Eastern Europe, Morocco, the UK, Nepal and Houston. See Venkateswaran, MacClune, Keating, and Szönyi, *The PERC Manual.*

monarchy had been abolished and the country had embraced a federal republican political order. The elected Constitution Assembly was drafting a new constitution to institutionalize the new federal governance architecture. The situation was one of transition, uncertainty and chaos. For knowledge-generating organizations, while opportunities existed to explore new research frontiers, the emerging order accorded primacy to state restructuring, peace processes and conflict resolution, all issues with more political relevance than research on the science–society interface.

For ISET-N, which relied on project-based sources of funding, this context raised many questions. The most important among these was the question of how to keep generating knowledge to benefit various stakeholders in Nepal. ISET-N would not only continue as an organization conducting research but also initiate activities that would help enhance efforts to build a research–policy ecosystem in Nepal. To meet this objective, ISET-N sought to become a 'catalytic think tank' that would work with organizations at different levels from governmental to grass roots. The logic behind this approach is the conviction that the society's well-being depends primarily on the health of its knowledge–policy–practice ecosystem.

IN A NEW TRAJECTORY

As it took its initial steps, ISET-N faced three challenges: (a) devising an institutional strategy, (b) putting in place a mechanism that would deliver administrative, financial, research, dissemination and policy outreach functions and (c) building its capacity to partner with other knowledge policy organizations. ISET-N resolved that it would endeavour to gain the required capacity to address these challenges through a continuous process of shared learning founded on contextualized evidence but was not sure about how to proceed or where to proceed from. The TTI's framework proposed three pillars of change: (a) improve the quality of research, (b) strengthen the policy engagement process and (c) develop robust administration and finance and human resource management mechanisms to support the first two pillars and serve as a practical point of entry. This framing of purpose helped ISET-N make a start. In line with the proposed framework,

ISET-N set three objectives for itself: (a) to strengthen organizational performance, (b) to enhance research quality and (c) to improve policy linkages, communication and outreach. Each of these objectives is still relevant today, and will remain so in the future.

1. **Organizational development:** Building organizational performance was an immediate need when we began implementing TTI activities; in particular, ISET-N's financial management system needed updating. To improve our financial and administrative performances, we hired a trained finance officer and upgraded our accounting software to a professional version. The organization hired a professional to oversee overall management, updated its human resource policy manual and employed a chartered accountancy firm to carry out auditing. Streamlining governance was our next major step, so ISET-N's executive committee created a conducive environment for both female and male professionals with years of experience and diverse backgrounds to serve as members of its governing board.

   We updated our management information system (MIS) and purchased a backup server to help better manage our library of knowledge products (research articles, peer-reviewed journals, digital layers of the geographical information system (GIS) and historical data on rainfall and temperature). Researchers were provided with capacity-building training on data analysis and visualization in GIS environment, article and report writing, and the delivery of presentations. As a result of this professional development, the number of published newspaper articles went up. A biometric attendance system was introduced and a 40-hour-per-week schedule implemented to boost productivity. Team-building activities and workshops on communication helped researchers and other staff work cooperatively, review each other's work and provide constructive feedback, which, in turn, helped produce good-quality products and see projects completed on time. The resultant synergy was evident in a new approach—the 360-degree appraisal of employees. ISET-N's official website was redesigned and updated, and it began to upload digital versions of its research products to improve ease of access.

2. **Research quality:** TTI support has helped systematize process for ensuring quality of research and knowledge products as well as

materials for policy engagement in a number of ways, including the development of a quality-assurance protocol and internal and external review processes, the capacity-building of research staff, mentoring and otherwise learning from the research environment, participation in and organization of seminars and conferences, field visits, and exchanges with researchers from collaborating partner organizations. We partnered with both educational and non-educational organizations within and outside the country, using these opportunities to boost cross-learning. ISET-N supported the Central Department of Environmental Science at Tribhuvan University (TU-CDES) in its effort to bring out a peer-reviewed journal, a step guided by our strategy of building a knowledge–research–policy ecosystem.

ISET-N broadened its research base and hired mid-level researchers to take the lead in thematic areas such as the right to information, climate, finance, trans-boundary water commons, ecosystem-based adaptation, earthquake resilience and information technology. ISET-N has leveraged funding support to other think tanks in Kathmandu so they could undertake research on issues that ISET-N believed to be critical. For example, ISET-N helped Martin Chautari, a social science research organization in Nepal, to conduct research on the status of the technology of building materials in Nepal after the 2015 Gorkha earthquake. ISET-N researchers also collaborated with the Center for Study of Science, Technology & Policy (CSTEP), Bengaluru; Public Affairs Centre (PAC), Bengaluru; Centre for Budget and Governance Accountability (CBGA), New Delhi; and Sustainable Development Policy Institute (SDPI), Islamabad, on climate change research and capacity-building activities. These short-lived endeavours emphasized the need for a more sustained sort of collaboration among think tanks and research groups in South Asia.

ISET-N's mid-level researchers have expanded the scale of their engagement with local community groups and, by doing so, have increased their appreciation of changing local dynamics and the importance of maintaining a dialogue with local stakeholders. Such a dialogue would begin the process of co-producing the knowledge crucial in Nepal to enhance societal recognition of the need for research. Currently, only a small group of enthusiasts and idealists in Nepal pursue research. The government does not support research unless it is absolutely necessary, and the support it does provide is largely externally funded. While we have taken steps to ensure quality of research, the organization needs to do much more to build research capacity and participate in global knowledge platforms such as peer-reviewed journals, engagements in expert panels and conferences.

3. **Dissemination, outreach and policy engagement:** Prior to TTI, ISET-N did not focus on repackaging knowledge for directly engaging the world of policy-making; this condition has begun to change gradually. ISET-N began using a variety of platforms to disseminate its products, expanded outreach and pursued new approaches to policy engagement. The organization used a variety of methods, including community FM radio, conferences, workshops, appearances on TV programmes, publications, policy briefs, articles in peer-reviewed journals and other publications, including books in the Nepali language, to reach the general public. The organization widened its partnerships with universities, academic institutions, government agencies (at the national and local levels), international non-governmental organizations (INGOs), civil society entities and local communities. It has started to narrow-cast research results to thought leaders, policy-makers and practitioners to maximize its impact and, in doing so, opened avenues for sustained dialogues with a range of stakeholders. Shared learning dialogues; one-to-one, continuous interactions; and follow-ups have been useful for making effective policy pitches. ISET-N's pitches were substantive when it established partnerships with policy-makers to identify a problem, design a study to investigate it and undertake the enquiry into that area of research.[5]

---

[5] In this support period, since 2010, we completed the following: 54 books and other reports, 20 policy briefs, 15 peer-reviewed articles, 13 working papers, 111 articles, 70 *Manthan* reviews, 6 TV appearances, 7 documentaries, 47 radio programmes, 42 conferences, 52 capacity-building trainings, 150 workshops and local-level meetings, 4,000+ Facebook and Twitter followers and 1,575 tweets. Prior to TTI, ISET-N's MIS was poorly maintained, and the outputs were as follows: 18 publications, 44 *Manthan* reviews and 75 articles.

NEW INITIATIVES

As the organization moved forward, it encountered a question: how could ISET-N use TTI support to incrementally build the research–knowledge–policy ecosystem, a step which, though it would have no immediate impact, would nonetheless result in a stronger ecosystem? It conceived new initiatives and partnered with other organizations to implement them. Thus, TTI support created space for ISET-N to move beyond its bounds and work with university students and teachers as carriers of knowledge, school teachers as creators of demand for knowledge at the local level, civil scientists for integrating high science, and producers of low science and book reviews to foster substantive and critical dialogue in the Nepali society. The specific initiatives are as follows:

- *Civic science:* ISET-N provides technical backstopping to Community-based Rainfall Measurement (CORAM), a network that works with high schools across the country to monitor rainfall using low-cost rain gauges. The partners of CORAM are the Department of Hydrology and Meteorology; Kathmandu Institute of Applied Sciences (KIAS); RECHAM Consultancy; the University of Wyoming, USA; and the Society of Hydrology and Meteorology. The members of CORAM monitor daily rainfall in rain gauges installed on school premises. While it inculcates scientific thinking in school children, CORAM also aims to complement the national rain gauge network. As a part of this process, ISET-N and CORAM organize annual discussion sessions and art competitions for students of community schools both in and outside of Kathmandu. These initiatives explore themes such as climate change, disaster reconstruction, and pollution.
- *Abishkar Fellowship:* ISET-N began offering the Abishkar Fellowship to undergraduate Nepali students in 2016. Students can compete for the fellowship either individually or in a group to undertake innovative projects on the environment, technology, adaptation, energy and disaster risk reduction, and ICTs. The fellowship includes a modest financial package, mentoring and opportunities for presentation in ISET-N's programmes. The fellowship is

announced publicly on ISET-N's website and social media platforms and through information sent to educational establishments.
The fellows are selected on the basis of merit of their proposals,
and the shortlisted candidates are required to make a presentation
before a panel. The Abishkar Fellowship helps inculcate a culture
of enquiry-based learning in the early stages of university education and thereby enables students to pursue innovative solutions.
As the private sector, government and donors in Nepal have started
to invest in start-up groups, their burgeoning capacity to innovate
will help them become policy entrepreneurs in both the private
sector and the community-based development arena.

- *Master's research grant:* ISET-N has been providing a research grant
to master's-level students from different Nepali universities since
2010. Proposals are evaluated on the basis of quality, relevance,
methodology, practicability and scientific/social importance. The
thematic areas for research include climate change and adaptation,
food security, water governance, disaster risk reduction, forest
management, energy, urbanization, migration, gender, poverty
and livelihood. So far, 34 students have been provided support,
which includes a financial package as well as input at different
stages of the research from senior researchers. Both this grant
and the Abishkar Fellowship hold value for the student community as few colleges and universities offer such support. Many
students consider research as a ritual to be performed to receive
a degree rather than a means to acquire knowledge and build
analytical capacity. The ISET-N's support has helped recipient
students expand the scope of their research and in-depth investigations. The selection process, which involves writing a proposal
and making presentations adhering to guidelines, also helps build
the capacity of the candidates.

- *Himalayan Knowledge Conclave:* ISET-N partnered with the Institute
of Science and Technology, CDES-TU, and the Resources
Himalaya Foundation (RHF) to organize a graduate conference
on environment and sustainable development named 'Himalayan
Knowledge Conclave' (HKC) on an annual basis in the first week
of April. The first conclave was held in 2015, and three more
have been held since. In 2018, the GoN's Ministry of Science and

Technology joined in the organizing of the conclave, as did the School of Environmental Science and Management (SchEMS), an affiliate of Pokhara University. The conclave aims to provide a platform for fresh Nepali graduates to share their research and build networks with peers and experts that promote creative discussions and learning. In Nepal, only a few conferences target students. Many fresh graduates feel that conferences are beyond their reach and that conferences are meant for academics and experts or are just rituals that development agencies carry out but that add little value to solving problems at hand.

While the conclave itself provides students a platform to critique each other's work, the orientation workshop for presenters prior to the conclave helps improve the format and delivery of presentations. The HKC engages students and their teachers as well as reviewers, judges, session chairs, volunteers, rapporteurs and staff members of the partners involved in its organizing. There have been noticeable changes since the first conclave in 2015. First, the participation of both junior and senior researchers and professionals has increased. Second, the quality of presentations has gradually improved. Third, a wide student community has accepted the initiative. Last, young researchers have taken the leadership in planning and organizing the conclave.

- *Manthan:* ISET-N's Nepali publication *Manthan*, which translates as 'reflective dialogue', presents both fiction and non-fiction reviews of English and Nepali books. Each review encapsulates the key arguments of the book it reviews and relates those arguments to the challenges faced by the Nepali society. Initially, the organization published and attempted to distribute copies of *Manthan* but found the strategy ineffective. After extensive discussions, ISET-N decided to publish and distribute *Manthan* in *Shikshak* (teacher), a monthly magazine in Nepali aimed at targeting more than 300,000 teachers across the country. In order to help them develop regular reading habits, think critically and build writing skills, we encourage young professionals to write reviews.

- *Local stories of change:* This initiative documents and publishes grassroots- and community-level innovations, which drive local-level change processes. Researchers at ISET-N and journalists from

Shikshak provide research on innovations while the journalists write stories in Nepali for the magazine. Thus far, eight stories variously about agricultural entrepreneurship, niche farming, stone water-spouts, aviation museum, community electrification, lake conservation and a local irrigation system have been published. It is expected that school teachers will use the stories as teaching materials to highlight examples of local-level changes. These stories are expected to catalyse similar innovations in other places and communities.

• *ISET Platform Lecture:* This lecture is another of ISET-N's important initiatives. The lecture is a reflective and theoretical exposition on a topical issue relevant to the contemporary era. Eminent Nepali and South Asian scholars and personalities who have made significant contributions in their professions are invited to deliver lectures on specific, relevant topics.

INFLUENCE STORIES

Policy influence is not a linear or direct outcome of research. Policy-making is a messy process and a political one too. It involves a continuum of activities consisting of opinion-building, discourse-setting, knowledge uptake and policy actions. A policy landscape involves many actors, including various knowledge-generating organizations, whose contribution to each element of the continuum is significant. While it is difficult to pinpoint how any specific lesson from a single study or organization leads to a policy reforms, below we present a few examples of such contributions:

• *Government support to HKC:* After three years of lobbying, the GoN's Ministry of Science and Technology has decided to allocate regular budget to HKC, thereby giving it both continuity and legitimacy. Support was made available for the organizing of the fourth HKC.

• *National Strategy for Resilient Local Communities:* Our learning underscores the fact that consistent participation in research can help foster policy uptake. By systematically repackaging knowledge products to target specific audiences, a window of opportunity can be created to influence the policy continuum mentioned above. The system-agent-institution framework, for example, is useful for assessing vulnerability to climate change and for preparing strategies for adaptation. Since the 2015 Gorkha earthquake, we have been using this framework to unpack the recovery efforts currently underway; ISET-N took a lead in formulating what became known as the National Strategy for Resilient Local Communities (NSRLC). With Practical Action Consultancy Pvt. Ltd and Genesis Consultancy Pvt. Ltd as its partners, this strategy, which falls under the aegis of Nepal's Ministry of Federal Affairs and Local Development (MoFALD), aims to help the country's municipalities to plan, develop and implement programmes for enhancing resilience.

- *Social enterprise in post-earthquake reconstruction:* ISET-N's work with the National Association of Community Electricity Users-Nepal (NACEUN) to restore the distribution systems managed by 26 community rural electricity entities (CREEs) in the four districts (Gorkha, Dhading, Kavrepalanchok and Lalitpur) severely affected by the 2015 Gorkha earthquake demonstrated the organization's flexibility and capacity to adapt to new circumstances. With support from Give2Asia and the facilitation by the Asia Foundation, local electricity distribution infrastructure was restored and the capacity of CREEs to manage the restored distribution system, strengthen internal governance and invest in preparedness was built. NACEUN facilitated the actual implementation, while ISET-N provided support for knowledge management and informed stakeholders' consultations. ISET-N continues to partner with NACEUN and CREEs, providing support to nudge them towards a better state of preparedness than existed in the past.

- *Community-led and local government-facilitated reconstruction:* ISET-N worked with the permanent reconstruction and rehabilitation committee formed by the earthquake-affected households of the village of Jarayatar in Melamchi Valley of Sindhupalchok District. The organization supported the committee to prepare a plan for building earthquake-safe shelters as well as for building livelihoods and local economic systems and implementing drinking water and sanitation, waste management, energy and communication schemes. The committee submitted this proposal to the National Reconstruction Authority (NRA), and in August 2017, the NRA approved a budget supporting the initiative.

ISSUES OF SUSTAINABILITY

Sustainability is the outcome of processes emerging from organizational dynamics and the external environment. While with TTI support ISET-N has made progress in improving organizational aspects, it needs additional support to continue its new initiatives and play its role as a catalytic think tank capable of contributing towards the building of Nepal's research-policy ecosystem. The organization needs to build on its brand and establish innovative collaborative programmes that translate ISET-N's efforts into better funding opportunities and research uptake while at the same time helping further a broad-based research agenda. Institutional sustainability is an unfinished agenda; it is always incremental and never complete.

ISET-N faces sustainability challenges at three fronts. One is that its ability to attract and maintain an interdisciplinary team of professionals, both at the leadership and the execution levels, continues to be a challenge, and this is likely to remain so for the foreseeable future. Like every other research–knowledge organization in the country, ISET-N faces a high staff turnover. Professionals joining the organization at the middle and lower levels move out once they get better opportunities, whether within the country or outside. A second challenge is securing access to an unrestricted funding base to build and expand its research–knowledge–policy engagements; right now, such opportunity is limited. Partnering with international development organizations within the country in areas of mutual interest is one way by which ISET-N maintains its fund flow and pursues research–policy interfaces. Its third hurdle is building the younger generation of researchers to produce high-quality knowledge products.

CONTINUING THE JOURNEY

ISET-N was successful in forging some new partnerships, but there were many others that it was not able to build despite its hopes for collaborative research in the country and in the region. Our failure stemmed in part from the fact that our request for funding was not forthcoming and that building such partnership involved a higher transaction cost. The country's ongoing transition further undermined our efforts. Nevertheless, our experience and the experience of groups like ours underscore the importance of continued partnership in pursuing collaborative activities across the board.

How will our learning be internalized and cemented in the post-TTI period? The answer to this question requires understanding the dynamics that everyone in the South Asian TTI cohort brought to the process. This understanding also applies to other think tanks working in Nepal and in the region as lessons from the TTI cohort are illustrative. After attending the formal launching of TTI in New Delhi in 2010, the participating members of the cohort travelled to Neemrana, Rajasthan, for a two-day meeting. At Neemrana, I met many old friends and made new ones. As the TTI cohort continued its journey, the group dynamics improved with meetings in Mysore, Marawila, Nagarkot, Gurgaon, Bangkok and Dhaka as well as in South Africa. The relationship between the members strengthened and new partnerships were developed.

These partnerships must continue. With the strengthened institutional capacity of the TTI cohort members, it is incumbent upon the think tanks to help the next generation of young South Asian scholars become actively engaged in collaborative research. My own learning accumulated over years of studying the issues confronting South Asia is illustrative. My learning grew gradually during formal meetings and seminars and while making presentations and participating in group work. It also came from my interactions with colleagues from India, the USA, Pakistan, Bangladesh, Sri Lanka, the UK, Canada and other countries during field visits, chats in tea shops, dinners and friendly banters, during a time of laughter and flared tempers on the banks of the Sabarmati, in the mountains and Terai of Nepal, on the Ganga and Indus plains, on the delta of Bangladesh, along the banks of the Palar and Kaveri rivers in Tamil Nadu, in the desert of Rajasthan and while walking in New Delhi's Lodhi Gardens and lanes of Patan in Nepal.

What had guided us then and continues to guide all of us now in our journey is a passion for exploring new frontiers of knowledge to inform policy-making and practices as new challenges are unfolding. Albert Einstein once said, 'Problems cannot be solved within the framework in which they were created.' In a sense, we endeavoured to envision an alternative framework, initially for water problems and then for assessing and minimizing vulnerabilities to climate change. ISET-N was a traveller in the journey to where we are now, and we are fully committed to continuing that journey.

Whether or not ISET-N and similar organizations in Nepal can continue this journey depends on how constructively the country's political system nurtures in-county efforts to consolidate knowledge-generation and policy-engagement platforms which can contribute in transforming the Nepali society. Creating and strengthening such platforms will not be a straightforward or linear process but must begin by allowing various ideas to be generated and expressed and for civic contestation to be fostered in the public sphere. In this journey, it is imperative that young generations of scholars are provided with opportunities for pursuing their passions for research, critical thinking and creative engagement.

Chapter 7

Sustainable Development Policy Institute

Abid Q. Suleri

INTRODUCTION, CONTEXT AND A BRIEF HISTORY

Established under the National Conservation Strategy (NCS) 1992, Sustainable Development Policy Institute (SDPI) pivoted its activities around environmental issues in its nascent period. The foresight of its founders is visible from the fact that they started talking of 'sustainable development' in the country two decades earlier than the formal introduction of Sustainable Development Goals (SDGs) in Pakistan.

In the beginning, SDPI's research programme featured sustainable agriculture and forestry, energy and environmental conservation, population, gender and other areas which helped in the accomplishment of NCS. Initiating or becoming a party to public interest litigations was how SDPI engaged itself with the society in its beginning phase. In addition, SDPI also started building a cadre of people who could help in delivering on the NCS through Canadian International Development Agency (CIDA) that funded Pakistan Environment Program.

After successfully performing its mandated role to become a knowledge and information hub for smooth implementation of NCS, the focus slightly shifted towards the economy during the late 1990s. By that period, the World Bank (WB)-funded 'structural adjustment programme (SAP)', which had begun in Pakistan during the early 1990s, had matured. SDPI vigorously published its work focusing on socio-economic impacts of SAP.

In late 1999, General Pervez Musharraf toppled the then democratically elected government. Being an independent policy think tank, SDPI shifted its focus on pro-democratic research policy initiatives in general and gender and human rights in particular. Initiation of World Trade Organization (WTO) Doha Round (2001) brought globalization, food security and regional trade into SDPI's sphere of work. By that time, SDPI had turned into a transdisciplinary think tank in a true sense.

In terms of funding, the decade of the 1990s was smooth and stable as it was also the post-Cold War period and there was sufficient supply of funding. By 2000, SDPI had grown in terms of size and scope and its expenses had also increased manifold. In the absence of an endowment or core funding, it was extremely difficult to meet organizational expenditures. Moreover, changing dynamics of the politico-economic environment in the country and the region during this decade did have an impact on the ability of SDPI to build a stable financial support base. In the later half of the previous decade, SDPI struggled to secure its funding since absence of funding impaired its human resource base. There was a point when SDPI even faced a threat of losing its existence.

By 2007, SDPI was in a state of financial loss. Most of the senior researchers had left the organization, and without them, it was difficult to fetch new research projects. Research quality also suffered, but not in terms of credibility. Rather it was difficult to adopt transdisciplinarity which was a key characteristic of SDPI and also a tool for remaining relevant.

To translate research into action, policy outreach remained part of SDPI's activities since its inception. Policy briefs, seminars and conferences were major tools used to successfully reach out to a wider audience. To cite a few, we were able to trigger the enactment of Pakistan Environmental Protection Act, 1997, through targeted campaign on an environmental conservation issue. SDPI also played a role in catalysing modifications in major hydropower projects as an outcome of its research-based critique of Ghazi Barotha project. We managed to prevent construction of an electricity grid station at a location designated for a park in Islamabad. Our study forced an industrial unit to abandon its proposed import of a hazardous technology. SDPI was also able to convince the Government of Pakistan (GoP) to abstain from endorsing WB's *Pakistan: Country Gender Assessment* report. The institute highlighted the technical deficiencies in the report. Through our advocacy, we successfully managed to get 33 per cent of seats reserved for women in the parliament of Pakistan.

WHERE IS THE THINK TANK NOW?

The period from 2008 to 2010 was the most difficult period for SDPI. To keep the organization alive, the team members along with the leader of the organization accepted cut in their salaries. However, by 2018, the think tank witnessed a turnaround and the University of Pennsylvania even placed SDPI among top 100 think tanks of the world in 13 different categories. Many factors helped in achieving this turnaround, including International Development Research Centre's (IDRC) multi-year competitive grant through the Think Tank Initiative (TTI).

ORGANIZATIONAL PERFORMANCE

Organizational performance is a function of human resource development, financial management, implementation of best policies and practices, and capacity enhancement. One of the lessons that SDPI learned from its financial crunch was the need for revision of policies and procedures (such as raising an endowment and not keeping gratuities and provident fund in SDPI's general accounts). Over the years, SDPI has improved its policies and procedures, and has strengthened its financial safeguards. IDRC's grant helped in breaking the vicious cycle between lack of trained human resources due to budgetary constraints and weak capacity of raising funds due to lack of skilled researchers. After receiving the TTI grant, SDPI was able to attract and retain trained human resources through monetary and non-monetary incentives. The systems of knowledge management and management information system (MIS) services were improved, and new programmes for capacity enhancement were introduced. These all collectively improved the organizational performance in different aspects discussed below in detail:

1. *Human resource development:* 'The IDRC grant enabled to strengthen our human resource base' which helped in the production of innovative policy solutions and cutting-edge quality research on sustainable development. Recruitment of senior-level staff not only built SDPI's profile externally but also helped bridge the gap in mentoring of junior and mid-career staff in research and support units. As a result, research quality and staff retention improved.

   Some new initiatives that took place at the beginning of TTI Phase 1 included establishment of a television (TV) station within SDPI. The station helped revitalize our policy outreach. SDPI revived its Urdu publications, complementing the formal policy outreach approaches with informal channels such as lobby meetings, book launches, holding commemorative references and a meticulously planned monitoring and evaluation framework. Our Strategic Work Plan documented the deliberations held in retreats. Towards the end of TTI Phase 1, Research Coordination and Proposal Development Units were established.

   The process of revival continued even during TTI Phase 2, whereby the English Editorial Board was strengthened for improving research writings. The Centre for Capacity was transformed into Centre for Learning and Development with a renewed and demand-driven capacity-building approach. The Human Resources Unit was remodelled as Human Resources and Organization Development Unit. This step helped systemize the mentorship activities and better stocktaking of the staff's training and capacity-building needs.

2. *Capacity enhancement:* TTI support was used in SDPI's capacity-enhancement programme as well as other assignments for its team of researchers. SDPI is part of different regional and international networks (Asia-Pacific Research and Training Network on Trade [ARTNeT] of United Nations Economic and Social Commission

for Asia and the Pacific [UNESCAP], Climate Action Network South Asia, etc.). The meetings/workshops/seminars held by those networks are also a source of capacity enhancement for SDPI staff. These opportunities are provided to all cadres of research faculty, whereas special exchange visits and capacity-building courses are arranged for research support staff. These measures have helped in better succession planning.

Exchange programmes helped research team become better and understand staff of other think tanks. Building of such relationship paved the way to plan and implement multi-country and consortium-based projects. Such projects also increased its financial stability.

In addition to learning through external platforms, internal knowledge sharing and brainstorming were promoted through regular brown bag research meetings (BBRMs) and mentorship programmes. Researchers share their research ideas with peers and get helpful feedback in BBRMs.

3. *Strengthening regulatory framework:* Since 2010, SDPI regularly (once in three years) conducts a policies and procedures audit. The findings of those audits are taken seriously and used to improve its regulatory framework (management practices). As a result, today, SDPI is using the latest version of accounting software, 'QuickBooks'. It also has an internal audit system. Ernst & Young, one of the big four auditing firms in Pakistan, audits SPDI's accounts. In 2016, Pakistan Centre for Philanthropy (PCP) thoroughly audited SDPI's finance system. PCP awards accreditation to non-profit organizations with sound structures and systems to deliver services effectively and efficiently. For last three years, SDPI has been placed among top 100 think tanks worldwide for their 'policies and practices on quality assurance and integrity' by University of Pennsylvania's Global Go To Think Tank Tanking.

4. *Changes in accountability, monitoring and evaluation:* Progress review of all the projects being implemented at SDPI started being carried out by Research Coordination Unit. It reviews the project's progress as per the contractually agreed implementation schedule. Progress reports of projects are directly shared with the executive director of SDPI and suggest recommendations on the basis of projects' progress. The project lead and team are accountable for delivery

and provide all sort of institutional support that project team needs to complete the project on time.

5. *Bridging research policy gaps:* With its 25 years of track record on research quality, credibility and intellectual independence, SDPI has earned the convening power to bridge research and policy gap in Pakistan. The TTI support further helped us undertake unsolicited and non-funded research projects, projects where SDPI team wanted to work but was not able to find a collaborator who would pay for the time of the researchers. Our flagship on unfunded work include Pakistan Power Sector Outlook: Appraisal of KESC in Post Privatization Period (2011), Multidimensional Poverty Assessment (2012), work on green economy for Rio+20 conference, resolution on mercury issues, Political Barometer, post-budget analysis, political parties manifesto series, Election Monitoring Cell, and policy contributions for Conference of the Parties (CoP) 20, COP 21 and COP 22. Likewise, the TTI support helped SDPI's senior researchers devote their time in gratis policy community services, such as serving on different high-level policy-making forums, advisory bodies and steering committees. This participation has significantly improved our research policy bridging capacity.

RESEARCH QUALITY

Research drives other pillars at SDPI, that is, policy engagement and capacity building.

1. *Consistency in research outputs:* During 2001–2010, the number of two important research outputs (policy briefs/papers and working papers) had declined (Figures 7.1 and 7.2). In 3 of the 10 years, no policy brief/paper was published. In the post-TTI period, this trend increased consistently. On an average, 5.9 policy briefs were published per year in the period 2011–2017.

Like policy briefs, the number of working papers also witnessed consistent rise. During last seven years, more working papers were published compared to the earlier period.

As we are approaching the culmination of TTI Phase 2, SDPI can claim that it has not only successfully increased the number of research outputs but also diversified its research outputs. In 2017,

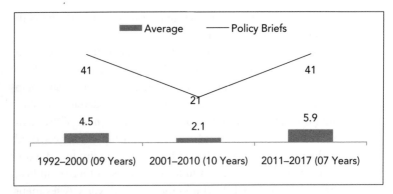

Figure 7.1 *Policy Briefs/Papers (1992–2017), SDPI*

Source: Data compiled from SDPI list of publications. Available at https://sdpi.org/publications/index.html (accessed on 27 September 2018).

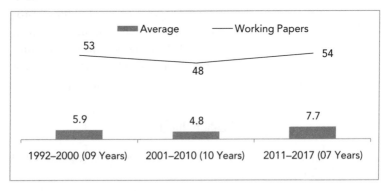

Figure 7.2 *Working Papers (1992–2017), SDPI*

Source: Data compiled from SDPI list of publications. Available at https://sdpi.org/publications/index.html (accessed on 27 September 2018).

the first volume of SDPI's *Journal of Development Policy, Research and Practice* was launched. This transdisciplinary scholarly annual journal aims to provide a diverse array of research and working papers, policy briefs and argumentative essays covering wide range of issues pertaining to sustainable development.

2. *Quality assurance mechanisms/indicators developed by the institution:* At SDPI, research quality is assured through a rigorous peer review process. Different categories of publications go through different types

of reviews, ranging from double-blind external peer review for SDPI journal publications to signing off by the executive director in case of policy briefs/reviews. Youngsters are encouraged to contribute their op-eds (or opinion pieces) in the mainstream newspapers. Supervisors review the op-ed pieces before they are submitted for publication.

3. *Quality of publications:* The quality of policy research-based publications is determined by not only the soundness of methodology or credibility of evidence but also the ability of that publication to bring about societal change. The other criteria used are the independence of facts and opinions used. The quality-assurance mechanisms in SDPI have helped achieve both the objectives. For instance, our food security research was translated into a nationwide Zero Hunger Programme. The recommendations of a study on institutional arrangements for managing climate change have been reflected in the Pakistan Climate Change Act, 2017, while a bill on non-Muslim-sensitive educational reforms, an outcome of SDPI's study, was tabled in the National Assembly (NA) in 2015.

   SDPI's Political Barometer publications are the best example of its transparency and independence. Although SDPI's representatives sit in various governmental task forces, advisory councils and steering committees, in one edition of Political Barometer we reported that the ruling party was losing its popularity demonstrating independence of the organization.

4. *Research ethics:* Research ethics are important contributors for SDPI's research credibility and quality. SDPI is a signatory of Anti Sexual Harassment (ASHA) at Workplace Code of Conduct. It also follows Higher Education Commission of Pakistan's guidelines on conducting research. We have zero tolerance for plagiarism, and our employees declare conflict of interest.

   Ethical concerns/issues are thought about from the beginning—when the research is being designed. For instance, even prior to data collection, the enumerators are sensitized about the ethical norms of administering a questionnaire. Voluntary participation of the respondents is ensured, and their permission is sought if their identities have to be disclosed. Survey coordinators conduct random inspections to monitor and ensure good quality of data collection.

5. *Collaborative research:* 'Since its inception, SDPI has been part of different national, regional and international networks. It has always

worked on collaborative research and advocacy projects.' It is member of a consortium comprising of Overseas Development Institute, London School of Economics and others that won a competitive grant on climate change, 'Pathways to Resilience in Semi-Arid Economies'. Short-term collaborations have also been made, with national and foreign institutes, including but not limited to Social Policy and Development Centre, Pakistan; Centre for Research in Rural and Industrial Development, India; Consumer Unity & Trust Society, India; South Asia Watch on Trade, Economics and Environment, Nepal; Institute of Policy Studies, Sri Lanka; and South Asia Network on Economic Modeling, Bangladesh.

SDPI is also reaching out to universities for collaborative research. We have begun submitting proposals in collaboration with academia to synergize. This approach involving high-quality, evidence-based research would help bring about policy changes.

The institute is member of networks such as Climate Action Network South Asia, International Union for Conservation of Nature and the International Society of Doctors for the Environment (ISDE). Keeping in view the recent developments in regional political–economic context, SDPI is a member of Central Asia Regional Economic Cooperation Program (CAREC) Think Tanks Network (CTTN) advisory panel.

6. *Shaping research agendas and adding new research areas/themes to portfolio such as gender and others:* Research agendas are regularly revisited and revised in the Policy Research and Advocacy Meetings and Annual Retreats. The research areas are prioritized according to the changing national and local contexts. For instance, in 2017, Pakistan was completing 70 years of independence and our overarching policy analysis pivoted around 70 years of Pakistan. This emphasis was also reflected in the thematic focus of the institute's annual Sustainable Development Conference (SDC). The theme of the 20th SDC was 'Seventy Years of Development'. Similarly, the advocacy events held in 2017 reflected upon the role of institutions in a democratic dispensation as the democratic process in Pakistan has become stable. For 2018, we focus on two major themes—regional connectivity through economic and knowledge corridors and SDGs.

Although the research priorities are revised according to national and international contexts, our focus does not shift away from the transdisciplinarity. We review the issues in totality and provide integrated solutions. Sustainability is the cross-cutting theme in every analysis that we do and every recommendation that we make. Our analysis and advice are always multipronged.

7. *Achievement and gaps:* SDPI is the oldest independent think tank of Pakistan. It ranks 14th among think tanks in East Asia (comprising East and South Asia excluding South Korea, Japan, China and India) and Pacific, and 1st in Pakistan. Its major achievement is its acceptability across the political spectrum in Pakistan. It is present on different high-level policy formulation bodies in Pakistan, in both public and private sectors.

POLICY ENGAGEMENT

Since its inception, SDPI has conducted policy research and engaged in policy dialogue. As the quality of our research improved, we devised new methods of policy engagement. Informality, ownership and proactivity were introduced in policy engagement approach without compromising on the research quality. Policy-makers, politicians, representatives from bilateral/multilateral institutions and academicians are invited to formal and informal meetings conceived as platform for communication. Such platforms are also used to disseminate policy advice in non-technical language. Movers and shakers of policy corridors are invited as keynote speakers in the high-profile events for ownership. SDPI remains proactive to meet knowledge demands of decision-makers. Our ways of policy engagement such as SDPI's online TV (started from TTI support in 2012) and use of social media have created our niche in policy outreach.

1. *Visibility and brand building:* These investments have helped SDPI develop its brand. SDPI's visibility is manifested in its think tank ranking.

2. *Achievements and gaps:* Experimentations have enabled SDPI carve its niche as a credible policy advocacy and outreach organization. But SDPI needs to further build its capacity for advocacy and outreach.

3. *Research uptake:* SDPI has many stories of impacts during the past eight years on the basis of our policy research and advocacy. The following list provides few according to different themes:

- **Bill on non-Muslim-sensitive educational reforms:** SDPI's analysis of curricula for a study 'The Subtle Subversion: The State of Curricula and Textbooks in Pakistan' showed that for over two decades, the curricula and the officially mandated textbooks contained materials that are directly contrary to the goals and values of a progressive, moderate and democratic Pakistan. In 2015, based on an SDPI study, a bill on non-Muslim-sensitive educational reforms was tabled in NA. Before it could be tabled in NA, SDPI continuously engaged with the members of Non-Muslim Parliamentarians Caucus. That engagement generated their buy-in to table the bill in NA. The bill proposed to establish a national commission on education for minorities in order to monitor the progress. The bill is lying with the parliamentary committee for further discussion and recommendations.

- **Pakistan Climate Change Act, 2017:** In 2011, SDPI published a report on *Institutional Arrangements for Climate Change in Pakistan.* The report proposed three institutional measures: (a) a Committee on Climate Change headed by the prime minister, (b) a National Authority on Climate Change and (c) a National Climate Change Fund. In 2017, NA of Pakistan enacted the Pakistan Climate Change Act. When the Ministry of Climate Change was in the process of enacting the law, it consulted with authors of the study on the institutional arrangements. Review of the Act would reveal that it also promulgated three institutional measures for more effective climate action, that is, Pakistan Climate Change Council chaired by the prime minister, Pakistan Climate Change Authority and Pakistan Climate Change Fund.

- **SDPI's research becomes part of curriculum:** The Institute of Business and Management, University of Engineering and Technology, Lahore, has included the SDPI study 'Pakistan Power Sector Outlook: Appraisal of KESC in Post Privatization Period' in its curriculum. A first of its kind, the report suggested measures for improving the power sector governance.

- **Affecting change in fiscal governance:** SDPI conducted extensive work on provincial tax reforms, trade policy reforms and improving private sector's voice in preparing election manifestos. The combined effects of research and advocacy carried under them are as follows:

  - In the Khyber Pakhtunkhwa (KP) budget 2017–2018, a key recommendation gleaned from SDPI consultations and official meetings in Peshawar, in which Khyber Pakhtunkhwa Revenue Authority had also participated, was included. The recommendation enhancing KP government's outreach towards potential taxpayers was to be carried out in public–private dialogue mode. Furthermore, we had noted that tax facilitation centres across the province were weak and too little in number. The KP government has announced an increase in tax facilitation centres across the province. Also, Finance Minister Muzafar Said has accepted that the province was slow in increasing tax collection through 'progressive' tax bases and committed that the provincial government would increase revenue base.

  - Following discussion, the Government of Punjab's Planning & Development Department has sent a letter to Federal Ministry of Finance in Islamabad to move towards streamlining/harmonization of federal and provincial tax regime in the interest of improving the cost of doing business. They are proposing the federal government to notify intergovernmental tax working groups—in line with the recommendations presented to the finance minister of Punjab.

  - Two provincial revenue authorities have signed memorandums of understanding (MoUs) for sharing resources and proceeding under input adjustment tax. The Federal Board of Revenue (FBR) has decided to expedite the streamlining of tax policy coordination and complete its MoUs with all the provincial tax authorities.

  - On the basis of SDPI's research on widening the formal economy of Pakistan, the corporate tax rate has been reduced to 30 per cent for 2018 and threshold level of advanced tax has been increased.

4. *Membership of policy-making group:* SPDI has presence on key policy forums such as National Economic Advisory Council; National Advisory Committee of Planning Commission; National Advisory Council of UNDP on Inclusive and Sustainable Growth; Higher Education Commission's Education Testing Council; National Advisory Committee on Food Security and Nutrition Strategic Review; and Climate Change Commission (formed by the Lahore High Court).

   In addition to the permanent bodies mentioned above, GoP recognizing our research on climate change has designated SDPI part of official delegations to CoP to Kyoto Protocol and Paris Agreement. Other achievements are as follows:

   - **Youth ambassador:** In 2015, SDPI's Ali Shahbaz was elected as the youth ambassador by the UN General Assembly president to speak at the 'High-Level Thematic Debate on Strengthening Cooperation Between the UN and Regional and Sub-regional Organizations', held in New York.
   - **Observer's status by International Monetary Fund (IMF) and WB:** SDPI is the only organization in Pakistan which was granted the civil society organization (CSO) fellow observer's status by IMF and WB. Under this status, SDPI representatives attended IMF and WB annual meetings in Washington, DC, and provided input on country-related issues.
   - **ISDE president:** SDPI's Senior Adviser Dr Mahmood A. Khwaja was unanimously elected as the president of ISDE for a two-year term. ISDE has its members in over 35 countries, mostly in Europe, Canada, the USA and Australia.

5. *Impact on enhancing public policy space, public discourse, narratives and public opinion:* In December 2017, GoP notified more than 20 international non-governmental organizations (INGOs) to quit their operations. SDPI led a campaign for convincing the government to provide an opportunity of explanation to those INGOs. In January 2018, GoP not only provided the INGOs an opportunity to present their case but also permitted them to operate until the final decision is made on their appeal.

6. *Other forms of contribution to policy, op-eds and media appearances:* Our researchers, seniors and juniors alike regularly place articles in the

popular press to reach out the wider audience with their policy advice. More than 50 articles are published in popular press every year. SDPI researchers also regularly appear on media to express their expert opinion on economy, energy, governance, international relations, environment, gender, health and other fields related to sustainable development. Now it has become an annual ritual for our researchers to capture the TV screens when federal and provincial governments announce budget.

SUSTAINABILITY: GAPS, CHALLENGES AND THINKING AHEAD

As the space for civil society is shrinking in terms of funding and freedom of choices/actions, SDPI will have to become more innovative and impactful. The infrastructural development made with TTI support has helped SDPI achieve financial sustainability. Our Strategic Plan (2015–2020) contains guidelines for the transition towards innovation and higher level of impact. The plan has identified pathways for the sustainability model for SDPI to adopt. This model prods the organization to keep looking for gaps in research. We will fill those gaps even if we have to use our savings for conducting research. This will make us leader of that particular subject and well positioned to engage with donors for long-term funding to conduct further research or put already conducted research into action.

Successful implementation of the plan would ensure financial and intellectual health of SDPI. This step is vital for materializing its vision to be a centre of excellence on sustainable development policy research, capacity development and advocacy in Pakistan.

We have created senior-level positions for resource mobilization and business development. Fresh monitoring evaluation and learning experts will support strengthening organizational monitoring/accountability, continuously learning about the best practices of peer think tanks. They will serve as internal knowledge managers and document strengths of SDPI for branding/marketing purposes.

Some changes have been brought in the top-tier management structure for ensuring a smooth succession and consistent leadership. To further improve some aspects of leadership such as effective decision-making, giving candid feedback and taking initiatives, SDPI will hold capacity-building courses for senior managers on leadership, management and governance with TTI support.

CONCLUSIONS

The TTI support helped SDPI mitigate the vulnerabilities induced by exogenous factors. That stability has helped the organization gain strength. We are optimistic that SDPI will remain strong enough to withstand the exogenous factors such as shrinking fiscal and intellectual space for think tanks.

In this endeavour, we will remain in close contact with the networks of the TTI cohort. We will seek room for synergizing with fellow think tanks. In that journey, they would find SDPI always ready to collaborate.

Chapter 8

Social Policy and Development Centre

Khalida Ghaus

INTRODUCTION, CONTEXT AND BRIEF HISTORY

Since its inception as a policy research organization in 1995, the Social Policy and Development Centre (SPDC) has made significant intellectual contributions to Pakistan's public policy agendas, especially those pertaining to issues of pro-poor economic growth and social development. The organization has prided itself on its hallmark effective policy advocacy based on quality research evidence.[1] More than 700 publications, the 100th research report recently published and over 300 citations in national/international peer-reviewed journals, books and publications bear testimony to its success.

Ranked as Pakistan's top research think tank by the University of Pennsylvania and 22nd in Asia-Pacific for two consecutive years (2012 and 2013), SPDC has created a well-defined niche within the national and international spaces for itself. The organization's impact on national and provincial policy levels has been substantial. Its capability

---

[1] The themes are development, poverty, inequality, governance, social sector policies, climate change, gender and pro-poor macroeconomic policies.

and capacity as a premier policy advising institute can be corroborated by the fact that its key staff members are nominated to commissions, committees, task forces and other forums established by the federal and provincial governments.

The thematic 'Annual Review of Social Development in Pakistan' is a flagship product of the centre and presents analyses and insights regarding contemporary issues in the country. Another activity that regularly features on SPDC's research agenda is the examination of federal and provincial budgets, particularly with respect to variables linked to the country's social development. Furthermore, research dissemination among policy-makers, academics and civil society organizations has been and continues to be a priority within its research focus.

SPDC's achievements are further bolstered by its unique contributions within the public sector. As a leading independent civil society research institute, SPDC played a significant role in placing development on the forefront of policy-making agenda in Pakistan. This is being reflected in the organization's expertise in social sector/macroeconomic modelling, where it pioneered the development of an Integrated Social Policy and Macroeconomic Model (ISPM). The model is used by the Central Board of Revenue (CBR), Planning Commission, the Economic Advisory Board, the Debt Reduction and Management Committee in the preparation of the 10-year Perspective Plan, and the Macroeconomic Framework of Pakistan's Ninth Five-Year Plan.

Moreover, SPDC's comprehensive 'database on public finances and social sectors' at federal, provincial and district levels of Pakistan is considered to be consistent and accurate time series. Research pertaining to the delivery mechanisms in the social sector has also influenced the designs of the Social Action Plans (SAPs I & II), and the National Devolution Plan. Additionally, the government has utilized SPDC's lessons on various aspects of poverty, inequality and pro-poor growth to prepare the Poverty Reduction Strategy Papers and to pioneer specialized training programmes on gender-responsive budgeting in Pakistan.

The centre also lent substantial technical assistance to Pakistan's federal and provincial governments in the formulation of National Finance Commission (NFC) Award of 1996. It has also provided similar assistance to the Government of Eritrea for capacity development of their National Statistics and Evaluation Office.

The centre was established through the support of funding from the erstwhile Canadian International Development Agency (CIDA). However, as the funding contract neared completion in 2010, sustainability became a major challenge confronting SPDC. This was further exacerbated by the changing geopolitical situation and the subsequent shift in priorities of international donors, who preferred funding short-term projects as opposed to programme funding. This lack of programme funding threated to compromise SPDC's main focus on research and informed advocacy. It was at this critical juncture in 2010 that SPDC became a recipient of the Think Tank Initiative (TTI) grant.

The TTI's support has been crucial in sustaining the organization's core research programme, which focuses on its 'Annual Review of Social Development in Pakistan' and analysis of the federal budget. Support under the programme led to an all-rounded improvement in areas pertaining to research communication, human resource development, organizational management, research quality and overall performance. Currently, the ratio of research and advocacy in the work mix is 60:40, as reflected by the increase in media appearances, targeted meetings with policy-makers and representation on various task forces.

With help from TTI, SPDC has continued to evolve and diversify its areas of research and expand its research focus to include climate change. SPDC also published research reports that analyse macroeconomic policies, economic growth, fiscal challenges and development priorities of the government. Keeping in mind Pakistan's sociopolitical turmoil, SPDC has completed two studies on[2] 'Social Impact of the Security Crisis'[3] and

---

[2] There are 13 in all; the 14th is currently being prepared.

[3] SPDC's 10th 'Annual Review of Social Development' probed aspects of security-related questions. Some of the questions are as follows: What is the economic cost of the war on Pakistan's economy? How have the priorities of the federal and provincial budgets been affected as a result of the security crisis? How has social development been affected by higher spending on security? How has local population been affected by the security threat? What socio-economic impact has the conflict had on the household? How has the civil society responded to the changed security environment?

'Devolution and Human Development'.[4] SPDC published six research reports on poverty in Pakistan, keeping track of inter-temporal changes in poverty incidence. Additionally, to bolster research studies, more nuanced measures were implemented to build capacity of research staff in areas of 'gender' and 'environment'. This initiative has not only resulted in further integrating the gender dimension in SPDC's research agenda but also helped it pursue research on gender-based topics. In addition, staff's capacity to investigate environmental questions was developed, integrating these issues within SPDC's wider research agenda.

ORGANIZATIONAL PERFORMANCE

The grant from TTI was used to support overall activities related to organizational performance, better research and analysis capacity of staff; financial and human resource management; and in building library facilities at SPDC. The centre also introduced significant improvement in its organizational governance as well as its financial and human resource management policies (e.g., gender and equal opportunities, anti-harassment, training and development, publications procedures, asset disposal policy and disciplinary action policy), enabling SPDC to receive certification from the Pakistan Centre for Philanthropy (PCP). In addition to all these protocols, SPDC follows a *Manual of Service Rules*. This regulatory framework has helped improve SPDC's institutional performance and integrity and indicates that the centre's internal workings are at par with the international norms and standards.

For improved management, computerized systems of financial and human capital management (HCM) were regularly upgraded, in accordance with amendments in tax and labour laws and other regulations by

---

[4] The 18th Amendment was a major charter of political rights as far as decentralization and devolution of power to the provinces in Pakistan is concerned. It contained far-reaching stipulations for empowering Pakistan's four federating units and intended to give them unprecedented autonomy. Devolution and social development in Pakistan, being 11th in the series of 'Annual Reviews' of SPDC, examined the design and implementation issues of the decentralization provisions of the 18th Constitutional Amendment and the 7th NFC Award, the two being major landmarks with the potential of having significant implications for the relations between intergovernmental relations in Pakistan.

competent authorities such as the Securities and Exchange Commission of Pakistan (SECP).[5] Additionally, financial accounts were maintained in accordance with guidelines of International Accounting Standards Board that sets the overall requirements for the presentation of financial statements, guidelines for their structure and minimum requirements for their content. As a result, the 2015 and 2016 Transparify reports[6] provided SPDC with a five-star rating and categorized it as a transparent organization among the 16 think tanks in South Asia and Oceania.

SPDC's programme support infrastructure was strengthened by improving IT facilities, software and the organization's website. Moreover, pay scales were revised to provide more incentives to the employees for retention, and the coverage of group life insurance, as well as hospitalization insurance, was enhanced. Additionally, a provident fund scheme was introduced. Under this scheme, each employee contributes to the fund and SPDC provides the matching amount. Furthermore, SPDC displayed progress on financial grounds through generation of revenue via contract research, resulting in an increase in the endowment fund by more than 50 per cent.

Having focused goals, objectives, strategies and tactics, coupled with a strong accountability system and organization's performance, enhances success. Therefore, 'a strategic planning exercise' was undertaken in 2014 to develop a specific set of goals, objectives, strategies and tactics to serve as a road map for planned growth at SPDC. Steps were taken to enhance human resource capacity through on-the-job training, external training programmes and networking opportunities with national, regional and international think tanks, universities and donors.

The flexible operation mechanism within the workplace contributed to an increase in confidence of staff, especially at the junior level. A more open and interactive work environment was created

---

[5] *SECP* is the financial regulatory agency whose objective is to develop a modern and efficient corporate sector and a capital market based on sound regulatory principles.

[6] Policy-relevant nonprofits disclose information—such as 'Who funds them?' 'With how much?' and 'For what purposes?'—publicly on their websites. This includes information contained in annual reports, provided that those reports are available on an organization's website.

where senior researchers guided mid/junior-level staff and helped improve their performance. In addition to senior- and mid-level research personnel, newly hired staff members underwent orientation programmes in order to broaden their research capacity along with analytical and networking skills. Staff also received research and communications capacity-enhancement training within the country and abroad. SPDC became a part of the Managing Global Governance (MGG) programme of the German Federal Ministry for Economic Cooperation and Development (BMZ). The programme provided staff exchange and learning opportunities in discussing sustainable, equitable and effective global governance architecture. SPDC staff members continue to participate in its activities as alumni[7] and in other training activities[8] organized by the German Development Institute (DIE) and the Federal Foreign Office, Germany. This exposure has helped the participants benefit from an international learning environment and integrate the experience resulting in a holistic study of development issues and more informed and evidence-based policy recommendations.

SPDC has also set up an outreach office in Islamabad to increase its visibility and create policy linkages with international donors and the federal government. Thus, the newly established contacts with several potential donors contribute in securing new research grants.

Currently, SPDC is working on the following multi-country projects with international academic institutions and donor organizations.

• **Study on tobacco taxation in Pakistan:** SPDC joined international research partnership on tobacco tax policies led by the University of Illinois, USA, with an aim to analyse the macroeconomic impacts of tobacco use in the country. Research protocols, methodology and secondary data collection were completed during the reporting period.

---

[7] The regional and international meetings and conferences held at MGG partner institutes.

[8] Such as the one on 'Peace Mediation and Crisis Diplomacy', offered by the Federal Foreign Office, Berlin, Germany; and 'Climate Change and Sustainable Development', organized by the Humboldt University, Berlin, Germany.

- **National University of Ireland (NUI) Galway—'Socio-Economic Costs of Violence Against Women and Girls in Pakistan':** SPDC is a partner of NUI Galway for conducting the study 'Socio-Economic Costs of Violence Against Women and Girls in Pakistan'. It is a three-year multi-country project undertaken in Ghana, Pakistan and South Sudan.
- **Comparative study of intergovernmental fiscal transfers in India and Pakistan:** SPDC, in collaboration with the National Institute of Public Finance and Policy (NIPFP), India, undertook a study, *A Comparative Study of Intergovernmental Fiscal Transfers in India and Pakistan*. The study looked into the similarities and dissimilarities between the systems of intergovernmental fiscal transfers in India and Pakistan with a purpose to draw lessons for devising a more equitable model of fiscal transfers.
- **Friedrich-Ebert-Stiftung (FES)—Linkages of trade and labour standards in key industries active in global supply chains:** SPDC has collaborated with FES in a multi-country project which mainly targets to promote the implementation of comprehensive labour and social standards in export-oriented industries in Asia. Countries included are Bangladesh, Cambodia, Pakistan and Vietnam. SPDC was a partner of FES Pakistan in this project.

RESEARCH QUALITY

The quality of SPDC's publications has consistently improved. Considering that a key aspect of SPDC research is its relevance to policy debate, topics for research are identified for the 'Annual Review of Social Development in Pakistan' and the country's priorities.[9] An experienced team of researchers, with diverse competencies, collaborates in its research activity. Over the past few years, Pakistan's GDP growth rate was slow, which resulted in increased macroeconomic imbalance, while the challenges posed by the war on terror had severe implications on socio-economic development. On the policy reforms front, the 18th Constitutional Amendment focused on devolution of

---

[9] To date, 13 have been published, whereas work on the 14th is in progress.

powers to the provinces, and 7th NFC brought significant changes in the resource distribution formula by increasing the share of provinces.

SPDC undertook research on these emerging issues and produced 'annual reviews' on social impact of security crisis, devolution and human development, and social development in urban and rural Pakistan'. Stakeholders including government, civil society, media and the donor community have provided positive feedback and reviews on the two reports. Furthermore, members of staff also produce other research reports, policy briefs, journals and newspaper articles.[10] Research quality is maintained through a robust peer review mechanism that varies for each category of publication. Under the guidance and mentorship of senior researchers, junior and mid-level researchers were encouraged to publish articles in national and international peer-reviewed journals, thereby building their capacity to write independently and increasing their research publications.

The centre studies federal and provincial budgets to examine government priorities with respect to social development in Pakistan, and the subsequent links between macroeconomic priorities and their impact on social development. Based on the feedback from parliamentarians, SPDC recently decided to produce an analytical brief on the key issues related to the state of the economy; this reflects SPDC's perspective on these issues in parliamentary debates on budgets and in public discourses.

The relevance and quality of research undertaken at SPDC is evident by the 'citations' in federal- and provincial-level policy documents and contributions made by its staff in policy-making processes. For instance, SPDC gave its input in the deliberations held in the 9th NFC at the provincial and federal levels. Its work was cited in the *Punjab Youth Policy 2012*, prepared by the Government of Punjab. Findings of its research were utilized in Pakistan's *Stocktaking Report* on sustainable development prepared for Rio+20. SPDC participated

---

[10] To date, a total of 700+ publications that include 100 research reports, 131 journal articles and 421 newspaper articles in Urdu, English and Sindhi languages have been published; further, SPDC's work is cited in 341 national and international journal articles and government reports.

in the consultative process on 'Post-2015 Development Agenda', organized by United Nations Development Programme (UNDP) and the Planning & Development Department, Government of Sindh. SPDC also provided support to build capacity legislators and government officials.[11] The improvement in the quality and relevance of SPDC's research[12] is also indicated by the fact that its senior research staff members are inducted as members of various governmental task forces/working groups.[13]

Moreover, SPDC staff is regularly invited to deliver lectures at various government training institutes. These institutes include National Institute of Management, Karachi; National Institute of Management, Quetta; Administrative Staff College, Lahore, for bureaucracy; National Defence University, Islamabad; and leadership programme of military institutes. SPDC has also been invited to talk shows, public and private universities, international/national non-governmental organizations (NGOs), and consultative group meetings held by financial/donor institutes such as World Bank and Asian Development Bank Institute. Similarly, various capacity development initiatives were taken for legislators and government officials, especially with regard to gender-responsive budgeting, gender mainstreaming, poverty alleviation and intergovernmental fiscal relations.

---

[11] A specialized training in gender-responsive budgeting was organized for members of the National Assembly.

[12] SPDC, in collaboration with the Women Development Department (WDD), Government of Balochistan, organized a capacity development workshop for the officers of the Government of Balochistan on 'Demystifying Gender Responsive Budgeting'; another three-day capacity development workshop on this topic was organized for officers of the Government of Gilgit-Baltistan.

[13] For instance, SPDC is a member of Punjab Economic Forum (PEF), Punjab Economic Research Institute, Planning and Development Department (P&DD), Government of Punjab; Core Group to oversee formulation of Sustainable Development Goals (SDGs), P&DD, Government of Sindh; Strategic Advisory Group (SAG) of the Enhanced Democratic Accountability and Civic Engagement (EDACE) project for Sindh; Chair, Research Committee (CRC), Shaheed Mohtarma Benazir Bhutto Chair, University of Karachi; Policy Advocacy Group on formation of non-tariff measures (NTMs)/non-tariff barriers (NTBs), Federation of Pakistan Chambers of Commerce & Industry (FPCCI); and Steering Committee on Sindh Social Protection Policy, P&DD, Government of Sindh.

In order to meet the above objectives, SPDC also invested in capacity development of its research staff in the areas of gender[14] and environment. Subsequently, a study to determine the level of gender sensitivity in previous research outputs and within SPDC was undertaken—'The Changing Landscape of Gender at SPDC: An Assessment'. The exercise provided an assessment of the extent to which SPDC meets the needs of both women and men in its research and contributes to an enhanced understanding of gender issues.

SPDC's organizational strategy has incorporated environmental and sustainable development issues in its research agenda. Thus, consequences of climate change were examined as cross-cutting issues for poverty and economic development. This step helped the institute obtain a three-year research grant for the project, *Gender and Social Vulnerability to Climate Change: A Study of Disaster Prone Areas in Sindh*. Such diversification of research was a milestone in SPDC's research, keeping in mind the contemporary importance of the topic. The findings of the study were disseminated through seminars, five newspaper articles (1 English, 2 Urdu and 2 Sindhi) and four working papers. In addition, two journal articles, four video documentaries and their abridged version with English subtitles, highlighting the effects of climate variability on the local communities, were prepared.

For any research study to gain credibility, it is important that it fulfils ethical requirements of research. SPDC has formed a four-member 'ethics approval committee'. This internal mechanism further ensures

---

[14] SPDC is a partner of NUI Galway for conducting the study 'Socio-Economic Costs of Violence Against Women and Girls in Pakistan'. It is a three-year study being undertaken in Pakistan, South Sudan and Ghana. The scope of the study is to estimate the social and economic costs of violence against women and girls (VAWG) and particularly capture the direct and indirect tangible costs as well as the direct intangible costs of the impact of VAWG on individual well-being and social cohesion. This study will be completed in 2018, and findings of the research will be taken forward for policy advocacy regarding costs of violence in Pakistan. Since this project also has a national advisory board consisting of representatives of the federal and provincial governments, leading gender experts and civil society organizations, it is hoped that policy recommendations coming out of this study will be included by the government in their policies and plans.

that the calibre of research conducted at the institute is maintained in line with international standards and requirements. SPDC successfully produced quality analyses and disseminated them through seminars, workshops, and print and electronic media. Specifically, dissemination was targeted towards academics, policy-makers, donors and civil society and media professionals.

Staff trainings and collaborative research initiatives have helped improve and expand the quality of research. For instance, SPDC became a part of a new global initiative called Southern Voice on Post-MDGs, which helps promote the centre's engagement with other think tanks in South Asia. The centre established relationship with King's College London for a research on social vulnerability. Recently, SPDC became a member of PCSD Partnership, an Organisation for Economic Co-operation and Development (OECD) initiative for enhancing policy coherence for sustainable development. The centre collaborated with the Lahore University of Management Sciences (LUMS), Institute of Public Policy, Leadership for Environment and Development (LEAD) Pakistan, Pakistan Institute of Legislative Development and Transparency, Sustainable Development Policy Institute (SDPI) and Global Change Impact Studies Centre for both research and outreach purposes. In 2017, SPDC's portfolio of research and collaborative activities with international organizations expanded further. The centre simultaneously worked on five multi-country projects, including two with international universities.

POLICY ENGAGEMENT

Effective dissemination of research and policy analysis to a wide spectrum of audience is essential to enhance comprehension and awareness of the issues and problems at hand, to impact public policy and implementation and to stimulate public debate.

Furthermore, windows of opportunity to position its evidence and research to inform policy-making (strike while the iron is hot) were used. Nevertheless, it was observed that despite all this, there was still the need to make communications multidirectional and multifaceted and to equip SPDC to deal effectively with the changing communications environment.

TTI's 'Policy Engagement and Communications (PEC) Program for Think Tanks in Latin America and South Asia'[15] provided SPDC with the opportunity to strengthen its policy engagement and communications (PEC) capacity and make its existing outreach approaches and products more effective and accessible. The annual meetings of the TTI cohort also helped in appreciating new and non-traditional methods of PEC and effective dissemination. SPDC's communication plan incorporates these learning.

In order to squeeze in our agenda into public discourse and improve visibility, existing networks with advocacy groups and organizations working on similar issues in Pakistan and abroad were strengthened. For instance, SPDC became a partner of the Allameh Tabataba'i University, Tehran (the largest public university specialized in humanities and social sciences in Iran), for holding their international conference on 'Social Policy in the Islamic World'. Additionally, with the objective of enhancing the research capacity of its staff, linkages were also developed with national and international research and academic institutions to expand SPDC's collaborative research network.[16] For instance, SPDC collaborated with NUI Galway and other organizations for research on the multi-country project 'Socio-Economic Costs of Violence Against Women and Girls in Pakistan'.

---

[15] Under this programme, the Institute of Development Studies (IDS) conducted a number of webinars on communicating with different audiences, focusing on policy-makers and the civil society; dealing with information overload; and monitoring and evaluation. The aim of these webinars was to share best practices on developing policy briefs, as well as to consider effective approaches for communicating with different audiences by sharing local insights and experiences. These capacity-building exercises enabled SPDC's PEC team and members of research staff to learn how to effectively communicate in today's policy environment and make better use of modern technology and tools.

[16] Such as NUI, Pakistan Institute of Development Economics (PIDE), LUMS, DIE, International Labour Organization (ILO)-Brussels and United Nations Framework Convention on Climate Change (UNFCCC)-Bonn.

SPDC is also a member of Local Governance Initiative and Network (LOGIN) Asia[17] and PCSD[18] on SDGs (17 and 14). Both networks work towards achieving policy coherence. Memberships of these networks provided opportunities not only for joint research and dissemination but also for enhancing the visibility of SPDC at an international level.

Moreover, seminars, conferences and workshops provide a platform to stimulate debate, exchange knowledge and build networks with other organizations. SPDC not only held dissemination seminars on the 'Annual Review of Social Development' and other key publications but also encouraged its staff to participate and read papers in such events organized by other institutions. A series of discussions on some of the core socio-economic issues were initiated, and interactive dialogues were conducted on topics such as 'Integrated Energy Policy' and 'Agenda for Sustained Economic Revival'.

To engage policy-makers and develop their capacity in areas such as gender, poverty and inequality and public finance, capacity development workshops were organized for officials of the provincial governments and legislators. Further technical assistance was also provided to the provincial governments of Sindh and Punjab in the 9th NFC Award. Implications of various options for intergovernmental fiscal transfers for provincial finances were suggested to the governments of Punjab and Sindh. The provinces used the suggestions for negotiations on the NFC Award. Further, SPDC also assisted the Government of Sindh in finalizing the draft on youth policy, and Government of Balochistan in beneficiary assessment of education expenditure. Moreover, new contacts were established with policy-makers to build

---

[17] A multi-stakeholder platform that brings together practitioners working in the field of decentralization and local governance to connect with one another and learn from knowledge exchange.

[18] It is a multi-stakeholder partnership for enhancing policy coherence for sustainable development. It is an initiative of OECD that brings together governments, international organizations, civil society, think tanks, the private sector and other stakeholders from all regions of the world, committed and working to enhance policy coherence for sustainable development (SDGs 17 and 14) as a key means of SDG implementation.

and improve their capacity on SDGs dealing with social development. As a result of being a member of Core Group on SDGs constituted by the Sindh government, SPDC's perspective is also reflected in the discussions in the province on SDGs.

The proliferation in the number of TV channels has increased the demand for independent researchers discussing social and economic development challenges in their programmes. TV anchors, politicians, parliamentarians and economists use the results to buttress their arguments.[19] This medium has created opportunities for think tanks to take part in informed public debates on developmental issues that would help influence policy formulation as alternative point of views are expressed. Senior and mid-level staff members at SPDC participate as guests in 'state and private sector radio and television channels'. They present their views on political issues, development, macroeconomic policies, gender and international affairs. See Boxes 8.1 and 8.2.

Box 8.1

In Pakistan, tax revenues are shared among the federal and provincial governments through a financial institution—NFC. The federal government collects more than 90 per cent of tax revenue. This creates overdependence of provincial governments on the federal government. In order to promote greater taxation at a provincial level, SPDC initially supported devolution of general sales tax (GST) on services to provinces, which was incorporated in the 18th Constitutional Amendment. This resulted in phenomenal growth in revenues from GST services. SPDC supported the view that GST on goods should be either devolved or collected by provinces.

Based on the successful experience of devolution of GST services, SPDC provided technical support to the Government of Sindh on strengthening the case for transferring the collection of GST on goods from federal to provincial governments. In this regard, SPDC prepared a report on *Devolved versus Integrated Tax Structure: Evolution of Tax Collection Framework in Pakistan* for the working group of the 9th NFC Award. Based on the

---

[19] For instance, SPDC's estimates on poverty and findings of its reports on security, women at work and devolution were quoted in various talk shows.

arguments and experiences of other developing countries, the report recommended that collection of GST on goods should also be transferred to the provinces.

The report initiated a new debate within the policy-makers about greater provincial fiscal autonomy with regard to the collection of GST on goods. Consequently, the Sindh government demanded that the federal government transfer collection powers of GST on goods. Thus, the debate initiated by SPDC triggered a process for change.

Source: 'Devolved versus Integrated Tax Structure: Evolution of Tax Collection Framework in Pakistan', Working Group for 9th NFC, Government of Sindh, 2016.

Box 8.2

Each year, SPDC publishes a report on the state of economy in Pakistan, using data related to economic performance published by the Federal Finance Ministry. The ministry makes this data public a day prior to the budget. SPDC received feedback from some parliamentarians that because its detailed report on economy is usually published few weeks after the budget is presented, the momentum of debate in the parliament slows down. The parliamentarians suggested that it would be useful for them if SPDC could publish a brief report quickly, which may be followed by a detailed report.

Based on the feedback suggested by the parliamentarians, SPDC decided to produce an analytical brief on the key issues related to the state of the economy. A five-member team of SPDC prepared it within three days of the budget, providing crisp and quality analysis of the key issues. It was published online and sent to the parliamentarians and media via email. The brief questioned some of the major claims made by the government regarding indicators of economic performance, such as GDP growth, investment and balance of payments. It was well received by the parliamentarians and news channels. They picked up the argument presented in the briefs in the discussions.

The initiative contributed to an informed debate on the budget by the parliamentarians not only in the National Assembly but also in the electronic and print media. It contributed to enhance the visibility of SPDC. However, because the federal government

(Continued)

(Continued)

> was put on the defensive by the media and the politicians in the opposition parties, SPDC was pressurized to change its analysis, but it assured the relevant authorities that it is a non-partisan organization and that its analysis aimed at contributing to the evidence-based debate.

Source: 'Key Issues in the State of Economy 2015–16', Social Policy and Development Centre, 2016.

Thus, support from TTI has enabled SPDC to build policy engagement and networking capacity. TTI has assisted SPDC in growing holistically as a leading policy and research institute in the country.

SUSTAINABILITY: GAPS, CHALLENGES AND THINKING AHEAD

Policy research organizations in developing countries face major challenges in expanding human resource base and maintaining their financial health. SPDC is no different and plans to address this challenge by adopting a multipronged approach, which includes the following:

- Increasing contract research and building endowment fund.
- Tapping alternative sources for institutional support, including local philanthropic organizations.
- Marketing with other donors to obtain research grants (consortium approach).
- Inducting senior expertise and continuing to build research capacity of junior staff in diversified areas of research.

The centre will continue making efforts to diversify its sources of funds. It aims to seek contract research (based on lump sum payments) that will allow surplus funds to be added to the endowment of the organization. Pursuing contract research beyond a certain limit may result in the organization deviating from its main research agenda. However, SPDC management is well aware of the risk of over dependency on contract research. It also plans to approach donors for core funding. We believe that the availability of research expertise within the organization will play a critical role in securing research grants. SPDC has conducted an exercise of mapping the priority areas of international donor agencies for development cooperation in Pakistan. The results showed that opportunities available are in line with the research priorities of SPDC, such as in health, women empowerment, environment and social sector. Further, expanding its research areas, SPDC has initiated studies on health issues. It was recently able to secure research grants on a research project of three-year duration. In line with this research priority, a senior professional staff has been hired.

The shift in priorities of international donors with respect to funding modalities shows preference to support consortiums financing. Further, donors favour a well-rounded organization that is engaged in research, advocacy and policy implementation. While this trend may force think tanks to seek exclusive research grants, it does provide opportunities to undertake collaborative activities. SPDC will look for synergies with other organizations, keeping in view the research–advocacy–implementation (RAI) model developed during its strategic planning exercise conducted in 2014 (Figures 8.1). A similar exercise is currently in progress and will hopefully be completed before the completion of the TTI support.

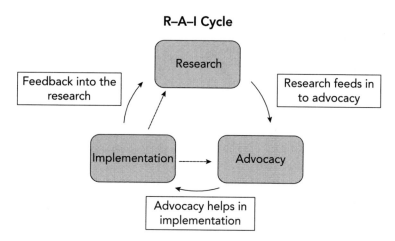

Figure 8.1 *Representation of RAI Model, SPDC*

Source: 'Report on SPDC's Strategic Planning Exercise', Social Policy and Development Centre, 2014.

In addition, SPDC is approaching philanthropic and corporate organizations working in Pakistan for funding support to pursue policy research and advocacy. This practice of funding policy research is not common in Pakistan. Yet, SPDC is making efforts to bridge this gap by inducting patrons of such organizations as members of its board of directors. This strategy is expected to help representatives of the corporate sector see the benefits of investing in research.

The Journey of
Think Tanks: India

PART III

The Journey of
Think Tanks: India

Chapter 9

Centre for Budget and Governance Accountability

Subrat Das and Happy Pant

BACKGROUND AND BRIEF HISTORY

Centre for Budget and Governance Accountability (CBGA) works towards enhancing transparency and accountability in governance. Towards this objective, CBGA uses rigorous analysis of policies and government budgets in India. CBGA carries out in-depth research on a range of issues relating to the governance accountability ecosystem and public policy priorities in India, with a particular focus on fiscal policy and processes. CBGA has simplified fiscal policy technicalities and governance issues so that a much broader group of people can connect with them. The organization is also ensuring a strong inter-face with civil society groups and networks. As a result, its work has strengthened civil society campaigns in the country on fiscal policy priorities for social sectors and the rights of disadvantaged sections.

CBGA was established in 2005 in New Delhi. In 2010, the organization witnessed a turning point in its evolution when it became a part of the Think Tank Initiative (TTI) programme. The impact of TTI on CBGA, over the last eight years, has been transformative.

The founding vision of CBGA was to carry out cutting-edge policy research and advocacy from the perspective of poor and underprivileged people. Ever since, its work has focused on bridging the gap between public finance and people in India through different interventions. However, until 2010, CBGA's research agenda had been somewhat limited, and it was oriented more like an advocacy organization.

As we began the TTI journey, framing policy issues and generating policy-relevant evidence and knowledge became more prominent in our work. CBGA optimized its strengths by carving out a fine balance between research and advocacy; today, it is an interesting blend of a think tank and an advocacy organization.

Evidence and policy alternatives generated by CBGA have successfully highlighted issues necessary to be included in the agenda for reforms in fiscal governance in India; and CBGA has established itself as a dependable think tank for many important actors across the country. The organization today combines in-depth and timely research with appropriate methods of dissemination and outreach. TTI support has been invaluable in helping CBGA emerge as a significant voice in the domains of public finance and governance in India. The support has played a crucial role in CBGA's work, acquiring a bigger scale, greater credibility and a stronger national profile. The organization has also established a foothold in relevant global platforms over the last eight years.

In the initial years of its journey, CBGA was dependent largely on core funding from the Ford Foundation. TTI's emphasis on sustainability of funding architecture pushed CBGA towards making stronger efforts to diversify its financial support base. As a result, we have successfully mobilized financial resources for our work from a combination of core and project funders. Efforts around this over the years paid off; the proportion of TTI funding to our overall annual budget has fallen from 35 per cent in 2010–2011 to around 15 per cent in 2017–2018, as the overall annual budget of CBGA grew significantly over this period, from ₹2.5 crore to ₹6.1 crore.

ORGANIZATIONAL PERFORMANCE

When CBGA was founded by a group of social activists and academicians, in response to the hegemony of a very few institutions and actors over the discourse on fiscal policy and governance in India, it had no support from the government at any level. In the early phase of our journey, while efforts to secure funding and leverage support for organizational sustainability were on, entry into TTI and access to stable and predictable core funds were crucial for CBGA's growth and consolidation. CBGA has evolved considerably during the last eight years and emerged as an organization that carries out mandated responsibilities by hitting on all cylinders.

Following the framework and objectives of TTI, CBGA has pursued significant improvements in some of the key parameters of organizational performance. Over the last eight years, we have invested in the strengthening of organizational systems and processes; human resource; policy; monitoring, evaluation and learning (MEL) practices; governance process; and our research infrastructure. These measures have made CBGA not only a better workplace but also a more accountable and efficient organization.

TTI has enabled CBGA to take important steps towards strengthening the leadership and organizational systems and processes. TTI's support led to increased efficiency by investing in process improvements; we built in processes where all members are able to contribute optimally with their strengths, skills and knowledge towards the organization's growth and success. It helped us in attracting more qualified, talented and dynamic staff to form a larger team; hiring appropriate premises and organizing suitable workspace for a bigger team after we expanded our work; and upgrading our research infrastructure. Along with supporting these measures, core funding also helped us in fulfilling all statutory requirements and regulations, including those pertaining to office premises. During this period, CBGA's human resource base has been strengthened with a number of highly qualified and talented members joining the organization. The centre has developed a competitive salary structure and introduced incentives for the staff; all of this helped improve our recruiting and retention efforts.

CBGA has carried out improvement in infrastructure for research through new subscriptions to relevant databases, software packages and journals. In the last eight years, the centre has invested to improve the capacity of the finance and administration section as well as provided the team several training opportunities.

A key takeaway from the entire process has been learning from the fellow travellers in TTI in the South Asia region. The sharing of experiences and strategies adopted by other think tanks in the region has helped CBGA in shaping its strategies. Focus on leadership development has been an important aspect of TTI support for CBGA. The learning opportunities through the regional conferences in South Asia and other conferences facilitated by TTI have been immensely useful.

TTI evaluations of CBGA also paid attention to the effectiveness of governance of the organization. This encouraged us to expedite some of the improvements in CBGA's governance architecture over the last few years; we expanded the Board of Trustees of CBGA in 2012 and modified the governance architecture of the organization in 2017.

Continuous and in-depth engagement with TTI staff at International Development Research Centre (IDRC) was helpful in a number of ways. Organizational development was all through an important parameter in the discussions with TTI staff, which pushed us towards enhancing our fundraising capacities and plans and put in place a number of measures for strengthening CBGA's systems and processes.

RESEARCH QUALITY

CBGA had already established its research credibility on issues relating to fiscal policy and budget at the Union level in India when it joined TTI in 2010. However, the support from TTI enabled CBGA to improve the capacity, quality and relevance of its research through strategic investments in a number of areas. The financial resources from TTI enabled us to work towards improving the organization's research agenda, research methods and research capacity.

Being able to attract and retain a greater number of qualified and talented professionals and invest in mentoring and capacity strengthening of the team at CBGA was certainly a key enabler for the organization. For instance, while we did not have any researcher with a PhD prior to joining TTI, we have had four researchers with PhD degrees and a few others with extensive research experience as part of our research team during the TTI years. The resources also facilitated strengthening capacity of the organization's existing research staff by roping in a senior economist as a special advisor/mentor for our team and giving our colleagues more exposure by facilitating their participation in a number of conferences and training workshops.

TTI gave CBGA the opportunity to include in its research agenda a number of themes that did not attract any project funding, expand its research to fiscal policy and processes at the sub-national level, and deepen its research methodologies. We were able to take up research projects, which necessarily required a relatively long time frame, but project funding for such studies was not available. Although ambitious, these long-term research projects have been received very well by most of our stakeholders and have garnered attention from experts and policy-makers. The flexibility we got from core funding, combined with the ability to raise additional funding that came with the increasing recognition for our work, helped us scale up our work strategically at the state and district levels. Thus, TTI support has helped us significantly in shaping a long-term and comprehensive research agenda better suited to the mandate of the organization.

The scale of our research has risen in the last few years, now covering a larger number of India's states and districts, allowing us to capture trends that would emerge from interstate comparisons. For instance, in a recent study that focused on budgeting for school education in India, we were able to address critical issues in this domain, covering all 29 states. The findings helped us contribute substantively towards the policy discourse on government financing for education in the country.

Quality assurance of research was another focus of TTI. Upholding the quality of research was always important in CBGA, and this was further strengthened along the TTI road. We developed and institutionalized a two-pronged review process: in the first step, the study design, research questions and methods are reviewed by CBGA's special advisors (experienced scholars); the second step comprises a two-layered peer review, first in-house and then an external one for extensive feedback on the draft outputs.

Thus, CBGA has made investments in enhancing the capacity of the research team, improving the quality of research outputs and developing a more comprehensive research agenda. In addition, CBGA has witnessed a significant increase in the demand for and uptake of its research work over the last eight years.

However, a somewhat unique development in this domain has been the adoption of information and communication technology (ICT) to expand research capacity on public finance in India, not just for the CBGA team but also for everyone interested in analysing the country's public finance data. With additional funding support mobilized from other funding institutions, CBGA has developed Open Budgets India,[1] an open data portal on government budgets in India. This portal makes available useful data relating to government budgets in the country in machine-readable formats. We believe that this would help expedite and considerably scale up analysis of such data. Through this project, CBGA is developing and applying technology-enabled tools to promote ways to make India's government budget data open, more accessible and easier to comprehend.

POLICY ENGAGEMENT

Back in 2010, we sought to strike a prudent balance between research and advocacy in our work; however, we realized over time that there are strong complementarities between the two. Improvements in research quality and strengthening of research agenda have contributed towards greater effectiveness of CBGA's policy advocacy, communications and outreach efforts. At the same time, stronger efforts in advocacy and communications have led to CBGA's research becoming more policy-relevant and rigorous in terms of the evidence generated.

Our advocacy, communications and outreach efforts are better planned and executed now; with an appropriate set of communication tools, we now engage with specific audiences in different areas of our work. Earlier, we faced the risk of becoming a Delhi-centric organization in terms of our outreach and stakeholder engagement; but TTI support has helped us engage with important stakeholders across the country. By reaching out to audiences outside Delhi in several states,

---

[1] www.openbudgetsindia.org

CBGA has been able to establish its national character. An extension of this process has been our engagement with think tanks and civil society organizations (CSOs) from other countries which focus on issues of transparency in the global financial system.

CBGA accords a significant emphasis to the voices of people, especially those from the underprivileged and vulnerable sections, on public spending priorities and processes in the country. One of the areas where TTI's core funding support was complemented with a comprehensive capacity development programme for the grantee organizations pertained to 'policy engagement and outreach'. Towards the end of Phase 1 of TTI, we received an opportunity to participate in a project on strengthening policy engagement and communications (PEC) plans and abilities of the think tanks. A facilitator appointed by TTI provided technical support such as guiding principles and tips that helped devise strategies to package and disseminate our research findings more effectively. The support also helped us develop the PEC approach best suited to our work. Equipped with a set of relevant skills and ideas, we introduced in CBGA a well-thought-out plan of action for revamping our outreach methods based on our priorities and stakeholders.

To become more effective in PEC, we increased our engagement with both key policy-making institutions, at the national and state levels, and civil society groups. We made concerted efforts to reach out to policy-makers and academicians while maintaining an interface with the larger civil society in the country. We ensured that our research was shared with civil society organizations (CSOs), networks and campaigns; we engaged continuously with CSOs and activists sharing evidence-based policy advocacy messages to answer their relevant questions. We engaged in several policy-influencing opportunities with both the executives and legislators around issues related to fiscal policy and governance. Our work led us to gain prominence in addressing some of the complex questions in fiscal governance in the country.

We worked on stepping up our visibility and media engagement for wider outreach. Some of the efforts included redesigning of our website and use of electronic dissemination through automated mechanisms and social network platform to disseminate our knowledge products. These efforts have contributed significantly to improve policy outreach and advocacy in a timely and effective manner. We now incorporate communications and policy outreach strategies in all our research projects from the stage of their conceptualization.

The TTI support helped us organize conferences, panel discussions, workshops, roundtables and consultations. These fora created platforms to present evidence from our research and solicit feedback on policy recommendations; key actors from different quarters participated in these discussions. In these platforms, we have covered themes such as gender responsiveness of budgets, taxation, global financial transparency, fiscal transparency and accountability, budgeting for social sectors and so on.

CHALLENGES

CBGA has covered a lot of ground over the last eight years, but it faces new challenges now. Achieving greater rigour and quality in our research remains an important goal for us. Improving accessibility of our work for CSOs which constitute a large part of our audience is another challenge to overcome. However, the biggest challenge has been bridging the differences between our perspective on fiscal policy and that of some of the policy-makers; this gap forces us to innovate and strengthen our outreach efforts.

POLICY CONTRIBUTION

Over the last decade, CBGA has made a number of contributions towards improvements in fiscal governance in India. It has generated useful evidence and analytical insights into both public expenditure and taxation. Its work has drawn public attention to the question of adequacy of government financing for social sectors in the country. CBGA's work on the responsiveness of budgets to disadvantaged sections of the population, such as women, children, Dalits, Adivasis, religious minorities and persons with disabilities, has strengthened the social inclusion perspectives in the discourse on budgets in the country.

CBGA's work has strengthened civil society campaigns in the country on social sectors and rights of the disadvantaged sections in fiscal governance. As stated earlier, CBGA has created Open Budgets India. As a result of the Open Budgets India project, Finance Departments of Assam, Jharkhand and Kerala have agreed to publish their respective State Budget data in machine-readable formats in future and the Union government has committed to publish all Detailed Demands for Grants of the Union ministries in open data format on its portal.[2]

Core funding from TTI provided us with the capacity, space and resources required to make concerted efforts towards influencing progressive changes in fiscal governance in the country, and in the following text, we provide a few specific examples of the impact of our work over the last eight years.

CBGA's analysis of budgets for social sectors has consistently drawn the attention of the media, academia, civil society and Parliament to the decisions and actions of the government vis-à-vis the challenges in this sphere. This, in turn, has strengthened the process of the Union government of India being held accountable by stakeholders for its decisions pertaining to public financing of social sectors in the country.

We were invited by the supreme audit institution in India, the office of the Comptroller and Auditor General (CAG) of India, for developing the background papers for the last two biennial Accountants General (AG) conferences organized by the office of CAG in 2014 and 2016.

CBGA provided pro bono research support to the CAG of India on both the occasions and developed the papers: 'Reporting in Public Interest: Value and Impact of CAG's Audit' in October 2014 and 'Public Auditing and Accounting: A Catalyst for Good Governance' in October 2016. We used the opportunities for effective advocacy with the office of the CAG on a number of issues and processes for improving the budget accountability ecosystem in India. In 2014–2015, we urged them to improve the accessibility and outreach of their audit reports as well as for stepping up their engagement with citizens at different stages of their work. Based on our recommendations, the CAG website was refurbished in 2015 and made more user-friendly

[2] www.data.gov.in

for enhanced engagement by different stakeholders and better uptake of their audit reports and accounts. In 2016, we helped the office of CAG draw the attention of a range of key policy-making and implementing institutions to the role of public auditing in promoting good governance. In this context, we also shared ideas and suggestions on improvements required in public accounts and audit effectiveness, emerging areas in audits, and the impact of e-governance on auditing and accounting. This engagement with the office of CAG required us to provide substantive analytical inputs in a pro bono arrangement at a very short notice on both occasions (in 2014 and 2016), which would not have been possible without the overall improvements in CBGA's organizational parameters and access to core funds.

Over the past eight years, CBGA has been working on and advocating for deepening of gender-responsive budgeting (GRB) at the level of state governments. In early 2017, when the Kerala government revived its process of GRB, CBGA provided research inputs to the State Planning Board in drafting a new format of the Gender Budget Statement. This new format of the Gender Budget Statement in Kerala, which follows the approach to GRB recommended by CBGA, has set in motion a process of re-examination of GRB in various states in the country. We must mention that CBGA had received project funding specifically for GRB work in 2011 and depended entirely on core funding from TTI to continue its work on GRB and engagement in the discourse on GRB as well as in strategic opportunities for advocacy in the subsequent years.

SUSTAINABILITY

TTI has created a positive impact for its grantees by strengthening them in the three important areas of organizational development, research quality, and policy linkages and communication. It has also ensured that the think tanks in this cohort pay adequate attention to sustainability. It has encouraged and led us into strengthening CBGA's leadership, systems and processes, capacities, research to policy linkages, and financial support base. All these have contributed towards enhancing CBGA's sustainability. Putting in place a strong MEL system has made the organization more resilient in terms of its ability to adapt to challenges in the funding and changing regulatory landscape for independent non-profit organizations in India.

CBGA now has access to a more diversified set of funders in India and is also raising project-based funding from a number of foreign funding institutions. Over the last 10 years, CBGA has generated useful evidence and analytical insights on both public expenditure and taxation issues, creating demand for its work, which is the most important factor underlying CBGA's sustainability; and we cannot overstate the contribution of TTI to this.

Yet there are major challenges before CBGA on the sustainability front. We need to ensure a reasonably adequate amount of predictable and stable core funding support for the organization for the coming years. In the current funding environment for think tanks in India, such support is elusive. Accessing core fund support of the kind provided by TTI will be a challenge in future, but the TTI journey has enabled CBGA to be prepared well to face and overcome the challenges ahead.

Chapter 10

Centre for Policy Research

Yamini Aiyar*

BACKGROUND

Centre for Policy Research (CPR) was founded in 1973 as an independent, non-partisan research institution focused on examining long-term policy questions emerging in South Asia at the time. The centre was partly intended to carry out high-quality academic research on wide-ranging policy issues and partly aimed at providing a forum for Indian policy-makers to develop and exchange ideas. Within a decade of its founding, the institution emerged as a leading think tank in India on a variety of fields, particularly developing core competence in the fields of economics, foreign policy and, later, political science. In the decade of the 1980s, CPR became one of the early proponents of economic liberalization and South Asia regional integration—both novel concepts at the time. In the 1990s, the centre emerged as one of the leading institutions in India, examining the health of its political institutions. By the 2000s, CPR had built core competence in five fields: urbanization and infrastructure; international affairs and security; governance and politics; environment and climate change; and law, regulation and society.

However, the early 2000s proved to be the watershed years for CPR. Its leadership went through quick changes and its faculty staff

---

* Special thanks to Mr Sandeep Bharadwaj, CPR.

suffered severe attrition. Then in 2004, under the leadership of its new president, Dr Pratap Bhanu Mehta, the centre embarked on a revitalization path. Broadly speaking, it aimed for three transformations. First, it sought to strengthen the academic side of its faculty and infuse it with greater intellectual rigour. Consequently, in the following years, the institution went on a hiring spree, recruiting many emerging scholars with internationally renowned reputation. Second, CPR expanded its public footprint by not only deepening its existing engagement with the policy-makers circles but also creating new networks with the academia, media, civil society and the larger public.

The third major transformation that CPR undertook was to shift its fundamental business model. Since its inception, the centre had been primarily funded by various government agencies and publicly owned corporations (although private funding had also played a crucial role). However, in the twenty-first century, this model was becoming unsustainable due to two major factors. First was the question of scalability. The post-liberalized Indian economy had opened up a gap between private sector spending and government expenditure markers. To be able to retain the best talent and maintain competitive infrastructure, CPR needed to move at a much higher pace than government outlays would have allowed for. Second, in the political atmosphere of the early 2000s, dependence on government funds had begun to threaten the institution's independence. Consequently, there was a concerted effort to shift the majority of the centre's funding away from government institutions and towards private sources.

The strategy proved enormously successful. By the end of the decade, CPR's annual budget had reached close to ₹10 crore, up from ₹2 crore in 2000. With this increased funding, the centre could attract new scholars, some of whom remain CPR's most consequential hires to this day. However, the new funding strategy also created unanticipated challenges. Most pertinent was the limiting restrictions attached with the private funding, most of which arrived tied to individual projects. While this strategy allowed for more expansive research undertakings, it narrowed the resources available to provide for the health of the institution as a whole. For instance, in FY 2009–2010, the difference between CPR's gross expenditure and specific project research expenditure was merely ₹4.39 lakh. The narrow gap between the centre's total resources and those tied to specific projects meant that the institution had very little to invest in its infrastructure or initiate unfunded projects.

The Think Tank Initiative (TTI) funding awarded to CPR in 2010 thus arrived at a propitious time and proved to be a boon for the long-term health of the centre. It provided much needed financial breathing space for the institution to grow organically, upgrade its infrastructure and experiment with new strategies. Further, in the last eight years, TTI has offered long-term stability to the centre, allowing it to retain its strengths in the face of sudden external shocks and moments of transition. TTI funds also allowed the centre to expand and aided in creation of wholly new departments such as CPR's economic research wing and its communication department.

In articulating CPR's vision while receiving the TTI award, the CPR president articulated the foremost goal that the centre had set for itself: to 'become undisputed leaders in CPR's areas of current research, recognised both domestically and internationally as such'. While it was a tall order in itself, CPR also aimed to expand its research into new areas (particularly economics), promote its long-term relevance by mentoring young researchers, scale up its infrastructure and 'enhance our convening power and outreach to better leverage our research'.

ORGANIZATIONAL PERFORMANCE

This vision may seem enormously ambitious, but it also proved to be a gamble that paid off. In recent years, the centre has cemented itself as one of the leading think tanks in South Asia and expanded its research into new and exciting fields. In the last decade, CPR had been consistently ranked as one of the leading think tanks in Asia by the University of Pennsylvania's Think Tanks and Civil Societies Program. In the field of climate change, it has been ranked among the top three think tanks (outside North America and Europe) by the International Center for Climate Governance. CPR's individual faculty members have amassed several plaudits on their own, including recently the prestigious Infosys Prize and T. N. Khoshoo Memorial Award.

In fact, it is CPR's ability to attract and retain the highest quality talent that has allowed it to maintain such high quality of research.

Today, the centre boasts a community of 30 internationally distinguished scholars working with over 50 young scholars. TTI funds played a crucial role in this accomplishment by allowing the centre bridge funds to hire and retain scholars in cases where specific project funding was temporarily unavailable. It is partly due to this stability that, aside from one exception, CPR has not lost any faculty members due to financial reasons in the last decade.

Moreover, in the last couple of decades, the centre has emerged as a magnet for attracting young scholars who are offered intimate mentorship and support by the senior faculty members. Many of these scholars have gone on to begin their own successful academic careers around the world. To take only one simple metric, in the last five years alone, 56 research associates from CPR have gone off to pursue higher studies in eight different countries. Over 11 of these CPR alumni are in Ivy League schools such as Harvard University, Yale University and Brown University. Others have gone on to prestigious universities such as Stanford University, University of Chicago, University of Cambridge, London School of Economics (LSE), John Hopkins University, Sciences Po, Sorbonne University, King's College London, Massachusetts Institute of Technology (MIT), University of California, Berkley, National University of Singapore and Carnegie Mellon University.

The TTI award also played a crucial role in re-establishing CPR's economics research wing. While the institution was a leading economics research centre in the 1970s and 1980s, at the turn of the century, it had lost its edge in this field due to severe manpower attrition. One of stated goals of the TTI award was to regain that lost strength. The unattached funding allowed CPR the flexibility needed for creating a new department from the scratch. Today, CPR is proud to host one of most vibrant economics research centres in the country. Perhaps nothing demonstrates this success more than the fact that only two years ago, one of CPR's faculty members was appointed vice chairman of National Institution for Transforming India (NITI Aayog), while another was appointed as the chairman of the Economic Advisory Council to the Prime Minister.

At the time of the TTI award in 2010, the centre also aimed to develop capacity in another area of research—China. Unfortunately, it was unable to find capable candidates to support this research, and the plan was temporarily shelved by the second round of funding in 2013. However, in the last few years, CPR has been able to attract new scholars working in the field of Chinese security policy and economy as well as expand the work of CPR's existing faculty to fold in various aspects of China studies. While it is still a bit early, the centre is also well on its way to establish a full-fledged research programme on China within the next couple of years.

In fact, in terms of its scope and depth, CPR has one of the largest research agendas in Asia today. Its agenda is broadly categorized into five fields: law, regulation and State; international relations and security; urbanization; environmental law and governance; and economic policy. Within each field are a plethora of research projects under way employing a variety of strategies. Under the same roof, the centre scholars are deliberating on the Indian Constitution; carrying large field surveys to track government expenditure; assessing the quality of school education; examining contours of globalization; evolving new solutions for India's sanitation policy; mapping India's foreign aid programme; analysing India's budget; developing recommendations for India's environment and energy policies; dissecting South Asian security situation; scrutinizing country's internal migration patterns; exploring the political philosophy of the Indian State; assessing the impact of caste on upward mobility; providing policy crash courses to sitting legislators and ministers; examining South Asia's river-sharing and management mechanisms; finding multi-stakeholder solutions for Delhi's pollution crisis; and carrying out historical research on India's past military adventures. These are only a few of the projects ongoing at the centre today.

RESEARCH OUTPUT AND QUALITY

Thanks to the effort of CPR's senior faculty members and these scholars, the centre has experienced one of the most prolific periods of its history. In the last three years alone, CPR faculty members have written over 23 books, 70 book chapters, 92 journal articles and 1,200 media articles and organized 200 seminars and conferences. In addition, CPR faculty members have performed invaluable public service by sitting on government committees, authoring policy briefs and providing expert technical advice to policy-makers on a range of issues.

Yet, while rapidly increasing the number of published outputs, the centre has also improved the research quality of its work which is now recognized and respected the world over. One indication of this high research quality is the number of internationally reputed academic publishers (Harvard University Press, Oxford University Press and Cambridge University Press) which are not only publishing books by CPR faculty members but also collaborating with the centre to develop mammoth edited volumes like the recently published *The Oxford Handbook of the Indian Constitution* and *The Oxford Handbook of Indian Foreign Policy*. Another indication of CPR's growing academic reputation is the litany of global research institutions which have recently partnered with it, including Georgetown University, Brown University, The New School, NITI Aayog, University of Cape Town and Centre National de la Recherche Scientifique. Furthermore, since the TTI award, several international foundations and organizations have found CPR worthy of grants, such as Bill & Melinda Gates Foundation, MacArthur Foundation, Ford Foundation, William and Flora Hewitt Foundation, World Bank, Asia Foundation, Chr. Michelsen Institute (CMI), Omidyar Network and Oak Foundation.

Over the years, the centre has tried to maintain a balance between ensuring high quality of research and allowing intellectual freedom to its scholars. The result has been high-standard quality assurance mechanisms which are largely normative. These are observed through a variety of strategies. First, CPR boasts a number of internationally recognized senior faculty members who not only produce high-quality research but also set the standards for research in their respective fields. Second, the centre has sought to inculcate an environment of academic excellence and self-motivation which encourages scholars to pursue the highest levels of research quality. Finally, due to its myriad of collaborative networks with research institutions across the world, centre's research is always embedded within the larger discourses occurring around the world which allows its scholars to self-evaluate their work against the cutting edge in any given field.

CPR's high-quality research has also been possible due to the infrastructure offered to its scholars by the institution. Here as well, TTI funding has played a crucial role. In the last eight years, the centre's Wi-Fi facilities have been updated regularly to maintain a state-of-the-art internal network and access to the Internet. The centre has nearly doubled its number of computers in the same period. Most of the PC workstations have been replaced with more mobile devices to allow greater flexibility to the centre's scholars. Moreover, CPR now has access to several online tools and resources as well as membership to many digital libraries, thereby enhancing the capacity of its research.

The TTI award has also played a critical role in helping the centre establish its communications department. At the time of the award, it was felt that while CPR's faculty was accomplished at communicating through the public sphere, engaging widely with media, government and policy circles, the centre as whole had not yet succeeded in crafting, maintaining and communicating its own institutional identity to a broad, global audience. It was believed that establishing a sound communications strategy is essential not only to building and maintaining the centre's brand but also to achieving its policy goals.

With TTI support, the centre established its communications department from the scratch, which manages CPR's web presence, its social media presence, its design needs and larger communications strategy. The centre rolled out a new dynamic website (with the homepage content refreshed at least three times a week), brand identity, mailing list, six social media channels, and outputs such as podcasts, blogs, interviews, research summaries and annual reports, and increased digital engagement via tools like Facebook Live, particularly on relevant topical issues. As a result of these efforts, the centre's reach has widened considerably. This expanded reach has led to wider consumption of CPR's research by policy-makers, coverage by media and mobilized community action. In the case of environmental justice, for instance and to quote one example, improved communication has directly impacted a proposed new law on coastal governance, which would have compromised earlier safeguards for affected communities.

POLICY ENGAGEMENT

While pursuing high standards of research, the centre has ensured effective dissemination of its work and repeatedly deployed its expertise to aid policy-making processes. Perhaps nothing can be a better testament to CPR's impact than the frequency and depth with which various government organizations have sought its participation. In the last three years alone, the centre has provided direct technical expertise to policy-makers though 188 targeted meetings with policy-makers. CPR also has membership in 107 task forces and working groups set up by state and central governments.

These engagements have been long-term and multifaceted in nature. Some of the centre's most successful, recent policy engagements include faculty participation in the Committee on Restructuring of Railways set up by the Ministry of Railways, Government of India; convening the Expert Committee to study alternatives for the new capital of Andhra Pradesh; engagement with government on building a strategy for India's long-term carbon and energy trajectory; preparing background papers for the Fourteenth Finance Commission recommendations on local government finances; and membership in the National Security Advisory Board.

Parallel to it, the centre has also increased its international engagement, working with multilateral agencies and foreign governments. Some of the recent engagements by CPR include the following: convening Track 1.5 trilateral meetings of India, the USA and China; engagement with UN-Habitat and World Urban Forum on the question of urbanization; participation and support for international climate governance activities such as United Nations Framework Convention on Climate Change and Intergovernmental Panel on Climate Change; and membership in international expert panels like Open Government Partnership.

Furthermore, the centre has also enhanced its efforts at strengthening the larger policy-making community in India. CPR faculty members regularly participate in teaching and training courses for civil servants. CPR has also been working closely with parliamentarians. In the last three years, CPR has engaged with 88 sitting Indian members of parliament (MPs) of 20 different political parties, including 9 sitting Cabinet ministers, 9 ministers of State and 1 chief minister. During the same period, CPR has organized 11 sessions to sensitize MPs on a variety of subjects including agriculture, digitization, malnutrition, children's welfare and banking. CPR has also organized 11 visits for Indian MPs to engage with foreign scholars in five countries–the USA, the UK, China, Israel and Australia.

CPR believes strongly that policy-making is not just about writing laws and policy rules but also about the ability to implement policy effectively on the ground. A number of CPR programmes are engaged with directly shaping implementation and strengthening governance capacity at the frontlines. To illustrate, in the last three years, CPR has engaged over 1,000 frontline officers at the panchayat, block and district levels on how to strengthen implementation of key social sector programmes related to health, education, sanitation and local government financing.

POLICY IMPACT: A CASE STUDY

To map out the impact of CPR's varied activities in its entirety would be impossible to achieve in these pages. A better strategy may be to consider one (of several dozens) CPR initiative currently under way to understand the scope and depth of the centre's engagement. PAISA (Planning, Allocations and Expenditures, Institutions Studies in Accountability) is one of CPR's projects operated by its team called Accountability Initiative (AI). It is India's largest expenditure tracking survey, which aids CPR researchers to study planning, decision-making and fund flows in key social sector schemes. Specifically, PAISA surveys are aimed at identifying implementation bottlenecks and through this understanding the factors that contribute to weak implementation and broken accountability systems on the ground.

In December 2015, AI conducted a PAISA survey focusing on three centrally sponsored schemes (CSSs): Sarva Shiksha Abhiyan (SSA), Integrated Child Development Services (ICDS) and Swachh Bharat Mission (SBM). The survey, conducted in 10 districts across 5 states (Bihar, Himachal Pradesh, Maharashtra, Madhya Pradesh and Rajasthan) in India, was undertaken against the backdrop of significant changes in fund flows to states, with the central government enhancing tax devolution (untied money) to state governments. Similar to PAISA surveys in the past, the 2015 survey also revealed the extent to which structural problems with the public finance management system, such as lack of transparency in fund releases, can impact the quality of programme implementation on the ground. However, the lack of predictability was exacerbated as a result of the changes in fiscal transfers. For instance, in 2015–2016, 31 per cent schools had not received their annual school grants, as compared to 5 per cent in the previous year.

Additionally, the PAISA survey collected information on progress in implementation, including achievement of Right to Education-related school outputs, teacher and student attendance, availability of toilets, implementation of sanitation-related awareness programmes and the prevalence of open defecation.

The survey results were disseminated at the policy level through the budget brief reports, AI's annual flagship research output. At the district level, AI adopted a new approach to dissemination. Rather than circulating reports, an attempt was made to share research findings through a dialogue with district- and block-level implementing officials. The objective was to leverage research findings to catalyse a ground-level discussion on 'how to' improve implementation and accountability—where it actually matters.

With this objective, between May 2016 and December 2016, a total of 40 PAISA dialogues were conducted across the 10 PAISA survey districts with sector-specific implementation officials. The dialogues were conducted by AI field researchers or PAISA associates (PA). In this bottom-up approach, government representatives on the ground level were engaged directly to foster a genuine feeling of partnership. The response was overwhelming. A senior official in the Elementary Education Department of Purnia district in Bihar said,

> The flow of funds through various levels of the government is very similar to the flow of blood from the heart to the various parts of the body. If there is blockage somewhere, it affects the entire body, so in that regard PAISA studies do the work of a physician.

The result of these engagements led to several small-scale localized transformations. For instance, in Himachal Pradesh, armed with PAISA surveys, frontline bureaucrats lobbied their senior officials to implement specific policy solutions to remove bottlenecks in the system. In Jhalawar, Rajasthan, local school officials developed informal communication networks with their funding sources to ensure smoother flow of funds.

PAISA dialogues were an experiment which paid off handsomely. These allowed the centre to move beyond its usual dissemination channels and attempt to affect change from the ground level. However, such an experiment had been possible only due to freedom and flexibility allowed to CPR by its financial base and intellectual resources. Contributions like the TTI Award have played a crucial role in affording the centre that freedom. Given such support, the centre is likely to continue experimenting in creative ways to bring about change.

THINKING AHEAD

In November 2018, CPR will turn 45 years old. For the centre's leadership, it has seemed like a propitious time to undertake another round of introspection and consider new ways of evolving this hallowed institution. Currently, the centre's administration is in the process of drawing up a vision plan entitled 'CPR@50' to consider the upcoming challenges and opportunities. While the plan continues to evolve, there are already several key issues which have become evident.

Foremost, it is recognized that to remain at the forefront of public policy research in India, CPR needs to significantly invest in building its institutional foundations. To do so will require at least three elements. First, the centre would have to double its faculty strength at the least. It will particularly have to focus on recruiting senior policy practitioners and build a new layer of junior faculty that will help grow the institution over the next decade. Second, CPR needs to build its research portfolio to address the new challenges confronting global policy-making today, especially in new fields including the following: technology and public policy, gender, jobs and the future of work. Finally, it needs to strengthen its communication and outreach. One important area of growth is in using new media tools. CPR has a well-established and widely regarded tradition of contributing to public argument through mainstream media. However, in this new age of digital communication, CPR needs to significantly upgrade its communication strategies to engage in the public domain through a wider range of media.

To meet these goals, CPR needs to address two institutional challenges. First and foremost is the funding. The centre needs long-term, predictable, core funding. Thus far, it has largely relied on international donors for financial resources. Eighty-seven per cent of CPR funding comes from international donors. These resources are linked to project-specific goals and timelines that make long-term, innovative research work difficult. Moreover, for a host of reasons linked to changes in domestic and global politics, funds from international foundations are likely to reduce significantly over the next few years. It is critical for CPR to diversify its funding model and focus its fundraising efforts on domestic philanthropy. However, domestic philanthropy in India is still nascent, and CPR will have to invest in raising visibility among domestic philanthropists and simultaneously building awareness on the critical role that think tanks and public policy research play in India's policy-making landscape.

The second challenge CPR faces is administrative. CPR's greatest organizational strength is the low burden of procedure and systems it places on faculty. This has allowed for much needed (and rare, in the Indian institutional context) flexibility and autonomy for faculty to shape their research projects. However, CPR's growth over the last decade (and future potential growth) has made some administrative and organizational standardization imperative. This includes building systems for human resource management, research protocols, quality control systems and project management. To achieve this, CPR needs to build a strong leadership team that works with the CPR president's office. In addition, CPR needs to upgrade its physical infrastructure to develop into a twenty-first-century workplace. Even the current CPR building is over 30 years old and in need of urgent repair and maintenance.

Over the next five years, in the run-up to CPR's 50th year landmark anniversary, CPR is launching a campaign to significantly expand the centre's financial resources. The objective of this campaign is to build a robust financial corpus that will allow CPR to retain existing faculty and attract new talent, build a strong institutional backbone (including upgrading infrastructure and administrative support systems) and expand our policy research into new domains.

Chapter 11

Centre for the Study of Developing Societies

Sanjay Kumar

INTRODUCTION

The Centre for the Study of Developing Societies (CSDS) is a premier social science research institute based in New Delhi. It is funded by the Indian Council of Social Science Research (ICSSR), Ministry of Human Resource Development, Government of India. CSDS works on interdisciplinary themes of political thought and philosophy, media and culture, democratic politics and its future, development paradigm and practices, spatial transformations, diversity, identity and violence, and social science in Indian languages.

Ever since its inception over 50 years ago, CSDS is recognized as one of the leading intellectual institutions of the global south. CSDS is one of the rare institutions that has accomplished generational transition by reinventing itself in the twenty-first century, with a fresh commitment to forging links between the social sciences and humanities and in building on non-European lineages of political and ethical thoughts in the Indian languages. CSDS greatly values its autonomy and critical presence in India's public domain and generates research products in the hope that it would shape public opinion, influence policy and facilitate meaningful interventions in society.

India, in the last decade, has witnessed a widespread contested civil society initiative against corruption, which radically interrogated the worlds of politics, law and public policy and raised several fundamental questions about the country's future. Together, these initiatives and questions forced us to redefine the criteria of research for our times. An altered environment necessitated the careful cultivation of research praxis in which long-term and theoretical investigation is in active dialogue with the conditions and problems of the emerging present. This reopening of the normative considerations has accompanied orientation towards practical action, questioning of the means and ends, and defining public policy as an element connected with societies and of concern to the wider public.

There has also been a significant change in the higher education context in India with several private research universities being opened up in the last 10 years. These universities have the potential to deter faculty away from existing public universities and research centres by providing globally benchmarked salaries, better benefits, advanced technology and communications facilities, infrastructure, and other kinds of professional and academic incentives. On the other hand, the pressure from large universities to absorb small independent research institutions has eased. This later trend has allowed CSDS to maintain its autonomy as a centre for advanced social science and humanities research while collaborating with the best traditions of research in Indian universities.

The funding environment for public research institutions has been fluctuating. When the International Development Research Centre (IDRC) Think Tank Initiative (TTI) was conceived, the economic crisis of 2008 had adversely affected research funding all over the world. This crunch made it difficult to seed projects and programmes in new areas. In this milieu, Indian academics lacked the financial support to undertake even minimal research, though they enjoyed the security of tenure. ICSSR was CSDS' primary source of funds, albeit with a degree of uncertainty about how steadily and how long it could continue to sustain the centre's research ecosystem. Private donors have remained largely project-oriented. In this conundrum, the institutional support provided by TTI was unique. The TTI support allowed CSDS to leverage other long-term funding commitments, which has had a major impact on research possibilities. CSDS is also aided by a substantial corpus that contributes to the institution's long-term stability and autonomy to pursue its research agenda.

RESEARCH QUALITY

The centre's objectives around 'research quality' are uniquely designed to promote cutting-edge individual research together with collaborative work and networking through projects and programmes. The value of research is deeply ingrained in the centre's non-partisan history, rigorous scholarship and extensive networks. These attributes aim to increase the outreach and communication of research results through policy dialogues and linkages. Mainly undertaken by programmes, projects and individual faculties, these platforms allow the centre to engage in a diverse range of public policy issues at multiple levels and strengthen the existing research value chain.

From the very outset, the CSDS research design has been based on collaboration within the centre, nationally, regionally and internationally. In addition to social science research networks, CSDS has long experience of setting up dialogues among academics, social movements, non-governmental organizations (NGOs) and policy institutions. In recent years, practitioners in the domains of culture and environment have also joined the centre's networks, thus enhancing the range of people that are connected with us. The centre reaches out to a larger public through various offline and online platforms, bringing in a whole new generation of younger scholars into our network. Our collaborative approach offers faculty members autonomy to scale up and across networks while maintaining scholarly rigour. We believe that our experience of developing diverse, cross-disciplinary collaborative platforms across many different publics (academics, activists and policy-makers) can be useful for other institutions.

There are several key areas in which TTI support has been invaluable for thematic research which include the following: (a) providing support to existing research projects and programmes that could not get adequate funding elsewhere, (b) supporting individual researchers with grants for conducting research and participating in research-related

156 | Sanjay Kumar

activities, (c) bringing in visiting scholars to strengthen existing lines of research and develop new ones, (d) acquisition of books, journals and databases, (e) developing an ambitious programme for engaging research results in local Indian languages, (f) organizing research activities such as conferences and workshops on a more regular basis and on a much larger scale than before, (g) developing national and global networks of researchers, (h) the publication of journals and (i) an expanded teaching programme to train younger (doctoral and postdoctoral) social science scholars.

TTI support also helped us strengthen our existing programmes: Lokniti and Sarai, research networks on election studies and media and urbanism, respectively. It has also helped us consolidate the Indian Languages Programme (ILP), which was started in 2001 with a limited agenda of translating works by CSDS faculty members and making them available in Hindi language. Over the years, TTI support has greatly enhanced this programme, and CSDS now engages with thinking about the entire domain of social sciences, seeking answer to the question: What it might mean to 'do social sciences in Indian languages?' The core idea behind asking this question is to think (a) beyond Hindi, in terms of Indian languages as a whole, and (b) beyond just translations from English and looking at the cognitive challenges of doing social sciences in these languages. Publications, lectures and fellowships are some of the key activities undertaken. 'An entirely new initiative on studies of Indian Thought which initially started with TTI funds has been enabled by core support from the Parekh trust.'

As a community of researchers, we have achieved considerable success in building and strengthening other networks and collaborative research possibilities. We have successfully hosted several national and international exchange programmes including co-hosting the 40th World Congress of the International Institute of Sociology on the theme 'After Western Hegemony' (2012) and setting up networks for cross-country analysis under the aegis of 'democracy in South Asia' and 'youth studies'. Reputed scholars, from India and abroad, have delivered 23 public lectures under the Golden Jubilee lecture series.

Attracting and retaining scholars is a key objective of CSDS. A major success in this regard was the setting up of an ambitious Visiting

Fellowships programme. CSDS undertook this initiative with great care and deliberation, conducting a wide range of public search and extensive interviews to select visiting scholars. Its peers hold CSDS in high esteem, and this is reflected in the large number of scholars from India and abroad who have applied for these fellowships. Several of these scholars, especially those in the early postdoctoral stage, have since moved on to regular positions at other academic institutions.

CSDS' profile as a premier research institute with a growing network also includes the teaching programmes offered by our faculty. 'Researching the Contemporary' is the centre's uniquely designed summer teaching programme, targeted at research students and independent scholars based in India. The programme started in 2010 with TTI support; it allows students to critically engage with the formation of the contemporary and its multiple histories, ideologies, forms and affects. The programme focuses on three thematic areas designed by faculty members of CSDS to enable participants to familiarize themselves with concepts and theories, and critically engage with different methodologies of analysis. These themes are determined annually by faculty members and are of a kind often unavailable in a university setting. The programme has been immensely successful, with the number of applications rising exponentially each year, with more than 700 serious applications received in the last fiscal year.

In addition, the centre's Lokniti programme offers a special summer course on 'Analyzing Quantitative Data on Indian Politics', initially in collaboration with the Indian Institute of Advanced Study (IIAS) in Shimla and currently with Jain University, Bengaluru. Over the last decade, this programme has contributed immensely to build the research capacity of young scholars, especially those based at universities where such a rigorous methodological course may not be offered. The research scholars' workshop on 'Mainstream and the Margins: Theory, Practice and Methods' was started in 2015 as a capacity-building workshop supported by the ICSSR and TTI funds for students of disadvantaged communities. Participants engaged in a range of readings, seminar-style discussions and special lectures, addressing (a) inequality and inclusion, (b) dissent and democracy, (c) vernacular modernities, (d) emergent histories, (e) technologies and media forms and (f) spaces and habitats. Each of these teaching initiatives provides CSDS an opportunity to strengthen linkages with the university system as well as to influence the future of social science and humanities research in India.

ORGANIZATIONAL PERFORMANCE

TTI support has enabled organizational transformation by supporting critical areas which include the following: (a) redesigning and upgrading the seminar room and meeting space, (b) upgrading technical infrastructure, including better computing facilities and web connectivity, (c) expanding storage facilities for library holdings, (d) instituting reforms in financial management, (e) better documentation, (f) in-house skill development and (g) enhanced social security for all members of the staff.

One of our key concerns is to make the CSDS' research available to a wider public. Besides establishing and publishing three peer-reviewed journals, we undertook an ambitious publicity programme. We hired a dedicated support staff to produce brochures, posters, invitations and other materials; design and maintain a new website[1]; and ensure widespread online and real-time publicity using traditional methods as well as social media, including Facebook, YouTube and Twitter.

Providing well-furnished workspaces and infrastructure for regular and visiting scholars has been another major challenge. Creating additional space for the increased library holdings has been equally critical. Several new measures have been taken with the aid of TTI funds, including the making of temporary structures for library holdings, renovation of the seminar room, making of a new meeting room to host small workshops, initiating the process of making CSDS more disabled-friendly and installing rooftop solar power plant for generating green energy.

Creating incentive structures for non-faculty employees and encouraging their participation are key challenges for any research institution. From the very inception of the TTI programme, we took special measures in this regard, including the enhancement of the Staff Welfare

[1] http://www.csds.in/

Fund and medical facilities available to staff members. Making soft loans available has been another important step. In-house training of staff members in dealing with audiovisual technologies and organizing events have contributed significantly to the enhancement of their skills.

POLICY ENGAGEMENT

The Publics and Policies programme was set up in 2011 with TTI support with the aim of making the centre's engagement with the public and policy spheres more relevant and deliberative by reinforc-ing its legacy of public intellectual interventions. While routine 'policy research' often lacks social scientific rigour, disengaged research too is deficient in relevance. As a think tank, CSDS sought to fill a signifi-cant gap in India's public sphere and make a difference by mobilizing research and knowledge for more inclusive public policies. It held consultations on participatory citizenship, pre-legislative transparency, communal violence, food security, electoral reforms, tribal self-rule and land transfers, the Lok Pal Bill, the issues of scavenger communities, India's road-use policy, genetically modified (GM) food and biosafety, and the future of affirmative action, besides a series of public lectures on diverse, policy-relevant issues.

The past years saw the centre develop new and important links and networks with several ministries of the Government of India, including Home Affairs, Rural Development, Human Resource Development and Youth Affairs and Sports. Other institutional links included those with the Planning Commission, the Election Commission, the National Advisory Council, University Grants Commission and National Council of Educational Research and Training.

CSDS, in partnership with Goa Foundation and the Inclusive Media for Change, held deliberations on 'Permanent Fund Model for Ethical Mining: Land, Livelihoods and Intergenerational Equity' on 18 February 2015 at India International Centre, New Delhi. It examined if perma-nent funds (PFs) are a viable cure for India's resource curse, a failure to benefit fully from its natural resources. It explored the practical implica-tions of applying such principles to manage resources from minerals to metal ores, oil and gases to more virtual public properties such as the spectrums and airwaves across all states. The participants were a coalition of people across states in order to discuss and take forward the idea of PFs as an alternative economic policy in India's extractive sectors. The main partners (CSDS, Goa Foundation and the Inclusive Media for Change) held an informal dialogue to strategize and take the initiative forward and to identify potential partners and collaborators.

A workshop on '(P)Reserving the Handloom Reservation Act' was organized by the programme in collaboration with the Federation of Handloom Organisations and Inclusive Media for Change on 14–15 March 2015 at CSDS. It was the culmination of efforts of a few handloom organizations to bring many of the issues hampering the growth of the handloom industry in India forefront. The idea was to bring a diverse set of groups and individuals to debate the relevance of legal protection to the sector in the backdrop of the new thinking by the State and civil society. The main aim of the workshop was to garner support for the cause of handlooms from new quarters. TTI funds received from IDRC supported the workshop (see Box 11.1).

A significant new development through TTI support has been the emergence of CSDS as a major publisher of peer-reviewed journals, in English and Hindi. These journals not only reflect the scholarly rigour of the institution but are also indicative of the diverse disciplinary and linguistic public that CSDS' research engages. *BioScope: South Asian Screen Studies* is a biannual peer-reviewed journal published by SAGE. In circulation since January 2010, this journal is primarily centred on film and media studies and also engages a wider orbit of images and sound practices. ILP launched a biannual, refereed journal, *Pratiman: Samay, Samaj, Sanskriti*, in February 2013 and published in collaboration with Vani Prakashan. The journal focuses on in-depth investigations in social sciences and humanities with an insistence on writing discursive text and articles originally in Hindi language. It represents a unique blend of quality in-house design, rigorous research content and innovative distribution strategies. The journal this year has brought out its 10th issue, having cumulatively published over 300 original research articles since its inception. Lokniti, one of the oldest programmes at the centre, launched its journal *Studies in Indian Politics* in July 2013 as a forum for those engaged in generating new knowledge in the analysis of Indian politics.

Box 11.1 *Revisiting Handloom Act*

CSDS' report on the Handloom Reservation Act of 1985 is another example. The Act is a serious attempt by the State to protect the interests of the handloom sector. In the past, powerful power loom lobby groups had made several attempts to undermine the Act and repeal the provisions. Although the implementation of the Act is far from ideal, its existence provides a genuine platform for opposing the power loom, maintaining handloom products and buttressing the survival struggle of handlooms in these changing times. The neglect of the industry's crucial requirements, such as the absence of adequate credit at reasonable interest rates and unregulated and ever-increasing yarn prices, has adversely affected the growth in the sector and led to large-scale migration of weavers. The report was submitted to the Ministry of Textiles and other concerned departments with the following policy pre-scriptions: proper implementation of the Handloom Reservation Act to increase the share of 'genuine' handloom products in textile production; formation of a handloom trust at the national level for research, advocacy and lobbying on behalf of the sector; better communication of the current story in handlooms; change the outlook and perception of handlooms in national media and bring handlooms into a larger public discourse. Building awareness of rights was recognized as part of this endeavour. One possible convergence that can easily be forged with consumers is to link handloom products to consumers preferring organic products. This was identified as a strategy to bolster handloom industry.

Source: CSDS Workshop Report March 2015. Report is available at https://www.csds.in/sites/default/files/final%20reportsmall.pdf (accessed on 27 September 2018).

CHALLENGES AND WAYS AHEAD

The raising of research funds remains one of the major challenges for CSDS, as funders are reluctant to provide support to build an institutional corpus. A consistent effort is being made to raise core support in addition to project funding. The implementation aspect of the resource mobilization plan remains a major challenge, as funding for social science research continues to be within the framework of short-term projects and quick deliverables. The resource mobilization plan for financial sustainability continues with meetings with potential funders, mostly Indian corporates, and we hope to generate funds in the future, with better publicity plan and improvement in the funding climate. The centre has engaged several professionals to help achieve better publicity and initiated the preparation of a new CSDS short audiovisual film, brochure and trailer for approaching the funders.

In the coming years, CSDS is expected to grow and develop at a brisk pace, as its objectives around 'research quality' are uniquely designed to promote cutting-edge individual research together with collaborative work through projects and programmes. The capacity-building programmes of CSDS to train young scholars (doctoral and postdoctoral) are expected to grow and become more intellectually engaging and help us in foregrounding and developing new emerging research themes. In the coming year, we plan to develop the practice of collaboration further, through initiatives such as a scholar-in-residence programme to bring scholars from outside to the centre and through online tools and platforms, such as moderated lists and curated blogs. Some faculty members and research programmes are already active in online platforms, and we seek to generalize such participation across the centre to become a major digital hub for knowledge production and exchange.

Chapter 12

Center for Study of Science, Technology and Policy

Anshu Bharadwaj

EARLY DAYS

It was just a regular day in office, in August 2009. The Center for Study of Science, Technology and Policy (CSTEP) was about a year old. I remember sitting in my office, with a handful of colleagues, which effectively represented the entire strength of CSTEP at the time. Jai Asundi, a fellow engineering and public policy PhD from Carnegie Mellon University, walked in with an excited look on his face. He showed us a newspaper clipping, which was a call for proposals for International Development Research Centre's (IDRC) Think Tank Initiative (TTI). We pondered over the article and then laughed, wondering what we had to do with this. At the time, CSTEP was a fledgling organization. We were full of ideas about how science and technology could solve India's problems but were not sure about how we would go about doing it. We felt that this call was for distinguished think tanks and not for a new kid on the block, like us. We put the clipping aside—but came back to it later in the day. After a prolonged discussion, we decided to apply for the call. Frankly, at that point, we thought of ourselves as a wild-card entry into the competition.

We spent the next few months intensely discussing the proposal. The thought-provoking process forced us to think through issues of building a research organization, such as research domains, connecting research to policy, human resources, financial management, and communications and outreach. Considering our occupation with bread-and-butter issues, we may not have thought of these issues in the near future, if not for the IDRC proposal. We realized that whether we got the grant or not, writing the proposal was a priceless experience and an opportunity for us to step back and think strategically about the organization we had committed to develop.

I vividly remember our uninhibited joy when we got to know that TTI had selected CSTEP as one of the 16 South Asian think tanks. It was even more gratifying to know that CSTEP was the youngest organization selected out of nearly 200 applicants through a highly competitive selection process—like an unseeded player, with a wild-card entry, going on to win the Grand Slam! Personally, for me the joy was similar to what I felt when I was selected into the highly competitive and prestigious Indian Administrative Services. It was a defining moment in CSTEP's history, and thus began our journey with TTI.

Our initial conversations with the then regional director of IDRC, Dr Steven McGurk, and senior programme officer, Dr Samar Verma, provided us excellent insights, which set the tone for our approach and work. They emphasized two main issues: One, TTI was a once-in-a-lifetime opportunity, and that it is very difficult to get such core grants. Two, TTI's main aspiration was to enable non-linear (and not incremental) improvement in the quality of institutions.

The message was loud and clear: TTI was a big 'leap of faith' grant on think tanks, especially CSTEP. We realized that we should, therefore, utilize the core grant judiciously to maximize its benefits. We also clearly understood that we are custodians of public money, which could have been put to various alternate uses. Thus, it was with a great sense of gratitude and humility that we began our journey with TTI.

CSTEP'S PROGRESS DURING TTI GRANT

During the last eight years, CSTEP has grown from an organization of just a handful of researchers to a vibrant and robust organization. In 2008–2009, we only had a couple of grants in energy and urban infrastructure. Today, not only is CSTEP recognized among India's reputed think tanks, but we have also made important contributions to policy through the research domains we work in. I can say with some pride and satisfaction that CSTEP illustrates how a core grant—if properly utilized—can make non-linear and transformational changes in an institution. The following section provides details of our progress in specific aspects.

BUILDING RESEARCH CAPACITY

In 2009, the Government of India had just announced the National Action Plan on Climate Change, which affirmed India's commitment to climate change. It included specific missions for energy efficiency and solar energy, and CSTEP had researchers with expertise in energy technology and policy studies. These national programmes provided an opportunity for CSTEP to work closely with policy-makers. For instance, CSTEP helped design the Perform Achieve and Trade (PAT) scheme, a market-based mechanism to improve the energy efficiency of manufacturing industries.

TTI's core grant enabled CSTEP to actively contribute in this policy agenda. We deepened our work in energy efficiency and initiated new programmes in renewables (wind and solar) and energy storage. The core grant helped us build capacities in these areas. We subsequently reached out to various funding agencies to support our research projects.

In urban infrastructure, we expanded our work to include other areas such as sanitation and transport. Recently, we have initiated work in air pollution, given that most cities are facing an acute crisis in this area.

We also started work in the use of artificial intelligence (AI) to improve governance and service delivery. We believe that India's developmental challenges are complex, and conventional solutions will take a long time to make an impact. AI could provide India an opportunity to leapfrog towards achieving its developmental goals.

As CSTEP is a technology policy think tank, it relies heavily on computational methods and tools. The TTI grant helped us procure and develop several such tools, which are being used in multiple projects. CSTEP developed an innovative computational visualization platform to model complex policy problems. This platform, Decision Analysis for Research and Planning (DARPAN), is used in most of our research projects, today. We find it to be highly effective for engaging policy-makers, more than submitting a report. The tool allows the users to play with a large number of scenarios, and thus have a meaningful dialogue.

FUNDING

At the beginning of TTI, CSTEP had an annual budget of USD 0.6 million. CSTEP effectively leveraged TTI support to raise multiple project grants, increasing our annual budget to over USD3 million in 2017–2018, which is a fivefold increase in the annual budget. In terms of financial support, the TTI core grant was helpful in the following ways:

- It provided us with the flexibility to have researchers spend time to develop research proposals on policy-relevant ideas and approach other funding agencies.
- TTI core grant was a great value addition to CSTEP's organizational profile. Other donors felt more confident to engage with CSTEP.
- The core grant allowed CSTEP to enter into high-level policy engagements with the government, which are usually pro bono. This increased the organization's visibility, and other donors provided funding for such engagements.

Our improved organizational capacity, quality of research and reputation within the think tank community enabled us to raise grants from donors such as Shakti Sustainable Energy Foundation; Oak Foundation; Global Green Growth Institute; Bill & Melinda Gates Foundation; European Union; Department of Science & Technology, Government of India; MacArthur Foundation; Good Energies Foundation; Government of Karnataka; Defence Research & Development Organisation, NITI Aayog, Ministry of New and Renewable Energy (MNRE), and Bureau of Energy Efficiency. This diversification of funding base illustrates that stakeholders found value

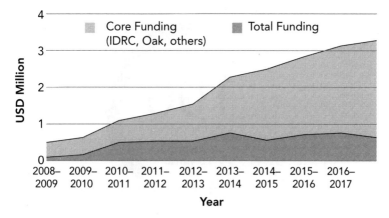

Figure 12.1 *CSTEP Successfully Used the Core Grants to Raise Project Grants for Growth*

in CSTEP's research. Interestingly, the share of the TTI core grant has progressively decreased, from 37 per cent in 2009–2010 to 19 per cent now (Figure 12.1). This highlights the fact that CSTEP did not slip into complacency upon getting the core grant. Instead, we used it effectively to raise more grants. We repeatedly reminded ourselves that TTI was a once-in-a-lifetime opportunity.

GENDER

Gender equity is an important component of CSTEP's ethos. We have consciously kept in mind the various challenges faced by women—discrimination, societal bias, harassment, lack of safety, inadequate representation in leadership roles, etc.—while developing the organizational structure and our research programmes.

Gender in the Organization

CSTEP has consistently maintained a high gender diversity in the organization. Of CSTEP's 106 employees, 42 are women and 64 are men.

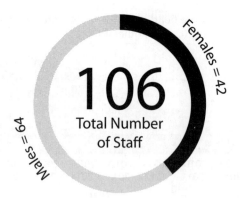

Research has identified a 'leaky pipeline' within organizations (including think tanks), where there were fewer women at every stage of the career ladder. According to data from TTI, while 43 per cent of think tank staff members are female, only 23 per cent of these organizations have female executive directors. While the dearth of women in leadership roles in most organizations is a matter of concern, the numbers at CSTEP are quite encouraging: women occupy 7 of the 16 leadership positions in CSTEP. This was achieved by proactively ensuring women's safety and dignity at the workplace and by providing opportunities for learning and mentorship from women in leadership positions within the workforce.

LEADERSHIP POSITIONS

CSTEP's Internal Complaints Committee (ICC) conducts yearly gender-sensitization workshops. Members are trained towards building awareness on sexual harassment and enhancing their ability to deal with cases of sexual harassment. Posters sensitizing employees on gender issues are posted in the office premises. Thus, the ICC members have been able to deal with all cases relating to sexual harassment and safety at workplace, swiftly and sensitively.

Gender in Research

In 2017, a CSTEP researcher wrote about a commonly held belief among urban planners—that improving the quality of life in cities would automatically address the gender equality agenda. 'Few acknowledged that improving the quality of life itself could be an outcome of more gender-inclusive planning,' she said in her blog.[1]

CSTEP, however, acknowledges the need to incorporate gender perspectives when designing and implementing research projects. For instance, CSTEP is working closely with the state government, using technology, especially machine learning, to address the malnutrition problem. The project SNEHA (Solution for Nutrition and Effective Health Access), a malnutrition management solution for children and women, adopts a technology-based approach to improving existing operations of 67,000 Anganwadis in Karnataka.[2] Malnutrition is a multi-generational issue, and ensuring the health of a child is possible only if the mother is healthy during her pregnancy and early care days. Thus, approaches to solutions take a two-pronged approach by targeting the needs of Anganwadi workers in addressing both child and maternal services.

In 'Understanding India's Peri-urban Resilience in the Context of Urbanisation and Climate Change', researchers studied various dimensions of poverty in Doddaballapur, on the outskirts of Bengaluru. Researchers assessed indicators of women empowerment, such as mobility and her role in household decision-making processes. Gender perspectives were incorporated when studying other indicators of poverty, such as water and sanitation, as well. For instance, focus group discussions with women from villages near Doddaballapur revealed that decreasing access to supply of water and sanitation had a bearing on women's safety, and this, in turn, can affect the water security of the household.

CSTEP, Centre for Advocacy and Research (CFAR) and Administrative Staff College of India (ASCI) are developing an implementable framework for strengthening institutional mechanisms to

---

[1] http://www.thinktankinitiative.org/blog/engendering-change-research-usual (accessed on 30 August 2018).

[2] The Government of Karnataka delivers nutrition and health services to about a million pregnant and nursing women and 4.5 million children under the age of six years, through a network of around 67,000 Anganwadis (day care centres).

address the gender gap across the sanitation value chain. The project is funded by the Bill & Melinda Gates Foundation. It looks at intersectionalities within gender in demonstrating a universal framework that includes the most marginalized in the formal planning processes. The objective of the project is to strengthen and advance policies, regulations, processes and agencies for increased accessibility to faecal sludge and septage management services. This is done through a demonstration of an intersectionality informed gender mainstreaming framework (IIGMF) in three towns of Andhra Pradesh, India.

Similarly, the United Nations Democracy Fund (UNDEF) is funding a project that looks at developing a spatial data system for the inclusive cities agenda in India. The project aims to enhance the claim-making and negotiation capabilities of an urban poor community in the water and sanitation sectors. The data collection and community engagement tools deployed have been designed with a strong gender-sensitive approach.

Our research on gender is also influencing policy change. The Gender Taskforce has taken forward a discussion paper, co-anchored by CSTEP, on mainstreaming gender in the National Urban Sanitation Policy (2008).

DEEPENING INTERDISCIPLINARY RESEARCH SKILLS

Keeping in line with CSTEP's mission of leveraging technology for human development, we initially hired researchers from science and engineering disciplines. However, we soon realized that the institution needed a holistic view to societal problems in order to solve them. Thus, we began recruiting researchers from various backgrounds, including economics, policy, developmental studies, etc. This was an interesting phase in CSTEP's journey. It was amusing to see how researchers with science–engineering backgrounds understood concepts such as cost, regulation and policy and, likewise, to see how economics and humanities researchers viewed technology from their perspective. There were often intense debates among the researchers.

CSTEP's research staff strength has doubled since the commencement of TTI. It was heartening that a number of young researchers trusted and joined us, even though CSTEP did not have a brand name. We provided these young researchers opportunities to lead projects and participate in meetings with high-level policy-makers. We feel proud that most of them rose up to the occasion and did well for the organization. They have built our research domains by raising project grants, successfully implementing projects and making important policy contributions. We will always remain grateful to these researchers for their faith in the organization.

DEVELOPING CORE VALUES

We realized that it was important to develop a set of core values, which would govern the functioning of the institution. We spent considerable time in discussions with the research staff to develop these values around four pillars:

- Research: The research should be scientifically motivated with a good understanding of related studies, and based on evidence. We perceive quality across three dimensions: quality of research, quality of writing and quality of presentation. Our focus is on a pragmatic approach that considers ground reality and provides implementable solutions to policy-makers.
- Organizational structure: Often think tanks tend to be personality centric, and there is a large gap between the founders and next layer of leadership. We took a conscious decision that CSTEP will not be personality centric; instead, it will be known by several outstanding professionals. This philosophy has reflected in our human resource practices and the establishment of a relatively flat organization.
- Engagement with stakeholders: This highlights the importance of sincerity, honesty and humility, and avoiding intellectual arrogance.
- Governance: This refers to ethical and transparent practices in operations, especially finance management, recruitments, performance appraisals and grievance redressal.

ADMINISTRATIVE PROCESSES

Before the commencement of TTI, CSTEP did not have any dedicated administrative personnel. Senior researchers were functioning as finance and human resource officers. TTI's support enabled CSTEP to establish dedicated administrative functions for finance, human resources and communications. Dr K. C. Bellarmine (Bell) joined us as our chief finance officer. He developed robust processes for managing finance and operations. This enabled researchers to focus on research projects, fundraising and policy engagements. CSTEP also learnt best practices in human resource management and finance management by being part of the TTI network. We learnt the importance of complying with statutory and regulatory issues such as filing of account statements, income tax and Foreign Contribution Regulation Act returns on a timely basis. We also understood the importance of managing human resource-related issues such as career growth path and redressal of grievances including sexual harassment at workplace. We now also have a dedicated staff for communications and outreach. Working with TTI helped them learn about the latest tools and technologies for outreach.

STORIES OF POLICY INFLUENCE

There have been several instances of CSTEP studies shaping policy. It validates our assumption that there is a demand for technology policy studies. The government departments are too preoccupied with day-to-day work to think of issues beyond immediate time horizons. They often also lack the skills for sophisticated policy research and analysis. However, it is important for think tanks to provide pragmatic and implementable policy options.

Our experience in the last several years suggests that most of our policy impact stories can be attributed to core grants. This is for the following reasons:

- Policy engagement is a complex and painstaking process. We normally use project grants to generate policy-relevant knowledge. However, these may or may not lead to immediate policy impact. Often, the policy environment may not be receptive. Or there could be a change in political or bureaucratic personnel. Therefore, we have to patiently continue to engage with policy-makers. We rely on the core grants for such engagements as these generally go beyond the duration of a project.
- Most of the high-impact government engagements are either pro bono or below the cost of research. Often, the policy-makers do

not have time to go through the complicated process of calling for proposals. They often request institutions to engage pro bono. Moreover, the government grants typically cover only a fraction of the actual cost of research. Therefore, we rely on core grants to take up such high-impact policy assignments.

- The participation in government committees and task forces is a fairly time-consuming process. The government typically provides only travel support but does not cover the time spent by researchers. Think tanks rely on their core support for such engagements.

We now provide a few examples of CSTEP's success stories which can directly be attributed to TTI's core funding:

1. CSTEP worked closely with the Bureau of Energy Efficiency to design and develop the PAT scheme, which was the government's flagship programme to improve the energy efficiency of manufacturing industries.

    While CSTEP developed the required domain knowledge through a project grant from Shakti Foundation, it was TTI's core grant that enabled CSTEP to engage with the relevant policy stakeholders, in the first place. CSTEP's contribution to the PAT scheme resulted in energy savings of 100 billion kWh (~8.67 million tonnes of oil equivalent), which is equivalent to avoiding 31 million tonnes of CO_2, thereby improving the avoided power generation capacity of 5,635 MW.

2. MNRE requested CSTEP to undertake a geographical information system (GIS)-based assessment of India's wind power potential. The government's official estimate was 50 GW. MNRE requested CSTEP to do a detailed reassessment of India's wind power potential, considering new technology wind turbines and different categories of land. It provided an impetus to MNRE to increase India's official wind power potential to 302 GW and provide an impetus to India's wind power programme. The MNRE engagement was pro bono, and CSTEP could work on it because of TTI's core support.

3. The National Security Advisor requested NITI Aayog to examine India's preparedness for indigenous manufacturing of rare earth and energy critical elements. NITI Aayog constituted a committee consisting of CSTEP and other institutions. This committee worked

for nearly a year and prepared a detailed road map for indigenous manufacturing of rare earth and energy critical elements. This report was presented to the National Security Advisor. The government is now acting on these recommendations. This study was pro bono, and CSTEP used TTI core grant to fund its involvement.

4. Recently, the Ministry of Environment, Forest and Climate Change (MoEFCC) has requested CSTEP to undertake studies in India's long-term CO_2 emission pathways, identify a likely peaking year and suggest alternate growth pathways. This is an important and prestigious assignment, which will help inform India's long-term climate policy. However, the government grant is much lower than the cost of research. CSTEP will use its core grants to partly bridge the gap.

BENEFITS OF TTI NETWORKS

CSTEP benefited immensely by being part of the TTI network of think tanks. As a relatively new institution, we learnt from the experience of other leading think tanks in the cohort. The regional meetings and TTI exchange provided us with a wonderful opportunity to rub shoulders with the best in the business. These intangible benefits were as priceless as the core grant itself. TTI stands out in its firm commitment to building institutions.

We are also happy that we actively contributed to the TTI network. We organized the first Regional Meeting in Mysore, India, in 2012. We actively participated in the various funding calls such as Opportunity Funds grants, Collaborative Adaptation Research Initiative in Africa and Asia (CARIAA) and capacity building. We initiated Aditi, a policy research bulletin, which discussed issues of common interest to think tanks. We are presently coordinating the course in capacity building, which seeks to deepen policy research skills in various think tanks.

LOOKING BACK: LESSONS LEARNT

CSTEP has come a long way since the commencement of the TTI grant. Have we made any mistakes? Is there anything we could have done better? The answer to both is 'Yes'. CSTEP started from scratch, and we learnt on the job. Therefore, it is natural to make mistakes. However, we have learnt from these mistakes and moved on.

Setting Benchmarks for Quality

We realized that in our business, quality is a non-negotiable attribute. We learnt the hard way how one mediocre study can cause long-term and often irreparable damage. During the initial days, we were still in the process of establishing our internal quality control processes. By oversight, one short report was published without rigorous quality control. This caused serious damage to the reputation of the organization and led to the cancellation of a contract. We realized that quality cannot be compromised even if there are pressing time constraints. We have now established robust processes to address this challenge.

Aligning Recruitments with Vision

We learnt that it is vital to be selective in recruitments. We learned the hard way that recruiting people with different visions for the organization can pull it in different directions. It is also important to be patient and selective. Often, because of pressure of project commitments, we tend to recruit without due consideration of the candidate's merit and the long-term career road map in the organization. It is better to leave the position vacant than recruit a misfit.

Selection of Projects and Partners

Another important lesson we learned was that we needed to be selective in taking projects. There is no dearth of research problems or funding agencies. In the initial days, when we were short of research grants, we often took up projects without seriously considering the relevance of the project. We soon realized that the availability of funding was not a sufficient reason to take up a project. In hindsight, we could have avoided doing a few studies which did not add much value to the policy discourse. Likewise, it is important to cautiously identify partners who are on the same wavelength.

We now follow a heuristic approach in deciding whether to take up a project. We ask ourselves three questions: (a) Is this among the most important policy problems facing the country? (b) Does CSTEP have expertise to conduct high-quality analysis in this area? (c) Do we have the confidence that we will be able to present the analysis to the highest level of stakeholders? We now take up studies only if we are convinced that the answers to above are in the affirmative.

Complacency Pitfall

It is also important to not let a sense of complacency creep into the organization. In any start-up, there is lot of energy and passion in the initial days. Often, the founders' vision and commitment drive the organization. However, with time, as the organization grows, there is a tendency for complacency to set in. The biggest challenge is to translate the founders' vision into a collective institutional vision. This takes time and effort. It can only be achieved by repeated discussions with the research staff. In CSTEP, this is still a work in progress, and we have to continuously set higher standards for ourselves. We also continuously remind ourselves that we exist because there is a policy problem, which requires a solution. Therefore, the policy problem is more important than our immediate and narrow interests. Hence, there is no space for intellectual arrogance.

FUTURE ROAD MAP

Where does CSTEP go from here? We have now completed a decade of our existence. While we are happy with the progress made by the institution, we are not satisfied. CSTEP's vision is 'To be the foremost institution in policy innovation and analysis'. We want to establish a 'CSTEP brand', which is synonymous with the highest quality of research. While we have achieved credibility, and are counted among India's leading think tanks, we are by no means the foremost institution, yet. However, the institution has a lot of potential, and the young research staff is enthusiastic and passionate. Hence, we are confident that CSTEP will blossom into an outstanding institution, and make meaningful and significant contributions to India's policy challenges. The following sections articulate our plans to achieve these objectives.

Developing Thought Leadership

In our experience, a think tank distinguishes itself from other institutions by providing thought leadership. Typically, researchers working on various projects acquire domain knowledge and subsequently provide thought leadership. However, we learned through experience that this can trap us into working only on 'project mode'. Considering that project grants provide sustenance to an institution, the researchers spend considerable time working on projects. However, as the researcher moves from one project to another, their knowledge in that domain ends with the completion of the project. Similarly, the researcher's immediate focus is to satisfy the funding agency's requirements. They lose track of the larger policy landscape, and often forget that their main stakeholder is the policy-maker; the funding agency is only an enabler.

Our aspiration is that CSTEP should continuously provide new and out-of-the-box policy ideas to policy-related and societal challenges. CSTEP should develop and nurture thought leaders who can provide fresh ideas to complex policy challenges. Therefore, there has to be a conscious effort to develop domain knowledge, going beyond the immediate project requirements. We recently undertook a detailed exercise in which we worked with our research staff and developed a long-term strategic plan for each research domain. We identified the areas where CSTEP can carve out a niche for itself. Our focus is to strengthen our knowledge in these areas and make important policy contributions.

Innovative Research Themes

CSTEP's main focus lies on how to use emerging technologies for the benefit of society. There is rapid progress in technological innovations in every sphere. For instance, AI technologies are growing at an exponential rate and are already impacting every aspect of human life. We believe that AI provides an opportunity to address India's complex developmental challenges, which are too large to be solved by conventional linear solutions. AI can potentially make game-changing interventions in education, agriculture, health, nutrition, managing natural disasters, etc. We have taken a conscious decision to initiate a long-term research programme in AI. We have already initiated a

project which uses AI to improve the delivery of child nutrition programmes in Karnataka. We plan to expand our work in other sectors,
such as public health and education.

In addition, we continue to extend our work in India's climate
policy landscape. We are working on several studies which attempt
to answer the question: Can India demonstrate a new and alternate
model of growth in which economic development is decoupled from
fossil fuels? India's experience will have profound implications for
other developing countries and will change the discourse in the global
climate policy debate.

FUNDING

CSTEP has grown rapidly and diversified its funding base. However,
there are two aspects of concern. One, most of CSTEP's funding comes
from international donors (Figure 12.2). This makes CSTEP vulnerable
to the vagaries of the global economic landscape. Moreover, since our
stakeholders are the government and society, ideally our funding should
mainly be from domestic sources. Two, our operations crucially depend
on the two core grants from TTI and Oak Foundation.

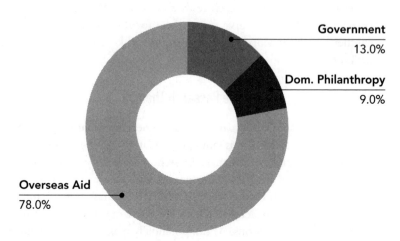

Figure 12.2 *Share of Government, Domestic and Foreign Funding
in CSTEP's Cumulative Funding*

It is, however, difficult to raise significant grants from the government. Therefore, engaging domestic philanthropy is crucial for the sustainability of Indian think tanks. Corporate entities have substantial potential funds available under their corporate social responsibility initiatives. However, they have to be convinced of the value proposition of think tanks and the need to invest in institution building. Going by past experience, this is a difficult task. However, this effort will have to start in order to develop a vibrant think tank ecosystem in India.

If the foreign philanthropies are willing to support Indian think tanks, it is time that the domestic philanthropy and the government do the same. One thought is to have a 'TTI-type' model, with domestic philanthropy. As the TTI grant is coming to an end in 2019, our immediate task on hand is to work on these alternate funding models.

We look forward to the day where we wake up to find an advertisement in our newspapers, placed by a local philanthropist, calling for applications from think tanks. At that time, thanks to the TTI grant, we will be adequately prepared to respond to the call and no longer be the wild-card entry we once were.

Chapter 13

Indian Institute of Dalit Studies

G. C. Pal and Sanghmitra S. Acharya

INTRODUCTION

The Indian Institute of Dalit Studies (IIDS) was established in 2003 to understand the problems of the marginalized groups, identify the causes of their marginalization and initiate policy engagement with different stakeholders to suggest policies for their empowerment. As a young policy research think tank, the institute came into existence at the time when there was growing recognition of a visible knowledge gap on the problems of excluded communities in India. Although there were a lot of debates and discussion on the problems of excluded groups, very often, these were not grounded on evidence.

With the mission centred on the study of 'marginality, social exclusion, social justice and inclusive policies', the institute came up with a specific research agenda revolving around certain key questions. Among others, some of them are as follows: What is the status of various marginalized groups in India, particularly Scheduled Castes (SCs; Dalits), with respect to human development indicators? What explains high poverty and underdevelopment among marginalized groups in India? Why social discrimination and exclusion, and violence and atrocities, against marginalized groups in general and Dalits in particular are unabated despite the provision of non-discrimination in the Constitution and specific legislation to deal with such gross human rights violations?

How do these human rights violations deny equal rights and entitlements, and result in deprivation and low development? Are there lessons from groups facing similar problems in other countries? What policies are necessary to address the problems of excluded groups in India? What knowledge support needs to be provided to various stakeholders so that they get effectively engaged with the issues of excluded groups? How to enhance the research capacity to undertake research on the issues pertaining to socially excluded groups?

However, the institute had enormous challenges in the pursuance of the research around the above questions. These mainly ranged from lack of infrastructure facilities to adequate resources and research capacity to conduct research on sensitive issues pertaining to marginalized and excluded groups. The research of the institute, therefore, came in stages. At the beginning, research focus revolved around Dalits and a few neglected themes. Given the challenges of lack of conceptual and methodological frameworks to understand the problems of socially excluded groups in India, the research work, however, heavily relied on the concepts and methods developed in other countries, particularly in the USA, in the context of excluded groups, of course with required modifications to make it relevant to the institution of caste, in particular.

These early research on discrimination and exclusion provided new insights into causes of inter-group disparities and gaps between an excluded group of Dalits and the rest. When the institute was able to validate certain research methods, it also extended its research to new themes around the core issues of marginalization, discrimination and exclusion associated with the social identities of caste, religion and other similar identities. This new body of research had definite policy implications. This drew the attention of various stakeholders, including few ministries. It also influenced the research agenda in universities and research institutes. The visibility of the institute as a policy research think tank increased. But the hardships in terms of resources and research capacity still continued. This was the time when the Think Tank Initiative (TTI) grant happened. The TTI support helped to take the institution's research agenda forward. IIDS had a renewed journey since then. The grant in the first phase of TTI brought some stability to the institute. In the course of the TTI grant period, IIDS has built on new initiatives and has achieved considerable success along the three pillars of TTI framework: research quality, organizational performance and policy engagement, and has been able to establish as a premier institution in the country.

RESEARCH QUALITY

Over the years, the institute has expanded its research both horizontally and vertically aligned with its vision. It has been able to undertake research in new spheres of the market and non-market discriminations such as employment, entrepreneurship, education, health and urban housing, and existing government policies and programmes for the socially excluded groups. It has also extended its new research on other excluded groups that include Scheduled Tribes (STs; Adivasis), nomadic and denotified tribes, differently abled, religious minorities, ethnic minorities, Dalits among religious groups such as Christians and Muslims, women and youth from socially excluded groups, sanitation workers, urban migrants and urban poor. Moreover, there has been a special research focus on new policy issues for excluded groups. The institute has undertaken several policy studies. Some of the policy studies in the context of recent policy debates include the following: impacts of reservation on marginalized communities, dimensions of caste-based violence and atrocities and its implications for laws, effectiveness of budgets for marginalized groups such as SCs and STs under Sub Plans, implementation gap in Sustainable Development Goals (SDGs) and role of policy research institutions in health-related SDGs. The research expansion has enabled the institute to fill the knowledge gap to an extent in areas of social exclusion, discrimination and inclusive policies, and to recommend appropriate group-specific policies for the development of excluded groups.

The TTI support enabled IIDS to evolve specific mechanisms to assure research quality. This was possible through providing stability to existing research staff, appointing professor-level adjunct faculty and scholars with specialization in advanced statistical techniques and strengthening the necessary research infrastructure. Besides, IIDS took initiatives for conducting specific capacity-building programmes to improve competencies and skill levels of the institute's researchers in new thematic areas, tools and techniques of research; promoting academic dialogue through special lectures on research focus of the institute; encouraging and providing financial support to researchers to participate in various academic events organized by other organizations on research areas of the institute; and providing opportunities for collaborative research initiatives and interacting with a number of civil society organizations at the community level and participating in policy advocacy.

As a part of its mandate to build research capacity of young researchers, the institute has conducted research methodology training programmes for the researchers in other universities/institutes to develop competencies in undertaking research on various aspects of social exclusion, discrimination and inclusive policies. Further, the institute has provided opportunities to young scholars from colleges and schools for internships to develop sensitivity towards the problems of excluded groups and have experiences of fundamentals of doing a research on these groups.

The institute has strengthened its institutional research capacity through the innovative strategy of expanding Community of Researchers (CoR), which is a network of researchers, distinguished scholars and experts from research institutions and universities in India and other countries working in the field of social exclusion, marginalization and inclusive policies. The CoR has been directly or indirectly involved in IIDS research on a wide range of themes and contributes to conceptual and methodological issues of social exclusion and policy engagement. Such a collaborative network has facilitated the institute to undertake more field-based research, evolve methodology on different dimensions of social exclusion and develop a new body of knowledge.

The institute has also strengthened its research infrastructure through a large collection of books on various aspects of inequality and exclusion and research methodology; strengthening the institute's data bank through purchase of new data sets from various sources on the issue of group disparities and field-level data on new marginalized groups and thematic areas based on large-scale household surveys; subscription of new journals; and collection of government documents and other study materials. In addition, the institute is reasonably equipped with technological facilities for the documentation process, and researchers are provided with essential technological facilities and essential service conditions. All these have contributed immensely towards improving research efficiency and capacity of researchers and, in turn, research quality.

The research quality is also ensured through formal and informal quality assurance mechanisms involving multiple review processes. The institute monitors the quality of research through the Research Advisory Committee as well as Project Advisory Committees. With the expansion of research on new areas and quality assurance mechanisms in place, the institute has been able to increase its research publications in various refereed academic journals besides publications of books by internationally reputed publishers. It also publishes two journals: *Journal of Social Inclusion Studies*, a peer-reviewed (biannual) interdisciplinary academic journal in English, and *Dalit Asmita*, a quarterly journal in Hindi with a focus on Dalit literature and arts. The former is published by SAGE in 2018. These journals have increased the institutional visibility on the issue of social exclusion and inclusive policies.

Within a short period of about eight years of TTI, the institute has considerably increased its research outputs and research publications. By the end of 2017, TTI support had covered about half of the total journey of the institute. How the support has helped to move closer to its research agenda could be understood from the research outputs before and during the TTI grant period. As per the institute's document 'Research and Publication—2003–17', the average number of research studies per year completed during the TTI period (2011–2017) increased than the earlier period. The increase was significantly higher for the research on the themes of 'discrimination and exclusion' and 'policy issues', more than twice and thrice respectively. However, there was not much change in the 'status studies'. Moreover, the TTI support enabled to take up more empirical research on the issues of discrimination and exclusion, and national policies and programmes, for marginalized groups. Similarly, expansion of research on new marginalized groups was visible from the increase in research on women from marginalized groups, STs and religious minorities. New studies were also carried out on groups such as Other Backward Classes (OBCs), differently abled, denotified tribes, adolescents and ethnic minorities. A glimpse of the change in the theme-wise number of research studies before and after the TTI period is illustrated in Table 13.1.

Given the expansion of research on new themes and new marginalized groups during the TTI period, the research publications of the

Table 13.1 *Percentage Change in Theme- and Group-Wise Completed Research Projects Before (2003–2010) and After (2011–2017) TTI*

Theme-Wise Research				Group-Wise Research			
Broad Themes	N	Before	After	Groups	N	Before	After
Status studies	47	42.6	57.4	SCs	16	68.8	31.2
Discrimination/ exclusion studies	33	33.3	66.7	Women from marginalized groups	4	50.0	50.0
Policy studies	29	24.1	75.9	Religious minorities	5	40.0	60.0
Collective action and governance	14	71.4	28.6	Others[a]	11	9.1	90.9

Source: 'Research and Publication—2003–17', IIDS, New Delhi.
Note: [a]Others include STs (Adivasis), OBCs, differently abled, denotified tribes, adolescents and youth, and other ethnic groups.

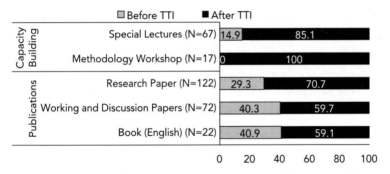

Figure 13.1 *Percentage Change in Publications and Capacity-Building Programmes Before (2003–2010) and After (2011–2017) TTI*
Source: 'Research and Publication—2003–17', IIDS, New Delhi.

institute in the forms of books and working and discussion papers and publication of research papers in edited books and journals disproportionately increased (Figure 13.1). As a part of the capacity-building initiatives for undertaking research on the issues of discrimination and exclusion, 17 research methodology workshops were organized. Of these, eight were organized for faculty and senior researchers from other universities and research institutions working on the issues of IIDS-focused research, and IIDS researchers also participated in these programmes. In fact, all the capacity-building programmes of IIDS were organized during the TTI period. Similarly, the number of special lectures increased by about six times. Moreover, paper presentation by the institute's researchers in national and international seminars/conferences increased about five times after the pre-TTI period. This has enabled them to strengthen their academic network with other researchers working on similar research themes.

ORGANIZATIONAL PERFORMANCE

The institute has been able to strengthen its overall organizational infrastructural facilities. It has been housed in two places to equip with the increase in the human resources. As mentioned earlier, it has been able to update its essential research infrastructure and other technological facilities to facilitate its research and teaching activities. Staff members have been provided with better service conditions through various welfare measures. The regulatory framework has been ensured through governance manuals. External auditing on a quarterly basis strengthens the financial matters of the institute. Administrative and financial personnel have been provided with opportunities to participate in capacity-building programmes to enhance their work-specific skills.

The institute has taken up specific initiatives at managerial and governance levels to ensure operation of day-to-day institutional activities and develop strategies for mobilization of resources. An administrative and finance advisor has been hired to manage the day-to-day administrative and finance matters. Besides the governing board at the helm of the governance, other committees address specific issues. While the institutional leadership takes initiatives to monitor the organizational performance, periodic local management committee meetings and staff meetings promote the accountability of staff members to achieve the targets of the institute.

POLICY ENGAGEMENT

Policy engagement has been a critical component in the structure of institute's research programmes. With the increase in institutional collaborative network, the scope for the dissemination of research output with larger audience has increased. The institute has set up a specific unit to deal with policy engagement activities. It has taken strategic initiatives for policy influence through various communication channels which include development of policy documents (policy briefs/memos/notes and other summary papers based on policy-research), targeted meetings with policy-makers, and engagement in policy discussion and debates. In addition, the institute has used networks and different platforms to disseminate research outputs with academics, international non-governmental organizations (INGOs) and policy advocacy communities at local levels. Such engagements contribute towards not only policy formulations on developmental issues for marginalized groups but also capacity building of organizations involved in human rights issues and policy advocacy at grass-roots level. Efforts have been made to initiate policy dialogue with key stakeholders and strengthen policy linkages through research-based knowledge support. As a result, the institute's research has increasingly been recognized as policy-relevant that has targeted governmental planning related to discrimination, social exclusion and inclusive policy.

With the increased focus on policy research and policy engagement during the TTI period, the institute has been able to bring a large number of policy briefs/memos for policy actors and other policy advocacy materials for civil society organizations. As a part of dissemination and outreach initiatives, the institute has organized about 50 seminars/workshops/roundtables, which has been significantly higher than the pre-TTI period. The change in the policy engagement outputs are shown in Figure 13.2.

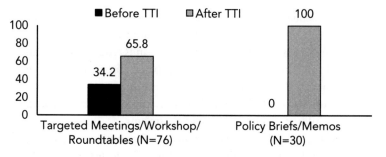

Figure 13.2 *Percentage Change in Policy Engagement Outputs Before (2003–2010) and After (2011–2017) TTI*

Source: 'Research and Publication—2003–17', IIDS, New Delhi.

POLICY IMPACTS

While the research of the institute has had a significant influence on policy, it cannot be fully traced because the research findings in effect become public goods over which the original researchers lose control. However, the institute, through timely input of research-based evidence, has assisted the government in the development of a few policies in recent times while playing a part in other policies as follows:

- *Affirmative Action in Public Procurement Policy for Scheduled Caste (SCs) and Scheduled Tribes (STs) in Micro and Small Enterprises (MSEs), 2012:* The institute's research emphasized on the need to support enterprise for SCs and STs. This led to a policy formulation by the Ministry of Social Justice and Empowerment that mandates public sector units to make 20 per cent of their purchases from MSEs owned by the SCs and STs.
- *Prevention of Caste-based Discrimination in Higher Educational Institutions Regulations by UGC, 2012:* The institute's research evidence emphasized on a need to ensure that SC and ST students are protected from discrimination and harassment in higher educational institutions. Academic support provided by the institute enabled the Ministry of Human Resource Development in formulating the policy guidelines for the prevention of caste-based discrimination, harassment and victimization and promotion of equality in higher educational institutions. This led to a formal gazette notification to develop an 'Equal Opportunity Cell' in all central universities.
- *NCERT Teacher's Training Module to Address Caste-based Discrimination Inside Schools and Classrooms, 2013:* Taking a note of the institute's research on discrimination experienced by Dalit children in schools, the Ministry of Human Resource Development issued guidelines against such caste-based discrimination. These guidelines ask states to take corrective measures and set up redressal mechanisms to address caste-based discrimination experienced by Dalit children inside schools and classrooms.
- *Strengthening and Leveraging Panchayati Raj Institutions for Effective and Non-discriminatory Delivery of Public Goods and Services, 2013:* The Ministry of Panchayati Raj took cognizance of the institute's

research on problems of the excluded groups in accessing public services and rural governance to make policy suggestions for non-discriminatory delivery of services in panchayati raj institutions.

In addition to the above policy influence, the institute's research has also informed to inclusive planning for SCs and STs in the Twelfth Five-Year Plan. Research on the access to and utilization of the government's national flagship programmes among socially excluded sections has drawn the attention of the government to take steps for delivery of services in a non-discriminatory manner. Similarly, the study on agriculture productivity in India and the concerns of the SC farmers has influenced the number of donor framework and strategy. The Food and Agriculture Organization's Country Programming Framework (2013–2017) for agriculture and rural development has been one such influence. The study on 'socially inclusive growth' has helped United Nations Development Programme (UNDP) to develop a strategy in funding pro-poor growth in India. The study has also influenced the World Bank's Country Program Strategy (2013–2016) for India, with a focus on the need for a comprehensive strategy to address discrimination faced by Dalits, especially in the sale of consumer products in rural markets. It also includes planning for the challenges faced by unequal benefit distribution based on caste and gender, among others. Based on the research outcomes on excluded groups, the institute has provided policy inputs to post-Millennium Development Goals (MDGs) 2015 discussion. The publication of the findings of the research on 'discrimination of Dalits and Muslims in urban housing market' has generated a lot of debate at various levels, drawing attention of the Ministry of Social Justice and Empowerment. This has also led to the filing of a public interest litigation (PIL) in the Supreme Court, demanding to frame a law against discrimination in the urban rental market. The Government of India passed the Scheduled Castes and the Scheduled Tribes (Prevention of Atrocities) Amendment Bill in December 2015. Before this bill was passed, the institute had shared findings of its series of research studies on caste-based atrocities with the Ministry of Social Justice and Empowerment. The institute, as a member of the National Confederation on the Amendments Bill, had also provided knowledge support to civil society organizations at various national consultations to strengthen the advocacy campaign on the Bill. The engagement partway had contributed towards formulation and passing of the Amendment Bill.

RECOGNITION AS THE RESEARCH INSTITUTE

The expansion of research agenda in the aftermath of TTI and, in turn, generation of new knowledge on the core issue of social exclusion and inclusive policies, and strengthening of its research and organizational capacity, increased the institutional visibility as a resource centre on the issue of social exclusion and inclusive policies. Taking the cognizance of the contribution of the institute towards this specialized area of social science research, the Indian Council of Social Science Research (ICSSR), through a rigorous process of selection based on research performance, recognized the institute under the new category of 'ICSSR Recognised Research Institutes' in 2014. Now, IIDS is one of over 30 ICSSR recognized research institutes in India. With the recognition, it receives financial support from ICSSR in the forms of PhD, postdoctoral and senior research fellowships, and also other academic supports for research and capacity-building activities. Further, recognizing the research expertise of the institute in the areas of social exclusion and marginalization, the Ministry of Human Resource Development through ICSSR has set up a Sub-Plan Research Centre at IIDS with an annual budget allocation to take up the responsibility of carrying out studies for identifying priorities of investments under the special component of Scheduled Castes Sub Plan (SCSP) and Tribal Sub Plan (TSP).

ACADEMIC RECOGNITIONS

With the recognition of the contribution of the institute in the fields of discrimination, social exclusion and inclusive policies, IIDS is bestowed with international academic recognitions, particularly during the TTI period. In 2010, the Economic and Social Research Council, UK, recognized the institute as a 'Centre with Potential for Excellence'. The institute got the recognition as an 'Emerging Centre for Social Science

Research' in 2011 by the South Asia Research Hub, Department for International Development, UK. In 2017, IIDS was identified as one of the 'Centres of Excellence under the Global Index of Think Tank among the 729 Think Tanks in the World and 20 Think Tanks in India' by Worldinz under the Think Tanks and Civil Societies Program, University of Pennsylvania. The institute is also identified as one of 'India's Most Admired Think Tanks' by *Education World*. These academic recognitions complement the institute's status as a policy research institute.

INSTITUTIONAL COLLABORATIONS

The institution has been able to strengthen its collaboration with other institutes and universities in India and abroad, particularly in Phase 2 of TTI. It has also collaborated with other international organizations. In this direction, there has been a formal agreement with some international research centres/universities such as the Heller School for Social Policy and Management in Brandeis University, Waltham, MA; University of Massachusetts Amherst (UMass Amherst), Amherst, MA; and British Academy, University College of London (UCL), Bloomsbury, in 2015, and Mahamakut Buddhist University, Bangkok, and University of Wisconsin-Eau Claire in 2016. These collaborations have created space for understanding social influences that aid or constrain inclusive policies and promote global academic dialogue to promote inclusion. Given these institutional arrangements, IIDS aims to undertake collaborative research and educational programmes of mutual interest and benefit and to strengthen the international character of the institute.

PhD PROGRAMME: A NEW INITIATIVE

The ICSSR recognition has created new opportunities for the institute to conduct its PhD programme in social sciences from the year 2016–2017 as per the norms and guidelines of the University Grants Commission of the country in affiliation with the Indira Gandhi National Tribal University (IGNTU), one of the central universities in India having a special focus on educational development of marginal-ized groups.

The PhD programme aims to provide high-quality academic training to scholars and prepare them as distinguished researchers in the areas of social exclusion, discrimination and inclusive policies. Setting up of the PhD programme has strengthened organizational capacity in research and teaching. The institute has developed an innovative course structure and methods of course transaction. There are two core courses: (a) interdisciplinary perspectives on inequality and discrimination and (b) research methodology to study inequality and discrimination. While the first course aims to enable scholars to understand the concepts of equality/inequality from the lens of social exclusion/discrimination through interdisciplinary perspectives, the second one aims to provide an understanding of general techniques besides other methods as how to study inequality, exclusion, discrimination and marginalization based on group identities. The institute, based on past research, has identified some emerging areas of research as 'optional courses' to enable students to pick any one of the research areas depending on the discipline and areas of interest. The courses have been designed to be predominantly interactive in nature where course transaction has a specific focus on discussions, reviews of book(s) and articles, presentations of assignments and research workshops. Besides, guest lectures by experts in the areas of the courses from other institutes/universities are organized periodically to develop critical thinking. The PhD scholars are also required to participate in various institutional academic events and in filed surveys conducted under institutional research projects to develop a strong orientation towards research in the areas of discrimination, exclusion and inclusive policies.

CHALLENGES AND ISSUE OF SUSTAINABILITY

Despite its success in the areas of policy research and policy influence, there are several potential risks in which the institute conducts its research and other activities. It functions in an atmosphere which is turning less encouraging to give due space to areas of institute's research focus. Given the discouraging sociopolitical situation to work on sensitive issues such as discrimination and social exclusion, especially with respect to specific marginalized communities such as Dalits and religious and ethnic minorities, the institute has to work with caution in carrying out research and disseminating the evidence. In the context of the new financial policy of the government, raising funds from international donors remains a critical issue. As a young organization, IIDS is still in the nascent stage of establishing itself; hence, it foresees challenges of building long-term support to secure a financial stability. All the constraints related to institutional stability are likely to pose many research and policy challenges in future.

Despite potential challenges, the institute looks for ways on the issue of its sustainability. Given an increasing demand for understanding group-specific problems and developing policies to address them, especially under the policy agenda of 'inclusive growth', the institute envisages to play a significant role in providing knowledge input in the areas of exclusion and inclusive policies to different stakeholders, the way it did in the past. It may draw attention of the government for the possible knowledge support from the institute. The international academic recognition that the institute has received recently has created the potential to engage with possible donors including corporate sectors. The institute also sees potential in collaborations with other organizations located within and outside the country in generating an endowment grant. Over the years, it has received support from various international donors; hence, it explores possibilities of receiving fund through project proposals.

LOOKING AHEAD

The institute has come a long way since its establishment in the initial days of the current century. It has witnessed enormous hardships in early years to conduct research on sensitive issues pertaining to marginalized and excluded groups. However, through the determined efforts and generous support from different originations, it has served the cause of the excluded and marginalized groups. With the TTI support, it renewed its journey and took new research initiatives. Over the years, it has achieved considerable success along the line of research quality and policy influence, in particular. The new body of knowledge created through research has had definite policy implications. It has drawn attention of various stakeholders in academic and policy domains.

It has received academic recognitions for its contributions towards unexplored areas of social science research and policy influence. The visibility of the institute as a policy research think tank has increased over the years. It has been able to establish as a premier institution in the country in the areas of discrimination, social exclusion and inclusive policy. With the introduction of the PhD programmes, the institute is also cognizant of the high expectations of young scholars. Despite the success, in the changing sociopolitical scenario, it foresees several potential risks to undertake various activities in the areas of teaching, research and policy engagement. As a young organization, the institute looks for long-term support for institutional sustainability. However, this modest journey allows the institute to dream of the day that will be socially just and inclusive and will also ensure to 'leave no one behind'.

Chapter 14

National Council of Applied Economic Research

Shekhar Shah*

REJUVENATING NCAER: THE TTI YEARS

These are exciting and challenging times, both in the life of the nation and in the life of an institution that is only nine years younger than the nation. An important part of Prime Minister Nehru's early vision for the institutions that an independent India needed, the National Council of Applied Economic Research (NCAER) was established in 1956 and is India's oldest and largest, independent, economic research institute. It was among several institutions that the Ford Foundation helped set up in India soon after it opened offices in New Delhi in 1952.[1]

NCAER's journey since those early days mirrors India's own evolving development, from central planning to now a vibrant market economy. Starting at a time when little systematic economic data was available about the newly formed states of India, NCAER's work over the years has covered every aspect of the economy. Its mandate

* The support of Dr Samar Verma, IDRC's Delhi-based TTI program officer from its inception, is gratefully acknowledged, as is the leadership of NCAER Senior Fellow Dr Anil K Sharma, who expertly steered the program through the TTI years, and the assistance of my former Special Assistant, Ms Akansha Dubey.
[1] George Rosen, *Western Economists and Eastern Societies.*

throughout has been to gather and analyse the data to assess the effectiveness of public policies in promoting economic growth, opportunity and service delivery. As the world's largest economic and social transformation gathers pace in India, NCAER's focus on evidence for policy-making, enshrined in the 'applied economic research' in its name, has never been more needed than it is today, its use of cutting-edge methods and uniquely focused data never more important.

It is into this mix that in 2010, the 54-year-old NCAER, along with 15 other South Asian think tanks, won its Think Tank Initiative (TTI) award from among 158 applicants from the region.[2] This was a time when independent, domestic think tanks had begun facing greater competition for funding and talent from for-profit consulting and data firms, investment banks, the on-shore arrival of global think tanks and private universities. By the late 2000s, these were all competitive threats, even as they presented opportunities to innovate and adapt.

The arrival of TTI at NCAER could not have been timelier. It coincided with a new phase of NCAER's journey, led by a newly appointed Director-General and an energized Governing Body led by President Nandan Nilekani. NCAER's September 2009 TTI Phase 1 application had noted that 'Our vision is to become one of the leading centres of independent socio-economic research in Asia...' and our 'mission ... [is] to uphold the importance of rigorous, data-based research as a critical, often overlooked input into decision-making and evaluation by both public and private actors'.

NCAER also could not have asked for better convergence between TTI's architecture and our growing aspirations to rejuvenate NCAER. Supported by the promise of TTI's long-term core support, NCAER's 10-year *2020 Renewal Strategy*, first proposed in late 2011 and approved by NCAER's Governing Body in 2012, was a road map for rejuvenation, based on assessing NCAER's analytical and data strengths, its

---

[2] The competitive selection process included proposals, site visits, peer reviews, evaluation by TTI's International Advisory Group and selection by TTI's Executive Committee comprising its original funders—International Development Research Centre (IDRC), William and Flora Hewlett Foundation, Bill & Melinda Gates Foundation, UK's Department for International Development (DFID) and the Netherlands' Directorate-General for International Cooperation.

relationships with governments and industry, its financial model, its competition, its growth potential, and its resilience.

Looking back on these TTI years, the timing of NCAER's TTI grants and the freedom to dovetail core support with NCAER's renewal strategy permitted exploration, piloting, world-class expert advice and learning by doing which would have been difficult otherwise. More than anything else, the TTI support worked to limit the institutional risk from such experimentation, helping NCAER bring about a culture of innovation, learning and resilience that will persist past the TTI years as NCAER continues to adapt to the changing climate for think tanks.

This chapter speaks to the journey NCAER took in the TTI years.

NCAER'S CHALLENGES AS TTI STARTED

The values that have animated NCAER since its creation include a focus on data collection, data quality and empirical methods; a mandate to serve both governments and industry; a commitment to evidence-based research; and engaging with a strong network of policy-makers, academics and opinion-makers. Our logo has the byline, 'Quality · Relevance · Impact'.

Against these values, two challenges stood out at the start of the TTI grant. First, NCAER, surprisingly given its size, had not received significant core support in recent decades, unlike most large Indian think tanks receiving such funding from government or industry. At the start, NCAER had received substantial core funding from the Ford Foundation, the Indian government, other overseas donors and Indian industry, particularly from the Tatas (J. R. D. Tata had been a founding Governing Body member, and Ratan Tata was NCAER's president during 1994–1998). But such funding had dried up, and NCAER had become reliant on shorter-term project funding. In 2010, NCAER had practically no longer-term programme funding, and its corpus had remained small, covering only a small part of operating costs.

The absence of core funding and the dependence on project revenues had some striking advantages, but also disadvantages. It had brought a project-by-project discipline to NCAER, focusing researchers on practical policy solutions. It also ensured that NCAER researchers had an ever-changing mix of work. Funding diversity also discouraged capture. But short-term project funding prevented sustained capacity building and risky upfront investments in new, long-term research initiatives. Sponsors sometimes hesitated to allow NCAER to publish its findings since these often went straight into policy-making, creating the erroneous impression that NCAER research did not have policy impact.

The second major challenge had been the recruitment of high-quality senior and mid-career researchers. Feedback from job candidates consistently suggested that NCAER offered unparalleled opportunities to research public policy. But offsetting that was the poor mobility of Indian researchers, which, combined with the growing competition for talent, was further adding to the problem.

Clearly, NCAER had to do more.

LOOKING BACK: THE TTI DECADE AT NCAER

TTI's designers had fixed on three objectives: enhancing research quality, strengthening organizational effectiveness and improving policy engagement. In all three areas, the decade of TTI support has made a seminal difference to the NCAER of today and is laying a strong foundation for the NCAER of tomorrow.

The shared learning in the TTI South Asia community, much in evidence at the seven TTI Regional Meetings, has shaped NCAER's appreciation of these objectives. Indeed, though not an explicit TTI aim, an unexpected benefit has been the powerful network effects TTI has produced, at least for NCAER.

INTEGRATING TTI WITH NCAER'S 2020 STRATEGY

NCAER's *2020 Strategy* was developed on the foundation of four assets: (a) NCAER's abiding interest in data-driven analysis and its long experience in data collection; (b) the coverage of almost all aspects of the Indian economy under one roof, making it natural to assess policies and programmes comprehensively; (c) its long-standing relationship of trust with government; and (d) its explicit mandate to partner with industry.

The *2020 Strategy* articulated a theory of change in four areas: growing NCAER's human capital, its social capital, its systems and physical capital, and its financial capital. The three TTI objectives meshed well with these goals. Although TTI started before NCAER developed its *2020 Strategy*, NCAER was able to align the two quickly because of the flexibility of core support.

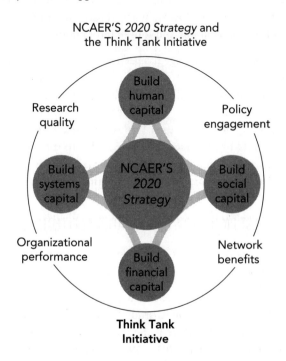

NCAER'S *2020 Strategy* and the Think Tank Initiative

Strengthening NCAER's human capital has had three objectives: creating an environment of excellence that attracts and retains research talent, working in a networked environment and creating the intellectual space for staff diversity.

NCAER also needed to strengthen its internal and external social capital. This meant collaborating more effectively internally and improving external communication.

Strengthening NCAER's systems and physical capital involved investments in IT and communications systems and improving financial and project management systems. NCAER had also drawn up plans by early 2012 to redevelop its centrally located—but by then 53-year-old—campus in the heart of New Delhi into a modern NCAER India Centre, with state-of-the-art 'green' buildings and world-class facilities for NCAER staff.

Finally, NCAER needed to strengthen its financial foundations, including growing its endowment and rebalancing its funding sources towards more core support and longer term grants.

A key integration challenge has been to ensure that the *2020 Strategy* and TTI implementation remain aligned. A mid-course, external validation arrived in mid-2014 in the shape of the news that NCAER had won a Phase 2 grant. The TTI Executive Committee had selected NCAER for 'a grant greater than 110% of the Phase 1 Grant [the maximum that could be requested for Phase 2] due to their appreciation of your organization's high quality research, proactive policy engagement, and the past and potential future contribution to the TTI cohort'.[3]

IMPACT ON NCAER'S ORGANIZATIONAL EFFECTIVENESS[4]

With TTI support, NCAER has invested in all four parts of our *2020 Strategy* to improve effectiveness.

We started with an approach document for a new HR strategy, followed by a pay and benefits study by Mercer, a global compensation firm, and then introduced a new compensation and performance evaluation system in 2013–2014. Work continues on the strategy to ensure market responsiveness. NCAER started recruiting internationally in Phase 2. This has improved research quality and lowered the average faculty age. It has also brought new rigour to our recruitment. TTI has supported capacity building, for instance, through greater

---

[3] Email from Peter Taylor, TTI Programme Manager, IDRC, Ottawa, 2 July 2014. NCAER's Phase 2 grant was 22 per cent higher than Phase 1.

[4] The sections on impact summarize developments on the core objectives of NCAER's TTI grants. Greater detail and data on these developments are available in the September 2014 *Final Technical Progress Report for Phase 1* and the *Annual TTI Monitoring Reports* submitted by NCAER to IDRC.

travel opportunities for professional conferences, time for writing up own research and communications training.

With technology partner Infosys Ltd providing pro bono help, NCAER started implementation of a three-phase IT strategy in 2012, including a new NCAER website, new IT systems and productivity enhancers such as video conferencing. In 2016, with pro bono help from NIIT Ltd, we started a full-scale revamp of our IT and communications infrastructure for the new NCAER India Centre. TTI support enabled us to hire EY, a global services firm, as our internal auditor, tasking it with preparing updated manuals for compliance, human resources, and operations and procurement. A TTI-supported Enterprise Resource Planning system is in the works for streamlining internal processes.

On fundraising, NCAER had modest success in Phase 1 with development work that yielded three generous contributions towards enlarging NCAER's small 2011 endowment and providing reprogrammable support for our construction project. With the decision to delay further major fundraising to leverage the completion of the campus, the focus in Phase 2 has been on longer-term grants and developing funding from corporate social responsibility. As part of this rebalancing, team leaders have also had to invest in new skills of grant writing and reporting and donor relationship management.

The end of Phase 1 coincided with the launching of NCAER's campus construction project. Managing many commercial contracts, regulatory and legal compliances, and large financial flows has led to a significant strengthening of our contracting, procurement, vendor management, accounting and legal skills. This institutional 'battle-hardening' has been an unexpected organizational bonus from our construction project.

IMPACT ON NCAER'S RESEARCH QUALITY

Three aspects of the improvement in research quality spurred by TTI stand out. First, TTI funding acted as venture capital, allowing NCAER to push harder on its own research compared to commissioned work. Breaking from past practice, NCAER started hosting workshops in 2013 on topics where we had made a tentative first entry, or had never ventured before, and no funder was in sight.

Early examples include workshops on macroeconomic modelling and policy analysis, land economics, and household survey research. Such workshops helped gauge policy-makers' interest when policy-makers—including cabinet ministers, parliament members, government secretaries and key international officials—joined them. Often, they led to further work. The workshop on land economics has led to a published volume, innovative grant-funded research on land titling done in collaboration with central and state governments, and now possibly a new NCAER initiative on land policy. The capacity analogue of this venture capital is TTI support for underwriting HR reforms, professional development, staff training, higher-quality international recruitment and better review processes at project entry and exit.

Second, a major shift during the TTI years has been the centrality of our data collection. The vast potential of NCAER's India Human Development Survey (IHDS), India's only national panel data set, has driven home the need to invest in data more systematically. Our older data sets, particularly the Rural Economic Demographic Survey (REDS), continue to be in great demand.[5] To that end, we entered a five-year partnership in 2013 with the global leader in survey methodology and operations at the University of Michigan. We followed that with a similar memorandum of understanding (MOU) with our IHDS partner, the University of Maryland, College Park (UMCP). And we established the NCAER National Data Innovation Centre in 2017 in partnership with UMCP and University of Michigan.

Third, a major change has been the shift in how we approach our research potential and its impact. In that sense, the biggest innovation that TTI has made possible is the spirit of innovation taking root at NCAER, allowing us to think with greater confidence about the journey ahead, what our researchers might need and how we go about getting it while dealing with uncertainty. We are also much less apprehensive about tackling ambitious goals such as creating new centres of research, investing deeply in technology that leverages research and starting a campus

---

[5] The government's *Economic Survey 2017–18* laments the fact that 'the only database on the effectiveness of Rural Local Governments in providing goods and services is the National Council of Applied Economic Research's Rural Economic and Demographic Database (REDS), which has not been updated since 2006–07'.

redevelopment project to alter the physical setting for our researchers, tasks that might have been difficult for us to handle just a few years back. We believe that this confidence comes from a clear strategy and the availability of core funding to innovate, learn and mitigate risk in improving the impact of NCAER's research. It also comes from having our work show increasing policy traction during the TTI years.[6]

IMPACT ON NCAER'S POLICY ENGAGEMENT

NCAER continues to enjoy deep and direct public policy engagement because of our work for government. NCAER faculty often contribute by joining or providing inputs to official policy-making or policy advisory groups and committees. These are usually unfunded time-consuming activities made possible by NCAER's core support. Examples include the Committee on Doubling Farmers' Incomes, Government Accounting Standards Advisory Board, the Prime Minister's Economic Advisory Council, the National Statistical Commission, the Finance Commission, the FRBM Review Committee and the Committee on Public–Private Partnerships in Infrastructure.

With TTI support, NCAER's outreach has broadened into the digital world. NCAER's academic, research and public policy events are now usually web-streamed, and we have strengthened our Facebook, YouTube and Twitter presence. Almost all our reports are published

---

[6] NCAER's Annual Reports to IDRC contain details about the policy impact of our work. Examples include the following: NCAER's Delhi land pooling study that led the Delhi government to implement its new policy; our strategy work for Vision Kerala 2030 has bridged successive changes of state governments; the recommendations of our confidential 'black money' report for the Finance Ministry continue to show up in initiatives to curb illicit funds; the annual Neemrana Conference, in its 20th year in 2018, continues to be the premier gathering of Indian and US policy-oriented economists who regularly engage with policy-makers at the highest levels; N-SIPI, the NCAER State Investment Potential Index, is gaining importance for investors and state and central policy-makers; our work on skilling is reframing the debate on acquiring, matching and anticipating skills; our state-level work on Direct Benefit Transfers (DBTs) is helping the government's DBT Mission to accelerate implementation; and our seminal work on now-casting short-term macroeconomic trends has piqued the interest of market economists, the RBI the World Bank and the IMF.

online and matrix-coded with multimedia links that simplify and bring alive complex policy issues. NCAER publishes two professional journals, the annual *India Policy Forum (IPF) Volume* and the *Journal of Applied Economic Research*. The *IPF Volume* is usually the highest ranked economics journal out of India based on citation counts.

With TTI support, NCAER has organized high-quality communications training for NCAER faculty by global experts on media and interviewing skills, presenting, and giving Ted talks. Our work with a US-based communications firm is teaching NCAER teams the art of crafting persuasive reports. Our multimedia productions have improved dramatically with TTI support.[7] Our grant proposals usually now feature an integral communication package for which we seek explicit support, often involving world-class, strategic communication partners.

TTI'S NETWORK IMPACT

The TTI South Asia community has generated strong positive externalities for its members and for the global funding community. These network effects were much in evidence in February 2018 at the 7th Savar TTI Regional Meeting, where in the final session there was universal support for staying together post TTI. NCAER has been a strong supporter of these network effects, participating in the planning of all major TTI-related meetings and contributing to them.[8]

---

[7] A good example is the Neemrana Conference video that NCAER showed at the 7th TTI Regional Meeting.

[8] In March 2013, at its 3rd Regional Meeting in Marawila, Sri Lanka, NCAER designed and led two sessions: a panel on 'Is There Life After TTI?' and a mock session with TTI directors and IDRC staff reversing roles in responding to a case on 'The Marawila Conclave: Clinching Agreement on a TTI Phase 2'. At the 4th TTI Regional Meeting in Nagarkot, Nepal, NCAER moderated the final plenary session on the 'Way Forward for South Asian TTI Grantee Organisations'. At the 6th TTI Regional Meeting in Bangkok, Thailand, NCAER was also on the final panel and similarly called the 'Way Forward for South Asian TTI Grantee Organisations'. And at the 7th Regional Meeting in Savar, Bangladesh, NCAER led the opening plenary session showcasing each institution's video of the institutional transformation TTI had supported, and thereafter participated prominently in the final plenary panel, 'Do We Meet Again? The Future of the South Asian Network'.

NCAER has also contributed to TTI in other ways. Early on, we posted on YouTube videos of conversations with TTI directors at the 2013 Marawila Regional Meeting to capture the value of core support for them. A 10-minute composite video of these conversations was an important element of IDRC's meeting with the TTI International Advisory Group and Executive Committee in London in June 2013 in deciding on Phase 2 funding.[9]

Illustrating Impact: The IHDS, Public-Use Data for Public Policy-Making

India has a long, pioneering and distinguished history of statistics and survey research. But most official household surveys are single-topic snapshots at a point in time, making it difficult to understand the interplay between economic, social and institutional factors and making the evidence for policy-making over time more tentative. NCAER has been collecting India's only national longitudinal panel data set, IHDS, led by a joint faculty member with UMCP. This is a mammoth, challenging task—for example, NCAER has to translate questionnaires into 13 languages.

IHDS data for 2004–2005 and 2011–2012 have been downloadable from the Inter-university Consortium for Political and Social Research (ICPSR) at the University of Michigan. In the two and a half years before October 2017, more than 7,800 unique users downloaded IHDS-2 data, and nearly 5,470 unique users downloaded IHDS-1 data, making them the second and third most downloaded data sets on ICPSR. Some 360 published journal papers and online working papers had used IHDS data as of January 2018: just in the four years before that date, some 170 newspapers or other media articles using the IHDS have appeared. The Government of India's *Economic Survey 2016–17* used IHDS data extensively to calculate the value of public subsidies in arguing the case for a universal basic income.

---

[9] The video can be viewed at https://youtu.be/d_WdPE0n3RU (accessed on 31 August 2018).

Our grant proposal for IHDS-3 has achieved a perfect 10 score from evaluators in the funding process as we await a final decision. In late 2017, NCAER won a Gates Foundation competitive bid for institutional support to promote data innovation from among 16 national and international applicants and has now established an NCAER Data Innovation Centre.

LOOKING AHEAD: OPPORTUNITIES, CHALLENGES AND RESILIENCE

NCAER's TTI experience, our conversations with the South Asia TTI directors, and our grant discussions with TTI staff and funders have provided incredibly rich guidance on enhancing NCAER's resilience while navigating its post-TTI future. TTI's end in 2019 will coincide with the closing years of NCAER's *2020 Renewal Strategy*. Work will start soon on a new *NCAER 2030 Strategy*, building on the lessons of the TTI years and providing the strategic bridge beyond TTI based on NCAER's changing opportunities and challenges.

For over 60 years, NCAER's 'opportunities' have been shaped by its long-standing relationship with government, its unmatched ability to collect data and its mandate to work with industry. The key to NCAER's future and its resilience will lie in building on all three assets, helped by the tremendous experience and network effects of having been a part of TTI. Some of this building has been under way for some time and has met with modest success; in other areas, there is much still undone.

The rebalancing of NCAER's research portfolio has advanced with several large, multi-year foundation and corporate social responsibility grants now at NCAER compared to when TTI started, for example, in our work on DBT and skilling. A challenge here is to continue this rebalancing without sacrificing NCAER's ability to deliver on high-quality, commissioned research to governments and industry.

A visible sign of our strength in data is the new Data Innovation Centre. Sustaining the centre beyond its three-year support and, in parallel, reviving NCAER's legacy national data sets, particularly REDS and National Survey of Household Income and Expenditure (NSHIE), will remain challenges.

As we get ready to move to our new quarters in the NCAER India Centre, the dramatic change in our physical work environment will present opportunities to change substantially the way we work and our social capital.

Not surprisingly, NCAER will continue to face 'challenges' on talent, outreach and fundraising. There are no magic bullets here. On recruitment, our focus is changing from entry to retention as we continue to build the intellectual environment that mentors talent and offers growth opportunities that motivate staff to stay. Technologies and the reach and limits of social media continue to change and will require public-facing institutions like NCAER to keep adjusting their communication strategy. Persistent hard work, good communications and seizing opportunities without compromising our values will remain the way forward.

Fundraising will remain a perennial challenge for an independent, non-profit institution like NCAER. The TTI years have shown us the power of core support, and through our 2020 Capital Campaign, we have learnt more. Developments at NCAER suggest fundraising opportunities that we have not had before. These opportunities relate to new research programmes that are taking shape with long-term funding, such as the new Data Innovation Centre and other programmes under discussion. They also relate to the physical development of the new NCAER India Centre, which will provide several fundraising opportunities such as naming rights and the revenue streams from sharing our new facilities.

NCAER's 'resilience' will come from both leveraging our opportunities and meeting our challenges. Since NCAER's *2020 Renewal Strategy* and TTI have coincided in intent and timing, the NCAER Governing Body's oversight and continuity on the *2020 Strategy* will ensure parallel accountability and oversight for an orderly conclusion of TTI support and NCAER's own transition to a *2030 Strategy*.

Finally, an important challenge relates not so much to NCAER as much as spreading the key messages of TTI. Core, non-earmarked funding from global donors went out of fashion in the early 2000s. TTI represents a unique global departure from this trend. The Hewlett Foundation initially approached IDRC in 2007 with the idea of TTI, which they then jointly designed, their respective boards approved and the TTI International Advisory Group endorsed in May 2008 in Oxford. Although the vision of returning to core support on a global scale was bold even back in 2008, little could the organizers have imagined that TTI would prove to be such a unique experiment over the next decade, with such dramatic impacts on the think tanks they chose for the Initiative.

Sharing this impact more widely, particularly from South Asia with its 14 TTI institutions, many of which we hope will remain closely affiliated even after TTI ends, is important for the future of core support globally. The challenge is to help grow the community of independent think tanks that can more credibly supply evidence that is high quality, relevant and impactful, at the same time engaging with policy-makers to learn their concerns. Reflecting the global tilt towards populism and the rolling back of evidence-based policy-making, the environment for such productive exchange is worsening. In the time that remains in the TTI journey, it seems vitally important to consider how the TTI institutions should prepare for the possibly difficult times ahead on policy engagement, including after TTI ends.

This will remain a key priority for NCAER. We look forward to working closely with our 13 TTI sister institutions in South Asia and the TTI consortium members to carry this important task forward.

Chapter 15

Public Affairs Centre

Meena Nair and Gurucharan Gollerkeri

INTRODUCTION, CONTEXT AND A BRIEF HISTORY

The birth of Public Affairs Centre (PAC) is a story in itself—it was born to pioneer a tool to measure public governance and help improve it. It all began with Dr Samuel Paul, who after stints as the director of Indian Institute of Management (IIM) Ahmedabad and advisor at the World Bank, decided to settle down in Bangalore. Dr Paul was troubled by the apathy of civic agencies not being accountable for their performance and civil society or citizens not knowing what to do to demand account-ability from them. With a selected group of friends, Dr Paul designed and implemented the first Citizen Report Card (CRC) that comprised a survey of users of various public services and used the data garnered to hold up a mirror to those civic agencies on the quality and adequacy of their services. Thus was born the process of measurable social account-ability of public governance in India. Acknowledging the demand for similar CRCs and recognizing the need to implement and propagate similar social accountability tools, Dr Paul founded PAC in 1994, with a vision to advancing good governance through active civil society engagement. From a two-member NGO that operated from Dr Paul's house, it is today a 30-member strong independent not-for-profit think tank located in its own campus, working at the cutting edge of action research across geographies, populations, sectors, services and schemes.

PAC is one of the 24 prestigious think tanks of South Asia to be represented on the Think Tank Map of the International Centre for Climate Governance (ICCG), Italy. PAC's strength is in engaging the community and leading evidence-based real-world research in sectors that impact society at large. In particular, PAC focuses on multi-stakeholder engagement to ensure that interventions occur at the intersection of the state–market–civil society, for equitable and sustainable solutions. Not only has the centre worked with international organizations such as the Asian Development Bank (ADB), the World Bank and the World Bank Institute, the Bill & Melinda Gates Foundation (BMGF), the International Development Research Centre (IDRC), the Department for International Development (DFID) and the European Union, but it has also worked closely with government at different levels in India on non-funding and funding bases. It is interesting to note that both Government of India and other state governments, especially the Government of Karnataka, have invited PAC to carry out assessments of their own services, displaying openness to constructive engagement and belief in PAC's non-partisanship.

PAC's vision is taken from a statement made by Dr Paul—'a leap of faith, guided by a vision to enhance the quality of our nation's governance through an active interaction of civil society with the State'. This is because the creation of PAC was among the first civil society-led institutional initiatives to mobilize a demand for good governance in India. PAC's mission equally reflects its commitment towards good governance. The Centre's mission is to identify and promote initiatives that facilitate a proactive role of citizens to enhance the level of 'public accountability and performance'.

Advocacy for any cause cannot be successful unless backed by evidence. PAC firmly believes that only evidence-led advocacy involving all stakeholders of a service delivery value chain can lead to change. Evidence comes from rigorous research, and advocacy or action through partnerships with the right stakeholders at the right point of the value chain. However, both research and action require a systematic application of tools that assess and analyse report findings and present pathways for actionable policies.

Table 15.1 *SATs Pioneered/Developed by PAC*

Tool	Explanation
Citizen Report Card (CRC)	A survey-based stakeholder feedback tool for service delivery improvement
CRC+	Enhances the diagnostic power of CRCs by going deeper into the factors that underline the problems, by using internal data from governments
Community Score Card (CSC)	A mixed approach tool using scoring of indicators to assess the quality of service delivery by both communities of users and service providers to create and implement joint action plans
Climate Change Score Card (CCSC)	Systematically integrates information on climate science, governance and livelihoods
Community-Led Environment Impact Assessment (CLEIA)	A community-led participatory tool used to generate and identify possible impacts on the environment of any activity/project
Citizen Monitoring System	A community-based monitoring tool of infrastructure such as roads
Public Affairs Index (PAI)	A data-based framework for ranking the states of India on selected governance indices

Source: Developed by PAC.

PAC has, in its history of more than two decades, pioneered and applied relevant tools that are now part of any repertoire of social accountability tools (SATs) used by development practitioners shown in Table 15.1.

PAC has tested these tools across diverse sectors, geographies, populations and services. The use of these tools both vertically, within various levels of government, and horizontally, across geographies and populations, has helped PAC identify priorities for investments. Such priorities can contribute towards the achievement of Sustainable Development Goals (SDGs). Other agencies have adopted these tools and modified them to suit their specific requirements.

A decade ago, in spite of its rich repertoire of tools and approaches, PAC was still seeking its niche in the development sector—it had a small team, irregular projects, lack of untied funds for carrying out research projects, lack of opportunities for experimenting with new tools, and informal management procedures and processes. PAC'S work lacked visibility. Even though PAC's strength as a credible organization with impeccable credentials and the presence of a stalwart like Dr Paul at its helm was attracting assignments from various funders, they were not enough to meet the centre's needs for growth. In 2009, in response to a call from IDRC, Canada, PAC was recognized as a potential think tank and was invited to be part of the Think Tank Initiative (TTI) managed by IDRC for four years. Responding to a call for Phase 2 of the same initiative, PAC was successfully included in the second phase as well.

WHERE IS PAC NOW?

The funds from IDRC were targeted towards improvement in three spheres of the development sector: research quality (RQ), organizational performance (OP) and policy linkage (PL). During the first phase, PAC paid more attention to improving its RQ and enhancing its OP. These are very well reflected in its operational objectives that it developed in the first phase (2010–2014).

During the first phase of TTI and into the second phase of the same, PAC systematically applied itself to achieving these objectives. Most of the initiatives turned out to be successful while some had to be toned down considering the centre's small pool of talent since it was a conscious decision to confine its employees to not more than 30 to avoid being unwieldy. Some of the successful initiatives were actual application of the new SATs developed with TTI funds in new projects; for example, CRC+ was used in a three-year project on rural sanitation in two states of India funded by BMGF, while CLEIA was applied on roads built under the Pradhan Mantri Gram Sadak Yojana (PMGSY) in a project funded by the National Rural Roads Development Agency (NRRDA); systems and processes in PAC were put in place and new software/hardware acquired to address needs of researchers. On the other hand, while PAC established relationships with various academic institutions, training on governance education had yet to take off.

In the second phase, in conjunction with the IDRC mandate to expand PLs based on improvement in RQ, PAC with technical support from IDRC went through a very rigorous capacity-building programme on policy engagement and communications (PEC). This led to the creation of an independent PEC team that now guides the quality, content and design of PAC's outputs and their targeted dissemination to ensure maximum visibility. A summary of PAC's achievements with IDRC–TTI's support is as follows:

- **RQ:** PAC has been able to successfully add new and influential tools to its repertoire of SATs that include CRC+, CCSC, CLEIA and PAI, and establish a new research group, the Environment Governance Group, that brings together the triumvirate of the state, communities and livelihoods and thus the human element into the technical realm of environment and climate change.
- **OP:** PAC has put in place systems and processes—protocols for all aspects of work (research, fieldwork, publication, communication and outreach), scientific human resource management, and appropriate hardware and software to support RQ improvement.
- **PEC:** PAC has established a three-member PEC team which ensures that all the work that PAC does is visible and engages the right stakeholders. PAC has successfully held workshops, colloquiums, roundtables and lectures and has been able to send its researchers to national and international conferences to present papers that highlight the relevance of primary data collection and the application of those findings in targeted interventions that seek to address challenges related to vulnerable populations and geographies.

The above three pillars helped PAC consolidate its research and engagement capacity in the areas of social accountability of public governance in India and in formulating approaches that help make governance accountable (Table 15.2).

Table 15.2 *PAC's Approaches and Their Applications*

Approach	Applications
Improve the scope and application of CRCs	• Revaluation of its core principles and analysis of similar instruments from other sources
	• Incorporation of fresh elements to arrive at CRC+, a fresh set of tools aiming at review and repair of public systems from a citizen's perspective
	• Application of CRC+ in selected areas of public interest such as environmental management and child rights
	• Promotion of citizen forums with the assistance of other field civil society organizations (CSOs), training organizations and community organizations to test and apply research findings from the application of CRC+
	• Promotion of CRC+ within government systems through active lobbying as well as presentations at key meetings and seminars
	• The positioning of CRC+ as an instrument of research enquiry, a locus for citizen and community organizations, and an evaluation tool
Expand PAC's familiarity with citizen enquiry	• Research and analysis of similar instruments through scanning and exploring potential of other tools such as CSCs
	• Public expenditure tracking systems (PETS)
	• Examine the feasibility of linking critical principles to citizen monitoring initiatives
	• Test fresh tools and instruments developed through above enquiry and research

Approach	Applications
Develop PAC as a think tank	• Review and refresh PAC's staff structure and systems through the establishment of new work groups focusing on new and emerging areas of concern • Strengthen existing work teams through the induction of professional support through consultants and select recruitments to meet emerging gaps • Provide opportunities for teams to interact and establish links with counterparts nationally and internationally • Training opportunities for team members to upgrade skills and meet other practitioners; develop a knowledge centre (online and offline) for the exchange of ideas between PAC and other organizations • Offer fellowships to external scholars to study and apply citizen monitoring methods to their own work
Identify potential areas for implementation of citizen monitoring tools	• Identify partners and engage in project activity including shortlisting of promising areas of intervention where the government is active and which are amenable to citizen monitoring, for example, road and infrastructure monitoring, child rights and environmental impact assessment • Develop appropriate tools and background research on policy and legislative frameworks • Identify donor and resource support for field activity to augment support from IDRC (for research and staff support) • Proposal of development, implementation and monitoring • Engage in policy dialogue with key stakeholders from government and the private sector

(Table 15.2 Continued)

(Table 15.2 Continued)

Approach	Applications
Identify and support critical areas of public policy analysis	• Shortlist promising areas of analysis such as the state of Indian cities and the contribution of the urban poor • Develop research plans and implement them • Present analysis to key opinion-makers at different governance levels
Active lobbying with policy-makers at central and state levels	• Work with policy-makers on emerging areas of public priority including identification of primary areas of intervention (e.g., urban governance and administration, criminal justice and police system reform, employment generation, food security, housing, education, health and child rights) • Prioritize potential areas; systematic engagement with government organizations and policy institutions • Establish common dialogue platforms: seminars, debates and conferences
Establish training resources and opportunities for governance education	• Alliance with national and international educational institutions • Course formulation for specific target groups: academics, policy formulators, CSO teams, etc. • Course delivery and monitoring; identification of resource pool for future training

Source: Developed by PAC.

POLICY ENGAGEMENT AND INFLUENCE: PAI

PAC research products have received widespread recognition from state governments, academics, academic institutions, the media and other eminent institutions engaged in governance. Of the tools that were experimented, peer-reviewed and finalized, the most visible one has been PAI. This unique flagship product from PAC has led the centre along two very critical pathways. First, PAI has made extensive and innovative use of secondary data collected from various sources in the public domain. Second, the use of PAI has challenged the nature of implementation of development policies and made both bureaucrats and elected representatives sit up and take notice.

PAI works on the premise that good governance is the process through which the desired outcomes in terms of better infrastructure, quality education, improved health, accountability, transparency, and law and order are attained optimally; however, measuring the quality of governance poses a challenge. PAC, therefore, pioneered and developed an evidence-based and data–driven framework to rank states on governance with the support of TTI. PAI, besides adding to the discourse on governance, enables one to measure the quality of governance. As a composite index, PAI captures the complexities of governance within and across the states of India. It is a statistical index that ranks the Indian states in standardized metrics, though they are socially, culturally, politically and economically diverse. The index is based on a scale of 0 to 1, 0 being the worst performing state and 1 being the best performer. Using a methodology, based on valid and reliable data, PAI adopts a rigorous process to calculate the PAI scores of the states and to derive their inter se rankings. The quantum of data sets that PAC has used to calculate the index, all drawn from the public domain and largely government data, are humungous, with each data set reflecting the diverse aspects of governance.

Former Chief Justice of India M. N. Venkatachaliah (former chairman of PAC) launched the first PAI report in March 2016,[1] which ranked the Indian states on the basis of 68 indicators, spread across 25 focus subjects, under 10 broad themes. Encouraged by the widespread

---

[1] see http://www.pai.pacindia.org

acceptance of the 2016 PAI report, it was decided to make PAI report an annual series. The grants given by TTI helped PAC in bringing out the second edition of PAI, which was released in May 2017 again by Justice Venkatachaliah. The 2017 report has 10 broad themes under 26 focus subjects and 82 indicators. In addition, PAI 2017 also included a separate study on 'inequality' that throws some light on the patterns of exclusion in India's development story and the widening gap between the rich and the poor. It also examines the social and gender disparities across the states.

The next PAI report was released in July 2018 and examines the quality of governance in the states, and their ranking, using 100 indicators. A special chapter focuses on 'Children of India'.

Since the launch of the PAI series, many eminent institutions engaged in governance such as the NITI Aayog, National Human Rights Commission (NHRC) and Lal Bahadur Shastri National Academy of Administration (LBSNAA), to name a few, have been approached and the findings shared with them. Learning institutions such as the National Law School, the Symbiosis University and the Central University of Rajasthan have hosted the PAC team while detailed presentations were made to their students and faculty.

The quality of this work and its relevance in the realm of governance have led to requests for similar studies across specific sectors and administrative levels. For example, NHRC has assigned a study to measure the quality of compliance of the states of India towards the principles of human rights, which is now ongoing. The Government of Himachal Pradesh has decided to carry the study to the sub-state level for comparison of good governance in 12 districts of the state; PAC is currently executing this project with full cooperation of the Himachal Pradesh government. The Government of Kerala has also requested a similar study, which is under consideration. The Government of Karnataka has expressed an interest to carry out similar indicator-based studies to measure rural development across gram panchayats and the well-being of Scheduled Caste and Scheduled Tribe populations in the state.

It is PAC's hope that this report would enthral students of public administration while at the same time enrich the literature on governance of the country. PAC also envisages that 2018 PAI report would motivate the states themselves to study it and encourage them to do better in the areas where they can make greater achievements. The support provided by TTI helped PAC in this innovative endeavour.

GROWTH AND SUSTAINABILITY

PAC is working towards developing a new business model that will harness multiple funding sources and would take into account the entire value chain of research to advocacy to action, for sustainable change. Some of the changes that PAC has witnessed and hopes will lead to its growth and sustainability are as follows:

- In February 2017, PAC underwent a leadership change, bringing in a new director, who belongs to the Indian Administrative Service (IAS) cadre and is well versed with the government machinery and systemic processes. The induction of the new director has brought in a better understanding of government requirements, as a result of which PAC has been able to successfully pitch for proposals that are critical for the improvement of the quality of life of people in the state. While this is being done aggressively in its home state Karnataka, PAC plans to pursue similar efforts in other states as well.
- PAC is also moving ahead to look for projects in the corporate social responsibility (CSR) space, where there is still a lot of ambiguity regarding projects carried out and the impact that they have had on the ground. PAC plans to move into this space of impact evaluation and recommendation for more effective initiatives.
- PAC continues to respond aggressively to requests for proposals (RfPs) from national and international funders for projects that echo its vision and mission. For this, PAC has also been able to successfully leverage its relationship with other TTI partners across South Asia to pitch for cross-country studies.

A new strategic framework (for 2017–2022) has been approved by its Board of Directors and has led to the reorganization of PAC in terms of groups that will encourage participation of sector expertise. This reorganization is based on the pursuit contributing to the realization of the SDGs. The new groups in PAC reflect the various aspects of development that SDGs reflect—the Development Action Research Group works with two programme groups on SDGs that encompass human development (SDGs 1–7), while the Environment Action Research Group works with two programme groups on SDGs that take into account environment challenges that need to be addressed.

PAC's 'Perspective Plan 2018–19' under the strategy further reinforces the importance of including SDGs into its project frameworks to achieve critical strategic outcomes as follows:

- *Enhancing RQ:* PAC clients will have more ready access to high-quality evidence-based policy analyses, contributing to improved policy discourse and programme interventions on some SDGs.
- *Enhancing policy engagement:* Some government agencies will review and change policies and approaches related to some programmes on the SDGs, on the basis of the evidence generated by PAC through its research.
- *Accountability:* Government agencies responsible for school education, primary health and rural livelihoods seek and respond to PAC inputs for improved participation and accountability in service delivery for achieving their programme objectives.
- *Deep and diversified client base:* With the reorganization, PAC will have an operational structure able to support the full range of planned products and activities; systems that encourage thematic specialization and self-organized groups to form and function effectively; and both core and project resources from a diverse range of clients.

PAC has also set for itself long-term, medium-term and short-term goals to maximize successful implementation of projects through good RQ, new insights and high visibility. To improve RQ and productivity, some institutional measures have been put in place which are as follows:

- Three protocols have been made mandatory—a research protocol, a fieldwork protocol, and editorial standards and guidelines.
- Three teams—RQ, editorial and data—have been constituted to explore new methodologies, products and applications and to enforce rigorous peer review processes.

- Objective performance evaluation criteria have been developed for individuals and team.
- A project proposal tracking system has been established to monitor project mobilization.

Similarly, to expand partnerships and networks, PAC has made efforts to strengthen interdisciplinary partnerships; memorandums of understanding have been concluded with academic institutions in Karnataka and other states as well.

In this trajectory of change, PAC's vision remains unchanged— enhance the quality of public governance through active civil society engagement. PAC's focus will continue to be on the last mile where the state's capacities are the weakest—by engaging in awareness and advocacy to enhance community agency. This means that advancing the data and evidence base through a process of co-generation of knowledge and knowledge sharing, giving voice to communities that are never heard, thus enhancing their ability to participate in the development process not only as a mere beneficiaries but also as active agents of change, mainstreaming gender equal praxis.

The most enduring legacy from the TTI support has been and will be the partnerships between and among think tanks with which PAC has built deep and abiding relationships over the last eight years. PAC has also developed similar relationships with other think tanks in neighbouring countries. The organization plans to continue to build partnerships with aims to contribute to the larger common goals that bind South Asians together.

PART IV

Social Science Research and TTI: Country-Level Synthesis

Chapter 16

Social Science Research and TTI: Bangladesh

Fahmida Khatun

CONTEXT

Since independence in 1971, Bangladesh has made remarkable progress in both the economic and social fronts. Economic growth had reached at 7.28 per cent in the fiscal year 2017, from only 3 per cent in the 1970s. Bangladesh's share in world gross domestic product (GDP) and world gross national income (GNI) has started to rise in recent years. Poverty headcount ratio (at USD1.90 a day, 2011 PPP; percentage of population) had declined from 31.6 per cent in 1983 to 14.8 per cent in 2016. The country has attained near sufficiency in food grain production for its 160 million people and had reduced its population growth from more than 3 per cent in 1970 to 1.16 per cent per annum in 2017. In the 2000s, notwithstanding the global meltdown during the latter part of the decade, and several major natural disasters and political disturbances, the country had attained a GDP growth rate of 6 per cent per annum on an average. The economy has undergone a structural change where the share of agriculture in employment had declined from 69.5 per cent in 1991 to 41.1 per cent in 2016, while the share of services in employment had increased from 16.9 per cent in 1991 to

38 per cent in 2016.[1] The main engine of growth in Bangladesh has been a resilient and vibrant private sector dominated largely by ready-made garments. Merchandise exports had increased by 175.39 per cent during the period FY 2007–2008 to FY 2016–2017, while remittances from overseas workers amounted to USD12.76 billion in FY 2016–2017.[2]

Similar strides have been attained in a number of social indicators. Primary schooling enrolment rate is 109.8 per cent, which also enjoys gender parity.[3] According to the Bangladesh Demographic and Health Survey 2014, 78 per cent of children aged 12–23 months had received all the recommended vaccinations before their first birthday.[4] For the five-year period before the survey, under-five mortality rate was 46 deaths per 1,000 live births, infant mortality rate was 38 deaths per 1,000 live births and neonatal mortality rate, that is, deaths in the first month of life, was 28 deaths per 1,000 live births.[5] The country's remarkable trajectory on the social front has been attributed, in large part, to aggressive supply-driven family planning programmes for reducing fertility as well as to a successful partnership between the government and non-governmental organizations (NGOs) for service delivery in the social sectors. Home-grown development initiatives such as non-formal primary education, micro credit, oral rehydration therapy, and village- and community-level health workers have contributed to reduction of poverty (Millennium Development Goal [MDG] 1) and child mortality (MDG 4).

Despite such impressive progress, the country faces several challenges. High growth has not been able to create adequate employment and income for its population. Data from the Household Income and Expenditure Survey for the period 1991–1992 to 2015–2016 show that the income share held by the richest 5 per cent of households in Bangladesh increased from 18.85 per cent in 1991–1992 to 27.89 per cent in 2015–2016, whilst the income share held by the poorest 5 per

---

[1] International Labour Organization, 'Employment by Sector'.

[2] Bangladesh Bank, *Monthly Economic Trends May 2018*.

[3] Ministry of Primary and Mass Education, *Annual Primary School Census 2017*.

[4] National Institute of Population Research and Training, *Bangladesh Demographic and Health Survey 2014*.

[5] Ibid.

cent of households in Bangladesh fell from 1.03 per cent in 1991–1992 to 0.23 per cent in 2015–2016.[6]

Additionally, environmental degradation and vulnerability to climate change constantly pose a threat to Bangladesh's progress in economic development. While the country has made commendable improvements in its natural disaster management efforts, the need to address environmental concerns as an integral part of the development discourse can no longer be ignored.

Thus, Bangladesh today is at the crossroads. On the one hand, there is a tremendous opportunity to reach the growth potential through diversification and structural changes in the economy, enhanced global and regional integration, and by tapping the potential of a youthful population which can be engaged in new areas of income generation; on the other hand, there remain the challenges of inadequate infrastructure, inefficient regulatory bodies and weak institutions. Given this scenario, it is crucial that the policy-makers and the civil society in Bangladesh together address the challenges faced by the country to enable it to continue to reap dividends of its recent growth trends. As the country is in the process of graduating from the least developed country (LDC) group to become a developing country by 2024 and also aspires to become a high-income country by 2041, there is a need of pragmatic and strategic policies responsive to the emerging realities of the country.

Bangladesh's development potential could be fully utilized through efficient functioning of institutions which protect and promote good governance. However, despite challenges of infrastructural constraints and corruption, the private sector in Bangladesh has demonstrated the resilience to drive the economy forward, while, at the same time, a few think tanks have established a track record in promoting accountability through social research. This effort for conducting in-depth and analytical research on pertinent issues concerning Bangladesh's social and economic development as well as governance is a prerequisite for engaging the public in policy dialogue.

---

[6] Bangladesh Bureau of Statistics, *Household Expenditure Survey*; Bangladesh Bureau of Statistics, *Household Income and Expenditure Survey*.

STATUS OF SOCIAL RESEARCH IN BANGLADESH

The rationale for a home-grown process of understanding the dynamics of development, and a platform for discussion and debate around issues of concern and interest in this context, cannot be overemphasized. This is indeed sine qua non for the various domestic constituencies promoting accountable developmental praxis, transparent policy-making process and inclusive governance, which are foundations of a democratic society. Think tanks are critical players in servicing these demands by generating new knowledge, analysis and evidence. The emergence of think tanks in Bangladesh is a relatively new phenomenon. Majority of the think tanks have come into existence in the post-1990s period which coincided with a juncture in the history of Bangladesh, when, after a protracted period of military rule, a democratic transition was taking place through national parliamentary elections. A new environment for open discussions and free thinking was created following the military rule, as the need for addressing the socio-economic challenges and improving the state of governance were felt most strongly.

However, the trajectory of social research in Bangladesh has been diverse. It has varied in accordance with institutional structures, developed coverage of issues, sources of funds and modality of engagement. Broadly speaking, think tanks engaged in undertaking social research in Bangladesh could be categorized into six types. First, there are a few government-funded research organizations which function as autonomous bodies. Understandably, because of their dependency on government resources, these organizations have limited independence in terms of coverage of issues and focus of analysis. Second, a number of public universities have research institutes affiliated with particular departments and faculties. However, these are limited in scale and size and cover only a limited number of issues. These organizations are supported either by a grant from the university or by external resources or both. Third, the NGOs also undertake social research on themes which fall within their areas of work. Supported mostly by development partners, charitable organizations and also the government, they carry out research as part of, and to support, their policy activism. Traditionally, their focus of research has been on areas such as health, education, environment, gender, human rights, anti-corruption and good governance. However, research capacity of NGOs is limited because of which they tend to collaborate with other think tanks from time to time. Fourth, there are think tanks that design their research agendas as per fund availability and tend to calibrate their views in anticipation of donor priorities and preferences. Fifth, there are think tanks which operate in consultancy mode with the support of donors on contractual research projects. These project reports are not for public consumption, and there is no quality control. Sixth, there are only a few think tanks which rely on programme- and project-specific support from donors, maintaining independence in the design of their own research agendas and policy focus.

Think tanks in Bangladesh have been taking part in policy debate primarily through research, dialogue, dissemination and publication. More specifically, they conduct research; analyse issues and prepare policy papers; publish op-eds, blogs, monographs and books; disseminate research findings by organizing dialogues, seminars and media briefing; and take part in policy debate through social media. The rigours of evidence, analytical depth and policy relevance vary across think tanks. The more credible ones are sensitive to quality issues of their outputs and blend research and outreach in a way that maximizes their effectiveness. The outputs of think tanks are used to raise awareness about public policies among the broader stakeholders and influence policy-makers in designing and implementing policies and programmes. There are think tanks that have considerable prestige and credibility, thanks to their influence on, and ability to mobilize, public opinion and track record of objective analysis and policy suggestions.

However, when views of think tanks do not correspond to views of policy-makers, the latter often tend to take hostile attitude towards think tanks. These relate particularly to issues of macroeconomic management, institutional performance, governance, corruption, etc. However, in general, government's openness and practice of consulting civil society think tanks has increased over the years. For example, the government invites members of think tanks for consultations during the formulation of important national policy documents such as budget and plans or includes representatives of think tanks in various government delegations. However, sometimes government officials are not tuned to a culture of reliance on evidence and research and find it challenging to use analyses of think tanks due to their lack of absorptive capacity. Politicians often tend to view think tanks as rivals contending for sway over public opinion and

support of civil society. The bureaucracy in the country has been increasingly politicized over the years; it depends on political signals for making
any decisions rather. Regrettably, over the last few years, the polarization
has intensified and tolerance of policy-makers to objective criticism has
declined to a large extent. The government has imposed rigid regulatory
measures, including stringent oversight on funding of civil society think
tanks. Hence, maintaining a balanced and working relationship with
the government has become more of a challenge at present. Reputed
think tanks are dealing with the emergent situation by maintaining a
non-confrontational attitude and by ensuring that their activities are of a
non-partisan nature, by being professionally competent and by producing
objective analytical, evidence-based reviews and comments. In all likeli-
hood, some of the aforesaid challenges facing think tanks in Bangladesh
will become increasingly more formidable. In view of the shrinking
space for civil society think tanks, think tanks in Bangladesh will have
to work under a more constraining environment at least in near future.
Hence, think tanks will be required to navigate the emerging situation
with caution and fortitude, by building broad-based partnerships with
other like-minded groups and organizations and being mindful about the
need to maintain high calibre of their outputs and activities. They will
also need to work more closely with print, electronic and social media to
take their messages to the stakeholders in a more effective way.

THE THREE PILLARS OF TTI: COUNTRY SYNTHESIS

One of the ways to improve organizational performance is through
recruitment, retention and capacity building. Most of the think tanks
in Bangladesh are weak in terms of organizational performance. They
struggle to recruit qualified researchers, as research as a profession has
lost its charm among the young generation for a number of reasons.
With the opening up of the economy, opportunities to seek jobs
in the private and multinational companies have increased. Higher
salary and faster career progression in these companies attract a section
of young job seekers. Those who join think tanks usually leave for
higher studies abroad, many of whom do not return to the country.
Other competing recruiters are universities, particularly the private
universities. Currently, there are 144 universities in Bangladesh,
out of which 40 are public universities, 101 are private universities
and 3 are foreign universities (University Grants Commission of

Bangladesh).[7] The advantage of being in the teaching profession is that teachers can be engaged in consultancy to earn additional income.

As for the think tanks themselves, many of them cannot provide predictability to the staff regarding their employment and career path within these organizations. Many think tanks are dependent on one person who is usually the founder, and promising staff members are not groomed to take up senior positions. Thus, they do not feel the need for a strong internal management system to monitor and evaluate individual performance to improve staff performance. Due to the dependence on solely project-based funding, several organizations do not think of improving organizational performance.

Quality of research primarily depends on the quality of human capital of think tanks. The think tank landscape of Bangladesh is mainly oriented towards project-based funding which does not allow for strengthening research capacity of these institutions. The Government of Bangladesh does not have a policy for social science research. Resource allocation by the government for social science research is also inadequate. The government established Bangladesh Social Science Research Council (BSSRC) in 1976. However, this council lacks the capacity to even perform the responsibility of facilitating social science research due to shortage of financial and human resources. In fiscal year 2017–2018, BSSRC received an allocation of little over BDT12.3 million or USD0.15 million.[8] Needless to say, this amount is insignificant compared to its objective to fund students, graduates, teachers, academics, professional researchers and also research institutes.

In order to ensure good research quality, resources for the education sector need to be increased. Unfortunately, the national budget allocates only 2.09 per cent of GDP for the education sector in fiscal year 2018–2019,[9] which is far below the internationally required level.[10] Such resource constraint limits the scope of research opportunities for students at universities which could have been useful in encouraging students to pursue a career in research.

---

[7] http://www.ugc.gov.bd/en

[8] Government of Bangladesh, *Budget of the Planning Division for FY2017–18*.

[9] Government of Bangladesh, *Budget for the Fiscal Year 2018–19*.

[10] Education 2030 Incheon Declaration, 'Towards Inclusive and Equitable Quality Education and Lifelong Learning for All'.

There is no study to understand the overall quality of research in Bangladesh. An indirect way to look at the quality of research is to analyse data on journals available on the Scimago website,[11] which contains publicly available data on scientific journals developed from the information contained in the Scopus database. According to Scimago, Bangladesh is ranked 61st in the world and 3rd in South Asia in terms of the number of published research documents in all disciplines. During the period 1996–2017, a total of 40,985 research documents, in all disciplines, were published in Bangladesh. This accounts for 0.08 per cent of the world and 2.45 per cent of South Asian research output. On an average, each of these research documents were cited 8.85 times, compared to the average of 13.35 times for the world and 9.47 times for South Asia. However, it must be kept in mind that many journals in Bangladesh are not Scopus indexed and are, therefore, not included on the Scimago website. Hence, the actual volume of research output is expected to be higher, although most of the research which is not included in Scimago is of poor quality. Figures 16.1 and 16.2 indicate Bangladesh's position vis-à-vis South Asian countries on published research documents, while Figure 16.3 shows the relationship between number of documents published and citations per document in Bangladesh during 1996–2017.

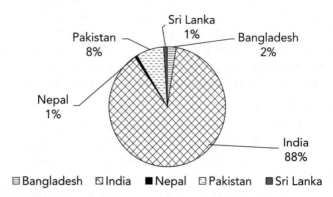

Figure 16.1 *Proportion of Published Research Documents in South Asia (1996–2017)*

Source: ScimagoJR (https://www.scimagojr.com/).

---

[11] https://www.scimagojr.com

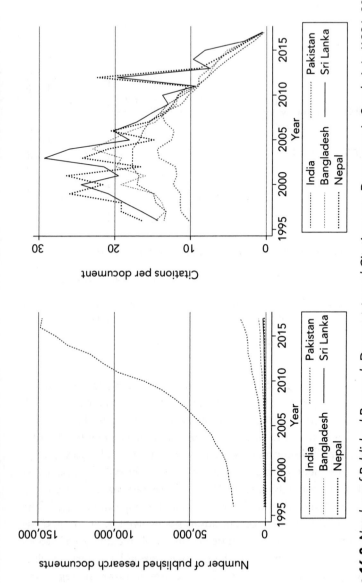

Figure 16.2 *Number of Published Research Documents and Citations per Document in South Asia (1996–2017)*

Source: ScimagoJR (https://www.scimagojr.com/).

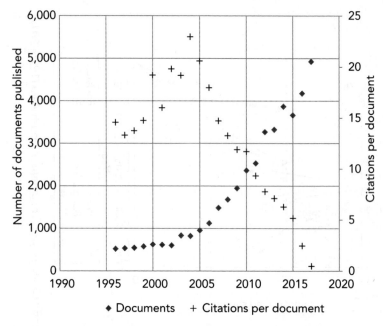

Figure 16.3 *Relationship Between Number of Documents Published and Citations per Document in Bangladesh (1996–2017)*

Source: ScimagoJR (https://www.scimagojr.com/).

The engagement of think tanks in disseminating the findings of research among the broader stakeholders and the government is limited. This is due to both demand and supply side constraints. The government takes note of the work accomplished by only a few think tanks. The business community, academics, researchers, advocacy groups and development partners also draw upon analyses of various issues conducted by some think tanks. Policy engagement has been expanded through various methods. Over the years, the scope and nature of the policy outreach of these organizations has evolved to encompass use of modern communication strategies and tools including web-based dissemination (e.g., streaming, blogs, Facebook and Twitter) as well as television and radio talk shows. These communication strategies and tools have helped the organizations to broaden their regional and global reach. However, such initiatives of policy outreach are undertaken by only a few think tanks. This is not only because of lack of capacity but also because this is not their objective. An effective policy outreach requires an effective communication strategy backed by a modern communication system. Additionally, a pool of staff should be engaged to carry out the activities whose skills should be upgraded on a continuous basis. This involves resource and commitment.

SUSTAINABILITY

Despite flourishing of think tanks, the growing demand for social science research in Bangladesh is not fully met by the existing think tanks. Moreover, the existing think tanks, particularly the civil society think tanks that do not have core support, have to continuously struggle to mobilize resources as project support does not cover their operational costs. Overheads of projects that are undertaken by these think tanks cover an insignificant portion of operational costs. Thus, in the absence of an endowment fund, financial sustainability of think tanks is a challenge. A few think tanks have managed to mobilize a continuous resource flow to carry out their activities, as they have elevated their reputation as think tanks by undertaking analytically rigorous, evidence-based and objective research on areas which are important for socio-economic development of Bangladesh and also by strengthening their organizational performance. Building on the success of their activities in areas of research, publication, and communication and outreach, they explore other funding opportunities.

However, as Bangladesh is on its way to graduate from an LDC, external fund for research may shrink. Think tanks will have to think of innovative ways to mobilize fund for undertaking their activities. Some potential sources for creating endowment fund for think tanks could be national and external philanthropic organizations and the private sector. They can also explore options for bidding on national and external research grants, both independently and in partnership with other national and global research institutes.

Chapter 17

Social Science Research and TTI: India

Sanghmitra S. Acharya, Chandrani Dutta and G. C. Pal

INTRODUCTION

In recognition of the role and importance of social science research (SSR) in India, there have been various initiatives to promote research infrastructure since the independence. The establishment of Planning Commission in 1950 had an immense impetus to the growth of SSR in India. However, it was only during the National Education Commission, popularly known as Kothari Commission (1964–1966), when social sciences were considered as one of the important pillars of social development in the country. While examining all aspects of the educational sector in India to evolve policies for the development of education, the commission envisaged the need for social sciences to be a significant part of the Indian universities and research institutions, and SSR can be a tool to bring social, economic and cultural transformation. The National Policy on Education, first promulgated in 1968, initiated the setting up of the premier institution Indian Council of Social Science Research in 1969 to address the foremost challenge faced by SSR in the country; the two main objectives being funding SSR and promoting institutions engaged in such research activities.[1] The need to

---

[1] Thorat and Verma, *Social Science Research in India*.

promote and fund such institutions arose due to the centralized planning, and the State's role in bringing social and economic development required large amount of data and information of the Indian society.

Over the years, the policy research institutions have grown with a large number of independent, autonomous centres, started under the initiatives of few individuals or a group of like-minded social and political thinkers. With the 1980s, the shift had occurred from public-funded to private-funded research institutions, and the country progressed towards a neoliberal regime in the 1990s. The need for a multidisciplinary approach in policy-making led to the ushering of non-economic social scientists in this domain.[2] With the growth of the research institutions, they also varied considerably in size, structure, policy ambit and significance. Despite the growth of institutes and large number of publications, the question of research quality (RQ) remains a crucial challenge, which is very often attributed to poor research infrastructure in the country. As argued, SSR in India could reach higher levels of standard with capacity enhancements of researchers and improvement of research infrastructure.[3]

However, SSR in India has a relatively moderate impact on policy-making. Policy-makers have engagement with social scientists to enhance the legitimacy of various policies. However, the tendency of the policy-makers to favour certain policies and provide less space for representatives from academic institutions results in a limited number of programmes of the ministries to have SSR references. For instance, review of a total of 52 documents from the Ministry of Social Justice and Empowerment revealed zero citations of SSR studies. There is a similar pattern in other ministries. However, SSR studies remain an important source of reference for various working groups of the Planning Commission and are used for analysis and policy designing. Policy research in universities rely more on self-motivation, while it is commissioned research in case of research think tanks. Moreover, interest in conducting research at universities has been dwindling with young researchers finding more prospects in lucrative non-research jobs on offer, and many a time, think tanks are considered as 'stepping stones' and means of advancement in a researcher's career.

---

[2] Mathur, 'Policy Research Institutions in South Asia'.
[3] Thorat and Verma, *Social Science Research in India*.

Thus, there are several issues to be considered in making SSR in India more relevant. Among others, important ones include the following: making the research more interdisciplinary with insights on policy issues, developing non-technical messages for improved understanding and sharing the research findings with appropriate dissemination strategies. In this, think tanks with a committed mission and vision bridge the gap between academia and policy-makers, while there need to be more impetus on capacity building and strengthening of research infrastructure. Greater attention is, therefore, 'desirable on developing communication links between social science researchers and policymakers to understand the policy priorities'.[4]

In India, many research institutions acquire the role of think tank institutions and mandate themselves with specific goals of feeding research-based policy inputs to the decision-making process and, in turn, become important drivers of change. SSR, therefore, has been an integral part of the system in which the decision-making agencies are located. Some of these institutions engage with economic concerns, governance and human capital, some delve with gender issues, resources, climate and environment, while others take upon themselves the mission to understand perpetual discrimination experienced by some sections of population. Some of these institutions were recognized for their zealous efforts by International Development Research Centre (IDRC) and were brought together under the umbrella of Think Tank Initiative (TTI) with the mandate of enhancing the RQ, organizational performance (OP) and policy engagement (PE). It is but imperative to trek down the memory lane and recap the journey.

This chapter on India would, therefore, try to encapsulate the memoirs of the seven think tanks' endeavour to profile their sojourn of becoming a part of TTI—achievements which were made possible and preparedness towards the road map ahead in sustaining themselves without the generous support under the programme. The untied funds from IDRC were targeted towards improvement in three spheres of the development sector: RQ, OP, and policy linkage (PL). During the first phase (2010–2014), most of the institutions paid more attention

[4] Joe et al., *Social Science Research in India*; Stone, 'Think Tanks and Policy Advice in Countries in Transition'.

towards improving their RQ and enhancing their OP. These are very well reflected in their operational objectives that they developed in the first phase.

RESEARCH QUALITY

Three aspects of the improvement in RQ spurred by TTI stand out. First, TTI funding acted as venture capital, allowing the institutions to push harder on their own research compared to commissioned work. Breaking from past practice, most institutions started hosting workshops on topics which were never ventured before, and no funder was in sight, and were relevant, due to which some institutions had made a tentative first entry. Early examples include workshops, consultative meetings and interactions with policy-makers and dialogue with grass-roots-level workers. Second, a major shift during the TTI years has been the centrality of data collection. The vast potential of National Council of Applied Economic Research's (NCAER) India Human Development Survey (IHDS), India's only national panel data set, has driven home the need to invest in data more systematically. Third, a major change has been the shift in how the institutions approached their research potential and its impact. In that sense, the biggest innovation that TTI has made possible is the spirit of innovation taking root at these institutions, allowing them to think with greater confidence about the journey ahead, what their researchers might need and how they go about getting it while dealing with uncertainty.

The institutions became much less apprehensive about tackling ambitious goals—such as creating new centres of research, investing in technology that leverages research and starting a campus redevelopment project to alter the physical setting for their researchers—tasks that might have been difficult to handle without TTI support for all these institutions. It engrained confidence that comes from a clear strategy and the availability of core funding to innovate, learn and mitigate risk in improving the impact of their respective research. It also was driven by the institutions' work which have shown increasing policy traction during the TTI years. Examples include the following: NCAER's Delhi land pooling study which led the Delhi government to implement its new policy; our strategy work for Vision Kerala 2030 has bridged successive changes of state governments; the recommendations of our confidential 'black money' report for the Finance Ministry continue to show up in initiatives to curb illicit funds; the annual Neemrana Conference, in its 20th year in 2018, continues to be the premier gathering of Indian and US policy-oriented economists who regularly engage with policy-makers at the highest levels; N-SIPI, the NCAER State Investment Potential Index, is gaining importance for investors and state and central policy-makers; work on skilling is reframing the debate on acquiring, matching and anticipating skills; state-level work on Direct Benefit Transfers (DBTs) is helping the government's DBT Mission to accelerate implementation; and seminal work on now-casting short-term macroeconomic trends has piqued the interest of market economists, the RBI, the World Bank and the IMF.

The TTI institutions' objectives around 'RQ' are uniquely designed to promote cutting-edge individual research together with collaborative work and networking through projects and programmes. The value of research is deeply engrained in the institutions' evolutionary history, rigorous scholarship and extensive networks which aim to increase the outreach and communication of research results through policy dialogues and linkages. Mainly undertaken by programmes, projects and individual faculty, these platforms allow the institutions to engage in a diverse range of policy regimes at multiple levels and strengthen the existing research value chain.

The research design for most of the TTI institutions has been based on collaboration within the institutions, as also nationally, regionally and internationally. In addition to SSR networks, they have engaged in setting up dialogues among academics, social movements, NGOs and policy institutions. The Centre for the Study of Developing Societies (CSDS), for example, in the recent years has encouraged practitioners in the domains of culture and environment who have also joined the centre's networks, thus enhancing the range of publics that connect with us. The centre has also innovated in reaching out to a larger public through various offline and online platforms. In addition, such collaborative model offers faculty members and research staff autonomy to scale up and across networks while maintaining scholarly rigour.

This has helped bring in a whole new generation of younger scholars into the network. Developing diverse, cross-disciplinary collaborative platforms across many different publics (academic, activist and policy) can be useful for other institutions.

There are several key areas in which TTI support has been invaluable for thematic research, which include the following:

1. Providing support to existing research projects and programmes that could not get adequate funding elsewhere
2. Supporting individual researchers with grants for conducting research and participating in research-related activities
3. Bringing in visiting scholars to strengthen existing lines of research and develop new ones
4. Acquisition of books, journals and databases
5. Developing an ambitious programme for Indian languages
6. Organization of research activities such as conferences and workshops on a more frequent basis and on a much larger scale than before
7. Developing national and global networks of researchers
8. Publication of journals
9. An expanded teaching programme to train younger (doctoral and postdoctoral) social science scholars

TTI-enabled support also helped the institutions to strengthen their existing programmes—Lokniti and Sarai, two research networks on election studies and on media and urbanism, respectively, are apt illustrations from CSDS. It also helped CSDS consolidate the Indian Languages Programme (ILP), which was started in 2001 with a limited agenda of translating and making available to the Hindi reading public works by CSDS faculty members. Over the years, the programme has been greatly enhanced through TTI support, and it now engages with thinking about the entire question of social sciences and what it might mean to 'do social sciences in Indian languages'. The core idea is to think (a) beyond Hindi, in terms of Indian languages as a whole, and (b) beyond just translations from English and looking at the cognitive challenges of doing social sciences in these languages. Publications, lectures and fellowships are some of the key activities undertaken. An entirely new initiative on studies of 'Indian thought' has been enabled by core support from the Parekh trust.

As a community of researchers, the TTI institutions have enjoyed considerable success in building and strengthening other networks and collaborative research possibilities. They have successfully hosted several national and international exchange programmes and have set up networks for cross-country analysis. Reputed scholars, from India and abroad, have participated in such programmes and events, and delivered public lectures.

Attracting and retaining scholars is a key objective. A major success in this regard has been that some of the TTI institutions could engage in setting up of Visiting Faculty and Fellowship programmes. The TTI institutions undertook this process with great care and deliberation, successfully conducting a wide-ranging public search and extensive interviews to select visiting scholars. The esteem in which these institutions are held by their peers may be seen in the large number of scholars from India and abroad who have applied for these fellowships. Several of these scholars, especially those in the early postdoctoral stage, have subsequently moved on to regular positions at other academic institutions.

The TTI institutions, with a growing network, also include the teaching and internship programmes offered by some of them such as the Indian Institute of Dalit Studies (IIDS) and CSDS. Uniquely designed internship and teaching programmes target research students and independent scholars based in India and abroad. These programmes, started with the TTI support, allow students to critically engage with the formation of the contemporary and its multiple histories, ideologies, forms and affects. The programmes focus on thematic areas to enable participants to familiarize themselves with concepts and theories, and critically engage with different methodologies of analysis. These programmes have been immensely successful, with the number of applications rising exponentially each year. The CSDS' Lokniti programme offers a special summer course on 'Analyzing Quantitative Data on Indian Politics', initially in collaboration with the Indian Institute of Advanced Study (IIAS) in Shimla and currently with Jain University, Bengaluru.

Over the last decade, these programmes have contributed immensely to building research capacity of young scholars, especially those based at universities where such a rigorous methodological course may not be on offer. The research scholars' workshop on capacity building supported by the TTI funds for students of disadvantaged communities has trained the participants to engage in a range of readings, seminar–style discussions and special lectures, addressing (a) inequality and inclusion, (b) dissent and democracy, (c) vernacular modernities, (d) emergent histories, (e) technologies and media forms and (f) spaces and habitats. Each of these teaching initiatives provide the TTI institutions an opportunity to strengthen linkages with the university system as well as to influence the future of social science and humanities research in India. See Table 17.1.

ORGANIZATIONAL PERFORMANCE

In the early phase of the journey, while efforts to secure funding and leverage support for organizational sustainability were on, entry into TTI and access to stable and predictable core funds were crucial for institutions' growth and consolidation. These organizations have evolved considerably during the two phases of TTI and have emerged as organizations that carry out mandated responsibilities.

Most of these institutions were founded by groups of social activists and academicians, in response to the hegemony of a very few institutions and actors over the discourse on social groups, economic and fiscal policies, and governance in India; it was mostly without any support from the government at any level.

Following the framework and objectives of TTI, these institutions have pursued significant improvements in some of the key parameters of OP. During the two phases of TTI, the institutions have invested in strengthening of organizational systems and processes; human resource policy; monitoring, evaluation and learning (MEL) practices; governance process; and their research infrastructure. These measures have made these institutions not only better workplaces but also more accountable and efficient organizations.

TTI has enabled the institutions to take important steps towards strengthening the leadership and institutional systems and processes.

Table 17.1 *Indian Think Tanks and Areas of Research*

Sl No.	Name of the Institute	Areas of Research
1	Centre for Budget and Governance Accountability (CBGA), New Delhi	Enhancing transparency and accountability in governance, rigorous analysis of policies and government budgets in India, and ensuring people's participation in public policy processes in India. Open Budgets India (www.openbudgetsindia.org), an open data portal on government budgets in India
2	Centre for Policy Research (CPR), New Delhi	Urbanization and infrastructure, international affairs and security, governance and politics, environment and climate change, and law, regulation and society
3	Centre for the Study of Developing Societies (CSDS), New Delhi	Political thought and philosophy, media and culture, democratic politics and its future, development paradigm and practices, spatial transformations, diversity, identity and violence, and social science in Indian languages
4	Centre for Study of Science, Technology and Policy (CSTEP), Bengaluru	Energy, infrastructure, security studies, materials, climate studies and governance, especially in areas of energy efficiency, urban infrastructure in sanitation and transport, and artificial intelligence in governance
5	Indian Institute of Dalit Studies (IIDS), New Delhi	Problems of the marginalized groups, causes of their marginalization and policy advocacy with stakeholders to suggest policies for their empowerment
6	National Council of Applied Economic Research (NCAER), New Delhi	Assess the effectiveness of public policies in promoting economic growth, opportunity and service delivery
7	Public Affairs Centre (PAC), Bengaluru	Social accountability: Social accountability tools—Citizen Report Card (CRC), Community Score Cards (CSCs), Climate Change Score Cards (CCSCs), Community-Led Environment Impact Assessment (CLEIA) and Citizen Monitoring System

TTI's core funding support has led to increased efficiency by investing in process improvements; institutions have built in strong processes where all members are able to contribute optimally with their strengths, skills and knowledge towards the organizations' growth and success. It has helped them in the following:

- Attracting more qualified, talented and dynamic staff to form a larger team
- Hiring appropriate premises
- Organizing suitable workspace for expanding bigger team with expanding work
- Upgrading their research infrastructure

Along with supporting these back-office functions, core funding has also helped in fulfilling all statutory requirements and regulations such as office premises, strengthening of human resource base with suitably qualified and talented members joining in, and developing a competitive salary structure and incentives for the staff. This has helped in improving recruitment and retention efforts. The TTI institutions have also carried out improvement in infrastructure for research through new subscriptions to relevant databases, software packages and journals.

TTI has also been instrumental in creating the enabling environment for learning from the colleagues from other institutions in TTI in the South Asia region. The sharing of experiences and strategies adopted by some think tanks in the region seems to have helped in shaping the strategies of the others. Focus on leadership development has been an important element of TTI support. The executives at the head of the institutions have significantly learnt from the leaders of other think tanks in the TTI cohort in the South Asia region. The learning and capacity development through the regional conferences in South Asia and other conferences facilitated by TTI have been immensely useful in this process. Personnel at other levels have also benefited a lot from such exposure over the last eight years.

In addition to leadership, TTI evaluations of the institutions have also directed towards effective governance in the organizations. This has encouraged many institutions to expedite some of the improvements in governance architecture over the last few years. Expansion of the governing board of trustees/governor, for instance, has yielded modified governance architecture of the organizations during the period of the two phases of TTI.

Continuous and in-depth engagement with TTI staff at IDRC has also been very helpful in a number of ways. Organizational development was all through an important parameter in the discussions with TTI staff; for example, CBGA made improvements in the capacity of the finance and administration team and facilitated a lot of exposure as well as training for them during the last eight years.

POLICY ENGAGEMENT

The TTI support enabled the institutions' engagement with the public and policy spheres more relevant and deliberative. TTI galvanized the process to fill a significant gap in India's public sphere and make a difference by mobilizing research and knowledge for more inclusive public policies. Institutions could hold consultations on a variety of issues with which they engaged. For instance, CSDS could hold on participatory citizenship, pre-legislative transparency, communal violence, food security, electoral reforms, tribal self-rule and land transfers, the Lok Pal Bill, the issues of scavenger communities, India's road-use policy, genetically modified (GM) food and biosafety, and the future of affirmative action, besides a series of public lectures on diverse, policy-relevant issues.

The TTI institutions developed new and important links and networks with several ministries of the Government of India, including Home Affairs, Rural Development, Human Resource Development and Youth Affairs and Sport; the Planning Commission which has reincarnated as NITI Aayog, the Election Commission, the National Advisory Council, University Grants Commission and National Council of Educational Research and Training. In this vein, CSDS, in partnership with Goa Foundation and the Inclusive Media for Change, held deliberations on 'Permanent Fund Model for Ethical Mining: Land, Livelihoods and Intergenerational Equity' on 18 February 2015 at India International Centre, New Delhi. It examined if permanent funds (PFs) are a viable cure for India's resource curse. It explored the practical implications of applying such principles to allocations across all states of all natural resources from minerals to metal ores and from oil and gases to more virtual public properties such as the spectrums and airwaves. The main partners held an informal dialogue to strategize to take the initiative forward and to identify potential partners and collaborators. The participants were a coalition of people across states in order to discuss and take forward the idea of PFs as an alternative economic policy in India's extractive sectors. A significant new development through TTI support has been the emergence of some institutions as publishers of peer-reviewed journals. These journals not only reflect the scholarly rigour of the institutions but are also indicative of the diverse disciplinary and linguistic publics and policies that the institutions' research engaged with. *BioScope: South Asian Screen Studies* is a biannual peer-reviewed journal published by SAGE for CSDS. In circulation since January 2010, this journal is primarily centred on film and media studies and also engages a wider orbit of image and sound practices. The Indian Languages Programme launched a biannual, refereed journal, *Pratiman: Samay, Samaj, Sanskriti*, in February 2013, published in collaboration with Vani Prakashan. The journal focuses on in-depth investigations in social sciences and humanities with insistence on writing discursive text and articles originally in Hindi language. It represents a unique blend of quality in-house design, rigorous research content and innovative distribution strategies. The journal has this year brought out its 10th issue, having cumulatively published over 300 original research articles since inception. Lokniti, one of the oldest programmes at CSDS, launched its journal *Studies in Indian Politics* in July 2013 as a forum for those engaged in generating new knowledge in the analysis of Indian politics.

While pursuing high standards of research, the TTI institutions have ensured effective dissemination of their work and repeatedly deployed their expertise to aid policy-making processes. TTI institutions' impact on policy-making is evident in that various government organizations have sought their participation in the process of formulation. These institutions have provided direct, technical expertise to policy-makers through targeted meetings with policy-makers and membership in task forces and working groups set up by state and central governments. These engagements have been long-term and multifaceted in nature. Some of the most successful, recent policy engagements, as illustrated by CPR, include faculty participation in the Committee on Restructuring of Railways set up by the Ministry of Railways, Government of India; convening the Expert Committee to study alternatives for the new capital of Andhra Pradesh; engagement with government on building a strategy for India's long-term carbon and energy trajectory; preparing background papers for the Fourteenth Finance Commission recommendations on local government finances; and membership in the National Security Advisory Board.

These institutions have also increased their international engagement, working with multilateral agencies and foreign governments. Some of the recent engagements include the following: convening Track 1.5 trilateral meetings of India, the USA and China; engagement with UN-Habitat and World Urban Forum on the question of urbanization; participation and support for international climate governance activities such as United Nations Framework Convention on Climate Change (UNFCC) and Intergovernmental Panel on Climate Change (IPCC); and membership in international expert panel such as Open Government Partnership. Furthermore, these institutions have also enhanced their efforts at strengthening the larger policy-making community in India. The faculty members and senior researchers regularly participate in teaching and training courses for civil servants, scholars and researchers. Some institutions such as CPR have also been working closely with parliamentarians. In the last three years, CPR has engaged with different political parties and organized sessions to sensitize members of parliament (MPs) on a variety of subjects including agriculture, digitization, malnutrition, children's welfare and banking. CPR has also organized 11 visits for Indian MPs to engage with foreign scholars in five countries—the USA, the UK, China, Israel and Australia.

These institutions strongly believe that policy-making is not only about writing laws and policy rules but also about the ability to implement policy effectively on the ground. A number of these institutions are engaged with directly shaping implementation and strengthening governance capacity at the frontlines. To illustrate, in the last three years, CPR has engaged over 1,000 frontline officers at the panchayat,

Table 17.2 *Ranking of SDGs as per Thematic Areas of Policy Influence by Think Tanks in India*

Rank	UN SDGs
1	Goal 16: Peace, Justice and Strong Institutions
2	Goal 4: Quality Education
3	Goal 1: No Poverty
4	Goal 2: Zero Hunger
5	Goal 3: Good Health and Well-Being
6	Goal 8: Decent Work and Economic Growth
7	Goal 10: Reduced Inequalities
8	Goal 7: Affordable and Clean Energy
9	Goal 13: Climate Action

Source: Based on individual think tank reports, India.

block and district levels on how to strengthen implementation of key social sector programmes related to health, education, sanitation and local government financing. The research outcome of seven Indian think tanks had wider policy implications. These are directly linked to various Sustainable Development Goals (SDGs). Table 17.2 presents a glimpse of the number of areas of policy influence under each SDG.

Policy Impact: Some Illustrations

The biggest achievement of CBGA was the Union government's commitment to publish all Detailed Demands for Grants of the Union ministries in open data format on its portal.[5] The other institution through which CBGA's work gained relevance in policy environment was the office of the Comptroller and Auditor General (CAG) of India. CBGA's association with the Kerala government helped in reviving gender-responsive policy research for the state of Kerala, which further extended across states throughout entire country.

CPR's initiative called PAISA (Planning, Allocations and Expenditures, Institutions Studies in Accountability) under the team

[5] www.data.gov.in

called Accountability Initiative (AI) can be considered India's largest expenditure tracking survey in addressing bottlenecks in the implementation of government schemes such as Sarva Shiksha Abhiyan (SSA), Integrated Child Development Services (ICDS) and Swachh Bharat Mission (SBM), conducted across five states (Bihar, Himachal Pradesh, Maharashtra, Madhya Pradesh and Rajasthan) in India, taking a bottom-up approach.

CSDS has tried to bring change in the working of the handloom sector which led to policy influence under the Ministry of Textiles, Government of India, addressing issues such as 'absence of adequate credit at reasonable interest rates and unregulated and ever-increasing yarn prices affecting the growth in the sector' by providing prescriptions of proper implementation of the Handloom Reservation Act.

CSTEP's collaborations with NITI Aayog, Ministry of Environment, Forest and Climate Change (MoEFCC), and Ministry of New and Renewable Energy (MNRE) have been noteworthy in influencing policy change in areas such as energy, CO_2 emissions, and improved power potential through alternative power. In most of these initiatives, TTI core grant helped CSTEP to fund its involvement in the area of energy policy-making.

IIDS' research led to a policy formulation in group-specific policies for development through their work with relevant ministries such as Ministry of Human Resource Development to address discrimination in educational institutions and Ministry of Panchayati Raj to address discrimination in implementation of welfare schemes and accessing public services, and its research helped mandate public sector units to make 20 per cent of their purchases from micro and small enterprises (MSEs) owned by SCs and STs.

NCAER's Delhi land pooling study got recognized in the form of a new policy by the Delhi government. NCAER influenced policy-making in the context of Vision Kerala 2030 to bridge successive changes of state governments; NCAER also worked for the Finance Ministry to curb illicit funds; N-SIPI is a noteworthy initiative along with state and central policy-makers. NCAER's state-level exercise on DBTs has been instrumental in the implementation of the government's

DBT Mission. NCAER's pioneer work on 'short-term macroeconomic trends' has found immense support among market economists, the RBI, the World Bank and the IMF.

The Public Affairs Index (PAI) series of PAC, Bengaluru, generated immense potential in the policy advocacy arena of the country, receiving recognition from State governments, academics, academic institutions, the media and other eminent institutions such as the NITI Aayog, National Human Rights Commission (NHRC), Lal Bahadur Shastri National Academy of Administration (LBSNAA), National Law School, Symbiosis University and the Central University of Rajasthan. Their work on public accountability has been found to be extremely popular, generating requests for similar studies across various levels of policy-making institutions like different state governments such as Himachal Pradesh, Kerala and Karnataka. PAC's current involvement with NHRC in measuring quality of compliance of the states of India as per the principles of human rights needs special mention.

WAY FORWARD: GROWTH AND SUSTAINABILITY

Before the second phase of TTI funding comes to an end, institutions are working towards a multiple-funding source business model that would take into account the entire value chain of research to advocacy to action for change. Some of the changes that these institutions have witnessed and hope will lead to their growth and sustainability are as follows:

- To put in place the leadership robust in research and well-versed with the government machinery and systemic processes. This will bring in a better understanding of government requirements, as a result of which institutions will be able to successfully pitch for proposals that are critical for the improvement of people.
- The TTI institutions are also moving ahead to look for projects in the corporate social responsibility (CSR) space, where there is still a lot of ambiguity regarding projects carried out and the impact that they have had on the ground. These institutions plan to move into this space of impact evaluation and recommendation for more effective initiatives.

- These institutions continue to respond aggressively to requests for proposals (RfPs) from national and international funders for projects that echo its vision and mission. For this, institutions have also been able to successfully leverage on their relationships with other TTI partners across South Asia to pitch for cross-country studies.

Some of the TTI institutions have evolved a new strategic framework for sustainability. For instance, PAC has a new strategic framework (for 2017–2022) based on the SDGs that encapsulate overall development. The new groups in PAC reflect the various aspects of development that SDGs reflect—the Development Action Research Group works with two programme groups on SDGs that encompass human development (SDGs 1–7), while the Environment Action Research Group works with two programme groups on SDGs that take into account environment challenges that need to be addressed.

CONCLUSIONS

The most enduring legacy from the IDRC's TTI support has been and will be the partnerships between and among think tanks who have built deep and abiding relationships over the last nine years. PAC has developed deep bonds with peer think tanks in neighbouring countries and plans to continue these partnerships long after TTI is over. After all, the common good must be common because that binds everyone.

The IDRC support under TTI has been extremely useful for the grantee institutions in building and strengthening their OP, RQ and policy engagements. TTI has given them the space to develop infrastructure, improve RQ and enhance policy engagement. This has connected the research with policy-makers and other stakeholders and influenced policy in the process. Therefore, it is important to conceive a programme which will support such activities of the institutions. From young organizations like CSTEP to older ones like NCAER, all have benefited from TTI in more than one way. Perhaps, a metamorphosed version of this programme has to be evolved to continue the unfinished agenda of leaving one behind through inclusive development across South Asia.

Chapter 18

Social Science Research and TTI: Nepal

Ajaya Dixit and Ashutosh Shukla

INTRODUCTION

How has knowledge production in Nepal been used for evidence-based policy-making and how healthy, grounded and vibrant is the ecosystem of knowledge production? The answer to these questions must be sought as we begin responding to the challenges Nepal is likely to face in its journey towards a just and prosperous society. These questions also raise additional questions: How do agencies with the responsibility for making policy value new knowledge? How is the knowledge produced used in policy-making? How has the knowledge produced in the past changed policies?

A public policy is formulated to achieve desirable social changes, but the impact of its implementation may not be direct and the process of implementation itself can lead to unintended consequences. It is also unlikely that knowledge based on certain data and evidence will automatically translate into policy. The relation between knowledge and policy-making is non-linear and determined by the political context of knowledge production and use. The actual use of evidence depends on claims and counterclaims, persuasion, and argumentation in defence of or in opposition to evidence in a social–political sphere. Knowledge tends to find salience in policy-making through public discourse, as assumptions and concepts are questioned, altered and refined. Often, it is political considerations, not evidence, that influence policy decisions. In fact, political interests appear to drive the misuse, manipulation and cherry-picking of evidence to promote one policy over another.[1]

Despite the problems outlined above, applying knowledge research to policy-making is necessary if Nepal is to fulfil its aspiration to prosperity. This aspiration began manifesting itself in significant ways in all sections of Nepali society following the promulgation of the 2015 constitution.[2] This constitution is expected to conclude the political transition that began in 1996 when the Maoist party declared 'People's War', though concerns relating to issues of regional autonomy, increments in the number of electoral constituencies, natural resource rights, and equitable representation in State institutions and agencies are still unmet with contestation going in various forms.[3] With the completion of the 2017 elections to the national, provincial and local assemblies and with the formation of the new local, provincial and federal

---

[1] This idea is based on Parkhurst, *The Politics of Evidence*.

[2] In a public opinion poll conducted by Himalmedia in 2018, respondents representing Nepal's demographic and geographic diversity said that the three levels of government that were elected would usher in an era of political stability, create employment opportunities, improve the delivery of basic services and address the lack of development. See Rai, 'Hoping Against Hope', as well as *A Survey of the Nepali People in 2017*, a survey carried out with support from the Australian government and the Asia Foundation Partnership on Subnational Governance in Nepal.

[3] The 2006 People's Movement, which was jointly led by both mainstream political parties and the Maoists, resulted in the abolition of the institution of monarchy and the establishment of Nepal as a republic. Then, following the promulgation of the Interim Constitution, Madhesis in the Terai started demanding a federal governance system, regional autonomy and an increment in the number of electoral constituencies in the Terai. For details on later political history, see Hachchethu, 'Madhesi Nationalism and Restructuring the Nepali State'.

governments, the narrative of development has transformed into that of prosperity as a dominant discourse.[4]

Indeed, the preamble of Nepal's 2015 constitution mentions this principle clearly: 'Ensure economic equality, prosperity, and social justice', while environmental integrity, a prerequisite for achieving prosperity, is incorporated in fundamental rights and duties.[5] Whose prosperity that will be, how it will be achieved and how it is different from the term 'development' are important questions. In this chapter, without debating the merits and demerits of using the term 'prosperity' rather than 'development', we will highlight the importance of a vibrant knowledge landscape as a precondition for Nepal to achieve the triad aims of 'sustainable development'—a healthy rate of economic growth, social inclusion and environmental stewardship—and thereby secure the well-being of Nepal and Nepali people.

Policies that increase and promote domestic production and exports, reduce imports, and create jobs while building the capacities of human resources will be key to Nepal's sustainable development. Achieving this goal will require attention to accountable governance, infrastructure development, investment in health services and education, as well as the creation of appropriate policies. But merely the existence of such policies will not suffice: their objectives cannot be met in an environment of institutional dysfunction or if their implementation is ineffective. They must be grounded in local reality and effectively implemented. In

---

[4] The term 'prosperity' is the platform of Nepali Prime Minister Khadga Prasad Oli, who has highlighted it along with other elements key to Nepal's new journey under his leadership: self-respect, democracy, social justice as well as peace and stability. Former Prime Minister Baburam Bhattarai has articulated the notion of prosperity thus, 'A dynamic process than a given or acquired condition. It is more than just the accumulation of material wealth: it is also joy of everyday life and the prospect of an even better life.' His propositions for prosperity are high economic growth, social justice, environmental conservation and spiritual enhancement. See Bhattarai, 'Proposition of Social Justice and Economic Prosperity'.

[5] Article 30 of the constitution says that 'every citizen shall have the right to live in a clean and healthy environment', that 'any injury caused from environmental pollution or degradation' shall be compensated in accordance with law and 'necessary legal provisions for a proper balance between the environment and development' be made.

addition, the impacts of these policies must be systematically monitored and necessary reforms introduced. At the same time, the Government of Nepal (GoN) must significantly improve its capacity and management mechanisms to ensure that it has rules-based procedures in place to fully utilize financial resources to meet the development goals as targeted. Otherwise, policies will remain as just expressions of intent, without making significant contribution to overall well-being.

To achieve prosperity, Nepal is currently emphasizing infrastructure-led path, partly because poor connectivity and mobility continue to be one of the nation's main weaknesses. Because Nepal is poorly connected to its neighbours and has no direct access to the sea, it finds it difficult to take advantage of global value chains and to bolster its manufacturing sector.[6] Besides boosting the national and local economies, improved infrastructure is key to delivering goods and services to suit people's needs. Developing infrastructure primarily requires the use of natural science-based knowledge from disciplines such as geology, engineering and technology to execute and manage projects. Because nature and societies are integrally linked through the natural ecosystem and people, both nature and societies adapt to the changes they undergo when infrastructure is built. When the scale of an intervention is large, its impacts on the dependent social and natural systems are large and, because of their complex and non-linear relationship, unpredictable. Often, the risks are transferred not only to local communities but also to the larger economy.

Thus, to minimize risks, policy-making need to be based on knowledge at the intersection of social and natural sciences. Such an approach to policy-making is important for two reasons. First, such knowledge has relevance, given the linkages between Nepal's development imperatives and its social and geographical diversity. Second, for policy resonance, knowledge based on natural science stream must be informed by disciplines such as economics, political science, social studies, law and concepts such as gender and inclusion. This knowledge should be packaged and communicated to various agents in the sociopolitical space using the right constellation of evidence. These

[6] See Di Battista, 'What's Next for Nepal's Economy?'

agents can be classified as belonging to one of three spheres—the government, private sector and civil society—each with a different worldview, perception of risk and style of using evidence.[7] While evidence-based policy-making can be a basis for development, there is no guarantee that such policy-making will bring desirable outcomes. Nepal's development journey is strewn with multiple risks, and well-being gains can be reversed at any point.[8]

This chapter examines the state of the knowledge policy landscape in Nepal by looking at the intersection of natural and social sciences with the understanding that building this landscape is an important investment for securing a future better than present through reforming policies and their effective implementation. We recognize policy-making as key in that process but do not discuss specific aspects of its formulation. The chapter is structured as follows. We first briefly encapsulate the geographical, climatic and social contexts of the country, which collectively set the stage for diverse social and cultural dimensions, past changes and future opportunities. Then we highlight factors that could debilitate Nepal's march towards well-being if overlooked. This consideration is followed by a discussion of the country's educational milieu, which sets the context and the opportunities for the demand and supply of various knowledge products. We then present the scale of Nepal's investment in the production and dissemination of knowledge. The next section presents the findings of a survey that we undertook at selected research centres and organizations engaged in knowledge production in Kathmandu, and summarize the challenges they face in analysing contemporary issues, informing policy and practices, and engaging the research knowledge policy environment. Finally, we make recommendations to strengthen the research policy landscape.

---

[7] This idea of plurality is based on Verweij, Thompson, and Engel, 'Clumsy Conclusions'.

[8] Solomon has argued, 'The journey of development takes time, incurs cost, requires choices to be made, and therefore demands a resolute collective determination not simply to cope with the risks arising from change, but to try in a long-term perspective to guide change in a particular direction'; see Solomon, 'The Uncertain Quest'. Nepal faced three major events that lowered the country's well-being: the Gorkha earthquake, the unofficial border blockade and 2017 Terai floods.

THE SETTING AND CHALLENGES

Nepal's biophysical characteristics, its climatic diversity and its social circumstances are interlinked, and together they determine the development opportunities and constraints within the country. Variations in altitude, temperature and precipitation have blessed Nepal, despite its relatively small area, with a wide variety of climate, from tropical to alpine and almost everything in between, thereby supporting diverse ecosystems and great biodiversity. Nepal's more than 123 caste and ethnic groups practise a vast array of livelihoods, each closely associated with a different culture and different practices.[9] These groups have developed the wherewithal to address and even adapt to the constraints on livelihoods imposed by the biophysical regimes in which they live. Local institutions that support adaptation have enabled them to address some aspects of climatic variability and other environmental challenges, but they face new forms of stresses as the climate continues to alter and the social and local institutional contexts change as well.

Over the past two decades, improvements in road access and air connectivity as well as the expansion of communication and information technology across the country have broken barriers once imposed by geography and climate, and combined with increased migration have had substantial social implications.[10] Push and pull factors, institutional

---

[9] Central Bureau of Statistics estimated Nepal's population to be 26.5 million, growing annually at the rate of 1.35 per cent; see Central Bureau of Statistics, *National Population and Housing Census*. Recent estimate of population ranges from 28 million (Ministry of Population and Environment, *Nepal Pollution Report 2016*) to 29.3 million (https://data.worldbank.org/indicator/SP.POP.TOTL?end=2017&locations=NP&start=1960&view=chart, accessed on 19 July 2018). The recent estimate of rate of population increase is 1.16 per cent.

[10] Indeed, the length of road in Nepal has increased and improved mobility, but most roads in the hills have been built very poorly and haphazardly that exacerbate landslides and other forms of erosion, flash floods and downstream sedimentation, often covering fields of small and marginalized farmers with debris. Poorly built roads have disturbed phreatic lines, affecting springs that feed local drinking water systems. Referring to the condition in Bajhang in Far-Western Development Region, Nepal, Singh writes,

> Finding details about new roads nationwide is impossible. Even the Department of Roads doesn't have proper records. Bajhang district

influences, and social networks have resulted in seasonal, temporary, long-distance and permanent migration. With migration from rural to urban areas on the rise, the number of slum dwellers and squatters is burgeoning in major cities and towns. While migration is a traditional strategy for coping with poverty, unsustainable livelihoods and insecurity stemming from recurrent disasters as well as for securing a stable income, the number of migrants has substantially increased since the mid-1990s.[11]

Today, rural–urban migration, haphazard urbanization and other drivers of change are altering the biophysical system and deepening linkages among economic, environmental and other realms. One distinct implication of this change is that the local community's traditional dependence on local natural ecosystems has shifted to dependence on products and services from outside its resource boundaries.[12] This trend is manifested in the country's macroeconomic context as well: Nepal is now a net importer of food, consumables and energy. Over the last two decades, the share of the service sector in the total GDP has continued to grow, while that of agriculture has declined. In 2017, for example, agriculture contributed 28.2 per cent, industry 14.2 per cent and the service sector 57.6, a substantial increase over its contribution

---

authorities have no idea where roads are being built, but unofficially we tallied at least 165 currently under construction. There are more than 75 heavy earthmovers in Bajhang alone.

See Singh, 'From Nowhere to Nowhere'. Bajhang is a microcosm of the haphazard roadbuilding process deployed ostensibly with the objective of achieving 'prosperity' across the country. An unholy nexus among politicians, contactors, real-estate agents and heavy equipment suppliers is fuelling this process without geographical, climatic, environmental and technological safeguards. Increased climate variability spawned by climate change has further exacerbated this landscape–community dynamics with serious consequence on livelihoods and natural ecosystem.

[11] For details on migration, see Ministry of Labour and Transport Management and Institute Organisation for Migration, *Contribution of Labour Migration and Remittance to Nepal's Economy*; Nepal Institute of Development Studies, *Migration Year Book 2012*; Adhikari and Hobley, *Everyone Is Leaving, Who Will Sow the Seeds?*

[12] For details, see Desakota Study Team, *Re-imagining the Rural–Urban Continuum*.

of 38.9 per cent in 2000. Remittances, which were less than 5 per cent of the GDP in 2000, increased sixfold to 32 per cent in 2016. Capital investment, however, averaged less than 20 per cent during the same period.[13] This expansion of the import-backed service sector is unlikely to be sustainable unless the nation adopts serious policy interventions to build productive capital.[14] When considered in light of Nepal's rising trade imbalance and its dependence on fossil fuel imports, the risk is clear.

Developing hydropower could help minimize the risks of increasing dependence on imported petroleum products, but despite calls for hydropower development-led prosperity that have been expressed since the 1960s, Nepal faces three challenges in doing so: (a) providing universal access to reliable clean energy at affordable prices, (b) contributing to economic and social development by increasing domestic production and creating jobs and (c) reducing the import of fossil fuels through substitution. How investment in hydropower development would help the nation meet the above objectives is unclear in absence of credible financing plan, but the priority placed on meeting domestic energy needs to support overall development and employment offers an opportunity for policy innovation.

Improving the quality of services, particularly water supply, sanitation, health and education, are other major challenges. In the hills, the depletion of water sources is an emerging constraint, while in the Terai, the lowering of groundwater tables has increased the physical scarcity of water for both drinking and irrigation purposes. Years of investment in irrigation infrastructures have had little impact on Nepal's low agricultural production and productivity. The high rate of urbanization, dependence on food imports, poor compliance with environmental safeguards and limited institutional capacity have resulted in the degradation of natural resources, a deterioration that in turn has adversely impacted water bodies, livelihoods, and the well-being of ecological and human communities, particularly among socially and economically marginalized groups.

---

[13] Lohani, '*Sukulgunda Chintan*'.

[14] See Pyakuryal and Acharya, 'Service Sector Needs Sustainable Base for Further Expansion'.

Other challenges Nepal faces are the risks associated with climatic hazards such as floods, droughts, and heat and cold waves as well as those associated with geophysical hazards like earthquakes. Climate change vulnerabilities are spiralling into disasters as local communities increasingly face snowstorms, cloudbursts, riverine and flash floods, and landslides that cost lives and properties. In the high Himalaya, rapid glacier-melt and the formation of glacial lakes have heightened the risk of glacial lake outburst floods, and the decline in snowfall has depleted the water sources needed for sustained low-season river flow. Both changes have had dire consequences for downstream ecosystems and the people.

Nepal's location between the juggernauts of India and China has impacted its foreign and development policies. In the era of the Cold War and the Non-Aligned Movement, Nepal's geopolitical dynamics involved countries such as India, the USA, China, the UK and the former USSR. Although the Cold War is ostensibly over, rivalry, particularly between India and China, both of whom are interested in expanding their markets in Nepal by investing in infrastructures such as hydropower and railways, is increasing. Their interest could be an opportunity for Nepal, provided that it handles the geopolitical competition with caution and skill. This emerging scenario promises to be different from the prevailing aid regime provided by Western governments and the Bretton Woods Institutions. To benefit, Nepal must focus on reforming national, provincial and local-level govern-ance by establishing a holistic and encompassing process. Doing so successfully requires having recourse to effective policies based on the generation of knowledge diffused both horizontally and vertically within the knowledge policy landscape.

INTERDISCIPLINARY RESEARCH AND PUBLIC POLICY-MAKING IN NEPAL

The demand for knowledge at the intersection of the social and the nat-ural sciences in order to inform policy-making began after the advent of democracy in 1951. During the 1960s, 1970s and 1980s, much of this demand was created and met through the involvement of bilateral

262 | Ajaya Dixit and Ashutosh Shukla

and multilateral agencies, which supported Nepal's social and economic development in the early periods of its quest to modernization. In the mid-1980s, the number of international and national non-governmental organizations (NGOs) working in Nepal began to increase. These organizations sought evidence they could use to decide which areas of development to support, how much grant money to provide and how to monitor the changes in the lives of people attributable to the programmatic and financial support they provided. Compared to these non-government actors, the Nepali State and State agencies were late entrants in appreciating the value of grounded research and learning to policy-making. In fact, State agencies used to and still do depend on information provided by bilateral and multilateral agencies and international non-governmental organizations (INGOs) to inform national policy-making. The Nepali State and State agencies did not consider investing in research and knowledge production either within the government or at academic institutions and independent think tanks.

Even though there have been no deliberate processes to invest in critical and creative learning and scholarship, opportunities to pursue a formal university-level degree in different social and natural sciences have increased in the country steadily since 1980. Subjects such as history, culture, geography, sociology, anthropology, psychology, economics and political sciences were traditionally taught at the undergraduate and postgraduate levels in Nepal's only university, Tribhuvan University, as well as at its constituent and affiliated campuses. Today, areas of learning such as development studies, engineering, agricultural science, human and natural resource management, rural development, environmental science, gender studies, medicine and social work have emerged as new themes. The demand for these new courses grew as national and international NGOs offered jobs in these areas. Kathmandu University, a private institution established in 1991 with a focus on core technical areas, began offering interdisciplinary courses in the social and environmental sciences. A few years later, a private engineering college began to offer a master's-level interdisciplinary course on water management.[15] Since then, many more universities have been established.

---

[15] See Dixit, Dahal, and Dixit, 'Bridging the Macro and Micro Dichotomy in Water Education'.

Nevertheless, the level of critical enquiry for knowledge production and its use in policy-making is low.

For the most part, the growth in the number of institutions that offer education in different social and environmental sciences and the number of graduates educated in them annually have made little contribution towards producing new knowledge for policy-making or informing the practices for the implementation of policy effectively. That said, there are a few examples of research that have contributed to policy-making. Past studies in social science have produced evidence that has informed public policies and helped develop a critical mass for social change. For example, the efforts of Nepali and foreign researchers in developing and communicating the status of women in Nepal during the 1980s influenced gender-sensitive policy in significant ways.[16] Today, gender equality is a theme and a key indicator for assessing the impacts of development investments and the health of society. Other tangible impacts of the gender-sensitive public policy include an increase in the enrolment of girls in primary, secondary and tertiary education; improvements in women's sexual and maternal health; and a greater proportion of women in government departments and in different levels of decision-making.

Participatory planning and the management of natural resources are other areas where evidence-based learning at the interface of social and natural sciences has contributed in significant ways. During the 1980s and 1990s, large numbers of scholars studied property rights, governance, equity and various common property resource regimes in Nepal, such as irrigation, drinking water supply, forests and watershed management.[17] Their work, taken as a whole, made two important contributions. First, it helped establish that irrigation and drinking water supply systems not only are matters of technology and infrastructure but also involve communities and their roles as the custodians, managers, and users of resources and systems. Thus, the sustainable management of natural resource depends on how actively communities participate

---

[16] See Acharya and Bennett, *An Aggregate Analysis and Summary of 8 Village Studies in the Status of Women in Nepal*; Acharya and Acharya, *Gender Equality and Empowerment of Women*.

[17] See Ostrom, *Governing the Commons*.

in making decisions about the use of resources. Second, the studies of community members and their organizations produced an alternative model of development that put value in community institutions such as social enterprises and cooperatives and on the co-production of knowledge in participatory irrigation, drinking water supply and sanitation, community forestry, and community electricity distribution.

Social science research between 1970 and 1990 also informed public policies on poverty, social inclusion and marginality to some extent. There was, in particular, a significant shift in the focus of development planning designed to address poverty: abandoning the trickle-down model to address income poverty and the government beginning to address poverty as a product of exclusion and marginality. At present, poverty alleviation programmes focus not only on promoting livelihoods and sources of income but also on empowerment, capacity building and inclusion.[18] The dividends of this shift are apparent; even in remote areas, people not heard from until a decade ago now speak out assertively. Research has also contributed to policy-making regarding disasters risk reduction. The Nepal Disaster Risk and Management Act 2074 (2017) is in part the result of research and advocacy carried out by organizations involved in disaster risk reduction activities in Nepal.[19]

---

[18] See Desakota Study Team, *Re-imagining the Rural–Urban Continuum*.

[19] According to the Save the Children Federation (https://nepal.savethechildren. net/news/much-awaited-disaster-risk-reduction-and-management-act-endorsed, accessed on 1 May 2018), 'ECHO's support to Save the Children lead consortium partner Mission East to execute an advocacy push for Disaster Management (DM) in the interest of the larger population could be seen as a contributing factor for the new act.' The Promoting Inclusive Community-Based Disaster Preparedness Project was a flagship that provided the final push for a decade-long initiative to make the new act a reality. That initiative was led by the Save the Children Federation, which developed an advocacy campaign involving all members of European Commission-Humanitarian Aid and Civil Protection (ECHO) and the Association of INGOs in Nepal (AIN). The project involved tapping into the influential national media to bring political commitment by summarizing the views of senior government officials and parliamentarians. The post further goes on to suggest that

The support from ECHO in the Inclusive Community-Based Disaster Preparedness Project with a media engagement angle is something the public is aware of. These weekly broadcasts have dug deep into the minds of the political class and thus the country has the DRRM Bill endorsed today after years of repeated hits and misses.

Space and respect for a plurality of voices and evidence-based arguments must be nurtured to consolidate democracy and the democratic institutions that will serve as a foundation for the country's well-being. The emergence of a critical mass of development policy, planning and practices, particularly after 1990, is yet another contribution of social science research. Civil society leaders have raised critical questions and maintained an independent position on public policy and debates on public issues, whether in parliament or in print or social or other electronic media.[20]

RESEARCH LANDSCAPE

The complex and evolving sociopolitical landscape highlighted above requires evidence-based lessons through analysis, synthesis and iteration, for adopting response strategies that minimize systemic vulnerabilities and improve well-being. Analysing the role of investment in education, learning, research, and the production and uptake of knowledge is critical in this endeavour. The following section provides a synthesis of the role of public and private sector agencies and the importance accrued by them to knowledge production to inform policy and practices.

- *University system:* In Nepal, universities were not conceived as centres of knowledge, and successive governments accorded low priority to improving the quality of education. Today, though the number of universities has increased to 11, from the one that existed in the early 1990s, the culture of research within them has remained stagnant or has even declined.[21] Education is more oriented towards securing jobs than towards enhancing the capacity to think, reflect

---

[20] Hagen, *Nepal: The Kingdom in the Himalaya.*

[21] These are the Agriculture and Forestry University, Far-Western University, Kathmandu University, Lumbini Buddhist University, Mid-Western University, Nepal Open University, Nepal Sanskrit University, Pokhara University, Purvanchal University, Rajarshi Janak University and Tribhuvan University. See *Education Management Information System: Report on Higher Education 2014/15.* Available at: http://www.ugcnepal.edu.np/reports/EMIS%2014%2015.pdf (accessed on 5 September 2018). There are also six other university-type institutions that offer courses in health.

and make informed judgements. This absence of critical thinking results from the general decline in the quality of the educational system and its inability to prepare future professionals who could participate in informing the public dialogue. At the same time, the government makes little use of evidence-based independent research to formulate policies.[22] In the late 1960s and early 1970s, research centres were established within Tribhuvan University to promote interdisciplinary research.[23] These centres did carry out research and published journals but largely remained independent entities that did not maintain links with teaching departments and, therefore, had minimal impact on fostering the culture of research and enquiry integral to higher education. These conditions continue to prevail today.

Partisan political influence has further compromised the quality of education and research within the tertiary education system. University departments have focused more on teaching and awarding degrees than on linking teaching with enquiry-based learning and critical enquiry. Only a few university faculty members are involved in research, and they pursue it more out of passion or as a hobby than as an academic endeavour. The career progression of faculty members is not linked to their contributions to furthering research and knowledge but to the number of years they have taught. The majority of teachers in universities and colleges seek consultancies or teach at private colleges rather than pursue research. Over the years, the research environment has narrowed and declined.

Exacerbating the problem is the fact that university students are limited in their capacity to undertake enquiry-based learning.

---

[22] We use this argument based on the analysis of the status of social science research in Nepal by Hachchethu, 'Social Sciences in Nepal'; Sharma, Baidya, and Dhungel, *Strategic Plan for the Proposed Social Science Research Council in Nepal*; and Dhungel and Adhikary, *Strategic Plan for a Social Science Research*. The other useful treatises are Subedi, *The State of Geography Teaching and Research in Nepal*, providing an extensive discussion of geography and Subedi and Uprety, *The State of Sociology and Anthropology: Teaching and Research in Nepal*, describing the state of teaching and research in sociology and anthropology in the country.

[23] The Centre for Nepal and Asian Studies, the Centre for Economic Development and Administration, and the Research Centre for Educational Innovation and Development.

First, the practices of enquiry-based learning, mentoring by faculty members and writing research papers, proposals and reports are hardly prioritized. Second, limited access to international journals and literature means that any research they do is rarely informed by emerging global knowledge. Since young researchers do not have access to supportive arrangements to fund their research, they are not motivated to undertake enquiries into areas that demand material, intellectual and financial resources for their graduate research. Third, the absence of an academic ambience and research culture in universities further stifles critical thought.

- *Government departments:* Research conducted by government agencies tends to be defined by the proclivities of the State rather than by a desire for critical understanding.[24] The products of such research, while they may be useful for drawing lessons, nonetheless remain grey literature and are rarely translated into knowledge products. In many cases, the in-house analytical capability of government agencies is limited and tasks are outsourced to external consultants. The quality of such outputs varies, but one characteristic is common: the absence of a sense of ownership.

- *Independent research organizations:* These organizations depend on donor funding to conduct research; thus, whether or not they conduct research and produce knowledge independent of the donors' agenda is a moot issue, especially changes in funding architecture as the twenty-first century has rendered competition for donor resources intense. Some organizations hire consultants, while others have their own research staff and infrastructure. Their human resource capacity may be in a constant state of flux as rates of staff attrition may be high, and, while many organizations have developed mechanisms to maintain the quality of outputs, that quality varies.

- *Private sector:* Private organizations conduct research primarily as consultants; thus, they are dependent on donors for funds, and the areas they study must complement donor priorities. Reports on such research are rarely available in the public domain and contribute

---

[24] National Planning Commission, Nepal Rastra Bank, Central Bureau of Statistics, Local Development Training Academy, Nepal Administrative Staff College, Trade Promotion Centre, Water and Energy Commission and ministries.

little to the body of knowledge that can inform discussions on contemporary issues. That said, this sector, by its very nature, is rarely involved in social science research, as there is no profit in such an enterprise. There is little incentive for the private sector to allocate resources to research and development (R&D) except as a gesture of corporate social responsibility or individual interest.

- *International non-governmental organizations:* According to the report of the Social Welfare Council that regulates INGOs and NGOs, there are 254 INGOs working in Nepal. The majority of INGOs work in the areas of community development, child health, maternal and neonatal care, emergency relief, reconstruction and rehabilitation, HIV/AIDS, education, water sanitation and hygiene, youth development, agriculture, empowerment, children's and women's rights, disaster resilience and climate change, livelihood diversification, and poverty reduction.[25] INGOs use external analysts to undertake research. Their products are mainly communication- and advocacy-oriented and based on single time-bound project-based analysis. Very few are converted into knowledge products, and most remain grey material within the organization that produces them.

- *Non-governmental organizations:* The Social Welfare Council lists as many as 39,000 NGOs working in different areas.[26] They implement programmes with financial support from INGOs, donors, donor governments, foreign private foundations, corporations, individual donors and faith-based entities. Their research is mostly programme-based and varies in quality. It remains grey literature and is not used to create knowledge products. The socio–political landscape in which these entities function is undergoing changes following the promulgation of the new constitution. How the dynamics will play out is unclear.

- *Donor agencies:* Major donor agencies support the government in various development sectors, including health, education, livelihoods, agriculture, disaster recovery and reconstruction, and

---

[25] See http://www.swc.org.np/wp-content/uploads/2016/03/INGOs-detail-information-2072_073-Falgun-Masant.pdf (accessed 27 September 2018).

[26] See http://www.swc.org.np/wp-content/uploads/2016/01/SWC_NGOs_2034_071-asadh_-Final-in-bhadra-2072.pdf (accessed 27 September 2018).

governance, and, in coordination with the government, are major actors in knowledge generation and use.[27] Their contribution to knowledge is largely development-oriented and is not linked to university systems.

Public Funding of Research

The amount of money allocated to research and innovation is an important indicator of the status of a country's research and innovation landscape. It is estimated that 0.3 per cent of Nepal's GDP was spent on R&D in 2010, less than a third of what neighbouring India spends and less than a tenth of what great innovators such as Japan and Taiwan spend.[28] Because there has been no policy shift designed to increase investment in R&D, it is likely that the level of investment will remain the same in 2018. Data available in the public domain and informal communications with the contact persons of different organizations suggest that about NPR 173.8 million is available annually for research and knowledge production.[29] The GoN's support for knowledge is limited and, rather than having its own budget head, research is implicitly embedded in the annual budget allocated to each sector.

The top three funding organizations based on the amount of money granted to research in 2017 were the National Agricultural Research and Development Fund (NPR 82.5 million), University Grants Commission (NPR 71.1 million) and National Health Research

---

[27] The major ones are the World Bank, Asian Development Bank, United Nations International Children's Emergency Fund, United Nations Development Programme, United States Agency for International Development, Department for International Development, Netherlands Development Organisation, Australian Aid, Korea International Cooperation Agency, Japan International Cooperation Agency, Norwegian Agency for Development Cooperation, German Technical Cooperation and Danish International Development Agency.

[28] See United Nations Educational Scientific and Cultural Organization, *UNESCO Science Report: Towards 2030*, 573–573.

[29] See Bhuju and Khadga, *Science Technology and Innovation in Nepal*. They classified R&D into the following fields: (a) natural sciences, (b) engineering and technology, (c) medical and health sciences, (d) agricultural and veterinary sciences, (e) social sciences and (f) humanities and the arts. Government funding supported 569 research grants in 29 categories.

Council (NPR 6.2 million). In terms of numbers of studies funded, the University Grants Commission again ranked top with 289 awards in six categories, while the National Agricultural Research and Development Fund followed with 82 awards under three categories and the National Health Research Council was third with 60 awards in two categories. In its 2018 budget speech, the GoN included funds for R&D in the general, financial, environment protection, health, cultural and religious, education, and social security sectors,[30] but grants are yet to be awarded and budget disbursed.

JOURNALS

One of the indicators of the health of the knowledge policy ecosystem in a country is the number and regularity with which academic journals are published in that country. Since the advent of multi-party democracy in Nepal in 1990 reintroduced the notion of participatory democracy and political rights as basic tenets of the political order, more than 100 journals in the social sciences have been established in the country.[31] Universities, academic NGOs, private research centres, commercial publishers and even government entities publish those journals. While this publication of journals is a reflection of the increasing capacity for research spreading to different parts of Nepal from its earlier concentration in the capital, Kathmandu, journals face numerous challenges. Their publications are not regular, quality of the articles in them vary and financial sustainable is a real concern. Along with addressing these issues, it is not clear how evidence in journal articles have contributed in public decision and policy-making. Some major barriers to the use of such research evidence are the decision-makers' perceptions of research evidence, the increasing gulf between researchers and decision-makers, the opaque culture of decision-making, competing influences on decision-making, and other practical constraints.[32]

---

[30] See GoN, *The Budget Speech*.

[31] This section is adapted from Onta, 'The Changing Research Landscape'.

[32] See Orton, Lloyd-Williams, Taylor-Robinson, O'Flaherty, and Capewell, 'The Use of Research Evidence in Public Health Decision Making Processes', e21704.

STATUS OF KATHMANDU-BASED RESEARCH ORGANIZATIONS

We purposively identified 16 organizations which conduct research on natural and social science-based themes in order to preliminarily assess the state of the knowledge policy landscape in the country.[33] Through semi-structured one-to-one interviews with the heads of each organization and their senior researchers, we tried to assess how organizations deal with performance, apply quality-assurance protocols, disseminate knowledge and engage in policy process as well as the challenges they face, particularly in terms of sustainability. The findings are as follows:

- *Organizational performance:* Most organizations have set procedures with regard to the management, recruitment and evaluation of staff. They annually appraise individual staff performance and have mechanisms for capacity building. Some have an autonomous recruitment committee of experts to recruit staff. The hiring of academic consultants is a common practice, and development practitioners are kept in the organizational loop. The rate of employee turnover is high, and financial incentives fail to prevent attrition as employees continually seek jobs in organizations with greater visibility and more perks.
- *Quality assurance:* All the organizations interviewed have set forth procedures to ensure the quality of their research and knowledge products. Methods include teamwork, in-house discussions segregated according to the nature or theme of research, mentoring by senior researchers, internal and external peer reviews, general feedback, and content- and copy-editing. Some monitor the citation and

---

[33] We visited the following organizations: Integrated Development Society Nepal; Nepal Development Research Institute; Martin Chautari; National Society for Earthquake Technology-Nepal; Nepal Economic Forum; South Asia Watch on Trade, Economics and Environment; Nepal Forum of Environmental Journalists; New ERA; Nepali Times; South Asia Institute of Advanced Studies; ForestAction, Center for Environmental and Agricultural Policy Research, Extension and Development; Niti Foundation; Social Science Baha; Nepal Center for Contemporary Research; Institute for Integrated Development studies and Nepal Institute of Development Studies.

the utilization of their published products too. A few organizations also maintain a dedicated roster of experts for peer review, but this is a culture yet to be inculcated by most. While discussion papers and policy briefs are subjected to internal reviews to ensure quality, these products cater to the priorities of specific users. Most organizations make use of the comments and feedback they receive during formal presentations made at international conferences by specialists and experts. All organizations review questionnaires for consistency and assess the validity of responses and the reliability of findings. They also focus on ensuring quality outputs during sample design, training and mobilization of field teams, monitoring, data collection, cleaning of metadata, analysis and presentation of findings, and development of recommendations. In recent years, organizations have started using software applications to carry out surveys, a switch that has made quality checks better and easier. Yet, most recognize inconsistencies in the data collected at official level and its limitation in forecasting and conducting analysis.

- *Knowledge dissemination and policy engagement:* Organizations use various channels to disseminate research products to different groups of users. They do circulate products to concerned governmental agencies. Then, through interaction programmes with concerned stakeholders, they solicit feedback, which they incorporate in order to improve the content and quality of their research products. Most organizations rely on social networking platforms such as Facebook and Twitter as well as their own websites and email lists to disseminate products, research information and presentations. Radio and video programmes are other common media used.

Most organizations do try to keep the government as well as donors and the private sector in the dialogue loop, but government agencies, which are key to policy processes, seldom show interest in research-based evidence. Some interviewees pointed out that focusing on a specific issue is strategically useful in engaging with government stakeholders and that organizations must be proactive in order to be effective. Working jointly with government departments to formulate approaches to research is equally helpful, but this strategy may incur transaction costs and even lead to a compromise in quality if the partnership becomes unequal, and research independence is compromised.

The officials of the organizations consulted recognized the importance of remaining independent of influence of funders of research. Indeed, many stated that they prefer to do policy research using their own funding to ensure that it is guided by the aim of building a bridge between the State and its citizens and not champion a State agenda. The organizations also recognized that effective policy-making is an outcome of the participation of the research community in the public discourse armed with rigorous research.

All organizations identify the language of delivery as a key issue for informing this dialogue. Most research reports are written in English, so they end up stacked on the shelves of the governed offices, of little or no use. Organizations do try to translate their outputs into local languages, but translating into the vernacular is a much larger enterprise than many assume. The challenge lies in capturing the content and concepts without losing their essence or meaning. Many research organizations attempt to expand the arena of research by allowing larger groups of people to become involved in co-production of knowledge. Most organizations recognize that the lack of coordination and cooperation among different agencies undermines the effectiveness of the implementation of policies. Institutional amnesia and lack of systematic documentation within governmental agencies further exacerbate this gap.[34] In the current federal administrative system, robust coordination among various governance tiers and departments must be maintained during policy-making and implementation of policies if either is to be effective.

- *Sustainability:* Sustainability is a challenge for almost all organizations. Even business groups that have regular sources of revenue do not break even financially and have to be subsidized by their

---

[34] Raj and Gautam write that such forgetfulness resulted in the Nepali State's not using the procedures it had developed for assessing losses in the 1934 earthquake in April 2015, when the Gorkha earthquake struck; see Raj and Gautam, *Courage in Chaos*, 86.

promoters. That said, organizations are cautiously optimistic that the new constitution will establish the rule of law, standard operating procedures and appropriate regulation, thereby making it easier for them to thrive. Organizations recognize that adequate resource mobilization is the key to sustainability. In addition, maintaining a core fund and initiating capacity-building activities can bolster an institution's financial sustainability. Those organizations that own a building and service infrastructures earn by leasing out part of the facility, and assets are much better placed than those who are forced to rent facilities.

WAY FORWARD

Our review reveals that Nepal's landscape of knowledge production is fragmented and vulnerable. Current allocations of financial and human resources to research are limited, a fact suggesting that knowledge and critical thinking have little priority.[35] This reality is unfortunate, given the challenges that achieving economic growth and simultaneously promoting social inclusivity and environmental sustainability entail. Without substantial outlay in enriching the knowledge landscape, it is unlikely that Nepal can achieve its vision of well-being in the future. Appropriate use of evidence can, in particular, help it better achieve its social goals and be a critical requirement for trust in a democratic society.[36]

Only if Nepal significantly increases its investments in social and natural science research can the country unpack and analyse the myriad challenges it faces and, after processing the evidence, shift towards a problem-solving mode. The GoN must institutionalize the agenda of pursuing high-quality research aimed at capturing ongoing social and environmental change dynamics. In terms of both its content

[35] Sharma, Baidya, and Dhungel, *Strategic Plan*, in their examination of social science research in Nepal, suggest that the currently low state of social science research reflects the lack of a national social science research policy and the consequent lack of governmental commitment to research, knowledge and ideas.

[36] See Parkhurst, *The Politics of Evidence*.

and quality, research must help improve practices, inform policies and contribute to knowledge building. Deliberate action is needed to make the research landscape more coherent, critical and constructive; otherwise, the quality of the entire ecosystem will continue to remain fragmented and vulnerable.

Among the actions that can enrich Nepal's knowledge-generation landscape are the following:

1. Disciplinary and interdisciplinary research must be creatively blended. While reductionist research does identify input at the level of a discipline, it must be supported by interdisciplinary synthesis if it is to be able to yield public policy lessons. The logic behind this requirement is straightforward: many societal, developmental and environmental issues cross their boundaries, so solutions need to be based on interdisciplinary analyses.

2. University education must be reformed so that it can impart context-sensitive knowledge through good-quality teaching backed by enquiry-based learning. Making this shift will require increasing investments and minimizing partisan political influence while at the same time inculcating the culture of reasoning and argumentation as the point of entry for critical analysis. Independent researchers studying Nepal's university education suggest that those Nepali citizens studying, doing research and teaching in foreign universities and also those involved in research within the country be hired as university faculty members.[37] At the same time, greater emphasis must be placed on incorporating research in postgraduate teaching, increasing cooperation between researchers and teaching staff, providing more funding for research within the university system, and encouraging and motivating university teachers to conduct research.[38] To build the human capital necessary for evidence-based knowledge, an exchange programme must be encouraged: Nepali scholars must work in foreign universities and foreign scholars in Nepali universities.

---

[37] See Parajuli and Onta, '*Taaxiyeka Biswabidhyalaya*' (Stunted Universities).
[38] Hachhethu, 'Social Sciences in Nepal'.

Providing material, finance and mentoring to students writing dissertation/thesis would be a good beginning.

3. The government must clarify the working space of independent research organizations. At present, organizations engaged in knowledge production and those involved in service delivery are all lumped into one category—NGOs—though they are conceptually and structurally different.[39] Knowledge organizations should be regulated using a different set of indicators than those used for organizations that implement social, community and infrastructure development programmes.

4. One possibility for implementing a new regulatory mechanism was mooted in 2014, when it was suggested that a social science research council be constituted to enhance the quality of public debate on critical social, economic and environmental issues as they related to Nepal's prosperity.[40] Forming such a council would be a starting point that could nudge the research ecosystem towards change and appropriate regulation of that change. Functioning as an umbrella entity regulating the various research organizations across the country, the council should make suggestions about research priorities and modalities and efficient means to mobilize resources as well as ensure that the quality of research improves and that research products are disseminated more effectively. One caveat must be observed: the council must be independent; no partisan political scheming can be allowed to influence its agenda.

5. The private sector must be given incentives like tax breaks to increase its investment in R&D and thereby promote

[39] The unwritten rule is that organizations must allocate 15 per cent of their operational resources to software (knowledge aimed at building capacity or inform policy and practices) and 85 per cent to hardware (infrastructure development). No organization engaged in knowledge production will be able to operate under such a regulatory regime. While hardware is important and targeted investments are necessary, knowledge production entities are conceptually and structurally different from other types of organizations. Regulating them needs very different metrics.

[40] See Sharma, Baidya, and Dhungel, *Strategic Plan*.

knowledge-based philanthropy. The State must enable the private sector to promote innovation in services such as information and communication technology, quality services and finance management to play complementary role in economic development.[41]

6. It is equally important that the critical social science perspective has space to incubate and evolve and that it be maintained by substantially increasing investment in R&D and, simultaneously, facilitating the growth of independent organizations that generate new knowledge.

7. Investments must target building the country's pool of human resources so that it has the capacity to synthesize and assimilate the insights offered by indigenous knowledge and practices as well as natural and social sciences streams, and use that wisdom as a pillar to build country's well-being.

IN THE END

It is crucial that research landscape must be nurtured to grow, as Nepal pursues infrastructure-led development in order to provide its people with goods and services. Education programmes in Nepal, however, do not focus on examining, much less assimilating the synergy among nature, technology and society. In the larger social–political sphere, the assumptions that solutions to all problems are technological and that the lack of social ethos and human capital in its use hardly matters prevail. Given that even in countries where modern technology developed, technological determinism does not work, adopting such an approach in a country such as Nepal where a technological ethos has not even taken root is fraught with major risks.

Without backing of interdisciplinary knowledge, infrastructure cannot be developed to provide effective goods and services to the people. Bhaskar Gautam, a researcher, has made a logical observation:

---

[41] Wagle, for example, has argued for making manufacturing in Nepal competitive by lowering costs, expanding sales, differentiating products and building brand loyalty; see Wagle, *Message to the Report Development of Manufacturing Industries in Nepal*.

Nepali government must begin to internalise deep connections between knowledge and infrastructure and invest in knowledge production so that we can build in-country capacity to prioritise development tasks. Simultaneously, universities must be improved to provide quality education while investments in social science research substantially increased.[42]

Indeed, increased investments in knowledge production and constructive policy engagement will be key aspects of Nepal's journey towards a better future, a future where Nepali citizens can become active participants and partners in creating.

[42] See Gautam, 'Oli lai Chiniya sikchya' (Chinese Education to Oli), 30–31.

Chapter 19

Social Science Research and TTI: Pakistan

Abid Q. Suleri

The critical and analytical faculties required in the highly interdisci-plinary field of policy research depend heavily upon the state of the social sciences. At the time of its inception, Pakistan inherited very weak infrastructure for social science training and research,[1] which continues to remain weak despite certain phases of development. The ideological context and political history of the country are often drawn upon by many analysts to explain the poor state of social sciences. The successive dictatorial and quasi-dictatorial political regimes had serious bearings for the autonomy of the academic institutions by absorbing them into bureaucratic procedures and subjecting them to the civil service rules.[2] Zaidi stratified the post-independence period into five distinct phases of social sciences in Pakistan.[3] Most of the pre-independence policies were followed in the first phase, 1947–1958. The second phase, 1958–1971, was characterized by a 'nexus' between bureaucracy and military with a strong US influence on the policies. Albeit a lack of independence, the development of social science picked up some momentum towards the end of the 1960s.

---

[1] Inayatullah, 'Social Sciences in Pakistan'.
[2] Ibid.
[3] Zaidi, 'Dismal State of Social Sciences in Pakistan'.

In Zaidi's view, the academic institutions started strengthening their roots from 1971 to 1977, which was the 'first democratic' era in the new Pakistan and was far freer and more liberal, and perhaps more creative as well. The subsequent military regime from 1977 to 1988, which constitutes the fourth phase, was a huge setback on the social and academic structure of the country through various tools including Islamization of the State and society including higher education. With a transitory period between 1988 and 1999, yet another military coup by General Pervez Musharraf put an end to the democratic era, however, with different implications for social sciences from the previous dictatorships. The establishment of the Higher Education Commission (HEC) promoted social sciences to some extent by sending a number of students and faculty members of universities abroad for doctoral training. While these investments are still being made, much of the research during and after this era has been produced outside universities, mainly in think tanks.

From Zaidi's perspective, the political culture of the country promoted a 'conformist' view instead of critical thinking necessary for the progress in social sciences.[4] The authoritative nature of the State has tended to be biased against a culture of debate and dissent, thus counterproductive for research. A fivefold increase in the number of social science teachers during 1963–2001 failed to yield any academic environment of debate and ideas[5] not the least because there is an offsetting increase in population and the number of educational institutions. Renowned educationist Rubina Saigol concluded a critical monograph by underscoring the key structural, ideological and institutional factors contributing to the poor state of social sciences in Pakistan by arguing that

> The overwhelming ideological orientation of teachers across the disciplinary spectrum revolves around religious and nationalist thinking. Most departments have courses in the Ideology of Pakistan and some form of religious teaching. These subjects are usually taught uncritically and from a single dominant viewpoint. Competing or alternative viewpoints on the subject are not entertained and there is seldom any debate over these issues (…). Even the suggestion that there may [be] competing

---

[4] Zaidi, 'Dismal State of Social Sciences in Pakistan'.
[5] Tahir, 'Quantitative Development of Social Sciences in Inayatullah', 459–560.

versions of ideology or alternative views about religion (say between the different sects and classes of people) causes hostility and defensiveness.[6]

Saigol further elaborates:

So deeply rooted are teachers and students in the hegemonic versions of state and society that even the social sciences, which are tasked to produce alternative visions, fail to do so. As a result one hardly finds any exponents of other schools of thought— say Marxist, socialist, feminist, subaltern or post-modernist. Very few faculty members are aware of other schools of thought so that there is seldom any ideological debate that could potentially generate new ideas. The absence of debate and controversy, discussion and contention, makes most of the universities very dull and insipid places where received knowledge from old books is transmitted from generation to generation in the same unchanging way. To some extent the problem is a consequence of a lack of basic research facilities, in particular in the public sector institutions.[7]

In Saigol's view, commodification of the knowledge under the neoliberal economic policies and the increased authoritarianism of the State over time have resulted in disciplines such as business and administration being preferred over the core disciplines such as history, philosophy and political science, which are critical to the understanding of the State, society and culture. Saigol lists several key factors responsible for the underdevelopment of social sciences in Pakistan. These include the following: little monetary reward for teachers, high student–teacher ratios, lack of academic facilities including libraries with up-to-date books and a general lack of community of researchers to reflect upon the research produced to generate the debate. The scarcity of academic conferences and seminars results in a behaviour of 'inwardness' rather than sharing of the ideas and cross-disciplinary communication and interaction. She highlights that the extent of training in research methods is extremely poor, inefficient and outdated. Social scientists trained in these conditions find it hard to secure jobs and the better paid jobs

---

[6] Saigol in Inayatullah, Saigol, and Tahir, 'Social Sciences in Pakistan', 477.
[7] Ibid.

are biased towards foreign-qualified social scientists: 'Locally qualified social scientists, even if they have greater insight and intelligence or first-hand knowledge of the local institutions, fail to compete with foreign qualified individuals owing to the lack of respect for the degrees awarded by Pakistani universities.'

Lastly, Saigol points towards the elitist nature of social sciences in the country by highlighting that despite the majority of the population of the country being rural, the positions of prestige and power in the knowledge system are dominated by the urban upper classes. This is increasingly visible as one observes the uprising of the few private sector universities providing better training to those who can afford it, albeit with some contrary evidences contradicting this general trend, at least in development sector.[8]

The current phase of social sciences in Pakistan is being affected by the recent transitions that Pakistan is going through for last one and a half decade (since 2008 to be precise). The era between 2008 and 2013 observed citizen's empowerment, restoration of independence of superior judiciary backed by common masses and end of quasi-dictatorship from Pakistan. During last 10 years, Pakistan has seen improved resilience in democratic forces. For the first time in the history of the country, two democratically elected national assemblies (lower house of the parliament) and governments have completed their respective five-year tenures. During last five years, security situation and energy crisis in the country have significantly improved. Partly due to the China–Pakistan Economic Corridor, the infrastructure development is taking place at an unprecedented speed. At societal level, mainly due to increased use of social media, citizens are more aware and empowered. Power is no more concentrated at a single source, rather parliament, judiciary, Election Commission of Pakistan, media, and civil and military establishments are the new power centres. Besides Pakistan Peoples Party and Pakistan Muslim League (Nawaz), Pakistan Tehreek-e-Insaf

---

[8] The text in the chapter till here is taken from Naveed and Suleri, 'Making "Impact Factor" Impactful'. This report was prepared for IDRC in 2014 and is available at: http://www.thinktankinitiative.org/sites/default/files/Pakistan%20 TT-university%20study_Final%20June%2022.pdf (accessed on 5 September 2018).

has emerged as third major political party in the country. A major development in last five years is demand and acceptability for a culture of accountability in the country.

Above-mentioned developments have brought mixed changes to the state of social sciences. On the one hand, citizens' empowerment, quest for accountability and increased political choice have given more room to new narratives. On the other hand, society has become further polarized. A major issue in today's Pakistan is not ensuring interfaith harmony but ensuring intrafaith harmony (among different sects of Muslims). Difference of opinion on religious or political grounds is often met with physical violence and more generally through hate campaigns on social media. This has further aggravated extremism and shrunk the thinking space for independent intellectuals.

Universities (academia) and think tanks are two important sources of input for social policy-making in Pakistan. Public sector universities have seen an increase of funding for their programmes (although more focused to basic sciences and other disciplines). However, with this funding comes the issue of self-imposed censorship, which raises the question of policy relevance of research produced in Pakistani universities. On the other hand, there is no mechanism for public sector funding to independent social scientists or independent interdisciplinary think tanks.

It can be argued that think tanks and universities are conceptually and structurally different organizations, hence are differently located in the landscape of knowledge systems for policy-making despite an overlap of the broader agenda of contributing to informed public policies. Thus, the interaction between think tanks and universities is understandably limited and informal. The existing regimes of funding policy research also tend to create and maintain separation between the two groups of institutions.[9] However, closed interaction and collaboration between the two is a key to promote social sciences research in Pakistan.

---

[9] Ibid.

COUNTRY SYNTHESIS OF THE THREE THINK THANK INITIATIVE (TTI) PILLARS
Organizational Performance

The think tanks in Pakistan operate in the above-mentioned social sciences context where appetite for critical thinking is lacking. In an environment, where 'if you are not my friend, you are my enemy', there is a huge cost for conducting objective analysis. These circumstances directly affect the sources of funding (in both public and private sectors) for independent research, which in turn affects the organization's capacity to attract and retain competent human resources and resultantly organizational performance gets affected.

Current development partners are reluctant to pay overhead costs and/or costs for improving operations. Think tanks cannot divert their restricted funding in meeting organizational operational expenditures. Lack of financial cushion for investing in organizational operations is another reason for erosion in organizational performance.

Research Quality

Research quality and quality of human resources have a chicken–egg relation. Most of the think tanks cannot attract and retain quality human resources due to lack of funds. This weakens their research capacities and due to weak research team, they fail to win research assignments through competitive bidding, and this cycle goes on. Another factor affecting quality of research in think tanks is Pakistan's education system, which encourages neither critical thinking nor creative writing.

Policy Outreach

When it comes to policy outreach and bridging research policy gaps, think tanks in Pakistan face a twin deficit of access and contents. Most of them lack access to the relevant decision-makers. Most of those who get an access to a 'champion of change' lack contents in politically correct language to convey. Another factor constraining effective policy outreach is growing intolerance in society at large against difference of opinion.

Sustainability

In the above-mentioned context, sustaining an independent think tank that is known for its objective research outputs is really a difficult task in Pakistan. International Development Research Centre's (IDRC) TTI was important to sustain independent think tanks generally in South Asia but especially in Pakistan, where promotion of culture of critical thinking and objective analysis is a prerequisite to develop an alternative narrative against extremism and counter violence.

The way forward can be an initiative to bring think tanks and universities closer and to support them to work jointly on promotion of social sciences. This would potentially offer both generators of knowledge the opportunities to overcome their weaknesses by building upon each other's strengths. The major benefit to universities would be increased relevance of their research to public policies and an improved dissemination of their research to policy world, while think tanks would be able to improve the quality of their research outputs by involving academics at various stages of their research projects cycles.

Our recommendation to IDRC and other development partners, for promotion of social science research in Pakistan, would be to start a new phase of TTI where think tanks may be matched with a public sector university.

Chapter 20

Social Science Research and TTI: Sri Lanka*

S. Sirimevan Colombage and
P. R. M. P. Dilrukshi Ranathunge

INTRODUCTION

Social science research in diverse fields in Sri Lanka reflects the complex social, cultural, political and economic changes the nation experienced during the post-independence period. During the pre-independence period, under the colonial administration, there was hardly any scope for research, and research in social science was particularly scarce. Although Sri Lanka (then known as Ceylon) had established a few professional and technical institutions in the late nineteenth century and opened a university college in 1921, it established a full-fledged university only in 1942. Since then, the university system has expanded, adding several new universities with ever more social science faculty members and departments, thereby establishing the institutional

* This is an updated version of the paper with the same title by the authors presented to the 2014 ICSSR/IDRC/TTI conference Status of Social Science Research in Asia. The editors express gratitude to the authors for support and updating the paper. Status of Social Science Research in Asia Emerging Challenges and Policy Lessons, Proceeding of ICSSR-IDRC Conference, ICSSR.

structure needed to support social science research. In addition, several government organizations and other institutes have evolved over the last five decades to carry out socio-economic research.

The objective of this chapter is to assess social science research in Sri Lanka and to identify the gaps between the supply and demand for such research. The second section of the chapter discusses Sri Lanka's social science research policy and institutional framework and the third section provides an account of the demand and supply sides of social science research. The fourth section explains the issues covered in social science research, the fifth section analyses the funding available for social science research and the sixth section presents challenges to social science research. Concluding remarks are given in the last section.

SOCIAL SCIENCE RESEARCH POLICY AND INSTITUTIONAL FRAMEWORK

A developing country reputed internationally as a model welfare state, Sri Lanka has monitored the country's socio-economic progress for the last several decades. To do so, it has established systems for collating, analysing and disseminating socio-economic information for use in policy formulation. The economic development strategies adopted by the government over the years have demanded more and more social data and research as time has passed. To meet this demand, the government has set up specific departments and institutes for data collection and research.

The government's policy on science and technology is embedded in its National Science and Technology Policy.[1] In this policy, 'science' refers to all sciences, including social science. With respect to research and development (R&D), the policy aims to promote basic, applied and developmental research, particularly in areas of national importance and priority. In order to achieve this objective, the policy document envisages six strategies, namely (a) prioritize R&D in water, food, energy, environment, nanotechnology, biotechnology, ICT and electronics, (b) establish world-class research centres, (c) improve facilities for

---

[1] National Science and Technology Commission, *National Science and Technology Policy*.

researchers, (d) encourage collaborative research partnerships, (e) ensure safe and ethical research practices and (f) establish a national research system to monitor state-funded R&D activities.

Four main organizations under the government directly provide funds for research in science and technology: (a) National Science Foundation (NSF), (b) National Research Council (NRC), (c) Council for Agricultural Research Policy (CARP), and (d) National Health Research Council (NHRC). NSF is under the purview of the Ministry of Technology and Research and directly funds research on social science. NRC, which is also under the same ministry, mainly funds research on hard science. CARP and NHRC support agriculture- and health-related research respectively. The University Grants Commission (UGC) provides finance to academia for postgraduate research in various disciplines, including social science. Other institutions, such as the Central Bank, the Institute of Policy Studies (IPS), the National Institute of Social Development, the National Institute of Education and the Institute of Archaeology, also undertake social science research independently or in collaboration with other institutions.

NSF was established in 1998 as the successor to the Natural Resources Energy & Science Authority (NARESA), which itself succeeded the National Science Council (NSC) set up in 1968. It has a mandate to support social science research and, indeed, does have several schemes to support the capacity building of human resources and institutions and to popularize science. These include offering (a) competitive research grants that openly advertise for applications twice a year, (b) thematic research grants to conduct research on nationally important themes proposed by NSF, (c) travel and overseas training grants that offer opportunities for scientists to participate in foreign training programmes, conferences and the like and (d) scholarships, fellowships and postdoctoral fellowships.

In order to coordinate and monitor its functions, NSF is equipped with a research advisory board as well as several working committees in different disciplines, each of which consists of subject experts drawn from different institutions. NSF's working committee on social science is designed to monitor, advise and conduct programmes to promote social science research in the country. This committee consists of senior university academics and experts specializing in different areas of social science.

In spite of the actions taken by the government to promote research, the nexus between research and policy-making is rather weak. This gap is partly due to the fact that research, in general, is not necessarily designed to address policy issues and even policy-oriented research may not be communicated properly to policy-makers. In addition, some policy-makers are not interested in research findings or cannot access research studies.

In recognition of this gap, NSF conducted a dialogue on the social science research–policy nexus designed to better understand and bridge the gap between the two domains. The dialogue focused on the influence of research on policy-making in the areas of society and culture, health, general and higher education, economic development, poverty reduction, science and technology, urban development, and waste management. The deliberations highlighted the need to develop a workable link between knowledge and policy-making. Participants in the dialogue recognized that policy decisions have to be evidence-based and, therefore, that field-level research is vital to building the link between social science and policy-making. They also declared that decision-makers in the public and private sectors have a responsibility to take into account the empirical findings of social science research in formulating their policy and business plans.

DEMAND AND SUPPLY OF SOCIAL SCIENCE RESEARCH

Vast arrays of complex social problems and issues have emerged in recent decades due to factors such as demographic shifts, economic liberalization, globalization, technological development and the growth of social media. Over the years, various organizations and individual researchers have addressed some of these issues as elements of social science research. The institutions engaged in social science research can be grouped into the following categories: (a) research institutes under government departments, (b) social science faculties and departments in universities, (c) non-governmental organizations, (d) international organizations, (e) think tanks and research institutes, (f) professional associations and (g) the research arms of commercial banks, credit rating agencies and other private enterprises.

Government departments play an active role in maintaining and updating databases for social science research. Some key data sets date back to the early 1900s. The Department of Census and Statistics and the Central Bank of Sri Lanka are the two main institutions officially responsible for regularly collecting and disseminating socio-economic data. The data series compiled by the department cover population and housing, household income and expenditure, human development indicators, poverty levels, national accounts, inflation, and the labour force. The databases maintained by the bank cover the monetary and financial sectors, balance of payments, foreign reserves and fiscal operations. The Central Bank also conducted periodic consumer finance and socio-economic surveys a few years ago.

Although social science research developed significantly over the last six decades, certain critical socio-economic issues have not been addressed adequately. These include social and economic inequalities, macroeconomic imbalances, environment degradation and climate change, and science and development.

The dearth of basic and theory-based social science research, particularly in Sri Lanka's universities, is a major lacuna. Universities are, in general, expected to engage in scholarly research contributing to the advancement of knowledge, rather than engaging in policy-oriented research. Bandaranayake argues that the universities have failed to bring about conditions for a 'generational leap' in the field of social science.[2] Indeed, he points out that much less work, assessed both quantitatively and qualitatively, was published in the 1980s and 1990s than in the 1960s and 1970s. He identifies five reasons for the decline: inadequate policy recognition, the failure of the university system to attract high-level and innovation-oriented human resources, the lack of basic theory-oriented research, institutional constraints and incompetence in English.

Reflecting on this context, Hettige argues that there has been little space for independent, critical sociological traditions to emerge largely due to the isolation of most Sri Lankan scholars from developments in

---

[2] Bandaranayake, *The University of the Future and the Culture of Learning.*

international sociological debates.[3] Sixty years after the country's independence, the pervasive influence of nationalist forces on educational institutions, including universities, has seen most university students divorce themselves from liberal Western academic traditions.[4] As most teachers are products of local universities, schoolchildren in general are not exposed to the secular, liberal ideas of the world's dominant social science traditions. Thus, nationalistic ideas linked to identity, nation state, history and development dominate the public discourse, politics and inter-group relations. Hettige opines that this state of affairs is a major challenge for Sri Lankan social scientists, but it can be addressed by building alternative networks of institutions which transcend national and regional boundaries.[5]

In addition to NSF, UGC has also implemented several measures to promote research in Sri Lankan universities, including an increase in annual funding allocations for research activities. In recent years, UGC has taken steps to improve the research capacity of university academics. In 2010, in order to inculcate a research culture in the university system, UGC began to provide a monthly research allowance to academics on the basis of their research output. This incentive saw government expenditure on academic research increase.

ISSUES COVERED IN SOCIAL SCIENCE RESEARCH

In its initial phase, sociological study showed great interest in issues such as caste, tribal groups and religion. Studies in the 1960s and 1970s demonstrated that the focus had changed. Since the government of the 1980s was promoting economic development, research focus shifted towards social changes in rural areas and began to expand in response to emerging complex social and economic issues. Early socio-economic studies focused on issues such as agriculture, foreign aid, traditional exports and economic growth. The studies were largely based on the prevalent development model. Following the election of a left-wing government in the second half of the 1950s, however, there was a shift in economic research towards issues associated with central economic planning, the welfare state and equity, and imports.

---

[3] Hettige, 'Sociological Enterprise at the Periphery'.
[4] Ibid.
[5] Ibid.

Like other societies, the Sri Lankan society is undergoing a significant transformation due to global integration and fast-developing information technologies. Ever since it first adopted economic liberalization policies in the late 1970s, the country has been open to free trade and international labour, both of which have had profound implications for social and cultural values. In response to this liberalization, the scope of social science research in Sri Lanka broadened considerably so it could address the socio-economic implications of a market-driven economy and global integration.

The civil war situation in the country during past 30 years resulted in gradual decline of investment in research while large proportion of funding had to deviate for defense and welfare activities. This directly affected the quality and the quantity of R&D work in the country. This conflict severely constrained the country's growth potential and negatively impacted well-being. Indeed, these negative effects still remain, and overcoming them is a major challenge. The research, which emerged from these changes, focuses on social disharmony and cohesion. Current studies reflect the social, cultural and economic dilemmas the nation encountered as a result, including social injustice, income inequality, poverty, gender disparity, child abuse, population ageing, livelihood development, microfinance, economic development, regional economic cooperation, ethnic conflict and social harmony.

Given the resource constraints Sri Lanka faces, conducting research on the entire gamut of social issues that have emerged is a major challenge. Thus, NSF has prioritized four major areas in its current social science research agenda, namely (a) managing social and economic change, (b) the social determinants of health and illness, (c) social and demographic shifts and (d) the social impact of science and technology. It expects that initiatives in these areas will provide the greatest opportunities for the widest group of social scientists to conduct research in collaboration with international agencies, foreign research institutes and universities.

FUNDING AVAILABLE FOR SOCIAL SCIENCE RESEARCH

In Sri Lanka, the gross expenditure on R&D (GERD) increased from USD 9.7 million in 1984 to USD 22.9 million in 2000 and then quadrupled to USD 83.8 million by 2015 (Table 20.1). GERD as a ratio of GDP, however, does not reflect this increase: It fluctuated between the

Table 20.1 *Gross Expenditure on R&D*

Year	Amount ₹ (Million)	USD (Million)	% of GDP
1984	257	9.7	0.18
1993	649	13.1	0.13
1996	1,410	23.0	0.18
2000	1,810	22.9	0.14
2004	3,808	40.9	0.21
2006	5,120	47.9	0.17
2008	5,048	46.1	0.11
2010	8,778	69.4	0.16
2013	9,670	73.3	0.11
2014	10,350	79.0	0.10
2015	11,904	83.8	0.11

Source: National Science Foundation, *Sri Lanka Science and Technology Innovation.*

range of 0.10 per cent and 0.21 per cent over the last three decades, and the ratio for Sri Lanka at 0.11 for 2015 is on the low side and lower than the ratios of the fast-growing countries in East Asia. For example, the GERD to GDP ratio was 3.74 per cent in South Korea in 2010, 2.09 per cent in Singapore in 2009 and 1.07 per cent in Malaysia in 2011.

The government is the largest contributor to R&D in Sri Lanka, accounting for around 60 per cent of GERD in 2015 (Table 20.2). Business enterprises contributed around 34 per cent of GERD, whereas foreign sources provided only about 2 per cent. The World Bank, the Asian Development Bank and the European Union were some of the key sources of foreign funds.

The government expenditure on R&D is allocated among different ministries through the annual budget (Table 20.3). In 2014, the total allocation for technology and research amounted to NPR 10.7 billion, or around 1 per cent of total government expenditure and 0.2 per cent of the GDP. By 2016, it was expected that the government's expenditure on R&D would rise to nearly NPR 12 billion. Each ministry

Table 20.2 National GERD by Sources of Funding, 2010

Source	Amount ₹			Percentage Share			Total as % of GDP
	Re-current	Capital	Total	Re-current	Capital	Total	
Government	6,181.5	918.0	7,099.5	59.1	63.3	59.6	0.063
Business Enterprises	3,737.6	362.3	4,099.9	35.7	24.9	34.4	0.037
Foreign	133.7	42.7	176.4	1.3	2.9	1.5	0.002
Other	400.8	127.5	528.3	3.8	8.8	4.4	0.004
Total	10,453.6	1,450.5	11,904.1	100.0	100.0	100.0	0.100

Source: National Science Foundation, *Sri Lanka Science, Technology and Innovation Statistical Handbook 2015.*

Table 20.3 Sector-Wise Allocation of Government Expenditure on Research and Collection of Statistics

Name of the Ministry	(Million SLR) 2005	2012	2013	2014	2015	2016
Technology and Research	665	2,347	4,370	3,768	3,999	4,228
Agriculture	976	1,759	2,280	2,397	2,513	2,619
Plantation Industries	445	704	937	1,075	1,104	1,154
Special Spending Units	456	1,070	1,260	744	200	210
Indigenous Medicine	68	114	483	311	368	410
Disaster Management	—	426	366	1,254	1,840	1,965
Finance and Planning (Census)	267	805	332	54	13	14
Health	189	228	321	339	378	410
Fisheries and Aquatic Resources Development	146	209	260	280	326	359
Traditional Industries	43	79	92	104	115	125
Environment	35	41	90	240	253	266
Defence	—	20	12	40	42	45
Livestock and Rural Community Development	—	22	32	35	48	49
Special Agencies (GIC, PTF)	—	6	66	26	28	29
Total	3,290	7,830	10,901	10,667	11,227	11,883

Source: Ministry of Finance and Planning, Annual Report 2016.

is expected to allocate part of its total allocation to socio-economic research, but it is almost impossible to determine the amount allocated for social research, as allocations are not categorized on a discipline-wise basis.

The discipline of social science and humanities accounts for only about 7 per cent of the total GERD (Table 20.4), an inadequate amount. The bulk of funds are spent for R&D in other disciplines, mainly agricultural science, engineering technologies and natural science, partly because they require expensive equipment and consumables for laboratory-based research.

CHALLENGES TO SOCIAL SCIENCE RESEARCH AND REMEDIAL MEASURES

The low level of funding has made it impossible for researchers to meet the growing demand for social science research from both public and private sectors. To begin with, the total government allocation for R&D for all disciplines is low, and then social science is not a priority area of research. Although the GERD in absolute terms rose from about USD 10 million in 1984 to USD 84 million in 2015, the GERD ratio of GDP declined from 0.18 to 0.11 in 2015. All disciplines have suffered. R&D facilities must be expanded to move the country to a knowledge-based economy with a wealth of knowledge-based inputs.

The low level of R&D expenditure on social science is partly a reflection of the limited number of research projects undertaken in this discipline. Funding organizations in Sri Lanka face several challenges in facilitating social science research. NSF receives far fewer research grant applications for funding research in social science than in other disciplines, despite the fact that it calls for applications at least twice a year. In 2013, out of 180 applications received, only 3 (1.6%) were in social science areas. The other difficulty the funding organizations face is the poor quality of the research proposals received, only few of which meet the evaluation criteria of funding agencies. Research objectives and methodologies were poorly constructed in the majority of proposals, and the ideas lacked originality and innovation.

Table 20.4 *Sri Lanka: GERD by Discipline*

Discipline	Amount (₹ Million)			Percentage Share		
	2010	2014	2015	2010	2014	2015
Natural Science	1,064	2,666	3,170	12.1	25.8	26.6
Engineering Technologies	1,771	2,448	2,991	20.2	23.5	25.1
Medical Science	499	371	1,019	5.7	3.7	8.6
Agriculture Science	2,926	4,078	3,746	33.3	39.4	31.5
Social Science and Humanities	578	604	647	6.6	5.8	5.4
Other	1,940	183	329	22.1	1.8	2.8
Total	8,778	10,350	11,904	100.0	100.0	100.0

Source: National Science Foundation, Sri Lanka Science, Technology and Innovation Statistical Handbook 2015.

Research proposals submitted to other funding organizations are little better. For instance, UGC reports that the inability of university academics in social science fields to prepare acceptable research proposals is a major constraint to their obtaining placements in universities abroad when they apply for grant financing for postgraduate research studies. As a result, the annual grants allocated by UGC for postgraduate studies in social science are underutilized. The major weaknesses of the research proposals include the areas of proposed research, the research questions set, and literature survey and research methods, as well as a lack of strong theoretical foundations. A large number of grant applicants in the field of economics, for instance, intend to conduct fieldwork in areas such as microfinance and livelihood development. While it is true that these are important research fields, postgraduate study candidates give inadequate attention to core subject areas of microeconomics and macroeconomics. It has also been observed that some candidates do not seem to receive adequate mentoring from senior academics to improve their research proposals.

In short, apart from limited funds, several other critical factors impede research in social science. Bandaranayke argues that funding is the fourth and last of his prerequisites for improving the research capacity of universities.[6] The other three are (a) correct policy orientation, vision and leadership, (b) far-reaching institutional changes and (c) the empowerment of researchers and the creation of space for young talent.

The poor quality of research proposals can be partly attributed to the fact that the social science research environment is less supportive for young social scientists than it is for youths in natural sciences, agriculture and medicine, fields in which a senior scientist almost always play a leading role in drafting research proposals and applying for grants. In the social science sector, such guidance is absent. Instead, social science students draft proposals on their own, with only marginal contributions from their supervisors. The quality of these proposals, therefore, rarely meets the standards that funding agencies demand. As a result, the rate of rejection is high.

---

[6] Bandaranayke, *The University of the Future and the Culture of Learning.*

In order to address the above problems, NSF's Working Committee on Social Science will conduct a package of programmes to upgrade the research capabilities of young social scientists. It will periodically conduct training programmes for young social scientists on topics such as research methodologies, data analysis, writing research proposals, writing research publications and research ethics.

The committee will conduct studies only after conducting awareness-building activities in the scientific community and stakeholders. Each research group it establishes will comprise researchers at different levels and be headed by a competent senior social scientist. The committee will also take initiatives to seek funds from potential collaborative research organizations and donor agencies abroad.

CONCLUSION

Sri Lanka has witnessed considerable progress in social science research over the last six decades. Importantly, social science research is recognized as a core component of the government's science and technology policy. Initiatives taken by the government to expand the university system and to establish specific research institutes over the years have contributed to the growth and diversification of social research. Autonomous research institutes established by the non-government sector have also contributed. In spite of these developments, the nexus between social science research and policy-making remains rather weak, and research findings need to be more effectively used in policy formulation.

The country's total expenditure on R&D for all disciplines is limited, and that for social science research is much lower than it is for other disciplines. Apart from the financial constraints, other factors such as the dearth of well-written research proposals constrains social science research.

In many instances, postgraduate aspirants and other researchers fail to obtain even those funds which are available at UGC and NSF due to weaknesses in their research proposals. For this reason, building capacity and developing research skills are crucial. Having recognized these problems, the Ministry of Technology and Research has given high priority to social science research in the 10-year research investment plan it is currently compiling. NSF will also take steps to formulate new strategies and plans to support and promote social science research in the country.

The supply of and demand for social science research are not balanced. Postgraduate candidates tend to choose rather vague and common research topics and to conduct empirical research without adequate theoretical foundations. This has led to a dearth of basic and theory-based research. Although different research organizations and individual researchers have addressed emerging socio-economic issues with numerous research studies, critical issues such as social and economic transformation, health and illnesses, social and demographic shifts, income disparity, environmental degradation, and science and technology need to be investigated in greater depth.

PART V

The Role of Think Tanks in South Asia: A Synthesis

Chapter 21

The Role of the Think Tank Initiative in South Asia

Sukhadeo Thorat, Ajaya Dixit and Samar Verma

INTRODUCTION

The preceding discussion presents the contribution of core, non-earmarked, predictable and (relatively) long-term funding through the multi-donor Think Tank Initiative (TTI) programme—managed by International Development Research Centre (IDRC) of Canada—to the 14 think tanks in five countries of South Asia. In the first part of this volume, progress made by grantee think tanks from Bangladesh, India, Nepal, Pakistan and Sri Lanka has been empirically presented over the duration of the TTI programme by the think tanks individually. The subsequent section presents a consolidated picture of social science research for each of the five countries where these think tanks are situated. These two sections together inform the regional synthesis that this chapter presents.

The TTI programme staff presented the case for the need to strengthen think tanks persuasively (as mentioned in Chapter 1 of this book):

The role of local actors and institutions, such as think tanks, in generating locally relevant evidence and knowledge, providing inputs into the design of policies and programs best suited to contextual realities, and engaging with a range of locally invested stakeholders is increasingly well-documented in development literature. Donors, both international and domestic, have increasingly recognised that local ownership is critical to successful development interventions and their future sustainability. Despite this recognition however, investments in local organisational capacities and their institutional landscapes to set, shape and implement locally relevant development agendas have not always been a high priority for donors. This increases the risk of ineffectiveness and failure of development interventions, no matter how well-meaning the intervention programs may be.

This observation is extremely relevant to South Asia too.

In the recent decades, there has been a steady increase in organisations seeking to influence or inform policy through research or evidence in South Asia. The supply of research for policy making in developing countries comes from a variety of institutions—think tanks, universities or academia, or studies undertaken by multilaterals, media reports, or even civil society organisations and advocacy groups. Further, in South Asia, the growth and influence of these organisations has been shaped by a variety of factors: democracy, strategy of economic development, and open socio-political systems which have greatly influenced the way policy research organisations have emerged. Initially, bureaucrats (non-elected government officials) and technocrats in line ministries (government departments) were the key source of knowledge, meant to aid policy formulation and decision-making, with experiential learning being a key factor. The planned economic development and reforms initiated from 1970s onwards in the South Asian region changed this modus operandi, when the demand for expertise, not necessarily available within the bureaucracy, began to grow. The first and modest state response was to incorporate experts within the government bureaucracy. It was only much later that external support from think tanks began to be recognised as a resource for policy making. Therefore, even though policy research institutions were encouraged by the government and several were housed in universities, due to shrinking government funding over time, external (bilateral/multilateral) funding sources assumed increasing importance.[1]

Governments in these countries face multiple pressing challenges and often lack the capacity for high-quality policy research to take

[1] Srinivasan and Verma, 'Public Policy Research in South Asia'.

informed decisions. Think tanks ... play a crucial role in supporting such informed decisions. However, most think tanks rely on project-based funding, which is often limited and project-specific. Therefore, think tanks are usually restricted to undertaking commissioned research instead of setting an agenda. Further, this prevents them from attracting high-quality talent and developing long-term research capacity, which in turn adversely affects the research quality.[2]

As a multi-donor global programme, TTI is an innovative experiment that attempted to break this vicious circle. It selected 43 think tanks in 20 countries in Latin America, Africa and South Asia—of which 14 were in South Asia (7 in India, 2 each in Pakistan, Bangladesh and Sri Lanka, and 1 in Nepal)—through a rigorous and competitive process of institutional assessment and selection. These think tanks were then provided predictable core—unrestricted—financial and technical support over a period of 10 years (in two phases of five years each). The objective was to help think tanks strengthen their research quality and outreach to improve their impact in shaping policy. At least three key features of the nature of support under TTI stand out, especially in stark contrast to project-funding modality that is the norm of funding in recent decades. These are discussed briefly in the succeeding paragraphs.

POLICY RESEARCH ORGANIZATIONS

It is important to note that the TTI programme made a clear distinction—even though not always explicitly—between policy research organization (think tanks) and research organizations. In addition to basic empirical research, think tanks specially focus on the policy and problem-solving research that is relevant to contemporary times, and address contemporary socio-economic and technological issues. In doing so, they are largely motivated by certain goals and the zeal to provide policy solution to pressing problems based on systematic empirical research. Unlike research organizations, think tanks actively leverage their research for effecting change by reaching out systematically and in a focused manner to undertake policy advocacy, and often assume the role of policy entrepreneur. The style of 'informing' policy

---

[2] Verma, Vaidyanathan, and Bharadwaj, 'Corporate Social Responsibility in India'.

debates or 'educating' public opinion takes multiple forms.[3] For policy advocacy, these organizations often not only use persuasive methods to convey their points of view on policy matters to the government and policy-making bodies but also take a bold position that involves taking a different stand—that differs from the official one. Thus, the differentiation between a 'research organization' and a 'think tank' revolves primarily around the role of advocacy or public engagement behaviour of the latter as opposed to pure research by the former.

CREDIBILITY AND INDEPENDENCE

Because of policy research and its advocacy, think tanks inevitably maintain some kind of engagement with government if they are to succeed in influencing policy while trying to balance the independence in policy suggestions and financial dependence on government. Their desire to preserve intellectual autonomy by maintaining a respectable distance from the government is fraught with difficulties and tension. Therefore, the precise nature of a think tank's 'independence' must be treated with flexibility. While many think tanks discussed in this volume are independent, non-government, non-profit organizations, depending on private and public funding, few were also set up with the support from the government of the day. However, a key learning from the experience of the functioning of the think tanks is indeed how fragile, and often mistaken, the notion can be of narrowly interpreting government support, or involvement in governance, as the sole determinant of think tank independence.

> Credibility is often narrowly interpreted as 'financial independence'[4] of TTs—the extent to which their research agenda and impact pathways are influenced by the source of funding. However, it is important to keep in view that 'financial independence' is only one dimension of the overall 'independence' of TTs.[5]

---

[3] Stone, 'Think Tanks and Policy Advice in Countries in Transition'.

[4] https://newrepublic.com/article/144818/credible-think-tank-dead (accessed on 12 September 2018).

[5] Verma, 'Think Tank Credibility', 26.

By the same token, it cannot always be assumed that government-created or -supported think tanks enjoy an automatic route to decision-makers and influence on policy-making process.

There is also an issue of independence from funding agencies. 'TTs have recently been accused—directly or implicitly—of acting as policy lobbyists on behalf of funders exposing them to allegations of being "foreign agents" or "corporate sector lobbyists".[6] Admittedly, active policy interlocution in seeking to influence policy is skating on thin ice.' Some funding organization sets the research agenda while others support with conditions on type of research. Here also, the think tanks have to steer their autonomy carefully from the funding organization's influence—real or perceived.

OWNERSHIP AND FLEXIBILITY

Core support from TTI clearly recognized these issues, and the programme design, delivery modalities and evaluations tools built its edifice on these principles. The entire support was fully owned by the think tanks themselves, and they developed their research agenda and programme objectives independently without conditionalities, though in close consultation with the programme staff. This was a bold, and unique, feature of the programme and strongly underlined the principle of relationship based on think tank ownership and mutual trust. The only guideline for the use of TTI resources was the requirement to define organizationally owned objectives for the use of grant in strengthening three dimensions of the think tank, namely research quality, policy engagement and organizational performance. And these objectives were to be outlined for the entire period of the programme, with complete flexibility to modify them as required during the programme tenure. Each organization, thus, had its unique, independently designed, fit to its own context set of objectives for the programme period, which formed the basis for monitoring and evaluation of their progress and performance.

---

[6] https://www.nytimes.com/2014/09/07/us/politics/foreign-powers-buy-influence-at-think-tanks.html?_r=0 (accessed on 12 September 2018).

In this chapter, we discuss and summarize the contribution of TTI on the strengthening of think tanks as organizations along the three dimensions of research quality, policy engagement and organizational performance. The programme also made a significant contribution to strengthening the policy research ecosystem, even though not all of those effects were fully foreseen initially. The remaining part of this chapter will highlight TTI's contribution in South Asia.

DIVERSITY OF THE THINK TANK COHORT

The chapter by TTI programme staff captures the diversity of the cohort in South Asia across multiple dimensions and states (as mentioned in Chapter 1 of this book) that

> A rigorous selection process across the globe produced a mixed portfolio consisting of independent think tanks that varied in size (large, mid-sized and small), age (young and established), areas of policy focus (themes as well as local, national, and international) and division of work between research and advocacy projects. Of the total 52 selected think tanks, 16 were based in South Asia.

Further, TTI did not select top performers only. While some were selected because they were top performers needing small support to strengthen some aspects of the organization, several others in the selected cohort displayed promise of performance. The choice of think tanks was also theme-agnostic by design, as a result of which collectively, the cohort represented a very wide variety in thematic engagement. The diversity of the selected South Asian cohort at the start of the initiative is reflected in the following dimensions as mentioned in the chapter:

1. The age of the think tanks selected ranged from 5 to 54 years, with total number of staff members ranging from 15 to 131. Full-time researchers also ranged from 8 to 51 across the cohort in 2010. While one think tank had less than 20 staff members, two had between 20 and 30, six had between 30 and 50, four had between 50 and 100, and three had over 100 staff members.
2. The annual budget of the grantee think tanks ranged from less than CAD 0.5 million to over CAD 2.5 million. Eight think tanks had

annual budgets less than CAD 1 million, whereas two had budgets exceeding CAD 2 million.

3. Of the 16 think tanks selected in the first phase, 4 had no previous relationship of working with IDRC, whereas many others had a long-standing relationship.

4. The huge dependence of think tanks on international sources of funding was also observed during the institutional visits to 34 think tanks as part of the selection process in the five South Asian countries. Fifty-four per cent of the total annual funding for all 34 think tanks combined came from international sources. While this was 44 per cent for Indian think tanks, it was significantly higher at 84 per cent for the other four countries combined. Only 20 per cent of all funding for Indian think tanks came from government, and it was much less at an average of 3 per cent for the other four countries in the region. While the share of domestic philanthropy in the annual budgets of think tanks in India was 12 per cent, it was only at an average of 3 per cent for the other four countries. This is evident from Table 21.1.

THINK TANK GROWTH IN SOUTH ASIA

The think tank growth in South Asia comprises a mix of old research institutes and new ones. While, by and large, the former were engaged in both basic and policy research, the latter were mostly set up with an explicit/predominant purpose of policy engagement. Table A21.1 presents an overview of the 14 think tanks' areas of research and policy engagement. Few features emerge quite clearly. The cohort comprises think tanks set up as early as in 1956 and as recently as in 2008 and 2009, with many emerging on the scene in the second half of the twentieth century and in the first decade of the twenty-first century. All think tanks in the cohort set up in the 1950s, 1960s and 1970s are from India (set up in 1956, 1963 and 1973). Five were set up in the 1980s and 1990s, and another six in the 2000s (between 2000 and 2009).

It is interesting to note that the think tanks set up during 1950–1970 were initiated by both the government and private individuals. In India, the National Council of Applied Economic Research (NCAER) reflects the vision of the then Prime Minister Jawaharlal Nehru, who

Table 21.1 *Main Sources of Funding for 34 Think Tanks in South Asia, 2009*

On an Average, Main Sources of Funding in 2009 for 34 Think Tanks in S. Asia	Source of Funding for India (in %)	Source of Funding for Rest of South Asia (in %)	Source of Funding for Total South Asia (in %)
1. Grants and contracts from international aid agencies (e.g., World Bank, United States Agency for International Development [USAID] and United Nations Development Programme [UNDP])	9.02	57.71	23.34
2. Grants from international foundations, programmes and NGOs (e.g., Global Development Network [GDN], International Budget Project, Revenue Watch Institute and Ford Foundation)	34.49	26.27	32.07
3. Grants from domestic foundations and organizations	12.17	2.65	9.37
4. Contracts from domestic government agencies	20.45	2.48	15.16
5. Contracts from private domestic for-profit organizations	6.00	0.39	4.35
6. Fees from training courses, conferences and other such activities	3.75	1.51	3.09
7. Income from publications	0.10	0.42	0.19
8. Other	14.03	8.57	12.42
Total	100.00	100.00	100.00

Source: IDRC internal background note prepared for TTI launch event, Delhi, October 2010.

recognized the need for policy research as back as in 1956, to meet the needs of the government of a newly independent country. This initiative was equally matched by the initiatives from individuals like Professor Rajani Kothari who set up the Centre for the Study of Developing Societies (CSDS) in 1963, while the Centre for Policy Research (CPR) was set up in 1973 with the help of a major support from the Indian Council of Social Science Research (ICSSR). Two institutes set up in Sri Lanka—Institute of Policy Studies (IPS) in 1988 and Centre for Poverty Analysis (CEPA) in 2001—reflected the combined initiative of both government and private individuals, guided by the recognition of the need for research to support policy formulation. Many motivated academicians in India, Pakistan, Bangladesh and Nepal established think tanks in the 1990s and 2000s. Of the 14 South Asian think tanks selected for the programme, if we exclude 5 which were established with the support of the respective national governments in India and Sri Lanka, the rest 9 think tanks were set up by motivated individuals or groups of individuals in the five Asian countries in the 1990s and 2000s. If the think tank cohort is any indicator, the think tank growth clearly accelerated during the 1990s and 2000s.

However, despite differences between the older ones and the ones set up in the past 20–30 years, there is a common thread that binds them. These institutes were established by motivated scholars and change-makers, whether inside or outside the government. This is the case both for the think tanks which were initially started with government support and those started by eminent individuals. In both cases, these individuals were immensely motivated by a desire to understand the contemporary social and economic challenges through empirical research and then suggest policy solutions. The institutions they set up were shaped by their vision and led by their energy. Compared with the old ones, the new think tanks are relatively more explicit in their engagement in policy research and policy advocacy.

Further, not surprisingly, given the need for policy engagement of think tanks, five of the seven think tanks in India are based in Delhi, the national capital, and two are in Bengaluru. Preponderance of Delhi-based think tanks reflects closely the national-level findings of the Centre for Social Studies (CSS) survey (Table 21.2).

Table 21.2 State-Wise Distribution of Autonomous Research Institutes with Social Science in India

SI No.	State	No. of Institutes
1.	Delhi	54
2.	Maharashtra	15
3.	Kerala	13
4.	West Bengal	11
5.	Gujarat	11
6.	Andhra Pradesh	7
7.	Karnataka	7
8.	Bihar	5
9.	Rajasthan	5
10.	Assam	3
11.	Tamil Nadu	3
12.	Himachal Pradesh	4
13.	Uttar Pradesh	3
14.	Madhya Pradesh	3
15.	Odisha	3
16.	Puducherry	3
17.	Chandigarh	2
18.	Punjab	2
19.	Jharkhand	1
20.	Telangana	1
21.	Sikkim	1
22.	Uttarakhand	1
23.	Haryana	1
Total		159

Source: CSS Survey, Table 3.1, p. 82, in Thorat and Verma, Social Science Research in India.

A look at the thematic cloud diagram (Figure 21.1) clearly indicates the huge variety of themes that the South Asian think tanks have been working on. Even though these themes are not mutually exclusively defined, it is clear that some themes such as public policy, urbanization, security, infrastructure, governance and poverty stand out, compared to many others where relatively fewer think tanks are engaged in.

Figure 21.1 *Thematic Diversity of South Asian Think Tanks Selected for TTI*

Source: TTI internal database.
Note: These themes are broadly reflective of organizational reporting for the period 2015–2017.

Given the diversity of subjects for research and advocacy, it is difficult to make a common statement about the themes. However, at the risk of generalization, the themes, which form the focus of policy research and advocacy of the think tanks, could be grouped into the following categories:

1. There are think tanks which focus on general economic growth or development, without specifying particular issues/topics within these broad themes. For instance, NCAER states its prime objectives 'to gather and analyse the data and to assess the effectiveness of public policies in promoting economic growth, opportunity, and to have improved service delivery'. In the same way, IPS (Sri Lanka) mentioned that 'Research has been mostly in matters related to

various issues of public policy in Sri Lanka.' The Centre for Policy Dialogue (CPD) in Bangladesh specifically mentions its objectives 'to strengthen the process of democratization in the country by promoting demand-driven developmental agendas and contributing to a process whereby stakeholders would have a say in the design, implementation, and monitoring of the developmental policies'.

2. The second category of think tanks seems to focus on specific development theme/topic. CPR (India) carries out academic research on wide-ranging policy issues with focus on urbanization and infrastructure, international affairs and security, governance and politics, environment and climate change, and issues related to law, regulation and society. Similarly, the Centre for Study of Science, Technology and Policy (CSTEP; India) works in areas such as energy, infrastructure, security studies, materials, climate studies and governance. It also works on issues related to urban infrastructure, sanitation and transport. The central focus of Sustainable Development Policy Institute (SDPI; Pakistan) is on issues of sustainable agriculture and forestry, energy and environmental conservation, population, gender, food security, and regional trade globalization. The Institute for Social and Environmental Transition-Nepal (ISET-N) identified climate change, water resources, energy, urbanization, urban and peri-urban food system, disaster risk reduction and resilience as issues for policy research and advocacy.

3. Among the think tanks, there are some which focus more on the issues related to inequality, poverty and social development. Although the Social Policy and Development Centre (SPDC) deals with the issues of policy research in development, it has specific focus on poverty, inequality, governance, social sector policies, climate change, gender and pro-poor macroeconomic policy in Pakistan. Similarly, CEPA (Sri Lanka) is mandated to develop both methodologies for poverty impact monitoring and a market-oriented service package for clients. It also provides services in the areas of applied research, advisory services, training and dialogue, and exchange within four programme areas: poverty impact monitoring, poverty and conflict, poverty and youth, and poverty assessment and knowledge. The Indian Institute of Dalit Studies (IIDS)

has a general focus on inequality, poverty and discrimination. But with these general issues,

> [It has a specific focus] to understand the problems of the marginalised groups which historically experienced discrimination and exclusion due to their ethnic, racial, and religious identity, identify the causes of their marginalisation and discrimination, do policy research in comparative (international) framework, and to undertake policy advocacy with stakeholders to suggest policies for the empowerment of the marginalised sections.[7]

There are some think tanks which are more focused on issues of accountability, monitoring and governance. For instance, the Centre for Budget and Governance Accountability (CBGA; India), in its goals, states, 'The central work of the institute has been to enhance transparency and accountability in governance through rigorous analysis of policies and government budgets in India, and fostering people's participation in public policy processes in the country.' CBGA has also developed Open Budgets India, an open data portal on government budgets in India for larger dissemination, understanding and utilization of data of such kind. The BRAC Institute of Governance and Development (BIGD; Bangladesh) focuses on the issues of quality research and advocacy on key governance and development issues of the country. Similarly, the Public Affairs Centre (PAC; (India) recognized the need for research in the areas of social accountability of public governance in the country. PAC has been instrumental in formulating social accountability tools such as Citizen Report Cards (CRC), Community Score Cards (CSCs), Climate Change Score Cards (CCSCs), Community-Led Environment Impact Assessment (CLEIA) and Citizen Monitoring System.

4. While most of the think tanks focus on economic development (and the issues related to inequality and poverty), there are only a few that have made political and social issues as areas of policy research. CPR mentioned international affairs, security, governance and politics as themes for its research and policy. Similarly, SDPI (Pakistan) also focuses on political change. However, the political

---

[7] http://dalitstudies.org.in/

and social issues are marginal themes in their research focus. The only think tank which exclusively focuses on interdisciplinary themes of political thought and philosophy, media and culture, democratic politics and its future, development paradigm and practices, spatial transformations, diversity, identity and violence is CSDS (India). ISET-N has worked extensively on disaster risk reduction and climate change vulnerability and adaptation at the national and regional levels. It seeks to achieve this objective by generating 'knowledge' at the intersections of the social and natural science disciplines through a collaborative global partnership informed by locally rooted research. ISET-N works with the young generation of researchers to build their capacity through education, training and interactions on challenges of adapting to impacts of global climate change and disaster risk reduction.

ROLE OF TTI

This section will not attempt to duplicate the extremely rich and varied experiences of the 14 think tanks but highlight some crucial issues that continue to emerge in discussions around policy research and its contribution to policy impact, and make an attempt to capture the highlights of changes that are reported by individual think tanks as a result of TTI support.

As a precursor to the discussion that follows, it is important to empha-size that even while the improvements in organizational sinews are reported as TTI contribution, TTI understands that most of these changes are not directly, or exclusively, attributable to TTI support. In that sense, as also reiterated by the TTI evaluation approach, we recognize that

> Multiple causal influences are at work and ... (we) do not try to impose simple, linear attribution of results to the program interven-tions ... (while appreciating) how it is the reasoning and decisions of actors in response to the resources and opportunities accompanying an intervention that ... determine whether or not, or to what extent (program interventions) work.[8]

---

[8] 'External Evaluation of TTI Phase 2', Second Interim Report, 5 December 2017 (TTI internal document).

It is also important to note that owing to the enormous flexibility offered to think tanks on their financial reporting and objective setting, there is no common template for capturing specific activities under a specific broad heading. So, for instance, some think tanks have listed hiring of researchers as organizational improvement, while others have listed that activity under research quality; or activities such as improved communication capacity of researchers are mentioned either as research quality improvement in some cases or as policy engagement in others. Arguably, it is difficult to make a crisp case of why activities such as these should be included in one, against another, heading. The TTI programme left it to the individual discretion of the think tanks to choose the dimension of the organizational strengthening under which they would like to include their activities. However, such digressions do not significantly alter most of the observations made in the following sections.

ORGANIZATIONAL STRENGTHENING

TTI considered organizational strengthening of think tanks as a critically important dimension for effective working of the think tank. All of organizational systems, structure, practices, and norms and values play a critical role in defining the brand, identity and attractiveness of the organization. These changes affect all staff—from research to administration and library as well as from governing board members down to the lowest rank of staff in support divisions.

The support did bring visible and significant improvement in the organizational performance of all think tanks. Table 21.3 shows the variety of activities that were primarily undertaken by different think tanks during the course of the TTI grant period as reported by them. These are clusters based on activities that most think tanks reported to undertake.

Just to illustrate some activities undertaken by think tanks, and their results as reported by them, SDPI has developed a programme under which it sends its researchers to various training courses within and outside the country to enhance their capabilities in specific areas of gender, macroeconomic modelling, environment and policy outreach. Bengaluru-based PAC developed a knowledge centre (online and offline) for exchange of ideas. The steps for relatively secure jobs have resulted in retention of researchers in CPR and checked the loss

318 | Sukhadeo Thorat, Ajaya Dixit and Samar Verma

Table 21.3 *Cluster of Activities That Grantees Undertook with the Funding*

Sl No.	Clusters	Number of Reporting Think Tanks
1.	Hiring of research and other staff	7
2.	Induction of consultants and new staff (mostly in administration)	5
3.	Training opportunities	4
4.	Research infrastructure (includes revamping libraries, audiovisual technologies, etc.)	7
5.	Employee incentives	4

of academic staff. CEPA in Sri Lanka established a management information system (MIS) to improve its administrative performance. The employment of senior faculty from outside the country in IIDS helped the enhancement of statistical techniques in the analysis of economic discrimination. CBGA could appoint four researchers with PhD degrees and a few others with extensive research experience as part of a research team for the first time during the TTI years.

So how did these activities help? Most importantly, the think tanks were able to improve their brand value—which not only helped them hire better quality staff but also helped retain good quality researchers during the period. These also helped improve the morale and motivation of the workforce at large, making most think tanks a happier place. This had a profound effect on organizational culture and efficiency. The retention was facilitated by increased salary structure, viable and interactive research environment, and social protection (such as staff welfare fund and medical insurance schemes). The capacity enhancement came through the training and participation of young researchers in methodology workshop. The capability enhancement came through attending national and international conferences, and networking. This had a direct link with organizational performances. The appointment of senior faculty also helped to increase the skill in research techniques and methodology of the younger researchers. Several think tanks also modernized and updated their governance manual and regulatory frameworks, which improved the working efficiency.

The grant has helped in building the research infrastructure of these think tanks in all the five countries of South Asia. While new additions were made, it also helped in revamping the older structures like libraries by increasing the number of books and print and online journals, newspapers, magazines and bulletins. The support aided in developing their websites and ICT to have better Internet connectivity, along with other audiovisual technologies like videoconferencing, to bring them at par with their counterparts in the developed world.

TTI also helped in strengthening the finance and administrative structure of these institutions. This became possible as the funding helped in inducting professional support for managing finance and operations of these institutes. For example, IPS introduced a new online financial accounting system and integrated its online human resources (HR) system. NCAER started a new HR development strategy and a performance evaluation system. It also hired a consultant—a global services firm—as an internal auditor, to prepare updated manuals for compliance, human resources, and operations and procurement. SPDC put in place a regulatory framework 'manual of service rules' that has helped maintain institutional performance and integrate strategic planning exercises.

At IIDS, the improved strength of faculty helped to launch a PhD programme affiliated to the Indira Gandhi National Tribal University. TTI also facilitated several improvements in the academic and financial administration of the institute. The programme has added more layers to the organization of the institute.

For ISET-N, improving organizational performance was an immediate need and it began with updating of their financial system, hiring of a trained finance officer and upgrading of their accounting software. The organization also hired a professional to oversee overall management. The other tasks included updating of its HR policy manual and employing a chartered accountancy firm to carry out auditing. Streamlining governance was its next major step, so ISET-N's executive committee managed to bring experienced female and male professionals from diverse backgrounds on its governing board.

Improved organizational structure and performance have led to an improved strategy of mobilizing resources so as to reduce dependence on a single source of funding. In case of BIGD, TTI supported the physical merger of two institutes—Institute of Governance Studies (IGS) and BRAC—into one. NCAER has also tried to focus on long-term grants and funding from the corporate social responsibility (CSR) component of firms.

RESEARCH QUALITY

Before delving into the wide variety of activities that think tanks have undertaken to strengthen their quality of research, it is important to address a key question that has been intensely debated within the cohort for the entire period of TTI support, and with no unanimous conclusion emerging.

What Does Research Quality Mean for Policy Research?

This, as the TTI programme learnt along the way, is not a trivial question. While tools and standards of assessing the quality of academic research are now fairly well established, such is not the case with assessing policy research. The *Second Interim Report* of TTI evaluation (December 2017) states that

> Research quality is in the eyes of the beholder. Few (TTI) supported think tanks (globally) put emphasis on conventional academic measures of quality such as peer-reviewed publications. Most described quality in relation to credibility among the users of research ... good policy research is research that is useful and used.[9]

Devesh Kapur[10] states that

> Custom-designed household surveys and randomized control trials have proliferated, most supported by external funding, which have

---

[9] 'External Evaluation of TTI Phase 2', Second Interim Report, 5 December 2017 (TTI internal document).

[10] Kapur, *The Study of India in the United States.*

generated new understandings about the country. But what has been the policy impact of this work? Suffice it to say the effects have been much more positive for the careers of US-based researchers than for India. Ironically, some of the very strengths, such as the stress on identification and causal inference, have been a source of weakness. The stress on these methods as 'the gold standard' comes at the cost of relevance and timeliness. Only certain types of questions can be addressed by these methodologies. This is not to say there aren't excellent studies that address important policy questions. But more often than not, even if they can address them, the costs and duration of these studies means they are more useful as citations than policy. When asked how many of these expensive RCTs had moved the policy needle in India, Arvind Subramanian, Chief Economic Advisor, GOI, was hard pressed to find a single one that had been helpful to him in addressing the dozens of pressing policy questions that came across his table. By contrast, the compiling of just some key facts on learning outcomes by Indian NGO, *Pratham*, has had a big impact on policy discussions in education, because it is backed by a degree of specific knowledge and engagement that is more credible and persuasive. One could question whether 'relevance' or 'timeliness' are a valid standard for good research—yes they are, when those are precisely the reasons given to funders for these projects.

Dominant techniques of research evaluation take a narrow view of what constitutes quality, thus undervaluing unique solutions to unique problems.... Peer review is by definition an opinion. Ways of measuring citations—both scholarly and social—tell us about the popularity of published research. They don't speak directly to its rigour, originality or usefulness. Such metrics tell us little or nothing about how to improve science and its stewardship.[11]

This approach and view is strongly endorsed by think tanks in their responses. Many factors were reported as strengthening research quality in think tanks.

Improved quality of research is, thus, indicated by the increase in the number of publications through reputed publishing houses and journals at both national and international levels, which included books, journals, memos, working papers and policy briefs. This has certainly gone

---

[11] Lebel and McLean, *A Better Measure of Research from the Global South.*

up in all grantee think tanks. Acceptance and use of research of these institutes by the government, civil society organizations, media, and the donor community also indicate the improved research standards, which most think tanks have credited to the TTI support.

The think tanks followed different methods to improve research quality. A summary of different approaches adopted by think tanks to strengthen organizational research quality is listed in Table 21.4. Please note that this data has been picked up only from what the think tanks highlighted in the chapters in this book. All think tanks have been—to a greater or lesser degree—following most, if not all, of the activities as listed in Table 21.4.

Table 21.4 Methods to Improve Research Quality

Sl No.	Mechanisms	Number of Reporting Think Tanks
1.	Pragmatic approach providing implementable solutions to policy-makers considering ground reality; quality of research, quality of writing and quality of presentation	1
2.	Induction of senior faculty members producing high-quality research and setting standards for junior researchers	4
3.	Rigorous and multiple review process (internal and external peer review)	5
4.	Sound methodology and credibility of evidence	2
5.	Importance of the whole research cycle (from conceptualization to dissemination of research findings)	1
6.	Maintaining global standards	2
7.	Committees to review research on the basis of ethics and plagiarism	3
8.	Ability to bring about societal change and transparency/independence of facts and opinions contained in it; non-partisan	2

Source: Reports by think tanks in this volume.

Table 21.5 *Internal Research Quality Control Process of Think Tanks, 2017*

Sl No.	Type of Products	Yes	No	Sometimes
1.	Report to clients	13	0	1
2.	Papers for conference presentation	8	1	5
3.	Papers being submitted to scientific journals	10	3	1
4.	Books being proposed for publication	11	2	1
5.	Articles for the popular press	9	2	3
6.	Documents to be distributed at press conferences	12	2	0
7.	Documents to be distributed at conferences	11	0	3
8.	Policy papers and memos prepared especially for government officials or members of parliament	13	0	1

Source: TTI internal database.

The varied approaches that think tanks use to assess their research outputs for different target groups also tell a similar story. Table 21.5 lists the number (out of 14 in South Asia) of think tanks that always, never or sometimes use their internal research quality mechanisms for different types of outputs targeted at different stakeholders.

Majority of think tanks subject their policy papers for government and reports to clients and press releases through quality assessment processes, but very few do that for conference presentations or newspaper publications. Interestingly, even papers submitted to scientific journals are not quality-reviewed by all think tanks in South Asia.

TTI has played a significant role in enabling adoption and strengthening of multiple approaches to improve organizational research quality. The set of activities undertaken by the think tanks could be clustered as in Table 21.6. Like in Table 21.4, the data in Table 21.6 has been picked up only from the think tanks highlighted in the chapters in this volume.

Table 21.6 *Activities Undertaken to Improve Research Quality*

SI No.	Cluster of Activities	Number of Reporting Think Tanks
1.	Rigour and extensive reach	5
2.	National and international collaborations	5
3.	Participation in capacity-building workshops	3
4.	Expansion in research	3
5.	Induction of senior academicians	4
6.	Quality-assurance mechanisms	7
7.	Increase in the number of publications	6

Source: Compiled from individual think tank chapters in this volume.

The CSDS collaborative model offers faculty members autonomy to scale up and network while maintaining scholarly rigour. IIDS has strengthened research through formation and expansion of its 'community of researchers', a network of researchers, distinguished scholars and experts from research organizations, institutes and universities in India and other countries working in the field of social exclusion, marginalization and inclusive policies. IPS, Sri Lanka, has been able to get its researchers back who had gone on postgraduate studies overseas to return full time to the institute, which has improved the quality of research. BIGD, Bangladesh, has launched the BIGD study group for researchers to discuss theories, learn research techniques, debate contemporary issues and watch relevant documentaries. It has tried to create a mentoring system from bottom up; younger researchers help seniors in the newest technical skills and the programming languages such as Python and R and different statistical software.

Quality was further strengthened by expanding research to the subnational levels and in non–traditional areas, moving beyond commissioned research interests. TTI funding has helped in generating new research with new methodologies by adapting to changing sociopolitical scenario in these countries. CBGA, India, has been able to scale up its research by covering more number of states and districts in the country. This has helped it to capture trends emerging from interstate comparisons. PAC, Bengaluru, with TTI support, has been able to improve the scope and application of CRCs, incorporating fresh elements for CRC+, a fresh set of tools to review public systems from a citizen perspective and extending application of CRC+ in areas such as environmental management and child rights.

CSDS has initiated a summer teaching programme called 'Researching the Contemporary', targeted at research students and independent scholars. TTI has also helped it in revamping two other programmes, Lokniti and Sarai, mainly catering to election studies, and on media and urbanism, respectively. CSTEP, Bengaluru, has come up with innovative research themes in the areas of artificial intelligence. IIDS, New Delhi, could expand its research in new spheres of market and non-market discrimination. It has extended its research on marginalized groups such as Scheduled Tribes (STs), nomadic and denotified tribes, differently abled, religious/ethnic minorities, women and youth from socially excluded groups, sanitation workers, urban migrants and urban poor, and filled the knowledge gap in areas of social exclusion existing in the country.

TTI support has helped ISET-N systematize research quality and knowledge products including the development of a quality-assurance protocol and internal and external review processes, capacity building of research staff, mentoring and otherwise learning from the research environment, participation in and organization of seminars and conferences, field visits, and exchanges with researchers from collaborating and partner organizations. It has partnered with both educational and non-educational organizations within and outside the country, using these opportunities to boost cross-learning. ISET-N has worked with Central Department of Environmental Science at Tribhuvan University (TU-CDES) in providing master's (postgraduation)-level grant and regularizing an annual conference for fresh graduates. TTI support has also helped ISET-N begin an Abishkar Fellowship for undergraduate students who did not have any such support in the country thus far. ISET-N has also supported TU-CDES in publishing its peer-reviewed journal.

CEPA has tried to focus on important areas of development in Sri Lanka, where it has built a clear niche in terms of knowledge and experience. CEPA has been involved in collaborative work, notably with Overseas Development Institute, London; the Universities of Oxford and Sussex; and the Commonwealth Foundation. The involvement with other TTI-supported think tanks through global initiatives such as the Organisational Capacity Building (OCB) project, the Southern Voice initiative and the reimagining development work, and more focused exchanges of ideas and partnerships have stimulated CEPA's thinking, broadened the skill base, contributed to greater research quality and increased its international visibility.

Further, the think tanks have been able to raise their research standards by introducing quality-assurance mechanisms in their research process and output. This has involved rigorous peer-review processes to have analytical rigour and thoroughness. Ethical consideration and technical guidance in publishing the research matter and conducting plagiarism checks have helped in improving the research standards. SDPI, Pakistan, has followed the Higher Education Commission of Pakistan's guidelines on conducting research. They have strict procedures before the inception of data collection where the enumerators are sensitized about ethical norms of administering a questionnaire.

Research at SDPI has contributed meaningfully to the national economy policy debates. The quantum of SDPI publications has gone up during the TTI years, and in 2017, SDPI launched its first *Journal of Development Policy, Research and Practice*. CPR, New Delhi, has reported publishing of their research by internationally reputed academic publishers such as Harvard University Press, Oxford University Press and Cambridge University Press—*The Oxford Handbook of the Indian Constitution* and *The Oxford Handbook of Indian Foreign Policy*.

IIDS has started its *Journal of Social Inclusion Studies* and has been publishing its own Hindi quarterly journal *Dalit Asmita*, which focuses on Dalit literature and art. The improved quality has enabled publication of books by renowned publication houses such as Oxford, Routledge and SAGE. NCAER could bring out the India Human Development Survey, based on India's only national panel data set. Lokniti, one of the oldest programmes at CSDS, India, launched its journal *Studies in Indian Politics* in July 2013. IPS started its flagship annual report *Sri Lanka: State of the Economy*, revamped and rebranded with original research based on an exclusive theme every year.

The think tanks have, thus, acknowledged the significant contribution of TTI support to enable creation of an ideal research environment with improved research infrastructure, including subscription of highly reputed journals and books and data to carry out meaningful research.

POLICY IMPACT

Think tanks are not only a source of policy ideas and innovation but also advocates of policies they believe in. They often give lead and set the policy agenda by fetching and carrying it into the public domain. Thus, their ability to establish links with the media, trade unions, pressure groups, political parties, bureaucrats and government departments is essential for policy impact. These formal and informal links create a route of access to decision-makers in order to promote ideas and influence and shape public policies.

MEASURING POLICY IMPACT

One of the most common questions associated with the assessment of policy impact is how to determine its influence. The attempts to measure this are plagued with methodological problems. The one-to-one correspondence between a think tank research and a policy adopted subsequently by government is not always straightforward. Besides, research has 'public good' character in the sense that it remains in public domain and, therefore, can be used by all without much cost. Its use is reflected in many ways and forms, which influence public opinion and policies. To capture the ultimate visible and invisible spread and impact of policy research is rather difficult to capture, especially in a relatively short time frame.

There is another more practical challenge of assessing impact, and that is to do with the question of what constitutes impact. Is it change in lives of real people that constitutes impact, in which case most illustrations of policy impact will fail by that standard, as they mostly limit themselves to effecting change in public policy formulation, and only very occasionally implementation? It is commonly known that major challenges in development lie more in implementation of policies, which think tanks rarely track.

A related challenge is of being able to provide evidence of influencing policy formulation, except through circumstantial incidences of membership in government committees, membership of government policy-making bodies, preparing background documents for government when solicited or engaged by policy-makers, etc. It is, therefore, important to retain the nuanced differences among access, influence and impact. Quite often, what gets reported as impact is at best access, or sometimes influence, and very rarely impact.

COMPLEX AND NON-LINEAR POLICY INFLUENCE PATHWAYS

Pathways to policy influence are multiple and multifaceted, with some routes visible and others not so visible, and some forms documented/cited and many others with no documentary evidence. Yet, the role and influence of think tanks on public policies are deep and powerful.

Each think tank seems to have developed its own methods and strategies to influence the policy process. Some have greater access as senior researchers are part of government policy formulation organization. Others have substantial influence through policy research sponsored by policy-making bodies of the government itself. Still others use several other strategies to take their research to the policy-making bodies, and make their research more visible for policy purpose by focusing more on dissemination to the wider policy stakeholders. Collectively, they often set the terms of debate, define problems and shape policy perception in one form or another.

Table 21.7 lists the broad cluster of strategies that think tanks are reported to have used for policy impact. Again, the data in Table 21.7 has been picked up only from what the think tanks highlighted in the chapters in this book, and nearly all think tanks have been—to a greater or lesser degree—following most, if not all, of the activities as listed in the table.

We have picked up few examples to illustrate the use of various strategies and then actual cases of policy influence by think tanks.

Table 21.7 *Cluster of Strategies Used by Think Tanks to Improve Policy Influence and Impact*

Sl No.	Cluster of Activities	Number of Reporting Think Tanks
1.	Visibility and accessibility	5
2a.	Platforms (workshop, conferences, lectures and roundtables)	4
2b.	Digital platforms (online portals, blogs, social media, radio and television [TV])	8
2c.	Dissemination through working papers, policy briefs and policy memos	4
3.	Part of policy-making bodies	8
4.	Senior representatives on communication platforms	6

Source: Compiled from individual think tank chapters in this volume.

STRATEGIES

Enabling digital access of the research generated in the form of policy briefs, executive summary sheets, memos and blogs and through social media channels has led to effective communication to various levels of audiences. For instance, CBGA has developed Open Budgets India, an open data portal on government budgets in India. This also includes the opinion on the general budget immediately after the budget presentation in Parliament. This receives immediate attention, influence and follow-up action by stakeholders. NCAER has taken pro bono help from leading Indian software company Infosys Ltd to implement a three-phase IT strategy in 2012, including a new NCAER website, new IT systems and productivity enhancers such as videoconferencing facilities. CEPA has initiated a three-language policy of communication to have a larger reach for its research. IPS started an in-house blog—Talking Economics—in 2009, which was still very much a work-in-progress and at a nascent stage in terms of the numbers of researchers who were engaged in writing blogs before TTI.

Research undertaken at these organizations has been presented at various platforms such as workshops, consultation meetings, colloquia, roundtable meets, public lectures and conferences, both national and international. Link and network with policy-making bodies like ministries and dialogues with policy-makers on a periodic basis have led to preparation of policy documents and national policy briefs.

SPDC set up an outreach office in Pakistan's capital city of Islamabad to increase its visibility and create new policy links with international donors and the federal government. PAC reports that the launch of the Public Affairs Index (PAI) series received widespread recognition from state governments, academics, academic institutions, the media and other eminent institutions engaged in governance such as the NITI Aayog, National Human Rights Commission and Lal Bahadur Shastri National Academy of Administration, to name a few. CSDS' workshop on '(P)Reserving the Handloom Reservation Act' in collaboration with the Federation of Handloom Organisations and Inclusive Media for Change focused on issues hampering the growth of the handloom industry in India. CPR has provided direct, technical expertise to policy-makers though 188 targeted meetings and has membership in 107 task forces and working groups set up by central and state governments in the country. CPR's PAISA (Planning, Allocations and Expenditures, Institutions Studies in Accountability) dialogues helped the centre to move beyond its usual dissemination channels and attempt to affect change from the ground level.

CSTEP worked closely with the Bureau of Energy Efficiency (BEE) to design and develop the Perform Achieve and Trade scheme, which was government's flagship programme to improve energy efficiency of manufacturing industries; it also worked in collaboration with the Ministry of New and Renewable Energy (MNRE), NITI Aayog and Ministry of Environment, Forest and Climate Change (MoEFCC). SDPI has its key personnel in important policy forums such as National Economic Advisory Council, National Advisory Committee of Planning Commission and National Advisory Council of UNDP on Inclusive and Sustainable Growth. CPD has been able to bring together cabinet ministers and opposition leaders even in times of conflict; it also takes credit for playing an important role in creating the tradition of multi-stakeholder consultations in Bangladesh.

Senior-level researchers of TTI, being a part of policy-making institutions, have helped in translating the research undertaken in these think tanks, feeding into landmark policies in these countries. For instance, erstwhile Planning Commission (NITI Aayog at present), Election Commission, National Advisory Council, University Grants Commission (UGC) and National Council of Educational Research and Training (NCERT) in India have been such organizations working with CSTEP, IIDS, CSDS and NCAER.

Representatives from these institutes, mostly the executive directors and senior researchers, are involved at disseminating relevant research through different mass communication channels such as TV, radio and newspapers, which influence public opinion and further help in policy formulation. ISET-N was able to begin its flagship programmes such as Himalaya Knowledge Conclave, master's-level thesis support and Abishkar Fellowship in partnership with monthly magazine *Shikshak* and community radio outlets to share its research products with diverse communities across the country. ISET-N has begun having 'more' targeted policy engagements with key stakeholders. NCAER's faculty contributes by joining or providing inputs to official policy-making or policy advisory groups and committees and has also been giving TED talks. SDPI's online TV station, Sustainable Development Television, and use of social media have created a potential platform for policy outreach. Their presence in the different channels of mass communication such as national and private sector TV and radio channels have made a significant difference in policy dissemination. CPD dialogues started by CPD provide platforms for frank and candid discussions on issues such as labour unrest, addressing input needs of farmers and price hike of essential commodities.

POLICY INFLUENCE

Here we present a few illustrative examples of how various strategies listed above enabled policy influence and impact. SDPI's major achievement is its acceptability across the political spectrum in Pakistan. In 2015, based on an SDPI study, a bill on non-Muslim-sensitive educational reforms was tabled in the National Assembly of Pakistan. SDPI also played a role in promulgating three institutional measures for better climate action, that is, Pakistan Climate Change Council to be chaired by the prime minister, Pakistan Climate Change Authority and Pakistan Climate Change Fund. One of the results of SDPI's extensive work on trade policy and provincial tax reforms was the Government of Punjab's Planning & Development Department sending a letter to Federal Ministry of Finance in Islamabad seeking the streamlining/harmonization of federal and provincial tax regime in the interest of improving cost of doing business in the country. SDPI's research further helped in widening the formal economy of Pakistan, resulting in reduction of corporate tax rate to 30 per cent for 2018.

Pakistan's other TTI-supported think tank, SPDC, engaged with policy-makers to develop their capacity in areas such as gender, poverty and inequality, and public finance. SPDC provided technical assistance to the provincial governments of Sindh and Punjab for the 9th National Finance Commission (NFC) award on intergovernmental financial transfer. SPDC also helped the Government of Sindh in finalizing the draft youth policy, and the Government of Baluchistan in assessing 'beneficiary' component of education expenditure. Furthermore, the think tank's initial support in the devolution of general sales tax (GST) on services to provinces got incorporated in the 18th constitutional amendment. SPDC also provided technical support to the Government of Sindh in strengthening the case for transferring the collection of GST on goods from federal to provincial governments. SPDC's analytical brief on the key issues related to the state of economy also shaped the parliamentary debate. The reports on the state of economy have created a platform for informed debate on budget not only in the National Assembly by parliamentarians but also in the electronic and print media.

In the case of CBGA, the result of the Open Budgets India project led the Finance Departments of Assam, Jharkhand and Kerala to publish their respective state budget data in machine-readable formats in future, while the Union government also committed to publish all detailed Demands for Grants of the Union ministries in open data format on its portal.[12] CBGA worked with the supreme audit institution in India, the office of the Comptroller and Auditor General (CAG) of India, to

---

[12] www.data.gov.in

develop the background papers for the last two biennial Accountants General (AG) conferences organized by the office of CAG, in 2014 and 2016. CBGA also provided pro bono research support to the CAG of India on both the occasions and developed the papers 'Reporting in Public Interest: Value and Impact of CAG's Audit' in October 2014 and 'Public Auditing and Accounting: A Catalyst for Good Governance' in October 2016.

CPR's PAISA initiative currently under way helps understand the scope and depth of the organization's engagement. This is India's largest expenditure tracking survey. The survey aimed at identifying implementation bottleneck in three centrally sponsored schemes—Sarva Shiksha Abhiyan, Integrated Child Development Services and Swachh Bharat Mission, conducted in 10 districts across 5 states (Bihar, Himachal Pradesh, Maharashtra, Madhya Pradesh and Rajasthan) in India. Thereby, CPR's dialogues helped the centre to move beyond its usual dissemination channels and attempt to affect change from the ground level.

CSDS submitted a report to the Ministry of Textiles and other concerned departments with prescriptions of proper implementation of the Handloom Reservation Act to increase the share of 'genuine' handloom products in textile production, formation of a handloom trust at the national level for research, and advocacy and lobbying on behalf of the sector. CSDS, in partnership with Goa Foundation and another think tank, Inclusive Media for Change, organized a discussion on 'Permanent Fund Model for Ethical Mining: Land, Livelihoods and Intergenerational Equity' on 18 February 2015 at India International Centre, New Delhi. The day-long deliberations brought to fore the practical implications of applying ethical mining principles across all states, and for all natural resources—from minerals to metal ores, and from oil and gases to more virtual properties such as telecom bandwidths and airwaves.

CSTEP has collaborated with NITI Aayog and other institutions to prepare a detailed road map for indigenous manufacture of rare earth and energy critical elements. The report has been presented to the National Security Advisor and the government is now acting on its recommendations. As this study was pro bono, the TTI core grant helped

CSTEP to fund its involvement in the area of energy policy-making. CSTEP is also collaborating with the Union (Federal) MoEFCC, which has requested the Bengaluru-based institute to study India's 'long-term CO_2 emission pathways, identify a likely peaking year and suggest alternative growth pathways'. This study has the potential to enable the government to formulate India's long-term climate policy. Here also, the TTI grant would be used to complement the limited government grant. During the TTI grant period, CSTEP was also involved with BEE to design and develop the 'Perform Achieve and Trade' scheme, which was the government's flagship programme to improve energy efficiency of manufacturing industries. MNRE also assigned CSTEP to undertake a geographic information system (GIS)-based assessment of India's wind power potential. The study findings enable MNRE to peg India's official wind power potential at 302 GW.

Research undertaken by IIDS has helped in framing appropriate group-specific policies. The Affirmative Action in Public Procurement Policies for Scheduled Castes (SCs) and Scheduled Tribes (STs) in Micro and Small Enterprises (MSEs), 2012, is one such policy outcome. The institute's research led to a policy formulation that mandates public sector units to make 20 per cent of their purchases from MSEs owned by SCs and STs. This policy was initiated by the Ministry of Social Justice and Empowerment, and its formulation was aided by IIDS. Another successful outcome of IIDS policy research is a UGC regulation for prevention of caste-based discrimination in higher educational institutions. Also, NCERT developed the Teacher's Training Module to address caste-based discrimination inside schools and classrooms in 2013, based on the evidence provided by IIDS. Taking cognizance of IIDS research on discrimination experienced by Dalit children, the Union Ministry of Human Resource Development issued guidelines against caste-based discrimination in schools. The guidelines obligate the states to take corrective measures and set up redressal mechanisms to address caste-based discrimination experienced by Dalit children inside schools and classrooms. The Ministry of Panchayati Raj recognized IIDS research on problems of the excluded and marginalized groups in accessing public services and rural governance bodies and incorporated its policy suggestions for non-discriminatory delivery of services in panchayati raj institutions (local governing bodies) in 2013. Following the research by IIDS on higher education policy, the Ministry of Human Resource Development has set up a unit to undertake policy studies for feedback to the ministry. IIDS has also prepared a *Dalit Human Development Report* for five states, which are directly used for policy framing by the state governments.

NCAER's Delhi land pooling study led to the implementation of a new policy by the Delhi government. Its strategy work for 'Vision Kerala 2030' has tried to bridge successive changes of state governments. Its recommendations based on confidential 'black money' report for the Union Finance Ministry helped in initiatives to curb illicit fund. NCAER State Investment Potential Index is helping investors and policy-makers at the centre and state levels. NCAER's exercise on Direct Benefit Transfers is helping the government's DBT Mission to accelerate its implementation; NCAER's seminal work on short-term macroeconomic trends has generated interest among market economists, the Reserve Bank of India (RBI), the World Bank and the International Monetary Fund.

Bengaluru-based PAC created immense policy relevance with their PAI series receiving recognition from state governments, academics, academic institutions, the media and other eminent institutions engaged in governance. This has led to requests for similar studies across specific sectors and administrative levels from different state governments such as Himachal Pradesh, Kerala and Karnataka.

Bangladesh's BIGD collaborated with the National Institute of Local Government to strengthen the guidelines set by ward *shobhas* (ward council) under the Helvetas-supported Sharique project. BIGD collaborated with the Copenhagen Consensus Center to identify smart solutions for Bangladesh, identifying village courts, land digitization and e-procurement as some key priorities. The findings generated got recognition in country's 7th Five-Year Plan and the national budget for FY 2016–2017. BIGD also partnered with the Central Procurement Technical Unit of the Ministry of Planning in strategizing citizen engagement in the implementation of public procurement, which was later approved for extension in the entire country.

Similarly, CPD played a significant role by advocating policy change against domestic violence. Its study on *Missing Dynamics of Spousal*

Violence Discourse in Bangladesh: Measuring the Economic Costs formed the basis of public and parliamentary debate on the economic costs of domestic violence. CPD organized a national dialogue on 9 August 2008 to disseminate the findings of the study in the presence of the then minister for women and children affairs. The Parliament of Bangladesh passed the Domestic Violence (Prevention and Protection) Bill, 2010, in order to protect women and children from physical, sexual and psychological abuse and other forms of domestic violence on 5 October 2010. Later, CPD organized a dialogue on 25 October 2014 to disseminate the findings of the study on *Estimating Women's Contribution to the Economy*. This study was also taken up for deliberation in the parliament. The Bangladesh Bureau of Statistics taking note of the findings informed the parliament about initiating the measurement of women's unaccounted work soon. CPD's first monitoring report on the infamous Rana Plaza garment catastrophe and subsequent dialogue titled *100 Days of Rana Plaza Tragedy: A Report on Commitments and Delivery* helped the government to improve the implementation.

Sri Lanka-based CEPA collaborated with international agencies such as Overseas Development Institute and Department for International Development (DFID) in terms of the Secure Livelihoods Research Consortium, a global research programme exploring livelihoods, basic services and social protection in conflict-affected situations. The communications and policy team could go beyond informing, influencing and inspiring stakeholders and decision-making bodies to position CEPA in the overall context and to allow the think tank to network with diverse actors.

IPS has set a mark in the area of urban policy research, especially in the areas of infrastructure development and urban regeneration efforts in the aftermath of post-war Sri Lanka. Training and guidance were also provided where required. This has extended in areas of migration and trade policy formulation in the island nation.

ISET-N has similar examples of influencing public policy and expenditure. After three years of lobbying, the Ministry of Science and Technology has decided to allocate budget to the Himalaya Knowledge Conclave, an annual conference for fresh graduates, thereby giving it both continuity and legitimacy. Its learning underscores the fact that consistent participation in research can help foster policy uptake. By systematically repackaging knowledge products to target specific audiences, a window of opportunity can be created to influence the policy continuum mentioned above. The system–agent–institution framework, which the ISET platform developed, for example, is useful for assessing vulnerability to climate change and for preparing strategies for adaptation. Since the 2015 earthquake, ISET-N has been using this framework to unpack the recovery efforts currently under way. It helped formulate what became known as the National Strategy for Resilient Local Communities (NSRLC) with the aim to help the country's municipalities to plan, develop and implement programmes for enhancing resilience. ISET-N also worked with the permanent reconstruction and rehabilitation committee formed by the earthquake-affected households of the Jarayatar village in Melamchi Valley of Sindhupalchok district. The organization supported the earthquake-affected households to prepare a plan for building resilient shelters as well as for building livelihoods and local economic systems and implementing drinking water and sanitation, waste management, energy, and communication schemes. The proposal this committee submitted to the National Reconstruction Authority (NRA) was approved for implementation with allocation of budget for reconstruction.

GENDER RESEARCH

With the need for more multidisciplinary research in South Asia, issues moving beyond economics became relevant in order to address the multidimensional aspect of development. Gender along with other identities came to prominence, especially from the 1980s, in case of India.[13] Research in other countries also correlated with the global situation. Instances of war, military rule, ethnic conflict and low human development during crisis led to strengthening of the need to study gender issues, especially women's status within the private as well as public sphere, their participation in education and economic activities, and their representation in the political spheres vis-à-vis men, issues of safety and violence. All the 14 think tanks have been proactive in their

---

[13] Mathur, 'Policy Research Organisations in South Asia'.

work towards the idea of development through a gendered praxis. It is important to note that the status of women vis-à-vis men in South Asia has been a result of patriarchal, cultural and social controls. Therefore, the work of the think tanks has also moved around these realms.

The activities of the 14 think tanks under TTI reflect much of the work taking place on women's livelihood needs, challenges and issues of safety within both the private and the public spheres. While most think tanks have tried to mainstream the factor of gender in all the research they have undertaken, there are some think tanks which have exclusively undertaken work on gender issues. This can be understood from the research themes designed by the individual think tanks; for instance, SDPI (women corner), SPDC (women at work) from Pakistan, IIDS (gender and social exclusion studies), CBGA (gender-responsive budgeting) from India, BIGD (gender cluster) from Bangladesh have exclusive units focusing on gender research. In addition, these think tanks, over the period of eight years, have had women in significant leadership positions who have further motivated and driven research on gender issues.

In addition, all think tanks have had some focus on gender work as part of their mainstream research to a lesser or greater degree. In Bangladesh, for instance, BIGD's work on 'Paradox of Change in Women's Capabilities: Case of Two Villages in Bangladesh' (2016), women's political representation and domestic violence against women in Bangladesh need to be noted along with one of the most important projects undertaken by them between 2014 and 2017 on 'Choice, Constraints and the Gender Dynamics of Labour Market in Bangladesh'. CPD has worked considerably (both research and advocacy) in the areas of workplace environment for women and contribution of women's household work in the country's GDP. Their work has influenced policies in the country. CPD has a number of publications on gender issues.

The seven Indian think tanks under TTI too have been quite active in their research as well as policy advocacy on issues related to many aspects of gender. CBGA's exclusive unit on gender-responsive budgeting is noteworthy. Its two most important research studies since 2012 are as follows: 'Safety of Women in Public Spaces in Delhi: Governance and Budgetary Challenges' (2017) and 'Recognising Gender Biases,

Rethinking Budgets' (2012). CPR has mostly worked at the interface of gender and basic amenities like urban sanitation ('Gender and Urban Sanitation Inequalities in Everyday Lives' [2017]) and gender and public transport, advocating the need for safety of women in the public spaces. CSDS has been working in the areas of electoral participation of women in India and also looking through a gendered lens on the attitudes, anxieties and aspirations of India's youth. CSTEP has worked by taking a mainstreaming gender approach. This has been reflected exclusively in their work on 'Localising the Gender Equality Goal Through Urban Planning Tools in South Asia'. IIDS also has an exclusive unit named 'Gender and Social Exclusion Studies', which deals with research on issues which are at the interface of gender and other social and religious identities, and their implications on access to livelihoods, education, health and political participation. 'Status of Dalit Women in India' (2015) and 'Gender and Caste-based Inequality in Health Outcomes in India' (2012) are some important research projects carried out under this head. The institute has also worked on experiences of discrimination intersecting with gender, caste, religion and ethnic identities in an urban space, in the access to government welfare schemes and also in education. NCAER has also worked on gender; most of their research has a strong gender component. However, the work 'Gender Impact of HIV and AIDS in India' (2012) and 'Does Inheritance Law Reform Improve Women's Access to Capital? Evidences from Urban India' (2012) need special mention. PAC has also kept gender as one of the important components of its activities. While ISET-N has been mostly working in the areas of environment related to crisis issues, its research on indigenous communities in the backdrop of climate change adaptation takes note of gender and social inclusion.

The two Pakistan-based think tanks under TTI have also been active in research on issues of gender and development. SDPI's 'Women Corner' showcases important research undertaken in the field of gender disparities in skill development and education, gender and environmental migration, gender situation analysis in the textile sector of Pakistan, and strategies to prevent violence against women. The following have been some important research on this count: 'The Gender Digital Divide in Rural Pakistan: To Measure and to Bridge It', 'Women's Land Rights in Pakistan', 'Country Gender Profile' and 'A Place for Women? Gender as a Social and Political Construct in Pakistan'. SPDC has contributed considerably towards 'changing gender roles in the labour force'. The think tank has mostly worked in the areas of enhanced female participation in workforce, access to credit, tax benefits, labour law reforms and social protection. It has been disseminating its *Women at Work* report since 2009. SPDC's findings led to the inclusion of 'harassment in public places' in the Pakistan's Protection Against Harassment at the Workplace Act, 2008. Findings from *Women at Work* report have led to strong, effective deliberations at the national platform on the limited workforce opportunities for women in Pakistan.

In Sri Lanka, CEPA has worked in the areas of poverty and environment and development by mainstreaming gender issues. Important research in this regard has been in the domain of livelihoods crisis (study of women beedi rollers) and women in conflict ('Social Control of Women in Post-war Sri Lanka: Its Effect on Women's Access to Secure Livelihoods'), and its work on 'changing family roles, gender roles in times of conflict'. IPS has mostly focused its work in the areas of women in labour force and women in work and caregiving sector. Both these think tanks have worked with a gender mainstream approach in their areas of activities.

STRENGTHENING THE RESEARCH ECOSYSTEM

As an organizational strengthening support programme, TTI neither had the direct mandate to support research ecosystem nor was it explicitly reflected in the programme design. Likewise, in the beginning, it had no mandate of directly supporting institutional collaboration or creating/supporting such activities. However, in recognition of the reality that the programme soon experienced and learnt of the need to strengthen the research ecosystem for sustainability of think tanks, TTI has catalysed and it continues to support and contribute to a regional initiative on a public policy discourse. These initiatives by TTI are a strong testimony to the progressive nature of programme donors' vision that allowed sufficient flexibility in programme design to learn and adapt the initiative as the TTI journey unfolded. Indeed, in South Asia, both of these types of activities—to strengthen research infrastructure as well as to create and strengthen an institutional network of 14

think tanks—have yielded very positive results. A third dimension of
the research ecosystem work was part of the TTI design, although the
purpose was rather limited to understanding the perception of *demandeurs* of public policy research in South Asia.

Collaboration with Research-granting Councils

The larger purpose of TTI was to eventually enable better-informed
policy-making through generation of good-quality research and evidence to bring about effective and sustainable change in the lives of
people, especially women and children.

> For social sciences to play their emancipatory as well as instrumen-
> tal role in public policy making, it is imperative that a well-designed
> national social science research policy steers and guides the creation of
> a vibrant research system under the leadership of adequately resourced
> and a well-governed national research council. A comprehensive set
> of data on social science research system was therefore, considered the
> starting point for informed decision-making to promote a social sci-
> ence research culture in the country.[14]

At the same time, early in the programme, it was becoming increasingly evident that a vibrant and sustainable think tank cannot be created
in a policy research environment that did not value their role and did
not support and strengthen their contribution. It was considered critical to work with the national research-granting councils as primary
public agencies responsible for strengthening social science research in
the selected countries and creating a national culture of innovation.
Fortuitously, under its leadership in 2014, ICSSR too was seized with
the idea of working towards a similar vision and larger national purpose.
TTI, therefore, joined hands under the ICSSR

> leadership—which has the mandate to enhance and promote good-
> quality research and teaching in India—to take stock of the current
> status of social sciences, identify challenges for emerging and develop-
> ing countries, make policy recommendations to address the challenges,
> and prepare for and feed into the growing demand for research-based

---

[14] Thorat and Verma, *Social Science Research in India.*

evidence as a basis for policy making at sub-national, national, regional, and global levels.[15]

This was the primary impetus for ICSSR to organize the first pan-Asian conference on 'Status and Role of Social Science Research in Asia'. TTI keenly joined hands. The conference was thus jointly held in March 2014 at New Delhi, with over 100 top social scientists and representatives of national research-granting councils, international and bilateral donors, and government agencies from 24 countries in Asia taking part. Together they assessed and deliberated the status of social science research in Asia and contemplated the need to set up a pan-Asian network for further coordination and support. The conference crucially highlighted 'the imperative for social science research-granting councils to adequately nurture social science research'. As a result of this beginning, and with active TTI support throughout the journey, ICSSR led the compilation of the first set of studies in India to comprehensively map the status of social science research, with contributions from over 29 top Indian social scientists from 9 ICSSR research institutes across India, subsequently published as an anthology.[16]

Further, following from the unanimous decision taken at the March 2014 conference, a pan-Asian platform of research-granting councils—the Asian Social Science Association (ASSA)—was formalized and launched at the follow-up conference in Bangkok in September 2014. Representatives of social science research-granting councils, government bodies, fraternal members and associate members signed the Bangkok Declaration establishing ASSA on 20 September 2014. The objective of ASSA, inter alia, is to create a pan-Asian knowledge platform for peer-learning and enhanced international and interdisciplinary collaboration, to identify emerging issues for Asian studies and scholarship, to promote social science research in Asia by addressing existing and emerging ecosystem and governance issues, and to disseminate good practices and advocate for adoption of evidence-based policy-making in Asian and other countries. ICSSR was selected as its first secretariat.[17]

---

[15] Thorat and Verma, *Social Science Research in India*, xxiii.
[16] Ibid.
[17] Ibid.

Social Capital Through Annual Regional Meetings

Following from an expressed need by the think tanks at the first regional meeting of the TTI South Asian cohort in Neemrana (India) in November 2010, seven annual regional meetings of the entire cohort have been organized by think tanks, supported by TTI, to discuss and deliberate on institutional matters (as opposed to thematic issues). The wide appreciation of the annual meetings is reflected in continued and rising demand for hosting such meetings every year of the TTI programme. Attempts to introduce thematic discussions as part of these regional meetings were not widely appreciated, owing to the unique nature of these meetings of executive directors and senior research and non-research staff, to discuss organizational matters pertaining to governance, management and operation of think tanks, and to share notes on emerging challenges and opportunities in the regional and national contexts for peer-learning. All of the think tanks have continued to express their deepest appreciation for the unique opportunity that this platform provided them to build social capital, much of which will continue beyond the TTI tenure. As the introductory chapter by TTI programme staff notes, 'We have consistently been told by TTs how valuable has this platform been, and how TTI RMs (Regional Meeting) were the only platform for discussion of institutional matters.'

As a matter of fact, the demand for documenting the TTI experience, the result of which is this book in readers' hands along with many other audiovisual outputs, emerged from the regional meetings, beginning at Mysore (India) in 2012, and reiterated in all subsequent meetings. It was widely felt that even though there is a rich history of institutional core funding in the past, especially in India, corporate philanthropists such as Ford Foundation have played an important role in creating an independent, social science intellectual system in the country. 'From the Law Institute to CSDS to CPR, Ford played a big role. The key is funding should not have any strings attached.'[18] Governments, domestic philanthropists and international foundations have set up some of the most vibrant institutions of higher learning and research, though very little of that experience is documented and available in public domain.

---

[18] Pratap Bhanu Mehta quoted in Jha, 'India's Most Influential Think Tanks'.

As a bold experiment in the recent donor environment where core funding had almost fully dried up, the executive directors of regional cohort strongly felt, articulated and have eventually led the documentation of their experiences and lessons from the TTI programme in the region.

The regional meetings have not only built a regional social capital but also enabled social relationships and personal bonding across think tanks that were remotely familiar with each other, and hardly knew of their work—and collaborative opportunities—in the past. Exchange of research and non-research staff among the think tanks has led to creation of accumulation of knowledge and mutual appreciation that will outlast TTI. Several collaborations on thematic research have also come about owing to the meeting of researchers at this platform. These platforms have also presented important opportunities to present a regional perspective at the TTI-hosted global exchange where all think tanks globally participate; two such global exchanges have been organized, and the last one is scheduled for November 2018. These systematic efforts spawning from the regional meetings have spurred global collaborations too. The Southern Voice Initiative,[19] led by CPD from Bangladesh, deserves special mention as a significant global collaboration that has had a notable impact on build-up to, and now monitoring of, SDGs.

Catalysing Regional Discourse on Public Policy

One of the notable offshoots of the TTI programme effort on strengthening research ecosystems in the region was the opportunity to catalyse and support the vision of leaders from Nepal, Bangladesh and India. The Nepal Administrative Staff College (NASC), the government agency which trains civil servants in the country, hosted the second conference on 'Public Policy and Governance in South Asia: Towards Justice and Prosperity' (28 and 29 June 2018) to develop a regional discourse on public policy that is home-grown and rooted in the local context, and hence more appropriate for effecting change relevant to the context. The conference was organized in partnership with ISET-N; Niti Foundation, Nepal; South Asia Institute of Advanced Studies (SIAS), Nepal; Institute of Public Enterprises (IPE), India; TTI/IDRC, India; BIGD, Bangladesh; and North South University (NSU), Bangladesh.

---

[19] For details, visit www.southernvoice.org

The concrete outcomes of the conference were a regular hosting of regional public policy conferences to bring together government agencies, scholars, eminent intellectuals and thought leaders from the region to deliberate on the contextual challenges and offer home-grown, native solutions to regional challenges. This platform is expected to build the regional social capital and mutual bonding among scholars and public officials through joint deliberations in non-official settings. The platform is also designed to provide opportunities to young scholars from the region to research and offer policy solutions to socio-economic, political and technological challenges in the region, enabled through a 'call for papers' from young research scholars. Understanding the significance of such meetings as 'public good', NASC continues to engage the highest levels of public policy-making community through its conferences and planning.[20]

A parallel effort is under way under this initiative to develop a regional course on public policy that draws upon the local context and challenges, and offers locally appropriate solutions.[21] BIGD and IPE already run similar courses for civil servants and scholars in their respective countries, and their experience is being used to develop this regional programme, aimed at triggering home-grown research and theory development based on local experiences and rooted in local context. The first such regional course on public policy is now proposed to be held in October 2018, hosted by IPE, Hyderabad, and jointly conducted by NASC, NITI, BIGD and TTI.

Conducting and Sharing Policy Community Surveys

As part of the programme design, TTI has supported the conduct of two community surveys,[22] while the third (and last) survey is scheduled to be conducted in September 2018. These surveys were 'designed to

---

[20] Ex-prime minister of Nepal and top civil servants from the country actively presented and participated in various sessions held on 28–29 June 2018 at Kathmandu. For details, see http://www.nasc.org.np/content/conference-public-policy-and-governance-south-asia (accessed on 12 September 2018).

[21] Nepal's Kathmandu University and Institute of Integrated Development Studies have also begun collaboration to begin similar educational programmes.

[22] They are available at TTI website: www.thinktankinitiative.org

gather views of senior-level policy actors within national policy communities on their need for research, perceptions of research quality
and think tank performance'. The surveys have been the only instruments to make an attempt to understand the demand side of policy
research. They help understand the general questions about the nature
of demand—such as what topics are demandeurs most interested in their
policy-making role, in what format are research outputs found most
useful by them, and what sources and mediums do they prefer when
looking for evidence and analyses. Additionally, the surveys enhance the
understanding about the perceptions of policy-makers about the roles,
strengths and challenges of think tanks in general, and for specific think
tanks that were supported by TTI in the region. Think tanks found
this information useful, even if it was perception-based and not always
complete or as robust as conclusions. Such information on demand
side is also rather—and surprisingly—rare in South Asia. 'The nature of
the research itself is based on a fuzzy understanding of the demand for
such research; an understanding that relies more on organisational or
individual experience, rather than on a scientific basis or comprehensive
evaluation of demand in the policy landscape.'[23]

This has been a modest but very critical contribution by TTI in raising awareness of the need to understand the demand side of the policy
research environment better, and prompted at least one—and first in
the region—study 'to systematically understand the policy impact of
social science research in countries of South Asia, exploring not only
the role of research in public policy, but—more importantly—public
policy makers' perception of the research they use, or not, in their
policy making activities'.[24]

SUSTAINABILITY OF THINK TANKS

The ultimate objective of TTI in strengthening organizations, quality of
research and policy impact is to bring think tanks on the path of long-
term sustainability such that they continue to provide good-quality
evidence for public policy-making in their countries and across the

---

[23] Srinivasan and Verma, 'Public Policy Research in South Asia'.
[24] IEG study in Thorat and Verma, *Social Science Research in India*.

world. The essays by different think tanks in the preceding chapters highlight steps taken by them towards sustainability beyond the TTI programme tenure, with varying degrees of success owing to different histories, strategies and efforts, and differing opportunities in their respective environments.

Sustainability is one of those fuzzy concepts that are better understood than defined, with different think tanks defining it differently in their local and organizational context. Based on the programme understanding and experience, TTI used a simple framework to define sustainability that essentially focuses on five dimensions, namely organization's value proposition, business models, governance and leadership, research quality, and policy impact. Table A21.2 lists the specific types of TTI contribution that was reported by think tanks on each of these dimensions in various TTI reporting tools. The overall message is clear—none of the activities towards think tank sustainability would have been possible in the absence of core, non-earmarked and predictable long-term funding.

Detailed case studies of few select think tanks also portray a rich tapestry of activities and approaches that they have employed to approach this concept in all of the five sustainability dimensions. Owing to confidentiality reasons, it is not possible to share details of those organizational strategies, but suffice it to say that think tanks have undertaken a significant variety of tasks under each of the five dimensions of sustainability and continue to make relentless effort drawing also on the contextual opportunities as they present themselves. The TTI programme has also worked jointly with several think tanks to support and catalyse achievement of think tanks' sustainability in general and that of its grantees in particular.[25] Table 21.8 lists a wide variety of strategies that TTI think tanks have followed to work towards sustainability.

---

[25] See, for instance, joint publications with CSTEP to highlight the need for and demand of institutional support to think tanks by public agencies as well as in partnership with corporate philanthropy: Bhardwaj, Asundi, and Verma, 'Creative Destruction'; Verma and Bhardwaj, 'Why Is India Freezing Out Policy Research?'; Verma, Vaidyanathan, and Bharadwaj, 'Corporate Social Responsibility In India'.

Table 21.8 *Strategies Adopted by Think Tanks for Sustainability*

Sl No.	Nature of Activity	Number of Think Tanks
1.	Collaborations, networking and peer-learning	6
2.	Creation of online portals and digital hubs to generate future demand	2
3.	Capacity-building programmes, training programmes and PhD programmes	2
4.	Strategic vision plan	2
5.	Engaging philanthropic organizations and corporate sector	2
6.	Consolidation of finances by professional fund managers	1
7.	Examining future grantees and mapping their research orientation	4
8.	More contractual positions	1

Source: Compiled from think tanks' chapters in this volume.

While most think tanks have adopted several strategies to achieve improved sustainability, the largest number of think tanks (6 out of 14) reported using 'collaboration, networking and peer-learning' as their strategy for improved sustainability. 'Regional meetings, combined with dedicated efforts by TTI to promote collaboration and peer-learning through bespoke capacity development mechanisms, also clearly played an important role in this strategy'. It is also noteworthy that most think tanks have used multiple strategies to achieve improved sustainability.

Apart from the activities listed in Table 21.8 that the think tanks claim to have undertaken for specifically enhancing organizational sustainability, they undertook crucial activities across all areas of strengthening sustainability—research quality, organizational performance and policy engagement. For instance, long-term commitment for funding under TTI enabled the think tanks to appoint researchers and staff on a long-term basis. The collaboration also helped in the appointment of senior researchers, which small think tanks could not do due to financial constraints. The presence of senior researchers improved the capabilities of junior researchers, particularly in methods and similar spheres. The capacity enhancement programme has helped young researchers and staff to receive training in methodology within the country and abroad. Appointment of senior staff and capacity enhancement of young faculty have resulted in improvement in the capacity of think tanks to undertake quality research. The grant also made research management more effective and, in multiple ways, improved the individual and collective capacities of research and non-research staff. The national and international networking opportunities also exposed researchers to new contacts and experience. Thus, together with increased number of researchers on a long-term basis, the appointment of senior researchers and the capacity enhancement of the junior researchers have resulted in more research output and improved quality. This, in turn, has earned them visibility and respectability, and networking opportunities with national and international organizations.

The TTI support to building the research infrastructure includes strengthening of libraries, purchase of new books, online and print journals, newspapers, magazines, and bulletins, and in developing ICT and the website of these institutions have all helped expand and improve research. The internal improvement in research capabilities has enabled some think tanks to start their own research journals. For instance, IIDS started its *Journal of Social Inclusion Studies*, and CSDS started the *Studies in Indian Politics*. This became possible due to the presence of senior researchers and capacity enhancement of junior researchers. The enhanced quality of research has resulted in increased publication of books by reputed international and national publishers such as Oxford, SAGE and Cambridge, among others. Some think tanks could introduce PhD programmes as a result of availability of good faculty. The improvement in quality of policy research has enabled the think tanks to influence the policies of the government more effectively. In many cases, the policy initiatives and advocacy have resulted in the adoption of policies based on the research conducted by them. All these go a long way in strengthening the credibility of a think tank and in significantly contributing to its sustainability. In part, this is reflected in high ratings received by TTI think tanks by national and international assessment agencies, who place them in the list of centres of excellence and/or institutes with potential of excellence.

The improvement in the standing of these think tanks has had a positive implication for fundraising from multiple sources. Some of them now have access to a more diversified set of funders. The improved demand for research work is an important factor enabling the think tanks to move towards sustainability. This has been possible owing to direct and indirect contribution of TTI. Sustainability depends on finding a reasonably adequate amount of predictable and stable core funding support, which continues to be elusive in the current funding environment for think tanks. TTI has helped to overcome this limitation to some extent. It has enabled many think tanks to lay a strong foundation for sustainability and effectiveness. The stable support for a period of eight years has enabled the grantee think tanks to work on their sustainability plans from the beginning of the second phase, and for some think tanks, it has started producing some positive results. Usually, sustainability is achieved incrementally.

The core support to organizational performance has also enabled improvement in think tanks' sustainability. The tangible and intangible infrastructural advancements have helped achieve some degree of financial sustainability and created new pathways for new business models. Some think tanks have created senior-level positions for resource mobilization and business development. Some have developed a strategy to consolidate and build financial savings base through professional fund managers. In some cases, their annual funding size has grown and improved. The improvement in credibility and visibility through TTI support for policy engagement and communications has invited funding from policy-making bodies. It is not surprising, therefore, that many think tanks in the cohort have reported that enhanced organizational capacity from TTI support served as a solid foundation to face the post-TTI future. They recognize that in-country initiatives aimed at dealing with emerging local problems must be bolstered by collaborative research across countries to produce insights that can lead to better practices and better formulation of public policies as well as contribute to the creation of new theories, or add to existing ones.

ANNEXURES

Table A21.1 *Think Tanks in South Asia: An Overview*

Sl No.	Name of the Institute	Year of Establishment	Areas of Research and Nature of Activities
1.	NCAER, Delhi, India	1956	It was established as an important part of former Prime Minister Jawaharlal Nehru's vision to gather and analyse the data to assess the effectiveness of public policies in promoting economic growth, opportunity and service delivery.
2.	CSDS, New Delhi, India	1963	It was founded by the eminent political scientist Professor Rajni Kothari to work in the areas of interdisciplinary themes of political thought and philosophy, media and culture, democratic politics and its future, development paradigm and practices, spatial transformations, diversity, identity and violence, and social science in Indian languages.
3.	CPR, New Delhi, India	1973	It was formed to carry out high-quality academic research on wide-ranging policy issues, and partly aimed at providing a forum for Indian policy-makers to develop and exchange ideas in the core fields of urbanization and infrastructure; international affairs and security; governance and politics; environment and climate change; and law, regulation and society.
4.	PAC, Bengaluru, India	1994	It was founded by Dr Samuel Paul to work in the areas of social accountability of public governance in India with the help of social accountability tools: CRCs, CSCs, CCSCs, CLEIA and Citizen Monitoring System.

(Table A21.1 Continued)

(Table A21.1 Continued)

Sl No.	Name of the Institute	Year of Establishment	Areas of Research and Nature of Activities
5.	IIDS, New Delhi, India	2003	The institute was established as a trust by senior social scientists and civil society activists in India in the backdrop of 2001 World Conference Against Racism (WCAR) held in Durban, South Africa. It aims to understand the problems of the marginalized groups, identify the causes of their marginalization and undertake policy advocacy with stakeholders to suggest policies for their inclusion and empowerment.
6.	CBGA, New Delhi, India	2005	It was started by a group of social activists and academicians. It aims at enhancing transparency and accountability in governance through a rigorous analysis of policies and government budgets in India and fostering people's participation in public policy processes in the country. CBGA has developed Open Budgets India,[a] an open data portal on government budgets in the country.
7.	CSTEP, Bengaluru, India	2008	Founded by Dr V. S. Arunachalam. Its areas of research are energy, infrastructure, security studies, materials, climate studies and governance especially in energy efficiency, urban infrastructure in sanitation and transport, and artificial intelligence in governance.
8.	SDPI, Pakistan	1992	It was established under the National Conservation Strategy (NCS) 1992 as a transdisciplinary think tank in its truest sense with research programmes on sustainable agriculture and forestry, energy and environmental conservation, population, gender, food security, and regional trade globalization. Initiating or becoming party to public interest litigations and building cadres of people who could help in delivering NCS were other strategies evolved.

Sl No.	Name of the Institute	Year of Establishment	Areas of Research and Nature of Activities
9.	SPDC, Pakistan	1995	Started with the support of Canadian International Development Agency (CIDA), SPDC specializes in policy research in development, poverty, inequality, governance, social sector policies, climate change, gender and pro-poor macroeconomic policy in Pakistan. The thematic 'Annual Review of Social Development in Pakistan' is a flagship product of the centre.
10.	ISET-N	2001	ISET-N's research focuses on climate change, water resources, migration, urbanization, urban and peri-urban agriculture, the economic integration of urban and rural areas, political change, and disaster risk reduction. It generates and disseminates new knowledge on policy-related issues concerning economic development, natural resource management and general well-being through field and policy research and through its engagement in public shared-learning dialogues.
11.	IPS, Sri Lanka	1988	IPS had the distinction of being the sole semi-autonomous organization, with formal financial and administrative links to the Government of Sri Lanka (GoSL) working in the areas of public policy.
12.	CEPA, Sri Lanka	2001	Poverty Impact Monitoring Unit (PIMU) of CEPA was mandated to develop both methodologies for poverty impact monitoring and a market-oriented service package for clients.[b] At its inception, CEPA was profiled as an 'independent service provider, to provide services in the areas of Applied Research, Advisory Services, Training and Dialogue & Exchange within four program areas: Poverty Impact Monitoring, Poverty & Conflict, Poverty & Youth and Poverty Assessment & Knowledge Management'.[c] In a generic sense, CEPA was also profiled as a 'professional' organization.

(Table A21.1 Continued)

(Table A21.1 Continued)

Sl No.	Name of the Institute	Year of Establishment	Areas of Research and Nature of Activities
13.	CPD, Bangladesh	1993	It was founded by Professor Rehman Sobhan, an eminent economist and civil society leader, to strengthen the process of democratization in the country by promoting demand-driven developmental agendas and contributing to a process whereby stakeholders would have a say in the design, implementation and monitoring of the developmental policies.
14.	BIGD, Bangladesh	2009	It was formed to undertake quality research and advocacy on key governance and development issues of the country.

Notes: [a] www.openbudgetsindia.org
      [b] Gunetilleke and Jafferjee, *Triangulation Squared*, 300.
      [c] Ibid., 273.

Table A21.2 *TTI Contribution Across Five Dimensions of Sustainability*

Dimensions of Sustainability	Outcomes	TTI Contribution
		TTI Contribution 1. Financial: core support + supplementary, targeted capacity-building funds 2. Technical: Program Officer's (PO) strategic engagement 3. Other: Facilitated peer-learning and exchange + stakeholder feedback (e.g., peer review and policy community survey)
Value Proposition	*Successes*	
	Think tanks positioned themselves as recognized experts (policy and services).	Enabled think tanks took risks such as exploring emerging research areas or conducted pro bono work to increase their visibility and showcase their expertise on a specific research area.
	Think tanks became recognized capacity-building centres, thereby contributing to: 1. Strengthen knowledge ecosystems 2. Enable evidence-to-policy processes.	Few think tanks set up their own in-house training centres Targeted capacity development projects in South Asia designed and administered by think tanks and allowed these to experiment with different models of capacity-building units.
	Think tanks provided competitive salaries to attract and train quality staff (research and support staff).	Enabled think tanks offered attractive salaries, benefits (maternity leave, medical and life insurance), salary advances and rewards for publications to senior researchers as well as hired financial and operational staff which contributed to strengthen their organizational performance.

(Table A21.2 Continued)

(Table A21.2 Continued)

	Think tanks are seen as a desirable workplace due to their infrastructure and policies.	Think tanks updated their IT infrastructure, purchased specialized software and office space, and improved their HR practices, financial units and internal audit and compliance units.
Challenges		
	On occasions, overtly displaying membership of TTI was challenging for working as members of alliances in certain contexts.	TTI allowed flexibility and space to each think tank to choose their own organizational strategy that worked best for them in their respective contexts.
Business Model	**Successes**	
	Increased credibility and recognition of the think tank helps to generate new funding.	Think tanks were able to focus their efforts in certain research areas and/or service areas (i.e., impact evaluation, data collection, etc.). This focus has in many cases responded to a particular policy need and has contributed to the institution becoming regarded as an expert in this area.
	Think tanks have broadened their resource mobilization strategy beyond traditional research work. This includes offering training and capacity-building support, launching an impact evaluation unit and a data collection unit, hosting conferences and workshops, etc.	Many think tanks pursued and instituted new funding sources beyond traditional research work.

	Think tanks have consciously and systematically begun to work towards achieving a balance between short-term research contracts and longer-term funding while ensuring alignment with their defined research agendas.	The experience of increased ability to risk taking and bandwidth to develop independent research agenda and work programme enabled by TTI.
	Think tanks invest in assets (equipment, technology, office space) for operational effectiveness.	Core support enabled this as well in investments made in the human resources required to manage assets over the long term.
	Challenges	
	Think tanks at different stages are presented with different challenges around managing growth and capacities. Through TTI support, many are better prepared to pursue and/or manage growth while taking into account the importance of 'right-sizing'.	Think tanks are empowered to make decisions around how to achieve manageable growth, with an eye to ensuring that sufficient capacities are available.
	Think tanks fund researchers solely through TTI funding.	Core support enabled this.
Governance and Leadership	*Successes*	
	Importance of governance transition and succession planning.	Strategic engagement from POs has helped think tanks to think strategically about transition and succession planning, and to set in place measures for addressing this.

(Table A21.2 Continued)

(Table A21.2 Continued)

Think tanks have a well-connected, diverse and engaged board who can help to navigate policy environments and bridge the institution with new and emerging funding opportunities.	In few cases, TTI highlighted the multiple roles of board members.
Think tanks have a well-connected and charismatic leader who can navigate context: 1. Internal: Builds trust with staff members, is able to delegate responsibilities, empowers staff members and promotes growth from within. 2. External: Understands how a change happens and is best to influence, has allies within the government (e.g., ministries, cabinet, parliament and president's office), and is trusted and well respected by many different stakeholders.	As an interlocutor and trustworthy knowledge broker, in few cases, TTI contributed to conducting organizational SWOT analysis jointly with think tanks.
Think tanks are better prepared to ensure that resource mobilization efforts are in alignment with the institutional strategy.	TTI contributed to highlighting the importance of developing an organizational strategic plan with in-built resource mobilization strategies.

Challenges	
Think tanks strive for gender diversity in board and management recruitment processes.	TTI has continued to raise awareness on the issue, fully acknowledging the think tanks' continuing efforts in this regard.
Constraints of boards being too engaged (or not enough engaged) in operational issues.	TTI engagement brought knowledge of funding, political and organizational management, and research contexts and has been able to facilitate thinking on the level of engagement and on redefining roles and responsibilities between boards and management teams.

Research Quality	Successes	
	Research quality was improved through attracting external researchers from the diaspora or adjunct professors on an associate basis.	TTI core funding and strategic engagement from POs allowed think tanks to reach out to senior researchers. This was also influenced by the strong value proposition created by the institution.
	Research quality was improved through mentoring junior and mid-level staff.	TTI core funding enabled certain think tanks to send their staff members for in-country training or abroad. Some think tanks were able to sponsor their researchers' doctoral studies with TTI core funding and even hire a visiting academic to assure quality, who provided hands-on training to research teams through the research process.
	Research quality was improved through in-house training.	Technical support provided by TTI through workshops contributed to better research quality.

(Table A21.2 Continued)

(Table A21.2 Continued)

Linking strategic plans and research agenda to relevant policy issues.	Peer networking opportunities at learning events such as the regional meeting and TTI exchange forums and facilitation of joint projects on relevant issues through the Opportunity and Matching Funds have helped create further opportunities for peer-learning.
Think tanks are scaling up specific projects.	TTI funding was utilized to pilot new areas of work, which was then scaled by other funders.
Research products regularly undergo peer review.	The annual peer-review exercise helped think tanks understand the challenges of assessing quality of policy research and also—within limitations of peer-review exercise that is better suited for academic work—some technical aspects of their submitted work/studies.
Challenges	
Attracting and retaining staff remain constant challenges for think tanks, recognizing that they are often in competition with international development organizations offering attractive employment prospects and packages.	TTI core funding has helped punctually, but this issue will remain at the end of TTI.

Successes		
Policy Engagement	Linking strategic plans and research agenda to relevant policy issues.	Targeted training such as on data visualization, peer-learning at regional meetings and through other think tank led capacity-building projects. The Policy Community Survey helped understand the broad trends to inform stakeholder engagement strategies.
	Importance of a well-connected and charismatic leader who can navigate context.	Core funding enabled bandwidth to undertake this task and enhanced the confidence of leaders and their organizations to engage with stakeholders more strategically, including enhanced ability to redefine their partner engagement landscape in the best interest of organizational effectiveness and credibility.
	Think tanks use innovative ways to engage with stakeholders and raise their profile in their national policy ecosystem such as setting up their own TV channel, making use of social media where appropriate and offering courses to civil servants.	TTI funding has been leveraged to buy material and equipment to facilitate this endeavour. TTI engagement underlined, encouraged and 'nudged' organizations as required to enhance their focus and investment on communications.

(Table A21.2 Continued)

(Table A21.2 Continued)

Challenges	
Continuing to resource communications team beyond TTI is likely to remain challenging.	TTI engagement is ongoing with think tanks on the modalities through which this core function may be funded in the future, for example, by monetizing specific communications activities and costing for this within overheads.

Source: TTI's internal analysis based on think tank reports and staff experience.

Note: Unlike in other four dimensions of TTI support, this is a dimension where TTI programme—fully respecting the autonomy of think tanks' governance—engaged as a responsive strategy, driven by demand from the leadership, or on rare occasions, when achievement of programme outcomes was at stake owing to challenges in this dimension. This is an area where most think tanks were already doing quite well and TTI enabled them to reassess their organizational strategy and develop long-term plans and space for developing strategic plans.

PART VI

Life After TTI: Challenges and the Way Forward

Chapter 22

Life After TTI: Challenges and the Way Forward

Ajaya Dixit, Samar Verma and Sukhadeo Thorat

THE INNOVATIVE EXPERIMENT CALLED TTI

During the latter part of the twentieth century and the early decades of the twenty-first century, core funding for institution building had nearly dried up, and many people had, in fact, even forgotten the significant role that core funding had played in setting up some of the top institutions of higher learning, especially those in India. Both international donor funding and government funding for research had shifted from core funding to project-type funding, with the focus on the timely delivery of outputs that were often decided by donors. Think tanks were expected to bid and then deliver on the outcomes of the associated project. Such funding allocated very little money to meeting indirect costs. In fact, there was rarely enough money to meet indirect costs, let alone meet other organizational costs associated with the delivery of the project. Project budgets are characterized by inflexible, detailed line items determined by the donor's organizational policies and rarely in line with the policies of the recipient organization. Such restrictive budgets not only fail to reimburse the cost of bidding and proposal writing that precedes the securing of a project grant, but they also do not allocate any money to strengthening the recipient's organizational systems or building the capacity of its research staff. Thus, most project funding benefit from existing capacities but rarely pay their full economic cost. The report of the seventh Think Tank Initiative (TTI) Regional Meeting held in Savar, Bangladesh, in February 2018 emphatically observes that

> Problems of the South cannot be resolved with solutions from the North. It is time for southern think tanks to step up—there is no need for northern votes for southern ideas.... To remain masters of their own voices, think tanks should responsibly be able to differentiate what they want to say, and what their fund-providers policy agendas are.[1]

The idea that think tanks ought to get core, non-earmarked, predictable and long-term funding was, therefore, a bold and unique idea at the time it was proposed. The fact that TTI chose to break new ground in its support of think tanks and thereby to promote evidence-based policy-making in developing countries testifies to the progressive vision of its funders. TTI was not only a unique programme and a bold experiment but also a gentle reminder to the world at large, especially to the donor community and public funding agencies, that institutions need core, non-earmarked, predictable and long-term support to ensure their credibility, protect their independence and promote the sort of rigorous evidence needed for effective policy-making. The uniqueness of the programme lays in its fundamental principles: demonstrated organizational owner-ship of the use of TTI support; flexibility of TTI resource allocation to suit evolution in requirements and needs amid changing contexts, organizational vision and leadership; emphasis on holistic growth and the strengthening of all aspects of think tanks from governance, leader-ship and management to operational systems and practices; programme monitoring designed as a tool of mutual learning; and demand-driven and bespoke capacity development modules and opportunities to develop national, regional and international social capital and collaborations. Trusted partnership based on mutual appreciation and learning character-ized the social relationship between think tanks and the TTI programme. The rich and diverse body of evidence and experience captured in this volume, narrated directly by think tank leaders themselves, demonstrates

---

[1] Report of the seventh South Asian Regional Meeting of TTI, held on 5–7 February 2018 at Savar, Bangladesh.

conclusively that the TTI support played a definitive role in strengthening think tanks and policy research ecosystems enough that they were able to have remarkable success in influencing policies and public discourse at all levels of public policy-making. Indeed, the report of the seventh TTI Regional Meeting asserts that 'Core funding from TTI has, without exception, helped all the fourteen think tanks in the South Asian region to improve as institutions by building upon their strengths, and overcoming weaknesses.'[2]

As a result of strategic decisions made by think tank leaders supported by the TTI programme over the last eight years—decisions enabled by TTI funding and technical support—grantee think tanks are now more efficient, more effective, more credible and more sustainable, a development that has in turn yielded better policies, deeper and wider collaborations, and more strategic partnerships. In addition to stronger organizations, the seventh Regional Meeting report concludes that 'The TTI network is a unique resource, and the TTs need to work together to preserve it…. The most critical distinctive feature of the TTI network was that it allowed TTs to discuss institution building activities.'

THE CHALLENGE

This success, by definition, has a flipside too. The sinews and successes of think tanks are not built in a short time or with project-type support. After the TTI programme comes to an end, the strength that think tanks have developed, thanks to TTI, will gradually atrophy unless they are able to secure the core support they need to maintain and continue to build institutional capacity and confidently embrace an independent research agenda. Almost all think tanks in the cohort have reported the lack of core funding in the form of endowment or corpus or regular annual grant as a main hurdle to cross if they are to achieve sustainability and credibility. Indeed, financial sustainability is their most pressing concern going forward.

The challenge is serious as the funding environment for research in the South Asian region is elusive and deteriorating due to changes in

---

[2] Ibid.

the regulatory regime of governments and declining space for dissent globally. The TTI Regional Meeting report explains this predicament:

> In South Asia, the space of think tanks in policy making had been shrinking due to nationalism and myopic political philosophy ... governments are not convinced about the significant role that think tanks play in helping government and policy makers ... solve practical problems.... Most of (funds) are project-specific rather than core fund which constrains the thinks tanks to be independent provider of sound policy advice. Due to immense growth in ICT sector in South Asia, focus has ... shifted from sound policy analysis to producing catchy bites without much evidence-based content. Ever-changing knowledge ecosystem and need for more policy-influencing makes it imperative for think tanks to address contemporary pressing issues and interests such as climate change, global warming, sustainable development, and at the same time continue to establish networking with national and international arena to enhance credibility.[3]

The increasingly challenging context notwithstanding, the role of think tanks will only increase. Wittrock points out how crucial research has become: 'Today, no public policy can be developed, no market interaction can occur, and no statement in the public sphere can be made, that does not refer explicitly or implicitly to the findings and concepts of social and human sciences.'[4]

This state of affairs is the result of the state of the world and, more specifically, of what has been called 'a confluence of crises', that is, contemporary crises that mutually reinforce one another.[5] Milton Friedman perhaps summed up the fundamental role of knowledge in a persuasive manner when he wrote:

> Only a crisis—actual or perceived—produces real change. When that crisis occurs, the actions that are taken depend on the ideas that are lying around. That, I believe, is our basic function: to develop alternatives to

---

[3] Ibid.

[4] Wittrock, 'Shifting Involvements', 205–208.

[5] United Nationals Educational, Scientific and Cultural Organization and International Social Science Council, *World Social Science Report: Knowledge Divides.*

existing policies, to keep them alive and available until the politically impossible becomes politically inevitable.[6]

The emerging development challenges in South Asian countries make conducting social science policy research imperative. Such research is needed for developing evidence-based policies that in turn ensure that the economic and social developments are founded on a sound footing and are capable of overcoming the high rates of poverty in the region and leading countries to sustainable future human development. Rapid and haphazard urbanization processes, fragile infrastructures, degraded natural ecosystems and complex institutional contexts add layers of stress that exacerbate systemic vulnerability and decrease well-being in all countries in South Asia. As the countries engage with each other and with the outside world, issues of geopolitics, security and trade acquire importance. To succeed, responses to the various stresses emerging from interactions among these elements and processes have to use different forms of knowledge from diverse sources. The TTI report underscores how critical the link between research and development is: 'South Asia is one of the final frontiers of development and think tanks are the last Jedi in the attainment of sustainable development goals (SDGs).'[7]

THE WAY FORWARD

Social science research is a public good, and governments globally are the largest users of this research. As a public good, research, particularly social science policy research, is accessible as 'public-domain information' without any restriction; it comprises 'sources and types of data and information whose uses are not restricted by intellectual property or other statutory regimes and that are accordingly available to the public for use without authorisation or restriction'.[8] The major sources of public-domain data and information for scientific research are academic institutes (sometimes universities) and not-for-profit institutions such

---

[6] Friedman, *Capitalism and Freedom*.

[7] Report of the seventh South Asian Regional Meeting of TTI, held on 5–7 February 2018 at Savar, Bangladesh.

[8] Esanu and Uhlir, 'The Role of Scientific and Technical Data and Information in the Public Domain', 4.

as think tanks dependent on government and philanthropic funding. It is, therefore, apt that the think tanks do what they do, that is, follow and advocate a policy of full and open access or exchange as 'data and information derived from publicly funded research are to be made available with as few restrictions as possible, on a nondiscriminatory basis'.[9] As an International Development Research Centre (IDRC) policy and a TTI programme requirement, all publications from all think tanks using TTI resources were made available as open-access material.

Public goods should be funded by public sources, and, indeed, all governments in South Asia provide public funding for social science research. That said, the amount of funding and the nature of support are inadequate and inappropriate. In India, for instance, the social science research budget for the year 2010–2011 was just 0.0062 per cent of its GDP. In the past, support by governmental and philanthropic funding agencies helped think tanks retain the public-good character of social science research by allowing them to set their own independent research agenda. Such public funding included modalities such as annual grants and other annual support, as well as one-time endowments which yield a regular flow of income through capital gains. In the funding context, there are obvious lessons to be learned from TTI.

The key lesson from the TTI—eloquently narrated by think tank leaders themselves—is that some minimum level of assured and autonomous funding over a reasonably long term is critical for sustainability. Such funding could either take the form of regular and assured annual grants or be an endowment of some kind which generates capital gain and regular income flow. The data from TTI on the level of funding in 2017 show that four think tanks got enough support to cover only 3 per cent–6 per cent of their total annual budgets and that another seven think tanks got annual TTI support worth 11–20 per cent of their budget. Only 3 think tanks out of the 14 in the South Asian cohort got over 32 per cent, and the greatest proportion funded was just 52 per cent. In most cases, however, even a small proportion of assured core support transformed the credibility and effectiveness of the recipient think tank.

---

[9] National Research Council, *Bits of Power.*

Philanthropic funding organizations must learn the lesson from TTI: If leading international donors of TTI can take a leap of trust in think tanks in developing countries, surely domestic philanthropists can rise to the occasion. Of course, the model must be modified to suit domestic priorities and be relevant to national contexts, but, other than that, nothing holds them back. The fact that, for example, the corporate social responsibility (CSR) budget of the top 250 companies in India was over ₹70,000 million for just one fiscal raises immense possibilities. One simple and effective approach for like-minded corporates seeking to fund similar endeavours would be to pool their resources to fund think tanks. This funding could be provided in the form of grants to think tanks identified through a rigorous competitive process, albeit the grant should at least in part be institutional in nature, such as to allow think tanks to work on core areas of policy-making and also help them to retain independence.[10]

TTI demonstrated a road map for strengthening policy research in developing countries through strengthening the think tanks in a way that has been an important lesson from history—that institutions and organizations are built through core and dedicated resources over a long period of time—but one that also seemed to have been mostly forgotten in the last half century. TTI serves as a useful and timely reminder in a world that is more tumultuous and in contexts that are more challenging than ever before, thus requiring ever more and better research to underpin public policy and public discourse more generally so that, in the true spirit of the call for global humanity, no one is left behind. South Asia, a region with huge numbers of poor people and high levels of diverse forms of inequality beset by great deprivation, nonetheless is a theatre of tremendous innovation. It is the home to rising aspirations, a place where all seek an opportunity to escape a life of destitution. If public policy needed to be strong and effective in any place, or at any time in history, it is here and now in South Asia. Local contexts must inform local solutions. Public agencies and corporate philanthropists must rise to the occasion and, committing themselves to the long term, work collectively and collaboratively with the best in the world to make the world a better place for us all. The experiences and evidences in this volume are a demonstrated pathway to success.

___
[10] Verma, Asundi, and Bharadwaj, 'Creative Destruction', 112–113.

Bibliography

Acharya, M., and L. Bennett. *An Aggregate Analysis and Summary of 8 Village Studies in the Status of Women in Nepal*. Kathmandu: CEDA, 1981.

Acharya, M., and P. Acharya. *Gender Equality and Empowerment of Women: A Status of Report*. Kathmandu: UNFPA, 1997.

Adhikari, J., and M. Hobley. *Everyone Is Leaving, Who Will Sow the Seeds? A Study of the Impact of Migration to Gulf States and Malaysia on the Livelihoods of Khotang District, Nepal*. Kathmandu: Swiss Agency for Development and Cooperation and Nepal Institute of Development Studies, 2012.

Bandaranayake, S. *The University of the Future and the Culture of Learning*. Kandy: Kandy Books, 2006.

Bangladesh Bank. *Monthly Economic Trends May 2018*. Dhaka: Bangladesh Bank, 2018.

BBS (Bangladesh Bureau of Statistics). *Consumer Price Index (CPI), Inflation Rate and Wage Rate Index (WRI) in Bangladesh*. 2016. Available at: http://bbs.portal. gov.bd/sites/default/files/files/bbs.portal.gov.bd/page/9ead9eb1_91ac_4998_ a1a3_a5caf4ddc4c6/CPI_January17.pdf (accessed on 11 September 2018).

———. *Household Expenditure Survey*. Dhaka: BBS, 1991–1992.

———. *Household Income and Expenditure Survey*. Dhaka: BBS, 2015–2016.

———. *Preliminary Report on Household Income and Expenditure Survey*. Dhaka: BBS, 2016.

Bastow S., P. Dunleavy, and J. Tinkler. *The Impact of the Social Sciences: How Academics and Their Research Make a Difference*. London: SAGE Publications, 2014.

Bhattarai, B. *Proposition of Social Justice & Economic Prosperity for Nepal*. Keynote speech delivered at Conference on Public Policy and Governance in South Asia: Towards Justice and Prosperity. Kathmandu: Nepal Administrative Staff College, 28–29 June 2018.

Bhuju, D. R., and D. K. Khadka. *Science Technology and Innovation in Nepal: Foundation for Development*, edited by D. R. Bhuju. Lalitpur: Academy of Science and Technology, Nepal, 2018.

Caplan, Nathan. 'A Minimal Set of Conditions Necessary for the Utilization of Social Science Knowledge in Policy Formulation at the National Level'. Paper presented at the Conference on Social Values and Social Engineering, International Sociological Association, Warsaw, 18–19 April 1975.

CBS (Central Bureau of Statistics). *National Population and Housing Census*. Kathmandu: CBS, 2011.

Central Bank of Sri Lanka. *Annual Report*. Colombo: Central Bank of Sri Lanka, various years.

———. *Consumer Finances and Socioeconomic Survey*. Colombo: Central Bank of Sri Lanka, various years.

———. *Economic and Social Statistics of Sri Lanka*. Colombo: Central Bank of Sri Lanka, various years.

Christoplos, Ian, Adam Pain, Jups Kluyskens, Francisco Sagasti, and Anna Liljelund Hedqvist. *External Evaluation of TTI Phase Two: Second Interim Report*. NIRAS Indevelop, 2017. Available at: https://www.niras.com/media/2685/tti-external-evaluation-2nd-interim-report-final_.pdf (accessed on 11 September 2018).

Department of Census and Statistics. *Census of Population*. Colombo: Department of Census and Statistics, various years.

———. *Demographic and Health Survey*. Colombo: Department of Census and Statistics, various years.

———. *Household Income and Expenditure Surveys*. Colombo: Department of Census and Statistics, various years.

———. *Poverty Indicators*. Colombo: Department of Census and Statistics, various years.

———. *Sri Lanka Poverty Preview*. Colombo: Department of Census and Statistics, 2009–2010.

———. *Statistical Abstract*. Colombo: Department of Census and Statistics, various years.

De Silva, N., and P. Fernando. 'Change from Within: A Self-Reflection of Action Research for Organisational Capacity Building at the Centre for Poverty Analysis (CEPA), Sri Lanka'. In *Action Research and Organisational Capacity Building: Journeys of Change in Southern Think Tanks*, 131–159. Lahore: SDPI and Sang-e-Meel Publications, 2014.

Di Battista, Attilio. 'What's Next for Nepal's Economy?' World Economic Forum, 16 October 2015. Available at: https://www.weforum.org/agenda/2015/10/whats-next-for-nepals-economy/ (accessed on 4 July 2018).

Dixit, A., N. Dahal, and K. M. Dixit. 'Bridging the Macro and Micro Dichotomy in Water Education: Perspectives from Nepal'. In *Higher Education on Water Resources in South Asia: Towards Capacity Building for IWRM*. Hyderabad: SaciWATERs, June 2002.

Dhungel, D. N., and U. P. Adhikary. 'Strategic Plan for a Social Science Research: Council in Nepal Status of Social Science Research in Asia Emerging Challenges and Policy Lessons'. In Proceedings of ICSSR–IDRC Conference. New Delhi: ICSSR, 2014.

DST (Desakota Study Team). 'Re-imagining the Rural–Urban Continuum: Understanding the Role Ecosystem Services Play in the Livelihoods of the Poor in Desakota Regions Undergoing Rapid Change'. Research gap analysis prepared by the Desakota Study Team (DST) for the Ecosystem Services for Poverty Alleviation (ESPA) Programme of Natural Environment Research Council (NERC). Kathmandu: Department for International Development

(DFID), Economic and Social Research Council (ESRC) of the United Kingdom and Institute for Social and Environmental Transition-Nepal (ISET-N), 2008.

Esanu, Julie M. and Paul F. Uhlir. 'The Role of Scientific and Technical Data and Information in the Public Domain'. Proceedings of a Symposium. Washington D.C.: The National Academic Press, 2003.

Friedman, Milton. *Capitalism and Freedom*. Chicago, IL: University of Chicago Press, 1982.

Gautam, B. 'Oli lai Chiniya sikchya (Chinese Education to Oli)'. *Nepal Magazine* (1 July 2018): 30–31. Kathmandu.

GoN (Government of Nepal). *National Framework on Local Adaptation Plans for Action*. Kathmandu: Government of Nepal, Ministry of Science Technology and Environment, Singha Durbar, 2011.

———. *The Budget Speech*. Kathmandu: Government of Nepal, 2018.

Government of Bangladesh. *Budget for the Fiscal Year 2018–19*. Government of Bangladesh, 2017. Available at: https://mof.portal.gov.bd/sites/default/files/files/mof.portal.gov.bd/page/e9e8a8c8_8a8b_4536_a18b_fc5ca696650a/St_2_en.pdf (accessed on 2 July 2018).

———. *Budget of the Planning Division for FY2017–18*. Government of Bangladesh, 2017. Available at: http://www.plandiv.gov.bd/site/files/9809aca9–6fda–45d5–9139–352855c9e303/Yearly-Budget-2017–18 (accessed on 11 September 2018).

———. *Health Bulletin 2017*. Dhaka: Government of Bangladesh, 2017. Available at: http://www.dghs.gov.bd/images/docs/Publicaations/HealthBulletin2017Final13_01_2018.pdf (accessed on 11 September 2018).

Grupo FARO. 'Influencing as a Learning Process: Think Tanks and the Challenge of Improving Polices and Promoting Social Change'. Working paper prepared for the conference 'Think Tank Exchange' organized by Think Tank Initiative in South Africa, 18–20 June 2012.

Gunetilleke, N., and A. Jafferjee, eds. *Triangulation Squared: Assessing Impacts of the Poverty Impact Monitoring Unit*, 300. Colombo: Centre for Poverty Analysis, 2005.

Hacchethu, K. 'Social Sciences in Nepal'. *CNAS Journal* 29, no. 1 (January 2002): 49–94. Kathmandu.

———. 'Madhesi Nationalism and Restructuring the Nepali State'. Paper presented at an international seminar on Constitutionalism and Diversity in Nepal, organised by the Centre for Nepal and Asian Studies, TU, in collaboration with MIDEA Project and ESP-Nepal, Kathmandu, 2007.

Hagen, T. *Nepal: The Kingdom in the Himalaya*. Kathmandu: Himal Books, 1998.

Hettige, S. 'Sociological Enterprise at the Periphery: The Case of Sri Lanka'. In *Facing an Unequal World: Challenges for a Global Sociology*, edited by M. Buraway, 300–315. Taiwan: Institute of Sociology, Academia Sinica, 2010.

ILO. *Employment by Sector: ILO Modelled Estimates*. ILO, 2 July 2018. Available at: ILOSTAT: http://www.ilo.org/ilostat/faces/oracle/webcenter/portalapp/pagehierarchy/Page3.jspx?MBI_ID=33&_afrLoop=87489089700809&_afrWindowMode=0&_afrWindowId=null#!%40%40%3F_

afrWindowId%3Dnull%26_afrLoop%3D87489089700809%26MBI_
ID%3D33%26_afrWindowMode%3D0%26_adf.c (accessed on 11 September
2018).

Inayatullah. 'Social Sciences in Pakistan: An Evaluation'. In *The State of Social Sciences
in Pakistan*, edited by S.H. Hashmi. Islamabad: Council of Social Sciences, 2001.

Inayatullah, R. Saigol, and P. Tahir, eds. *Social Sciences in Pakistan: A Profile*.
Islamabad: Council of Social Sciences, 2005.

Janowitz, Morris. 'Sociological Models and Social Policy'. *ARSP: Archiv für Rechts-
und Sozialphilosophie/Archives for Philosophy of Law and Social Philosophy* 55,
no. 3 (1969): 305–321.

Jha, Prashant. 'India's Most Influential Think Tanks'. *The Hindustan Times*, 16
August 2015. Available at: https://www.hindustantimes.com/india/india-s-
most-influential-think-tanks/story-emb0db2lmqltL8pKeYuZiL.html (accessed
on 13 July 2018).

Joe, William, Aakshi Kalra, and Manoj Panda. 2017. 'Policy Impact: Evidence on
Central Government Policies'. In *Social Science Research in India: Status, Issues
and Policies*, edited by Sukhadeo Thorat and Samar Verma. New Delhi: Oxford
University Press, 2017.

Kapur, D. *The Study of India in The United States*. 29 June 2018. Available at:
https://casi.sas.upenn.edu/iit/deveshkapur2018 (accessed on 6 July 2018).

Knorr, Karin D. 'Policymakers' Use of Social Science Knowledge: Symbolic or
Instrumental?' In *Using Social Research in Public Policy Making*, edited by Carol
H. Weiss, 165–182. Lexington/Toronto: Lexington Books, 1977.

Lebel, J., and R. McLean. 'A Better Measure of Research from the Global South.'
Nature 559, (5 July 2018): 23–26. Available at: https://www.nature.com/arti-
cles/d41586–018–05581–4?utm_source=twt_na&utm_medium=social&utm_
campaign=NNPnature (accessed on 11 September 2018).

Lohani, P. C. 'Sukulgunda Chintan' (Street Hero Thinking). *Kantipur*, 4 January 2018.

Mathur, Kuldeep. 'Policy Research Institutions in South Asia'. Working Paper
Series No. CSLG/WP/13, Centre for the Study of Law and Governance.
Jawaharlal Nehru University, New Delhi, 2009.

Ministry of Finance and Planning, Government of Sri Lanka. *Government Estimates:
2014*. Colombo: Ministry of Finance and Planning, 2014.

Ministry of Finance and Planning. *Annual Report 2016*. Colombo: Sri Lanka
Central Bank, 2016.

MoPE (Ministry of Population and Environment). *Nepal Pollution Report 2016*.
Kathmandu: Government of Nepal, MoPE, 2016.MoPME (Ministry of
Primary and Mass Education). *Annual Primary School Census 2017*. Dhaka:
MoPME, 2017. Available at: http://dpe.portal.gov.bd/sites/default/files/files/
dpe.portal.gov.bd/publications/94a597e2_4d46_427f_842c_300f78d2a7d7/
Final_Draft_APSC_2017_.pdf (accessed on 24 March 2018).

Nachiappan, Karthik, Enrique Mendizabal, and Ajoy Datta. 2010. *Think Tanks in
East and South East Asia: Bringing Politics Back into the Picture*. London: Overseas
Development Institute, 2017.

NASTEC (National Science and Technology Commission). *National Science and Technology Policy.* Colombo: NASTEC, 2008.

National Research Council. *Bits of Power: Issues in Global Access to Scientific Data.* Washington, DC: The National Academies Press, 1997. Available at: https://doi.org/10.17226/5504 (accessed on 12 September 2018).

National Science Foundation. *Sri Lanka Science, Technology and Innovation Statistical Handbook 2015.* Colombo: National Science Foundation, 2015.

Naveed, A., and A. Q. Suleri. *Making 'Impact Factor' Impactful: Universities, Think Tanks and Policy Research in Pakistan.* IDRC–SDPI, 2014. Available at: http://www.thinktankinitiative.org/sites/default/files/Pakistan%20TT-university%20study_Final%20June%2022.pdf (accessed on 11 September 2018).

NIPORT (National Institute of Population Research and Training). *Bangladesh Demographic and Health Survey 2014.* Dhaka: NIPORT, Ministry of Health and Family Welfare, 2014.

NIDS (Nepal Institute of Development Studies). *Migration Year Book 2012.* Kathmandu: NIDS, 2012.

NSF (National Science Foundation). *National Survey on Research and Development and Innovation.* Colombo: NSF, 2008.

———. *Sri Lanka Science and Technology Innovation: Statistical Handbook.* Colombo: NSF, 2010.

Onta, P. 'The Changing Research Landscape: Silver Lining Celebrating 25 Years'. *The Kathmandu Post,* 2018, Kathmandu.

Orton, L., F. Lloyd-Williams, D. Taylor-Robinson, M. O'Flaherty, and S. Capewell. 'The Use of Research Evidence in Public Health Decision Making Processes: Systematic Review'. *PLoS ONE* 6, no. 7 (2011): e21704. Available at: https://doi.org/10.1371/journal.pone.0021704 (accessed on 11 September 2018).

Ostrom, E. *Governing the Commons.* Cambridge: Cambridge University Press, 1990.

Parajuli, L. R., and P. Onta. 'Taaxiyeka Biswabidhyalaya' (Stunted Universities). *Kantipur,* 6 June 2018. Kathmandu.

Parkhurst, J. *The Politics of Evidence: From Evidence-based Policy to the Good Governance of Evidence.* Routledge Studies in Governance and Public Policy. Abingdon: Routledge, 2017.

Pyakuryal, B., and K. Acharya. 'Service Sector Needs Sustainable Base for Further Expansion'. *The Himalayan Times,* 4 May 2017. Available at: https://thehimalayantimes.com/business/service-sector-needs-sustainable-base-expansion/ (accessed on 5 September 2018).

Rai, O. A. 'Hoping Against Hope'. *Nepali Times,* 2–8 February 2018. Kathmandu.

Raj, Y., and B. Gautam. *Courage in Chaos: Early Rescue and Relief After the April Earthquake.* Chautari Book Series, 86. Kathmandu: Martin Chautari, 2015.

Rich, Andrew. *Think Tanks, Public Policy, and the Politics of Expertise,* 258. New York, NY: Cambridge University Press, 2004.

Rich, Andrew, James McGann, Kent Weaver, Mark Garnett, Martin Thunert, Rudolf Speth, Rudolf Traub-Merz, and Yang Ye. 'Think Tanks in Policy Making: Do They Matter?' Briefing Paper Special Issue, Shanghai, September 2011.

Rosen, George. *Western Economists and Eastern Societies: Agents of Change in South Asia, 1950–1970.* Johns Hopkins Studies in Development, 1985.

Sharma, P., B. G. Baidya, and D. N. Dhungel. *Strategic Plan for the Proposed Social Science Research Council in Nepal.* Report Submitted to the Ad hoc Council, Ministry of Women, Children and Social Welfare, Government of Nepal, and Social Inclusion Research Fund (SIRF). Revised on the basis of Regional and National Consultations. Kathmandu, Ad hoc Council of Ministry of Women, Children and Social Welfare, Government of Nepal, and SIRF, March 2014.

Singh, B. P. 'From Nowhere to Nowhere: Haphazard Road Construction Is Ravaging the Nepali Countryside (in Bajhang)'. *Nepali Times*, 6 July 2018. Kathmandu.

Solomon, J. J. 'The Uncertain Quest: Science, Development and the South'. Paper presented at the conference 'Developing Countries and the World Order', Indian Centre for International Cooperation, New Delhi, 9–11 December 1994.

Srinivasan, S., and S. Verma. 'Public Policy Research in South Asia'. *Economic & Political Weekly* 51, no. 13 (2016): 58–61. Mumbai: Sameeksha Trust.

Srinivastava, J. *Think Tanks in South Asia: Analyzing the Knowledge–Power Interface.* London: Overseas Development Institute, 2011.

Subedi, B.P. *The State of Geography Teaching and Research in Nepal: A Review and Reflection.* Kathmandu: Martin Chautari, 2014.

Stone, Diane. 'Think Tanks and Policy Advice in Countries in Transition'. Paper prepared for the Asian Development Bank Institute Symposium 'How to Strengthen Policy-oriented Research and Training', Hanoi, Vietnam, 31 August 2005.

Subedi, M., and D. Uprety. *The State of Sociology and Anthropology: Teaching and Research in Nepal.* Kathmandu: Martin Chautari, 2014.

Tahir, P. 'Quantitative Development of Social Sciences in Inayatullah'. 2005. In *Social Sciences in Pakistan: A Profile*, edited by R. Saigol and P. Tahir. Islamabad: Council of Social Sciences, Pakistan.

Think Tank Initiative. *Policy Community Survey: South Asia.* Canada: Think Tank Initiative, 2011.

———. *Policy Community Survey: South Asia.* Canada: Think Tank Initiative, 2013.

———. *Final Technical Progress Report for Phase 1*, 22. Canada: Think Tank Initiative, 2014.

———. *Technical Progress Report 2016–17*, 7. Canada: Think Tank Initiative, 2017.

Thorat, Sukhadeo, and Samar Verma. *Social Science Research in India: Status, Issues and Policies.* New Delhi: Oxford University Press, 2017.

UNESCO. *Education 2030 Incheon Declaration: Towards Inclusive and Equitable Quality Education and Lifelong Learning for All.* UNESCO, 2015. Available at: http://www.uis.unesco.org/Education/Documents/incheon-framework-for-action-en.pdf (accessed on 11 September 2018).

———. *Institute for Statistics 2015: Science Report Towards 2030*, 573. UNESCO, 3 June 2015. Available at http://unesdoc.unesco.org/images/0023/002354/235406e.pdf (accessed on 11 September 2018).

Venkateswaran, Kanmani, Karen MacClune, Adriana Keating, and Michael Szönyi. *The PERC Manual: Learning from Disasters to Build Resilience: A Simple Guide to Conducting a Post-event Review*. Zurich: Zurich Insurance and ISET-I, 2015.

Verma, S. 'Social Science Research: Status, Emerging Trends and Interdisciplinary Research'. *Journal of Governance & Public Policy* 7, no. 1 (2017): 88–102.

———. *Think Tank Credibility: Lessons for Funding Agencies*, 26. 2017. Available at: https://onthinktanks.org/wp-content/uploads/2018/03/OTT_AnnualReview_2017.pdf (accessed on 11 September 2018).

Verma S., and A. Bharadwaj. 'Why Is India Freezing Out Policy Research?' *Business Standard*, 21 January 2013. Available at: https://www.business-standard.com/article/opinion/samar-verma-anshu-bharadwaj-why-is-india-freezing-out-policy-research-112021900007_1.html (accessed on 11 September 2018).

Verma, S., V. Vaidyanathan, and A. Bharadwaj, A. 'Corporate Social Responsibility in India: Case for Supporting Think Tanks'. In *Corporate Social Responsibility: Driving a Sustainable Future*, edited by R.K. Mishra and S. Sarkar. New Delhi: Academic Foundation, 2017.

Verma, Samar, Jai Asundi, and Anshu Bharadwaj. 'Creative Destruction: Towards a National Think Tank'. *Economic & Political Weekly* 49, nos. 43–44 (2014): 112–113. Mumbai: Sameeksha Trust.

Verweij, M., M. Thompson, and C. Engel. 'Clumsy Conclusions: How to Do Policy and Research in a Complex World'. In *Clumsy Solutions for a Complex World: Governance, Politics and Plural Perceptions*, edited by M. Verweij and M. Thompson. New York, NY: Palgrave Macmillan, 2006.

Wagle, S. *Message to the Report Development of Manufacturing Industries in Nepal Current State and Future Challenges*. Kathmandu: Central Bureau of Statistics (CBS), 2014.

Weiss, Carol H. 'Research for Policy's Sake: The Enlightenment Function of Social Research'. *Policy Analysis* 3, no. 4 (Fall 1977): 531–545.

Wittrock, Bjorn. 'Shifting Involvements: Rethinking the Social, the Human, the Natural'. In *International Social Science Council World Social Science Report 2010: Knowledge Divides*, 205–208. Paris: UNESCO, 2010.

WSSR (World Social Science Report). *Knowledge Divides*. France: UNESCO and International Social Science Council, 2010.

World Bank. *World Development Indicators*. World Bank, 2018. Available at: http://databank.worldbank.org/data/reports.aspx?source=world-development-indicators&l=en# (accessed on 11 September 2018).

———. *World Development Indicators*. World Bank, 2018. Available at: https://data.worldbank.org/indicator/SL.UEM.1524.ZS?locations=BD (accessed on 11 September 2018).

Zaidi, A. S. 'Dismal State of Social Sciences in Pakistan'. *Economic & Political Weekly* 37, no. 35 (31 August 2002): 3644–3661.

About the Editors and Contributors

EDITORS

Sukhadeo Thorat is Chairman, Indian Institute of Dalit Studies (IIDS), and Emeritus Professor, Jawaharlal Nehru University, India. He is an economist by training, who has worked extensively in the areas of agricultural development, economic institutions and development, poverty, social exclusion and inequality, caste and economic discrimination, labour market discrimination, economic problems of excluded groups (Scheduled Castes and Scheduled Tribes), higher education, urban slums, human rights, and economic ideas of Babasaheb Ambedkar in his previous roles at Jawaharlal Nehru University (1973–2014) and as the founder director of IIDS (2003–2006). He was also chairman of the University Grants Commission (2006–2011) and of Indian Council of Social Science Research (ICSSR; 2011–2017). He has been awarded honorary DLitt, DSc, DS (Doctor of Education) and LLD degrees by 12 universities from India and 1 university from outside India. In 2008, Professor Thorat was awarded the Padma Shri, India's fourth-highest civilian award; he was also awarded the Mother Teresa International Award and Babasaheb Ambedkar Ratna Award by the Delhi government.

Ajaya Dixit works as an analyst of water resources and environmental themes in Nepal and South Asia. He taught water resource engineering at Nepal's Institute of Engineering and worked with a team to establish a Master's-level interdisciplinary water education course in Nepal. His current research focuses on exploring the approaches to develop strategies for resilience building against shocks due to climate change and other hazards at the sub-national scale. He is studying the role systems play in building societal resilience and using the knowledge generated to engage the policy-making domain. He has written extensively on water resources, transboundary cooperation, flood management, environment and climate change adaptation.

Samar Verma is Senior Program Specialist at International Development Research Centre (IDRC) of Canada. He manages the Think Tank Initiative (TTI) programme in South Asia (and more recently a similar support to think tanks in Myanmar). Before joining IDRC, he was the global head of the economic justice policy team at Oxfam Great Britain, based at Oxford, UK. He was also the founder director and chairman of Consortium of Trade and Development, a not-for-profit think tank. Previously, he had been Oxfam's South Asia advisor on trade policy. As Senior Fellow with the Indian Council for Research on International Economic Relations (ICRIER), he has published widely on international trade and competitiveness. Most recently, with Professor Sukhadeo Thorat, he jointly edited a seminal book on *Social Science Research in India: Status, Issues, and Policies*. With over two decades of professional experience in corporate sector, conducting policy research, international development and research grant management based in India and in the UK, Samar holds a PhD in economics and an MBA.

CONTRIBUTORS

Sanghmitra S. Acharya has been the Director of IIDS, New Delhi. Currently, she is a Professor in the Centre of Social Medicine and Community Health. She obtained her MA, MPhil and doctoral degrees from Jawaharlal Nehru University. She has been a Visiting Fellow at Chinese Academy of Social Sciences (CASS), Beijing, China (2012); Ball State University, Muncie, USA (2008–2009); University of the Philippines Population Institute (UPPI), Manila, Philippines (2005); and University of Botswana, Botswana, South Africa (1995–1996). She was awarded Asian Scholarship Foundation (ASF) fellowship in 2005 to study youth in the Philippines. She has published extensively in peer-reviewed journals on the issues of youth, gender in urban spaces, Northeast India and social discrimination in health. Her recent work includes a co-edited book titled *Marginalization in Globalizing Delhi: Issues of Land, Livelihoods and Health*.

Yamini Aiyar, the President and Chief Executive of Centre for Policy Research (CPR), founded the Accountability Initiative (AI) at CPR. Under her leadership, AI has produced significant research in the areas of governance, state capacity and social policy. It pioneered a new approach to tracking public expenditures for social policy programmes and is widely recognized for running the country's largest expenditure-tracking survey in elementary education. Yamini Aiyar is also a TED fellow and a founding member of the International Experts Panel of the Open Government Partnership. She has worked with the World Bank's Water and Sanitation Program and Rural Development Unit in Delhi at strengthening mechanisms for citizen engagement in local government. As a member of the decentralization team at the World Bank, she provided policy support to strengthen Panchayati Raj in India. She is an alumna of the London School of Economics, St Edmund's College, University of Cambridge, and St Stephen's College, Delhi University.

Anshu Bharadwaj is the Executive Director of the Centre for Study of Science, Technology and Policy (CSTEP), Bengaluru, and is also a member on the CSTEP Board. His research interests include technology and policy options for India's clean energy. He specializes in computational modelling of energy systems. He is a member of several committees at national and state levels and has made important contributions in clean energy technology policy subjects. He is a former member of the Indian Administrative Service (IAS; 1992 batch—Karnataka) and has worked with the Government of Karnataka in various capacities. He holds a PhD from the Departments of Engineering and Public Policy and Mechanical Engineering, Carnegie Mellon University. He also has a BTech in mechanical engineering from the Indian Institute of Technology Kanpur and a management degree from the Indian Institute of Management Calcutta.

Seema Bhatia-Panthaki is a Senior Program Officer for TTI, based in IDRC's New Delhi office. She manages a portfolio of TTI grants in India, Sri Lanka and Pakistan and was most recently involved in the selection of think tanks for core support in Myanmar. She is also a part of the IDRC's internal working groups on gender issues, and on options for support to think tanks post 2019. Seema holds an MSc in development economics and a PhD in economics and business from the University of Reading, UK. She has previously worked with the Department for International Development (DFID) and ICRIER (India), the Overseas Development Institute (ODI, UK) and in Malawi, Libya, Zambia and the UAE.

S. Sirimevan Colombage is a resource person for the Faculty of Graduate Studies and Board member, Social Policy Analysis and Research Centre, University of Colombo. A postgraduate and PhD in economics from the University of Manchester, he is a member of the Sri Lanka Economic Association and co-editor of the *Sri Lanka Journal of Social Sciences*. Professor Colombage also served as a chair professor of social studies at the Open University of Sri Lanka and as director of statistics at the Central Bank of Sri Lanka. His research interests include macroeconomics, policies, econometric modelling, international finance and financial inclusion. He has published a large number of books, monographs and articles on different economic trade, poverty and social issues. He has also conducted research on key economic issues with several multilateral agencies and foreign universities.

Subrat Das is serving as the Executive Director of the Centre for Budget and Governance Accountability (CBGA), New Delhi, since 2010. He has worked on government financing of social sectors, fiscal policy and social inclusion, and some of the structural issues in the federal fiscal architecture in India. A major part of his work in these areas has been towards creating spaces for transparency and accountability through rigorous analysis of government budgets, and he has tried to foster people's participation on these complex issues by demystifying them.

Chandrani Dutta is an Assistant Professor at IIDS. Her areas of interests include the field of marginal communities living in slums and contemporary urban policies. She is working on the status of development of Dalits in selected states of India, and interface of gender/ethnicity and caste. She has an MPhil and PhD in population studies and an MA in geography from Jawaharlal Nehru University, New Delhi.

Udan Fernando has held leadership positions in Sri Lankan development organizations over the past 20 years and was a senior staff member in a research and consultancy organization in the Netherlands, working in Europe, East and West Africa, and Southeast Asia. He has also functioned as a freelance consultant in Sri Lanka and abroad. He has had academic and professional training in management, law, labour studies and international development cooperation. He has taught in universities in Sri Lanka and the Netherlands as a visiting academic.

Khalida Ghaus is a former Director, Centre of Excellence for Women's Studies, Chairperson, Department of International Relations, University of Karachi, and Director, Pakistan Centre for Democracy Studies. With a teaching/research experience of 30+ years, Dr Ghaus has extensively worked on foreign policy, development and gender issues, besides being actively involved in the Neemrana process (Track II initiative). Author of a book and several monographs, she has given lectures in Canadian and American universities besides attending the sessions of the United Nations High Commissioner for Refugees (UNHCR). She has been involved in policy-making with both the federal and provincial governments on gender-related issues and is a member of several technical committees, public policy committees, academic boards, advisory committees and professional bodies.

Gurucharan Gollerkeri is Director, Public Affairs Centre (PAC), Bengaluru. A civil servant from IAS, in the higher echelons of the government for over 34 years, he retired as secretary to the Government of India in 2016. He served with distinction as the first director of the India Centre for Migration (ICM), a policy 'think tank' on international migration, during 2010–2013. Based on his work at ICM, he co-authored *Migration Matters: Mobility in a Globalizing World* (2016). In 2004–2005, Mr Gollerkeri was a visiting fellow at the Centre for Public Policy at the Indian Institute of Management Bangalore.

Andrew Hurst is Program Leader for TTI, based at IDRC. He has spent most of the last 20 years in policy positions in various Canadian federal government departments. He has lived in Tanzania and Ethiopia, and worked in many other countries in Africa, South Asia and Latin America. Andrew has taught at Oxford University and Carleton University, and has a doctorate (geography) and a Master's in science (environmental change) from Oxford University, a Master's (political philosophy and African politics) from McGill University and a Bachelor's in arts (political studies) from Queen's University, Kingston.

Fahmida Khatun is the Executive Director of the Centre for Policy Dialogue (CPD), Bangladesh. She is a leading think tank in South Asia. She has accomplished Master's in economics from Jahangirnagar University, Bangladesh. She did her second Master's in environmental and natural resource economics and PhD in economics from the University College London, UK. She did her postdoctoral research at the Earth Institute, Columbia University, USA, as a Fulbright Scholar in 2015. She worked on ICT and SDGs with Professor Jeffery Sachs during her fellowship at Columbia University. She was a visiting fellow at Chr. Michelsen Institute (CMI), Norway (1994); Korea Institute for Industrial Economics and Trade (KIET), South Korea (2012); and CSTEP, India (2016).

Sanjay Kumar, Professor and Director at the Centre for the Study of Developing Societies, has expertise in electoral politics. He has been conducting research on a wide range of themes: Indian youth, state of democracy in South Asia, state of Indian farmers, slums of Delhi and electoral violence. He has published widely, written several books, edited volumes, contributed chapters for several edited volumes, and published articles in various national and international research journals. His most recent book is *Post-Mandal Politics in Bihar: Changing Electoral Patterns*. His new volume on Indian youth based on his latest research is forthcoming.

Meena Nair has specialized in the field of geography with her MPhil and PhD from the Centre of the Study of Regional Development, Jawaharlal Nehru University, New Delhi. She is the Head of the Participatory Governance Research Group (PGRG) of PAC. She coordinates most of the research activities of the centre, especially those related to the implementation of Citizen Report Cards (CRCs) in various spheres of governance and levels of public service delivery. Dr Nair joined PAC in February 2005 as a research consultant. She has an experience of working as a researcher at various levels in the Social and Environment Research Centre (SERC) for Synovate on projects related to health.

G. C. Pal is an Associate Professor and is currently serving as the Director, IIDS. He has an MPhil/PhD in social psychology. He was a postdoctoral visiting fellow at Tata Institute of Fundamental Research and senior fellow at ICSSR. His academic interest is to understand development issues from sociopsychological perspectives, with a focus on marginalized groups, and explore research methodology. He has been engaged in interdisciplinary research which include social psychology of unemployment; cognitive bases of learning and teaching; identity-based exclusion, discrimination and violence; disability, intersectionality and deprivation; and impact evaluation and public policies.

Happy Pant, with her Master's degree in economics from the University of Lucknow, has substantive professional experience in the development sector, specializing in areas of governance, knowledge management and civil society empowerment. As Head of Advocacy in CBGA, she spearheads efforts aimed at advocating for pro-poor budgetary policies and greater transparency in governance processes. She also serves as the organization lead on CBGA's communication and media work. She has an experience of working with UNDP country office in India.

Sultan Hafeez Rahman, Executive Director of BRAC Institute of Governance and Development (BIGD), BRAC University, is leading the restructuring of BIGD and is involved in research and academic issues of the institute. In Asian Development Bank (ADB), which he led until 2012 as director-general, he supervised the preparation and financing of development projects, country and sector strategies, economic integration, thematic and sector studies and analysis of macroeconomic policy issues, and made seminar contributions to programmes in South Asia and Southeast Asia. He presented papers, and participated in and organized many workshops, seminars and conferences around the world throughout his professional career spanning 40 years. Dr Rahman has worked on Cambodia, Thailand, Vietnam, Malaysia, the Republic of Korea, Indonesia, Kazakhstan, Uzbekistan, India, Pakistan, Afghanistan, Nepal, Bhutan, Sri Lanka, Maldives, Bangladesh and Timor–Leste, as well as 14 Pacific Island countries.

P. R. M. P. Dilrukshi Ranathunge is a senior scientific officer at National Science Foundation of Sri Lanka. She has a PhD in zoological sciences from Postgraduate Institute of Science (PGIS), Faculty of Science University of Peradeniya, Sri Lanka. She was a principal investigator to the tracer study of S&T postgraduates passed out from national universities.

Shekhar Shah is Director-General of the National Council of Applied Economic Research, India's oldest and largest, independent, economic think tank. During a World Bank career spanning 1989–2011, he was the bank's South Asia regional economic adviser, a principal author of the *2004 World Development Report*, sector manager for Europe/Central Asia, Bangladesh lead economist and deputy research administrator. He was the Ford Foundation's South Asia Program Officer for Economics during 1984–1989. He worked earlier on US banking and financial services with Golembe Associates in Washington, DC. Shah received his Bachelor's degree in economics from St Stephen's College and Master's and PhD from Columbia University.

Ashutosh Shukla is a senior research faculty at the Institute for Social and Environmental Transition-Nepal (ISET-N). He completed his Master's degree in agricultural engineering from the University of the Philippines. His specialized research interests are on water engineering, agriculture and climate change. He has 30 years' experience in teaching as a lecturer in different engineering institutions of Nepal. His interdisciplinary research publications are generally based on agriculture, animal science, irrigation management, climate change and sustainable development.

Abid Q. Suleri, Executive Director, Sustainable Development Policy Institute (SDPI), Pakistan earned his PhD in food security from the University of Greenwich, UK. He has conceptualized and managed research-based programmes and projects on the transition towards sustainable development. He serves on Prime Ministers' Economic Advisory Council and Planning Commission's National Advisory Committee. He has served on three judicial commissions on environmental issues and as the member of Board of Management of Pakistan

State Oil. He has represented Pakistan in official delegations and is serving on different international policy-making forums. He is also editor-in-chief of the *Journal of Development Policy, Research and Practice*.

Dushni Weerakoon, Executive Director and Head of Macroeconomic Policy Research at Institute of Policy Studies (IPS), Sri Lanka, has over 23 years of experience at IPS and functioned as its deputy director from 2005 to 2017. Her research and publications cover areas related to macroeconomic policy, regional trade integration and international economics. She has extensive experience in the arena of public policy through her research and direct engagements in policy formulation. Dushni Weerakoon holds a BSc in economics with first class honours from the Queen's University Belfast, UK, and an MA and PhD in economics from the University of Manchester, UK.

Kaneta Zillur is a Research Associate in BIGD, based in Dhaka, Bangladesh. At BIGD, she has worked on urban and governance issues, including urban poverty housing, citizen engagement, taxation and democratic practices. Ms Zillur is currently working on a collaborative research on economics of tobacco, supported by the University of Illinois. She joined BIGD after receiving her Bachelor of Arts degree in economics from Boston University, USA. During her studies, her prime area of interest was in international development and macro theory.

Index

Adapting to Climate Change in Asia
ISET-N, 79

Bangladesh, SSR and TTI, 225–235
    least developed country (LDC), 227
    Millennium Development Goal
        (MDG), 226
    organizational performance, 231
    policy debate, 229
    policy engagement, 234
    research quality, 231–232
    social research, 228–230
    SSR, 225–230
    sustainability, 235
    three pillars of TTI, 230–235
        published research documents,
            232–233
        relationship between, 234
BRAC Institute of Governance and
    Development (BIGD), 30
    organizational performance, 31–33
    policy engagement and influence,
        37–40
    strengthening of research quality,
        33–37
    sustainability, 40–41
    TTI, support from, 30

Center for Study of Science,
    Technology and Policy (CSTEP),
    163–164
    administrative processes, 171–172
    benefits of TTI networks, 174
    building research capacity, 165–166
    deepening interdisciplinary research
        skills, 170–171

developing core values, 171
funding, 166–167, 178–179
future road map, 176
    developing thought leadership,
        177
    innovative research themes,
        177–178
gender, 167
    organization, 167–168
    research, 169–170
lessons learnt, 174–175
    aligning recruitments with vision,
        175
    benchmarks for quality, 175
    complacency pitfall, 176
    selection of projects and partners,
        175–176
progress during TTI grant, 164–165
stories of policy influence, 172–174
Centre for Budget and Governance
    Accountability (CBGA), 129
    challenges, 136
    evidence and policy alternatives
        generated by, 130
    founding vision of, 129–130
    organizational performance, 130–132
    policy
        contribution, 136–138
        engagement, 134–136
    research quality, 132–134
    sustainability, 138–139
Centre for Policy Dialogue (CPD)
    challenges and lessons learnt,
        49–50
    citizen's platform on SDGs, 54
    collaboration, 45–46

contributions, 51
global leadership, 53–54
improving regional connectivity, 52
issues critical to Bangladesh, 43
media as strategic partner, 50–51
operational areas, 42
organizational performance, 43–44
policy engagement
  dialogue activities, 47–48
  linkages, 48–49
publication and dissemination, 51
research quality, 46
strategy and focus, 44–45
success stories
  monitoring of Rana Plaza
    Collapse, 51–52
sustainability, 54–56
  participation of more youth in
    dialogues, 55
  proactive engagement in gender-
    sensitive issues, 55
  publish more in Bangla, 54
  women's contribution to economy,
    52–53
Centre for Policy Research (CPR),
  140
organizational performance,
  142–144
policy engagement, 147–148
policy impact, 148–150
research output and quality,
  144–146
thinking ahead, 150–152
transformation, 141
TTI funding awarded to, 142
ups and downs, 140–141
Centre for Poverty Analysis (CEPA), 57
credibility and visibility, 65
formative years and orientation,
  57–59
journey with TTI, 65–66
reimagining development, 62–63
sectoral support, 59–60
significant changes, 61–62
strengthening of research agenda, 65

think tanks
  being part of fraternity of, 63–64
  enter, 59
TTI support, 64–65
Centre for the Study of Developing
  Societies (CSDS), 153–155
challenges and ways ahead, 161–162
organizational performance, 158–159
policy engagement, 159–161
research quality, 155–158
revisiting Handloom Act, 161
Citizen Report Card (CRC), 209
Community-based Rainfall
  Measurement (CORAM), 86

Friedrich-Ebert-Stiftung (FES), 115

Handloom Reservation Act of 1985,
  161
Himalayan Knowledge Conclave
  (HKC), 87–88

India, SSR and TTI, 236–239
growth and sustainability, 251–252
organizational performance, 243–246
  Indian think tanks and areas of
    research, 244
policy engagement, 246–249
  ranking of SDGs, 249
policy impact, 249–251
research quality, 239–243
TTI
  aspects of improvement, 239
  attracting and retaining scholars,
    242
  core funding support, 245
  key areas, 241
  objectives around RQ, 240
  research design, 240
Indian Institute of Dalit Studies
  (IIDS), 180
academic recognitions, 190–191
challenges and issue of
  sustainability, 192–193
challenges faced, 181

institutional collaborations, 191
looking into future, 193–194
mission, 180
organizational performance, 186
PhD programme, 191–192
policy engagement, 186–187
policy impacts, 188–190
    affirmative action, 188
    NCERT teacher's training
        module, 188
    prevention of caste-based
        discrimination, 188
    strengthening and leveraging
        panchayati raj institutions,
        188–189
recognition as the research institute,
    190
research quality, 182–186
    publications and capacity-
        building programmes, 185
    theme- and group-wise completed
        research projects, 185
TTI support, 181–182
Institute for Social and Environmental
    Transition-Nepal (ISET-N), 79
Adapting to Climate Change in
    Asia, 79
influence stories
    community-led, 90
    government support to HKC, 89
    local government-facilitated
        reconstruction, 90
    national strategy for resilient local
        communities, 89–90
    social enterprise in post-
        earthquake reconstruction, 90
journey continuous, 91–93
new initiatives
    Abishkar Fellowship, 86–87
    civic science, 86
    Himalayan Knowledge
        Conclave, 87–88
    local stories of change, 88–89
    Manthan, 88
    master's research grant, 87

platform lecture, 89
new trajectory, 82–85
    challenges, 82
    dissemination, 85
    objectives, 83
    organizational development, 83
    research quality, 83–85
    TTI's framework, three pillars of
        change, 82
sustainability issues, 91
Institute of Policy Studies (IPS), 67
    context and brief history, 67–68
    organizational performance, 68–71
    policy
        contribution, 75–77
        engagement, 73–75
    research quality, 71–73
    sustainability, 77–78

life after TTI
    challenge, 367–369
    corporate social responsibility
        (CSR), 371
    future, 369–371
    innovative experiment, 365–367
    public agencies, 371

Maoist-led armed rebellion, 81–82

National Conservation Strategy
    (NCS), 94
National Council of Applied
    Economic Research (NCAER), 195
    2020 strategy, integrating TTI with
        areas, 199
        assets, 198
        strengthening, 199–200
    arrival of TTI, 196–197
    challenges as TTI started, 197–198
    illustrating impact, 205–206
    impact on
        organizational effectiveness,
            200–201
        policy engagement, 203–204
        research quality, 201–203

journey, 195–196
looking back, 198
opportunities, challenges and
resilience, 206–208
TTI's network impact, 204–205
National University of Ireland (NUI)
Galway, 115
Nepal, SSR and TTI, 253–257
disciplinary and interdisciplinary
research, 275
interdisciplinary research and public
policy, 261–264
investments, 277
journals, 270
Kathmandu-based research
organizations, status
knowledge dissemination, 272–273
organizational performance, 271
policy engagement, 272–273
quality assurance, 271–272
sustainability, 273–274
private sector, 276–277
public funding of research, 269–270
quality of public debate, 276
research landscape, 265–269
donor agencies, 268–269
government departments, 267
independent research
organizations, 267
international non-governmental
organizations, 268
non-governmental organizations,
268
private sector, 267–268
university system, 265–267
setting and challenges, 258–261
university education, 275–276
working space, 276

Pakistan Climate Change Act, 2017,
104
Pakistan, SSR and TTI
country synthesis
organizational performance, 284
policy outreach, 284

research quality, 284
sustainability, 285
current phase, 282–283
Rubina Saigol's views, 280–282
universities (academia) and think
tanks, 283
universities and think tanks, 283
Zaidi's views, 279–280
policy community survey (PCS), 13
Public Affairs Centre (PAC),
209–212
CRC, 209
focuses, 210
growth and sustainability, 219–221
accountability, 220
deep and diversified client base,
220
enhancing RQ, 220
institutional measures, 220–221
strategic framework, 219–220
policy engagement and influence,
217–219
SATs developed by, 211
today's situation, 212–216
achievements with IDRC–TTI's
support, 213
approaches and their applications,
214–216
first phase of TTI, 212–213
second phase of TTI, 213
vision, 210

research–advocacy–implementation
(RAI) model, 125

Social Policy and Development
Centre (SPDC), 109
achievements, 110
database, 110
organizational performance,
112–115
FRS, linkages, 115
NUI Galway, 115
study of intergovernmental fiscal
transfers, 115

tobacco taxation in Pakistan,
study, 114
policy engagement, 119–124
RAI model, 125
report on state of economy,
123–124
research quality, 115–119
sustainability, 124–126
TTI's support, 111–112
South Asia, role of TTI, 303–305,
316–317
credibility and independence,
306–307
gender research, 337–340
growth in, 309, 311–316
main sources of funding, 310
state-wise distribution, 312
thematic diversity, 313
organizational strengthening,
317–320
cluster of activities, 318
overview, 351–354
ownership and flexibility, 307–308
policy impact, 327
measuring, 327–328
policy influence, 328, 331–337
policy research organizations,
305–306
research quality, 320
activities undertaken, 324
CSDS initiative, 325
Devesh Kapur's statement,
320–321
IIDS role, 326–327
internal control process, 323
methods, 322
research at SDPI, 326
Second Interim Report, 320
strategies used, 329–331
strengthening support programme,
340–341
annual regional meetings,
343–344
catalysing regional discourse,
344–345

collaboration, 341–342
sharing policy community
surveys, 345–346
sustainability, 346–350
contribution across five
dimensions, 355–362
Sri Lanka, SSR and TTI, 286–287
challenges to, 296, 298–299
demand and supply, 289–291
funding available, 292–293, 296
national GERD, 294
sector-wise allocation of
government expenditure, 295
GERD by discipline, 297
institutional framework, 287–289
issues covered, 291–292
Sustainable Development Policy
Institute (SDPI), 94
Sustainable Development Goals
(SDGs), 94
bill on non-Muslim-sensitive
educational reforms, 104
catalysing modifications, role,
95–96
financial loss, 95
fiscal governance, change
Khyber Pakhtunkhwa (KP)
budget 2017–2018, 105
focus, 94–95
International Monetary Fund
(IMF) and WB, 106
ISDE president, 106
organizational performance,
96–97
bridging research policy gaps,
99
capacity enhancement, 97–98
changes in accountability,
98–99
human resource development,
97
strengthening regulatory
framework, 98
Pakistan Climate Change Act,
2017, 104

policy engagement
  achievements and gaps,
    103–105
  enhancing public policy space,
    impact, 106
  membership of policy-making
    group, 106
  visibility and brand building,
    103
research quality
  achievement and gaps, 103
  collaborative research, 101–102
  consistency in outputs, 99–100
  quality assurance mechanisms,
    100–101
  quality of publications, 101
  research ethics, 101
  shaping research agendas,
    102–103
research, part of curriculum,
  104–105
sustainability, 107–108
think tank, presence, 96
youth ambassador, 106

tax revenues in Pakistan, 122–123
Think Tank Initiative (TTI), 3
  aims, 3–4
  balancing learning and
    accountability within, 21–22
  core funding, on, 15–16
    long-term sustainability, 18–19
    ownership, 17–18
    size, 16–17
  funders, 4
  governance structure, 8
  grantee-level tools, 10–11
    annual monitoring questionnaire
      (AMQ), 11
    annual technical and financial
      reports, 11

institutional monitoring visits, 11
journey continuing, 25–26
learning tools, 12
  grantee scorecard, 12
  PCS, 13
  peer review, 12–13
mid-program phase 2 review
  (2014), 9
mission, design and approach, 4
  core funding support, 5
  technical support, 5–6
programme evaluation, 13–14
  capacity-building component,
    design, 14–15
  cohort selection and flexibility,
    15
  collaboration, 14
  data collection, 14
programme-level tools
  snapshot, 11–12
  technical and financial reports to
    donors, 12
programme monitoring, 10
programme officer accompaniment
  model, 22–24
programme tools, including
  evaluation, 19–20
reflections on programme's
  implementation in South Asia,
  15
RM platform, 20–21
selection process
  aims, 6
  geographic clusters of countries,
    6–7
  selected South Asian cohort,
    diversity, 7–8
think tanks, 3

Vulnerability Through the Eyes of the
  Vulnerable, 80